WILLIAM BERGER

Puccini

WITHOUT EXCUSES

William Berger was born in California and studied Romance languages and music at the University of California at Santa Cruz. He worked for five years at the San Francisco Opera Company, where he acquired for the company's recorded music collection. He is the author of *Wagner Without Fear: Learning to Love—and Even Enjoy—Opera's Most Demanding Genius* and *Verdi with a Vengeance: An Energetic Guide to the Life and Complete Works of the King of Opera.* He is a frequent lecturer and radio commentator and has recently been a regular host for New York Public Radio's *Overnight Music.* He has written libretti, performance pieces, and articles on a wide variety of topics including architecture, religion, and, of course, music. He is a music host for WNYC radio and lives in New York.

ALSO BY WILLIAM BERGER

Wagner Without Fear

Verdi with a Vengeance

Puccini

WITHOUT EXCUSES

*A Refreshing Reassessment
of the World's Most Popular Composer*

WILLIAM BERGER

*Vintage Books
A Division of Random House, Inc.
New York*

A VINTAGE ORIGINAL, NOVEMBER 2005

Copyright © 2005 by William Berger

All rights reserved. Published in the United States
by Vintage Books, a division of Random House, Inc.,
New York, and in Canada by Random House
of Canada Limited, Toronto.

Vintage and colophon are registered trademarks
of Random House, Inc.

Library of Congress Cataloging-in-Publication Data
Berger, William, 1961–
Puccini without excuses : a refreshing reassessment of the world's
most popular composer / William Berger.
p.   cm.
Includes bibliographical references (p.) and index.
1. Puccini, Giacomo, 1858–1924. Operas. 2. Operas—Stories, plots,
etc. I. Title.
ML410.P89 B46 2005
782.1′092—dc22
2005046157

Vintage ISBN-10: 1-4000-7778-8
Vintage ISBN-13: 978-1-4000-7778-6

Author photograph © Scott DiPerna
Book design by Rebecca Aidlin

www.vintagebooks.com

Printed in the United States of America
10 9 8 7 6 5 4 3 2 1

For Stephen
"Si, si, ci voglio andare . . ." (Gianni Schicchi)

Contents

PART THREE | THE PUCCINI CODE
Issues in Puccini and the Perception of His Works

PART FOUR | EXPLORING PUCCINI

Part One

THE CASE OF PUCCINI

Why Puccini? Why Now?
An Introduction

WITHOUT PUCCINI, there is no opera; without opera, the world is an even drearier place than the evening news would have us think. This book is aimed, firstly, at people who would have trouble agreeing with either part of that sentence.

To begin with, there is the issue of opera in general. I do not hold with those who believe that opera is a dying art form. The same things have been said about opera almost since its invention. Opera was said to be doomed when the castrati disappeared in the eighteenth century, when the Napoleonic Wars shut down the conservatories in the early nineteenth century, when tonality was redefined in the twentieth century, and so on. Movies, television, radio, and the Internet were each supposed to nail the coffin lid shut, and all of those media have become part of the opera story. If opera were mortal, it would have died by now.

Yet opera has been neatly contained in an obscure corner, thought to be only for, ahem, "certain" people, and this riles me. I believe opera is the most important art form. It is not the most important because, as is always said, it subsumes every other art form (which happens to be true), but because at its best it has the ability to probe deeper into the human experience than any other art form. There are never any easy answers in opera, and it promotes critical thinking. This is why fans are always said to be so passionate. While I can celebrate the high profile of opera in America today, I wish it were even higher—much higher.

There are, however, impediments to raising this profile. Opera will always be considered a foreign art form, and we see all our national neuroses about things foreign in our approach to opera. It will always be marginalized to some degree. Opera continues to attract the elitist label. That there are rich people who support and attend the opera is beyond question, but I must wonder why it is that opera remains the single great signifier of the effete elite. You have all seen the images on television: overdressed, ancient, white audiences wielding lorgnettes while overfed woman onstage hits earsplitting high note. It doesn't matter that this image has little basis in reality—it exists and is with us forever. Had there never been this "opera house of the imagination," it would have been necessary to invent it. And the image continues to keep opera, and all its considerable power, away from many, many people.

Conversely, the arts marketing people have been working overtime for a generation or so to combat this idea, and in doing so have perhaps overstepped their bounds. Opera is not elite, they have maintained. It's fun, and (worst of all), it's good for you, like cultural cod liver oil. This is America. We have to believe, or pretend, that something has an uplifting moral effect in order to support it (cf. baseball). I doubt that opera has ever made anyone a better person. I don't think baseball has either, but I love it all the same. Quality should be an end in itself. Furthermore, opera is elitist, but not in the way it is assumed by detractors to be. It is phenomenally expensive to produce and always has been, and therefore must be funded by someone (the king, corporate foundations, whomever). It is elitist in its performers: only about one in a million people (by one estimate) is born with the instrument necessary to make the sounds required, and only very few of them can follow through on their gift. And it is elitist in its requirements of its audience. We are expected to pay attention if we are to cull what can be culled from the experience. We seem to be able to assimilate these ideas in sports. We ought to be able to do something analogous for opera.

Leaving aside, for now, the issue of opera's continuing, illogical, and urgent validity in the world today, we must focus on Puccini within that world. On the one hand, a Puccini fan should have no cause for complaint. Puccini's works are in the repertory of every company, major and minor, and are hugely available on recordings and video. The numbers are unreliable, but I have read that one-fourth of all opera performances in the United States are of three of Puccini's most popular operas (*La bohème*, *Tosca*, and *Madama Butterfly*). The number seems plausible. Yet this alone can be a cause for complaint among fans. There is a tendency toward either fossilization of performance or hysterical attempts to "revitalize" these works, both of which have the effect of reducing their inherent vitality. In general, critics, performers, directors, and audiences have reached a stalemate on this man's art. People like Puccini, and many love him, but one gets the feeling that he is approached in this country as a sort of guilty pleasure, like dessert. I never understood this stance, and let me say right off that I am absolutely allergic to anything that reeks of the sentimental. So how could I stomach Puccini? I have always found a huge degree of insight in his works, and was shocked to discover that there were others who didn't.

A hundred years ago, there may have been something "old-fashioned" about Puccini. He relied heavily on melody, with which he was ostentatiously gifted, and much of the popularity of his operas was due to the "hit tunes," the big arias, in his work. The general movement of opera composers at the time was away from a reliance on the aria and toward an absolute horror of melody. This was a huge issue of debate at the time. It need be less so now. Audiences seem to comprehend that there are different styles of opera, and no one in their right mind posits one form only as the right way. Furthermore, Puccini's arias, magnificent though they may be, are not the whole of the story. There was recently an interesting movie called π ("Pi"). In it, a young mathematician is on the verge of discovering a sequence of numbers that forms the numerical identity of God. Naturally, everyone wants to wring the secret out of him, from Wall Street to religious factions. At one point, our hero is captured and tortured to reveal the equation. He attempts to explain to his captors, "It's not the numbers . . . they're just numbers! It's the spaces in between them and their relationship to each other—THAT'S where God is!" It occurred to me that this was the most elegant explanation of opera I had ever heard. The numbers—that is, the arias, or the hits, or the "big" moments—are not the point. Of course, as in π, they have to be the "right" numbers, but those are not the essence. The point is the work as a whole. Example: Musetta's famous waltz from Act II of *La bohème*. This, by any standards, is a hit. Snippets of it are heard everywhere. Fine. But later in the opera, Musetta's sometime lover Marcello will include phrases of the waltz while he is pondering how much he misses her. It is the same music, yet it is entirely different. And we in the audience can experience the relation of the two moments to each other, how there is always something a little painful in joyous moments because we will know they will pass, and something a little sweet in painful moments because they cause us to remember the times of fulfillment. This is how one can best appreciate Puccini's genius. There are lots of great waltzes in the world, but there is only one *Bohème*.

Another large problem with the perception of Puccini, I came to realize, is the issue of verismo. This is the name given to a genre of opera current around the turn of the last century. It is hard to define: in fact, I address the issue on nearly every page of this book and must warn you right off that I never come close to defining it. Suffice it to say for now that composers like Puccini were seeking a direct communication with their audiences, avoiding everything that looked like "artistry" or "technique." Of course, they used tons of artistry and technique in their works, but they still had the elusive ideal of verismo to guide them. In cinema, this trend became known as neoverismo in a slew of Italian masterpieces from the mid-twentieth century. (It is called "neo" verismo because the operatic and literary output in the genre fifty years previously was the original verismo.) Any film student can tell you that most of the films thus categorized are not "pure" in their usage of the techniques of the genre, which stress the "invisible hand of the creator." In *Bicycle Thief*, for example, there is a crowd scene during a sudden rainstorm. The intended effect is to show people caught, quite casually, in the rain. The few seconds of film took an entire day and a squadron of Rome's fire department to get the exact "impromptu" effect the director wanted. The same is true for our contemporary films of the "Dogma" school: only one or two films from Denmark truly qualify as "Dogma" films, but their effect on filmmaking in general is enormous. So while Puccini is not a "pure" verismo composer, we must consider the issues at stake in the genre in order to understand him. (These issues are explored throughout the book.)

The verismo school of opera is not particularly well understood today. Times change, and audiences and performers naturally respond to certain styles more easily than to others. Right now, baroque opera is very well represented in theaters. There are exciting, well-sung productions of long-neglected works by Handel and others given to enthusiastic audiences. No one in their right mind could have seen this coming forty years ago. Furthermore, I see more diverse audiences at those performances than I do at the standard repertory, all eating it up without the slightest bit of explanation necessary. Fifty years ago, it would have taken the average music fan a week of lectures just to be able to sit through such a "static" opera without pulling out his or her hair. Today's audiences take it all in stride.

Handel's operas are stylized in the extreme and conform to certain conventions that draw a neon light, so to speak, around the staginess of the work being given. This is the very opposite of verismo, which seeks to show life as it is among people as they are. All good and well, but how can we look for life as it is at the opera house, of all crazy places? Furthermore, it takes a certain kind of performance to make verismo come alive. The traditions of performing verismo are quite unacceptable in the world today—they seem like overacting, overscreeching, and so forth. It simply doesn't work. But what will work instead? Very, very few performers have found a formula. While Handel's operas can come to life with the talents and temperaments of today's performers, verismo eludes a great many of them. Go and see a master class given by a great retired diva—Renata Scotto's spring to mind immediately. You can see her working with the young artists, who are all very talented and who know the techniques of operatic singing quite well. But when there is a piece of Puccini to be sung and evaluated, watch her literally trying to pull something out from inside the young singers! Just hitting the notes will simply not do. You need to feel them, live them, BE them, and of course deliver them across the footlights. Verismo is often translated as "realism" but the word is closer to "truth" in Italian.

Truth—there's a big word, and a big part of the problem. One can find truth in opera as long as it is fake enough (stylized enough) to allow us to draw a frame around it. But the direct, in-your-face work of Puccini is strangely elusive for today's performers and audiences. Puccini is considered "easy" opera and the classic composer to use when introducing new audiences to the medium. I seriously doubt if that is true in quite the same way it was fifty years ago. There is something in the frank emotions and lack of intellectual pretense that makes Puccini remarkably difficult for a modern audience. Furthermore, there is a remarkable subtlety (yes, subtlety) in his works. Melodies are driven home when necessary, but many of his most excellent effects are achieved with a superb economy of expression—a few notes here and there. We are not equipped to listen as closely as people were a couple of generations ago, and we miss a lot. Puccini's operas are not short because they are trivial. They are short because he says what he needs to efficiently and quickly. In this way, Puccini has become more "difficult" to fathom, while, ironically, a composer such as Wagner has become much easier for modern audiences than he was a few decades ago. It's time for a new look at Puccini. All the traditional assumptions have changed.

Beyond provoking the groups of people outlined in the first paragraph of this chapter, the main thrust of this book is aimed at those who want to delve, or delve more deeply, into the art of Giacomo Puccini. A certain amount has already been written, from quite specific points of view. And everyone seems to have a point of view. The musicologists, after a century of benign neglect or outright hostility, have been forced by the paying public to admit that Puccini has some musical validity after all. Since all their contempt (much of which, I will repeat throughout this book, seems based on thinly veiled racism, or at least on cultural assumptions so insidious that they border on racism) did not consign Puccini to the dustbin of history, they have, for a few years now, been turning themselves around to analyze this music with the same tools they applied to much of the abstract and emotionally retarded music of the twentieth century and have managed to discover a vocabulary that allows them to enjoy it without feeling that they have compromised their values. To be sure, much of what has been written lately is fine and long overdue: it is my hope that the reader will be inspired to research such works for his or her own deeper understanding of the music. I am especially indebted, and will refer continually, to the great musicological efforts of Mosco Carner, William Ashbrook, Julian Budden, and, more recently, Michele Girardi, and the fine biographical work (which contains a good deal more musical insight than some of the musical commentaries out there) of Mary Jane Philips-Matz. I am also indebted to and inspired by the wonderful work of Susan Vandiver Nicassio, whose work opens up greater vistas by using Puccini as a departure point. But I intend to address the issue in a slightly different way: What is the art of Puccini about? Why does it continue to captivate people, either directly in the opera house or in the many other forms where it is experienced? Since opera is the total performing arts experience, what is the most total way to experience it?

Let's look at one famous example: *La bohème*, the most popular of Puccini's popular operas. In Act I, the two lovers are brought together when their hands touch as they paw the floor of the hero's dark garret to find the heroine's lost key. Everyone has a different way of explaining what makes this moment so celebrated. The musicologist will be impressed by the deft arioso and the little ostinato on the strings pizzicato (Mosco Carner). To the stage manager, it is the pleasure of getting two singers to make hand gestures on cue with the music. To the lighting designer, it is the magic of creating vision within a palpable darkness, relieved only by pulses of indirect moonlight appearing between passing clouds (an effect, I am told by those who know, that is one of the pinnacles of the lighting designer's art). To a tenor, it is but a prelude to one of the great tenor arias of all time; to the soprano, a chance to show her ability to listen, act charmed, and prepare mentally for her great subsequent aria. To the "conservative" director, it is a chance to reinforce the Great Tradition of Opera; to the "progressive" director, the irregular lifestyles of the protagonists are a clear instruction to offend, yet again, the bourgeoisie in the audience. All of which is relevant, but no one aspect of which is the whole story from the audience's point of view. And since it is the audience, rather than the specialists, who have preserved Puccini for posterity, then it is to the audience's mind that we must turn to unpack the treasures of Puccini.

I am a member of that audience—a fanatical one, to be sure, but that is my only relevant credential. That, and a lifelong allegiance to the towering figure who, directly or indirectly, is the progenitor of all art that can be called in any sense "Italian." When asked by semicelestial authorities to define his credentials as a poet, Dante replied simply, "I'm just someone who takes note when love inspires me, and by that manner dictated from within, I go making signs." I have taken note of the feelings Puccini's art has inspired in me. I have honored them with the respect I think they merit. This book is the sign of that love.

The next chapter is a biography of Giacomo Puccini's life and the times he lived in, which attempts to give a context for the operas and also a context for many of our inherited assumptions about them. The second part of the book is devoted to his mature operas themselves. My general format is to present the synopses with frequent interruptions I honor with the name of commentary. (Half the time my comments are only expressions of what I would like to say during performances but am forbidden by custom to articulate.) In general, I dislike the emphasis placed on synopses (story outlines) in opera books because I am convinced the opera is not "about" the plot in the same way that a movie might be. (This disconnect results in, I am sure, a huge gulf between audiences and the ability to enjoy an opera.) This is not a literal art form—far from it. And yet, one must have a road map to the work in question. Thus I have chosen this method of "deconstructing" operas, and I hope the reader finds it useful. The third and fourth parts of the book are devoted to the many directions one can go after a slight familiarity with the operas, from explorations of "issues" within the operas to lists of performers, recordings, and books one might wish to pursue. I have also included a glossary of terms one must, willy-nilly, use when discussing this admittedly strange art form. This glossary also includes some of the places discussed throughout the book. Much of the "story" of Puccini comes out in the chapters on singers and recordings and even in the glossary, and I hope you will read these rather than simply keeping them around for reference.

Some readers will be annoyed, while others will be relieved, when I tell you that your present author is absolutely unencumbered by musicological erudition. I resort to the erudition of others when it is appropriate, but I do not seek to justify my love of these works, or yours, by a string of what Shaw so aptly called "Mesopotamian words." I will admit straight off that I am compelled, at two points in the narrative, to discuss the mixolydian mode, but I assure you that I will do so with all the humility I must employ when confronted with such an awesome terminology.

Puccini's operas are beautiful, touching, and rewarding. Most people would concur. But I believe they are much more as well. In their ability to examine the truest emotions of the human condition, and in the human dignity they inherently uphold, his operas convey a message of hope in humankind that is quite rare even in the greatest works of art. I am convinced they are crucial for our world today.

Puccini in Context:
His Life, Times, and Artistic Matrix

THE OPERAS OF PUCCINI have an excellent capacity to make a marvelous first impression. They can, in a way, be appreciated by any person walking in off the street. Yet they also hold up to deeper scrutiny, as time has shown, and anyone who would like more than a nodding acquaintance with them would do well to consider the circumstances in which they were created. A closer look at the ideas current in Puccini's time is crucial to understanding what these operas are, and, equally important, what they are not. Puccini's life story, in and of itself, does not provide the most instantly impressive biographical material. He did not place himself in the center of world events, as Wagner did, nor did he seek out fame anywhere but in the opera house. His life was hardly without incident, but it is interesting on the human rather than the epic level (much the same could be said about his operas). He furthermore lived through an era of awesome creative (and destructive) activity, and responded to all these currents in his own fashion.

Roots

The city of Lucca is now officially part of Tuscany, but it is far from the Tuscany of rolling hills and villas populated by English dilettantes discovering their sex drives, students with backpacks, or divorced Americans in midlife crises. Lucca lies in a flat plain by the Tyrrhenian Sea that also includes Pisa, an ancient city with a long and proud tradition of independence. Although Pisa is officially in Tuscany now as well, the intensity of local prejudices can be seen in the still-current Florentine proverb "é meglio avere un morto nella casa che un pisano all'uscio" (it's better to have a dead man in the house than a Pisano at the door). For most of its history Pisa was a maritime republic whose power once rivaled that of Venice. Lucca, likewise, was an independent republic with its own traditions and institutions dating back to the Dark Ages. A series of fortifications built in the Renaissance still rings the town, adding to a sense of insularity. The Lucchesi are known throughout Italy as being industrious, rather bourgeois in their tastes, and very self-sufficient. South of these two cities lie swampy wetlands, an area abundant in waterfowl and popular among hunters since anyone can remember. It is a melancholy landscape, traditionally considered unhealthy, and relatively primitive despite its proximity to the two sophisticated cities of Lucca and Pisa. Still farther south are the hills of the Maremma, now a protected "wilderness."

A certain Domenico Puccini moved from the small hilltop village of Celle in the late seventeenth century to Lucca. His son Giacomo (1712–81) was born in the city and studied music there and in Bologna, where he received honors. In 1740, Giacomo returned to Lucca where he was named organist of the San Martino Cathedral, built in the eleventh century, and *maestro di capella* (basically, "music-master") of the Republic of Lucca. The job would have kept him busy. Besides the tonnage of new music required by cathedrals at that time, the republic additionally required music for public celebrations. Notable among these celebrations were the *tasche*, pageants accompanying the various rituals of election days in the republic. The *tasche* grew quite elaborate in the decades before the republic's demise under Napoleon in 1799, and were not unlike little outdoor operas. Giacomo's son Antonio (1747–1832) followed in his father's footsteps, becoming organist of the cathedral and *maestro di capella*. He married Caterina Tesei, an organist in her own right who took over her husband's duties after his death and who filled in for their son Domenico when he was away and after his premature death. Domenico's son Michele (1813–64) became the next Puccini to lead the musical life in Lucca, still thriving despite the city's loss of independence and attachment to the Grand Duchy of Tuscany. In 1848 or 1849, Michele married Albina Magi, who was nineteen at the time but already a proud woman known to all as Donna Albina. Michele tried his hand at composing operas, as his father had, but was more successful with his civic and church compositions and as a teacher and organist. He and Albina had a large family: Otilia (b. 1851), Tomaide (b. 1852), a third daughter who died in infancy, Nitteti (b. 1854), and Iginia (b. 1856). Their first son, baptized Giacomo Antonio Domenico Michele Secondo Maria, was born on the night of December 22–23, 1858. Two more daughters followed: Ramelde (b. 1859), and Macrina (b. 1862 and who died at the age of eight). A second son, Michele, was born after Michele Sr.'s death in 1864.

Michele's death left Albina with a large brood and a public position to uphold. The Puccinis had led the musical life of Lucca for over a century and had worked with the brightest musical names of Italy, including Padre Martini of Bologna, their fellow Lucchese Luigi Boccherini, and the opera composers Mercadante, Paisiello, Pacini, and Donizetti. If the position of *maestro di capella* did not mean quite what it had at one time, it was still an honorable calling and a respectable livelihood. And although a few of the Puccini children showed musical aptitude, it was clear from his baptismal names that young Giacomo was meant from the start to carry the family torch. Albina scrimped and saved, borrowed money from relatives, and wrote endless grant proposals to the city authorities and, later, to the national government. She focused her attentions on Giacomo, assuming the daughters could marry or be otherwise settled. Indeed, Nitteti and Iginia were packed off to a convent in 1865, the latter eventually taking holy orders. Giacomo was a born musician if left to his own devices, but there must have been many times when Albina wondered if her efforts were in vain. Giacomo was not a good student. One teacher said, "He comes to class only to wear out the seat of his pants." Albina wanted him educated in the classics as well as music, but he never could apply himself to any subject that did not hold immediate interest. Even the basics of counterpoint and rules of music eluded him. He simply could not pretend to be interested in abstract subjects, and so he would remain for the rest of his life. He did excel, however, in practical jokes and adolescent pranks, once being called before the authorities for having stolen a pipe from the organ and sold it as scrap metal to buy tobacco. And he was introduced to the carnal pleasures at a young age, although biographers quibble as to the exact date of the encounter with the generous lady. Puccini the man was already formed.

One other formative incident of note occurred in these days. He and a group of friends walked the long road to Pisa to attend a performance of Giuseppe Verdi's opera *Aida* at the theater there, larger than anything in Lucca. As he wrote later, a new musical "window" had opened for him. Whether he was aware of it at the time or not, his heart was already moving away from the musical course set out for him at birth, toward a broader horizon. He would later say that God touched him on the shoulder once and promised him great success if he wrote for the theater, but only for the theater. Puccini was never a man to speak of curious conversations with the Almighty, and tended to keep matters we describe as religious or spiritual at arm's length. His later comment is all the more striking, then, and we might assume that the beginnings of his new "calling" were planted on that arduous trip to Pisa.

Milan

Albina was of the opinion that Puccini needed to complete his studies at the Milan Conservatory, the center of musical life in Italy.

Through connections, she petitioned Queen Margherita of Italy for a scholarship for her son and won it. It was a small amount of money, but it was filled out by some well-situated relatives and was enough for a student to live on. Giacomo was packed off to Milan in October 1880. Puccini had been something of a big fish in a small pond in Lucca. His name drew attention and created expectations, and his few early compositions, including a Mass for four voices, showed great promise. Milan, however, was another story. This metropolis boasted a heritage as old as anywhere in Italy, more or less, but was now the most modern and prosperous city as well. Situated in the middle of a fertile plain at a crossroads dating from before the time of the Roman Empire, Milan was a cultural crossroads as well for traders, travelers, and invaders. The Lombards made it their capital at the time of the fall of the Roman Empire, and French, Spanish, and various German powers occupied it at one time or another. Milan was dominated by the Austrian Hapsburgs from the early eighteenth century until uniting with Piedmont in 1859, save for a brief period when it was one of the capitals (Venice was the other) of the Napoleonic Kingdom of Italy in the early nineteenth century. The city's outlook was cosmopolitan and sophisticated. It had Italy's largest and most important theater, La Scala, as well as its largest cathedral, the famous Duomo (St. Peter's in Rome is not officially a cathedral). It also boasted the marvelous Galleria Vittorio Emanuele, a sort of protoshopping mall with elegant shops and restaurants and cafés bustling with all the latest ideas. Industry was booming, producing its wealth for a few and misery for the many. The 300,000 inhabitants considered themselves the most forward-thinking, industrious, and best-dressed people in Italy, as their descendants still do.

Puccini passed his examinations and entered the Conservatory. The forward-thinkers there were looking at Germany and the development of symphonic music as the path of the future, the traditionalists were seeking to maintain a strictly Italian profile in their art, while the young were simply eager to absorb everything. And there was plenty to absorb in Milan just then beyond electricity and streetcars.

There were ideas buzzing as well. The Kingdom of Italy had been formed by the previous generation: what would become of it now? Opera had been Italy's chief export for over two hundred years. What form would it take now? The Grand Old Man of Italian opera, Giuseppe Verdi, seemed, to all outward appearances, to be retired on his farm in the province of Parma. Verdi's trips to Milan were quiet and infrequent at this point. The younger people looked abroad for inspiration. The music of Richard Wagner was on everybody's lips, even if very little of it actually made it to their ears. Producing Wagner's operas was too expensive and risky a proposition in Italy, and there was even doubt that Italian musicians could play it adequately. (The fear was not merely cultural chauvinism. The best musicians of Paris were quite unable to play the prelude to Wagner's opera *Tristan und Isolde* when a series of concerts was arranged there in 1861.) Many of the new musical ideas were coming from France, to which Milan had ancient cultural and economic ties. Giacomo Meyerbeer's formula for Grand Opéra was no longer new in Italy, but his works remained popular and impressive with their demanding solos and marvelous spectacle. Puccini attended performances of at least *La stella del Norte* (*L'étoile du Nord*) at La Scala as a student, although he wrote little about his impressions. Others, however, were quite impressed. Meyerbeer's operas seemed ambitious and grand, worthy of a rich, modern nation like France and a model toward which Italians should aspire if they could dare to imagine their own cultural heritage in the same large terms. The French, meanwhile, were beginning to look beyond the rigid confines of the Grand Opéra and to redefine themselves after their own country suffered a traumatic shock in the war with Prussia and its aftermath in 1870 and 1871. Another whole world seemed to open up with the arrival of Georges Bizet's opera *Carmen* in 1875. While coldly received by the public at first, the novelty of *Carmen* soon captured much of the world's imagination. Here were earthy common people, their outfits as tattered and inelegant as their emotions, who lived out their violent destinies without appearing to give a moment's thought to the rules of counterpoint or notions of good taste in art. Audiences, after the first few, were shocked, disgusted, transported, and enthralled. Even the mercurial young philosopher Friedrich Nietzsche, who had so recently proclaimed Richard Wagner as something just short of the Second Coming, decided Wagner was a disease threatening the health of the world and recommended universal renewal through the emulation of *Carmen*. Opera was not confined to the opera house in those days.

Indeed, the irresistible grunginess of *Carmen* followed corollaries that had long been developing in French literature and were reaching their fullest bloom in the 1880s. The novels of authors such as Honoré de Balzac, Émile Zola, and Gustave Flaubert had opened the floodgate of what would come to be called naturalism. The rhetorical artistry of the author was subdued in favor of a clear outline of the characters and their psychological motivations. The favored subjects were everyday characters of the present times: businessmen, housewives, shopkeepers, farmers. There were nobles and there were rustics in these novels, but they were presented as people one might meet in the street with all their human foibles rather than as idealized archetypes or thorough embodiments of evil from a romanticized past. Many readers felt these writings were closer to journalism than art, but there was no denying they seemed to encapsulate the modern era, with all its prosaic, industrialized reality. Clearly, romanticism was out and realism was in.

Italians soon followed suit. The Sicilian author Giovanni Verga published his short story *Cavalleria rusticana* ("Rustic chivalry") in 1880. Its four pages of direct, unadulterated prose slapped readers across the face with its simple tale of jealousy and passion in a Sicilian village. (Describing Alfio, the "other man" in the story, Verga wrote simply, "He was rich. He had four mules.") Verga followed this success with a novel, *I Malavoglia*, which used the same methods to narrate the fortunes and miseries of oppressed fishermen in the villages of Sicily. Verga's work became the beacon of what became known in Italy as verismo, an untranslatable term usually rendered as "realism." *Cavalleria rusticana* was transformed into a play and toured

Italy with tremendous success. It played in Milan in 1884. Everyone knew these ideas would somehow be transported to music and opera, but no one was yet quite sure how.

The groundwork had actually been laid in opera, and not only by *Carmen*. Verdi had already scored a worldwide hit with *La traviata*, a love story about the doomed affair between a consumptive and elegant prostitute and a bourgeois young man. It may have been romantic in the modern sense, but it told of real people with some real problems: disease, annoying middle-class families, and overdrawn bank accounts, for example. In 1876, La Scala audiences flocked to see Amilcare Ponchielli's *La gioconda*, which remained in the repertory. *Gioconda* was adapted from a play by the Frenchman Victor Hugo. On the surface, Ponchielli's opera had many of the traits of French Grand Opéra: nobles of yore committing murder to preserve honor, religious pageantry, a full ballet in the middle of the proceedings. Yet *Gioconda* had an immediacy (some would call it vulgarity) that was a break from previous tradition. The tenor sings one of the most gorgeous arias in the repertory and then blows up an entire ship. When the title character decides to commit suicide, she does not sing of lofty abstract concepts, but walks to the front center of the stage and cries "Suicidio!" at the top of her lungs. The much-derided libretto was a miracle of incisive words and phrases that jumped out at the audience, even beyond the classic "Suicidio!" (Best line: "I love him like a lion loves blood!" The final line is another classic of Italian opera: "And furthermore, I killed your mother!") In fact, there seem to be more exclamation points in the libretto of *Gioconda* than in all other libretti combined.

This libretto came from the pen of a young man named Arrigo Boito, son of a Polish countess and an Italian artist, who was educated around Europe. Boito returned to Milan in 1864 full of ideas and a healthy contempt for the old order. He found his inspiration from beyond the Alps, believing the French and the Germans held the keys to the future. As the most visible member of a group called the *scapigliati* (the disheveled ones, known for their lack of bourgeois niceties like combing their hair), Boito once composed an ode in honor of "New Italian Art" calling for renewal and a sweeping away of the old, which was tainted like the urine-drenched wall of a whorehouse. Verdi understood the jibe as squarely against him and avoided Boito for years. Meanwhile, Boito espoused theories in short-lived literary magazines, aided by abundant energy, a sense of mission, and a fondness for hashish. He wrote the words and music for his opera *Mefistofele* (based, significantly, on Goethe's *Faust*, the towering masterpiece of German literature), which was booed off the La Scala stage in 1868. It was revised and presented with success at forward-thinking Bologna in 1875. He set to work on his next opera, *Nerone*. He would still be working on it, as we shall see, at his death in 1918.

Ponchielli was the chair of composition at the Milan Conservatory when Puccini arrived there in 1880. Boito had mellowed since his radical days, as his friendship with the amiable Ponchielli would demonstrate. In fact, Boito was even working with Giuseppe Verdi, of all people, on a revision of an earlier, unsuccessful opera, *Simon Boccanegra*, to be given at La Scala in 1881. This was a notable collaboration: the very emblem of the Old Guard and the soul of Italy working with the internationalist, multicultural enfant terrible! *Boccanegra* was a success, and for a moment it seemed as though the extreme poles of Italian culture might find some common ground after all.

Ponchielli was instantly aware of the young Puccini's extraordinary talent and did everything he could to help him. He even corresponded at length with Albina back in Lucca, keeping her updated on her son's progress. Like every other teacher Puccini had, Ponchielli did not hesitate to inform Albina of her son's propensity toward carelessness in his studies. The student was undisciplined and overly casual in his attitude toward many of the fundamental courses. None of this was news to Albina. Puccini had written her that his Dramatic Literature class "bored him to death." In other notebooks, he scribbled in the margins, "Help! Enough! I'm dying!" But Ponchielli's interest in the tepid student was not dissuaded. He invited Puccini to the villa he and his wife opened to the literary and musical celebrities of Milan (including Boito) every summer on Lake Como.

Besides the established celebrities, there were plenty of other young men making their mark on the music world or just about to. There was his fellow Lucchese, Alfredo Catalani, only four years older than Puccini but already on the verge of a major career. Catalani's elegant chamber compositions were popular, and his first opera had been given at Turin just before Puccini arrived in Milan. And there was Puccini's fellow student Pietro Mascagni, who hailed from nearby Livorno, and with whom Puccini shared lodgings for a while. Together, the two indulged in plenty of pranks and adventures typical of starving students everywhere.

Puccini may have been undisciplined but he was not unproductive in these years. He graduated in 1883 and composed a *Capriccio sinfonico* for the end-of-the-year concert. The piece, written, Puccini claimed, on scraps of paper wherever the inspiration grabbed him, got attention from the foremost critics. It was included on a concert program at La Scala and was well received. Puccini wrote to Albina with obvious pride in his success.

The Professional World

The musical establishment in Italy was dominated by the House of Ricordi, a publishing house whose catalogue included Rossini and the greats of Italian opera as well as their current cash cow, Verdi. Publishers at that time invested a great deal of time and resources into "their" composers, and even acted as personal advisers. They loaned money, gave pep talks, and often handled the most complicated imbroglios that free-living composers frequently got into. Though Ricordi sat on the top of the heap, others were trying to break into the market with new and imported composers, and for a while there was healthy competition. The "upstart" House of Sonzogno (founded 1874) sought new talent among the younger composers and announced a competition for a one-act opera in August 1883. Ponchielli was determined to get Puccini entered into the competition and connected him with a poet and playwright named Ferdinando Fontana who had a handy libretto by the unwieldy name of *Le willis*. It was a "ballet-opera" based on a German legend, northern stories still being the mark of "progressive" thought among Italian artistic circles at this time. It also included many opportunities for orchestral interludes, at which Puccini showed an early aptitude. Ballet audiences already knew the story from the popular *Giselle, ou les Wilis* of Adolphe Adam. There were a few obstacles facing Puccini: Fontana had already promised his libretto to another young composer, but he was persuaded to favor Puccini instead (an interesting situation that would repeat frequently in Puccini's career). Furthermore, Puccini had no money to pay for the libretto, as was customary at the time. Still, Ponchielli's patronage counted for something, and Fontana was persuaded to reduce his fee. Excited from having heard the *Capriccio sinfonico*, Fontana agreed, and Puccini returned home to Lucca to work on the project.

Or not to work, as the case may have been. . . . Puccini wrote Ponchielli and admitted he was being lazy, doing nothing. One biographer remains convinced that the whole of the opera was written a couple of weeks before the deadline. Yet his sister Ramelde later reminisced that Puccini threw himself into the task with astounding energy. Perhaps there was truth in both points of view: Puccini would always accuse himself of laziness and later critics would take this at face value, accusing him of the same. But we know from his constant revising of scores—even very successful ones—that he had a healthy artistic hunger to improve his work, and self-castigation was an integral part of his personality. His letters from Milan to his mother, Albina, are full of references to the sorrow he had caused, his acknowledgments of what a disappointment he was, and even requests for forgiveness for being a bad person. He clearly expected great things from himself, and must have always been a little disappointed, as great artists always are.

Whether he was lazy or a firebrand, he was slow in producing his first opera. In fact, he finished it at midnight on the day of the deadline to submit. There wasn't even time to copy the score over in a legible hand, and it was sent, mistakes, cross-outs, and all. The judges were not impressed. Even before the verdict was read out a couple of months later, Puccini knew he had no chance to win. (He didn't. The prize went to others whose names have not made operatic history.) Puccini returned to Milan with fewer prospects than before. Albina wrote Ponchielli asking for help, and Ponchielli introduced Puccini to Giulio Ricordi, the head of the titan firm. Puccini's younger brother, Michele, the darling of the family and another budding musician, joined him in Milan to share his bohemian life, and for a while the brothers shared quarters again with Mascagni, who had even less money than the Puccinis. The three divided their humble meals of beans made on a hot plate in their room and wandered around the Galleria Vittorio Emanuele in search of ideas, women, and lunch. Still, it must have lifted Puccini's spirits, since Michele seems to have been a bit of a charmer. And Fontana was determined not to let *Le willis* disappear. Albina did what she could to raise money for her sons among supporters and relatives in Lucca, but her health was failing. She would not be able to help her sons much longer. Fontana was comfortable among the artistic salons of Milan, and dragged the shy, tongue-tied Puccini to soirees and musicales. He even bluntly asked for money to get the opera produced in a theater, something Puccini would never have been able to do. Fontana knew all the aging *scapigliati* of the town, and money came forth, including a modest investment from Boito himself. With at least the verbal support of Giulio Ricordi and Arrigo Boito, Puccini was practically blessed in "apostolic succession" to the great Verdi. He could not have asked for more.

Le willis was produced as part of a triple bill at the Teatro dal

Verme on May 31, 1884, and received rave reviews. Puccini, embarrassed as ever by public appearances, was brought out on stage, cheered, and given a silver wreath. The next day Puccini telegrammed Albina with a glowing, crowing account of his success. Soon there was even more cause to celebrate: Giulio Ricordi announced that his firm had acquired the rights to *Le willis*, which effectively meant Puccini was the new, hot commodity on the Italian music scene. There was little chance to celebrate, however. Albina Puccini died on July 17, 1884. Puccini made no effort to hide his emotions. He adored his mother and was fully aware of all the long years of sacrifice she had made for him and his career. No wonder he always felt a bit guilty for not working hard enough! As a touching tribute to her contributions, he laid the silver wreath he had been given at the Teatro dal Verme on Albina's coffin.

Edgar *and Elvira*

Puccini lingered on in Lucca, arranging family matters as best he could, corresponding with Fontana about new productions of their opera, now definitively titled *Le villi*. But most of the time he simply drifted in his grief until he found solace in a passion with a married woman, Elvira Bonturi Gemignani. She was married to an old acquaintance of Puccini's, a former schoolmate and amateur musician, in fact, named Narciso Gemignani. Puccini, who was now responsible for his family after Albina's death, was supplementing his income by giving music lessons in his native town, and Gemignani hired him to teach piano to his wife. The Gemignanis had two children, a daughter, Fosca, five, and a son, Renato, two. Yet somehow in this bustling household there was some flirting on the piano bench, and soon Puccini and Elvira were lovers. Puccini confided this to his brother Michele in Milan, but Gemignani did not catch on for about a year. When the cat finally came out of the bag, Elvira was pregnant and showing with Puccini's child. Puccini had much to fear: Gemignani had both the law and public opinion squarely on his side (despite the fact that he was a known womanizer), and no one would have raised an eyebrow if Gemignani challenged Puccini to a duel or even had him murdered outright. Puccini, as we might say, may have been a lover but was never a fighter, quite contrary to the mores of his society. He and Elvira fled to the town of Monza, a day's trip out of Milan, and rented furnished rooms. He had his sisters, whose position in their town was severely compromised by this escapade, write him, not from the general post office, where Gemignani could have tracked down his new address, but from the train station, which kept private records.

In their humble dwelling in Monza (since there was still no more money than there had been previously), there was an air of gaiety and friendship for a while. We have a record of an afternoon when a group of friends from Milan, including Catalani, Mascagni, Fontana, and the playwright and budding librettist Luigi Illica, along with Michele Puccini, paid a surprise visit to Puccini and Elvira. She put out what few snacks she could muster from the vacant pantry, but between all of them there was not enough money to buy a slab of meat for her to cook. Michele came to the rescue, hitting up a young lady of his acquaintance for some stamps to write a publisher in London. The stamps were then traded at the butcher for a piece of meat, and Elvira created a hearty stew for the delighted guests. On December 22, 1886, Puccini's and Elvira's son, Antonio, was born. He would be called Tonio for the rest of his life. For the next few years, Elvira lived sometimes with Puccini, wherever they could afford to set up a house together, sometimes with her sister in Florence, and occasionally wherever she could find a lodging for herself and her son.

There was also work to be done. Ricordi had supplied Puccini with a libretto by Fontana called *Edgar*, a full-blooded opera of murder and deception in the grand manner. There was even a "bad girl" in it, like Carmen but much, much worse, named Tigrana, no less. Puccini had the full backing of the Ricordi machine. He could write the most difficult roles without regard to making them manageable for local talent, since Ricordi could guarantee him the best singers in Italy. The same was true for the orchestral score, since it was understood that *Edgar* would be premiered at La Scala. Publicity and production would all be handled by the most experienced team in the country, if not the world. Puccini received a monthly stipend from Ricordi, which of course was insufficient for his growing needs but was still a salary, something many composers search for their entire lives in vain. All he had to do was produce.

Edgar was not finished after a year passed and his contract elapsed. Giulio Ricordi had to "go to bat" for the young man with his own board of directors, who were skeptical. And Signor Giulio had other priorities: wrangling new music out of the temperamental Verdi had been no easy matter, and, although few knew it, the "Bear of Busseto" (as Verdi was known) was working on yet another opera, *Otello*, with Arrigo Boito. There were resentments as well from Puccini's other colleagues, who were ignored, or feeling ignored, by Ricordi. There was Catalani, growing thinner and more ill by the year, and Mascagni, who had no contract from Ricordi or anyone else. And there was the Baron Alberto Franchetti, who was no mere dilettante but a composer of great promise. Franchetti had enormous wealth and was born connected, advantages he used unblushingly. He entertained lavishly at his many homes. These included the celebrated Ca' d'oro on Venice's Grand Canal, arguably the most beautiful home in Venice and therefore the world. Franchetti had the palace refurbished by the architect Camillo Boito, Arrigo's brother. As a sort of "aesthetic supervisor" on this most visible of private homes, Franchetti turned to a very remarkable, very short (5'4") budding poet, author, womanizer, patriot, self-promoter, and all-around arty person named Gabriele D'Annunzio. Yet even Franchetti, with all his resources, remained relatively ignored by Ricordi in favor of Puccini. Franchetti did not grumble, and in fact remained generous to all his colleagues, even if he did make disparaging comments about Puccini's music once at a dinner party, knowing it would get back to Puccini. He invited Puccini to pass the summer at one of his estates, but Puccini declined. It may not have been due to Franchetti's bitchy after-dinner chatter. Puccini did not seek out brilliant company. In fact, he was a bit of a loner, which made Ricordi's confidence in him all the more marked.

Edgar was finally completed and given the first-class treatment by La Scala. The singers were the best, the scenery top-notch, the publicity state of the art. Verdi was rumored to be making a rare public appearance at the premiere, which proved to be false. Everything was set for a brilliant night on April 21, 1889. It wasn't. The audience yawned collectively. The critics were judicious, and almost all expressed an interest in hearing more from the young Puccini. Even Verdi, presumably having read the score, noted sound theatrical instincts in the young composer. But *Edgar* was withdrawn after two performances. Ricordi was not quite done with Puccini yet. He sent the young man to the Wagner Festival at Bayreuth to attend a performance of *Die Meistersinger von Nürnberg* and make recommendations for cuts to the long work that could make it presentable to the Milan public. Ricordi had bought out Giovannina Lucca's publishing house, which originally owned Wagner's rights in Italy. Wagner died in 1883, but his famous festival, dedicated exclusively to his own music in his specially designed theater, resumed under his widow Cosima's direction in 1886. Wagner's final masterpiece, *Parsifal*, was written expressly for the unique acoustics of the Bayreuth Festival House and could only be performed there by special agreement with the German government. Other opera houses either respected Wagner's wishes or couldn't get their paws on a complete score until the Metropolitan Opera of New York produced a "pirated" version in 1903. In Bayreuth, Puccini attended a performance of *Parsifal* as well as *Meistersinger*, and was duly impressed with both. It is one thing to read Wagner's music on a score or at a piano, but quite another to experience a professional production.

Catalani was ill with tuberculosis, a death sentence. He was bitter and angry, and vented a lot of his understandable frustration on Puccini, the new "Golden Boy." How did this upstart presume to make cuts in Wagner's work? Catalani ignored the fact that Ricordi ordered Puccini to make the cuts he, Ricordi, was convinced were necessary to sell Wagner's work to an Italian public. (In fact, Wagner's mammoth *Die Meistersinger von Nürnberg* was given with substantial cuts everywhere except at Bayreuth until recent memory.) Nor was Ricordi being uniquely philistine in his desire to cut Wagner. Wagner's previous Italian publisher, Giovannina Lucca, kept pestering Wagner to cut down his epic, four-day-long *Ring of the Nibelung* to a single evening's entertainment, and a relatively short one at that. Wagner's reply to Sra. Lucca was the priceless comment to the effect that she was welcome to try it herself if she thought she could pull it off, but he would certainly not wield the scissors himself. Ricordi himself never truly developed a love for Wagner's music, but he owned it all the same. None of this mattered to Catalani, who was also hallucinating an intimate relationship between Verdi and Puccini and imagining the two of them planning the rosy future at Catalani's expense. (Of course none of this was happening in reality.) All he saw was his own work languishing while Puccini was receiving every indulgence from the Ricordis.

Arturo Toscanini

Catalani was not without powerful friends of his own, particularly a young man of extreme intelligence and energy named Arturo Toscanini. He was born in Parma (which is "Verdi country") in 1867, and studied the cello there at the Conservatory. His defining traits were apparent at a young age: he was brusque, incapable of suffering fools or people who he judged were not applying themselves to the sacred art of music with their full capacities, and, above all, had an astounding memory. The young cellist joined a touring company bound for South America in the spring of 1886, a typical feature of the opera world in those days that allowed extra income for musicians when the theaters closed in the Northern Hemisphere summers. Toscanini turned nineteen on the passage over. The conductor was a Brazilian whom no one had met until they arrived. He was judged incompetent by the musicians from Italy, and the company was in an uproar. In Rio de Janeiro, the musicians were in a near-riot, and the conductor stepped aside, citing reasons of ill-health. (It remains astounding to this day how suddenly ill-health can strike in an opera house.) A substitute was summoned from the Italian company for the evening's performance of Verdi's *Aida*, but the audience took the sudden departure of the original conductor as an affront to their national pride and booed the substitute off the podium. What was to be done? If everyone simply left the theater right then, there wouldn't even be enough money to book passages back home (not an unknown occurrence with touring opera companies). Toscanini ascended the podium, remaining perfectly still until he impressed the raucous audience with his composure, and conducted the mammoth piece from memory (as would become his habit). The evening was a triumph (opera audiences love to have their derision shoved back at them) and the Rio newspapers were ecstatic. Toscanini conducted eleven different operas for the balance of the season, all from memory, and was loaded with honors and presents, including a diamond ring from the opera-loving emperor of Brazil. (All the gifts were stolen from his hotel in Rio.) He returned to Italy, the subject of much talk among those who had been to Rio but having little else to his name. He returned to his cello and auditioned for the Scala orchestra simply to be able to play in the world premiere of Verdi and Boito's long-awaited *Otello* in February 1887. He never forgot the experience (he never forgot anything) and was so moved that he ran home after the opening and ordered his startled mother to get on her knees and give thanks to and for Verdi.

The act of humility in rejoining an orchestra was remarkable, since Toscanini had already made his Italian conducting debut the previous

November. The event was the premiere of Catalani's opera *Edmea* at Turin. Giovannina Lucca had invited the young phenom to her villa, where he had impressed her with his playing of Wagner (from memory, of course, but this was a feat Wagner himself could rarely accomplish). Toscanini was recognized as a rare talent by the press, and he and the serious Catalani formed an intense friendship.

Friends and Enemies

Puccini's life did not relax after the disappointment of *Edgar*. Giulio Ricordi was calm: the third opera had been the lucky charm for Verdi and for Wagner; perhaps Puccini was following the same operatic destiny. But from Puccini's point of view, both personally and professionally, things must have looked dire. Elvira and little Tonio kept up their peregrinations, Puccini and she trying not to spend too much time together to mollify their families. Puccini himself floated between Lucca and Milan and whatever summer homes he could find. His brother Michele emigrated to Argentina in 1889, and Puccini had hopes he would make some money in that prosperous nation. He even hit up Michele for cash by mail "no matter what the rate of exchange is." Michele had enough problems without having to send money back home to Italy. He loved bustling Buenos Aires with its large Italian population and even found many familiar faces from Lucca there, but he accepted a position in far-off, provincial Jujuy in the Andes. In a strange reenactment of Puccini's destiny, Michele got involved with a married lady to whom he was giving piano lessons. This particular husband managed to track down Michele, there was a duel, Michele shot the husband (who recovered) and fled the country. He went to Rio de Janeiro, but died there of yellow fever. The Puccini family was distraught over the loss of their youngest sibling. The one silver lining was that Puccini's sisters eased their stern attitude somewhat toward their remaining brother and his socially unacceptable position. His favorite sister, Ramelde, even consented to meet the bastard Tonio, and relations improved in that important direction.

In 1888, Mascagni had won another one-act opera competition from the House of Sonzogno. His entry was an operatic setting of Verga's groundbreaking play *Cavalleria rusticana*. Puccini was happy for his friend's success, but no one was prepared for the *furore* that ensued at the opera's premiere in May 1890, at the Teatro Costanzi in Rome. Italy had not seen a triumph of this magnitude from a young composer in almost half a century, since the heady days of Verdi's youth. Verismo, the Italian catchall term for the naturalist trends in literature, had found an expression in opera. It was more than a success in the opera house—it was a national success as well. For decades, words like "new" and "exciting" had been applied only to art and music from Germany and France, and even from more exotic claimants to innovation such as Russia, Bohemia, Hungary, and elsewhere. Finally, there was something entirely new (well, almost entirely new, since we have seen harbingers in Verdi, Ponchielli, and Bizet) from tired old Italy. *Cavalleria* packed a punch in about an hour, with a brash, even vulgar score leading the audience in an inexorable sweep to its finale, which was an actual scream from the stage. It was repeated everywhere, discussed everywhere, derided and applauded everywhere. Within a year it had crossed the Alps and the ocean, and the chatter covered the whole music world.

Puccini, still smarting from the big yawn of *Edgar*, was working on an opera based on *Manon Lescaut*, the protonovel of French literature. It was a risky proposition for a number of reasons, primarily because the opera *Manon* by the Frenchman Jules Massenet was immensely popular everywhere, including in Italy. But Puccini was not deterred. Massenet had written a beautiful and utterly French opera, while Puccini would fill his with purely Italian passion. Hadn't Verdi been warned by the old-timers to avoid *Otello*, since the mighty Rossini had used the same subject and he could never hope to compete with a legend like Rossini? All right, Massenet was still very much alive while Rossini was dead many years when Verdi set to work on *Otello*, but what of that? Hadn't Rossini himself set *The Barber of Seville* while Giovanni Paisiello was still alive and whose own *Barber of Seville* remained popular? That was not the problem for Puccini. The problem was getting the libretto just right.

This proved to be a major problem for Puccini, as it would remain for his entire life. Puccini rejected working with Fontana again, although he never fully explained why, and Fontana felt, not without reason, that Puccini owed him a thing or two. They never collaborated again. Instead, Puccini was paired with Ruggero Leoncavallo, a man of many talents and many more tall tales. Leoncavallo was a composer and a poet who had been around quite a bit, from Egypt to Paris and Naples and elsewhere. He claimed to have met Wagner in Bologna and expounded to him on his own ideas for an Italian answer to the *Ring of the Nibelung*, which he said Wagner enthusiastically encouraged. (Nobody believed this, then or now.) In any case, his path crossed Puccini's in Milan in 1890 and they set to work on *Manon Lescaut*. Puccini was unsatisfied with the results and unceremoniously dumped Leoncavallo. He then met a literary man while hanging out in the Galleria in Milan and asked him on the spot to help him with his opera. The man, named Praga, said he was not a good poet but had a friend who was, Oliva, and the three got to work. Ricordi approved the libretto as rearranged by Praga and Oliva, but Puccini then requested major changes—drop an entire act and add another new one. First Praga quit, then Oliva. Ricordi, who must have pulled out his remaining hairs by this time, decided to bring in the heavy artillery and, if necessary, start over. He hired the outstanding man of letters Giuseppe Giacosa, a highly honored intellectual and good friend of Boito's, as well as Luigi Illica, a brash and temperamental young playwright. The plan was that the theatrical Illica would develop the scenario, while the educated Giacosa would provide the polished poetry that was still expected in Italian opera (even in the verismo *Cavalleria rusticana*). Nobody knew it at the time, but Giacosa and Illica would collaborate with Puccini on his most successful operas. Still, the classic triumvirate of Puccini/Gia-cosa/Illica was not yet solidified. Puccini himself contributed some lines, and even Giulio Ricordi supplied four lines to the final libretto! Before it was finally set, Puccini even returned to Leoncavallo to ask for a few bits and alterations. Perhaps by that time he had forgotten ever working with Leoncavallo in the first place.

Leoncavallo might well have forgotten *Manon Lescaut*, since he was off on a new compositional adventure of his own. Always one to sense which way the wind was blowing, he pitched Sonzogno with an idea for a one-act chunk of verismo, for which he would supply both the libretto and the score, about a jealous clown who murders his wife onstage. Leoncavallo later claimed the incident was drawn from real life, and his father, a judge, had heard the case. (This claim came in handy when Leoncavallo was shortly thereafter accused of plagia-rism by French author Catulle Mendès.) Sonzogno jumped at the plan, although it eventually expanded to two acts, albeit still in the brief and hard-hitting style of *Cavalleria*. He worked with admirable speed, and *I pagliacci* was given to a frenzied audience at the Teatro dal Verme in Milan in May 1892. Toscanini was the conductor. The cast was spectacular as well, but the work itself had undeniable punch, and within two years had been given in every European coun-try and many overseas.

Puccini (not to mention Ricordi) must have wondered if he was barking up the wrong tree. His *Manon Lescaut* had everything going against it, from a French rival to a patchwork libretto. There were some signs of hope, however. *Edgar*, of all things, turned out to be a success in Ferrara in a three-act version, and Puccini even traveled to Madrid to oversee a production of it there. The Madrid production was not a howling success, even though Puccini was introduced to the queen of Spain. (He was unimpressed with the queen and with Madrid, only writing a twisted letter to Elvira about how beautiful the women were in that city and then adding that of course he was remaining faithful.) Puccini rediscovered the village of Torre del Lago in the wetlands of the plains south of Pisa, and decided this was where he belonged. Only someone of Puccini's melancholy character could have found the place an "earthly paradise," as he called it, since it is an eerie, swampy landscape and certainly not the tourists' ideal of "Bella Tuscany." It afforded great opportunities for hunting and fishing, which appealed to Puccini, and it was quiet. He moved to a rented cottage with Elvira. She promptly hated it, and the locals, very simple folk living a rather primitive existence, instantly disliked her. But she did manage to talk her husband into letting her daughter come live with her and Puccini, and little Fosca brought some much-needed joy into the house.

Manon Lescaut was scheduled for Turin on February 3, 1893. Turin was not La Scala, but Ricordi knew what he was doing. *Edgar*'s failure in Milan made another venue more practical. Besides, La Scala had bigger priorities: the seventy-nine-year-old Verdi, in collaboration with Boito, had written yet another opera, *Falstaff*, to be given there on February 9. After the dizzying triumph of *Otello*, the entire musical world was focused on this living legend who paradoxically seemed to be getting younger, artistically and in every other way, as he approached the century mark. Giulio had his hands full with the grumpy Verdi, and barely made it down to Turin between rehearsals to attend the opening night of *Manon Lescaut*. He must have been glad he did. *Manon Lescaut* was the biggest success of the season. The progressive use of the orchestra seemed to absorb all the latest German ideas while remaining unflinchingly Italian in tone. And everyone was astounded at the genuine feel for the human voice in the opera. Puccini had arrived.

The Successor to Verdi

A lot was happening in these few years. Catalani's masterpiece, *La Wally*, debuted in 1892. It was a distant cry from *Cavalleria* and *Pagliacci*, which were eating up the world's stages, and *Manon Lescaut*, with its clear mastery of both voice and orchestra and its

wealth of melody. Italian opera seemed to be going in several directions at once, but which would prevail? George Bernard Shaw, familiar with all the goings-on in Italy, saw *Manon Lescaut* at the Royal
Opera House in London and stated bluntly that Puccini struck him
as the "successor to Verdi" more than any of Puccini's contemporaries. It was an honor, a victory, and a burden to be so named. Verdi,
it must be stressed, was much, much more than the greatest living
Italian composer. His status in Italian history was assured just by the
important symbolic role he had played in the Risorgimento, the unification of an independent Italy. But for all the subsequent mythifica-
tion of the Risorgimento, the reality of the Kingdom of Italy was
quite different. Count Cavour, the political genius behind creating
the Italian nation, died shortly after that birth—a great calamity for
all involved. Without Cavour's guidance, his creation foundered.
Verdi himself resigned from parliament and "retired" to his farm,
leaving the other notable figures of the era to lose public esteem over
time. Garibaldi wore everyone out with his constant ravings and drew
the ire of public opinion against himself when he forced the national
army to engage his irregulars at Aspromonte. The new king, Victor
Emanuel II, did everything possible to lose the affection of the
nation after unification. Even his title, "the Second," showed he considered himself primarily the king of Piedmont-Sardinia and only the
king of Italy as a sort of afterthought. The long-awaited annexation
of Rome was also anticlimactic. The new government brought in an
administration from the north and failed to ingratiate itself with the
Romans. The pope locked himself in the Vatican and declared he was
a prisoner of a foreign occupying power. The king hated Rome and
locked himself in his palace, and he and the pope glared at each
other across the Tiber for years. Meanwhile, the city itself was over-
run with new development to make room for the new government,
and the sleepy but gorgeous city of 200,000 became a dirty metropolis of half a million within twenty years. The sense of loss was
inevitable. Nor was it limited to the capital. The southern half of the
country waited in vain for the modernization and prosperity that was

promised with the new unification: it is still waiting. The mass emigrations began, to Buenos Aires, to New York, and elsewhere. Nor were the emigrations only from the impoverished South. Genoa and the surrounding areas lost inhabitants to the New World. Verdi thought it worth boasting about that his own district had almost no emigration. Michele Puccini commented on how many fellow Lucchesi he recognized in the streets of Buenos Aires in 1889.

The industry in the northern cities such as Turin and Milan was supposed to propel the new nation into modernity, but it was not long before this proved to be a disappointment as well. Wealth, as usual, was concentrated in the hands of the few, while the many workers found their lives even more wretched than before. Finally, in 1898, troops were ordered to fire on disgruntled workers in Milan, and the bloodshed was far greater than it had been when Milan was crushed under Austrian occupation two generations before. It must have been small consolation to the victims that their assassins spoke Italian rather than German.

The disillusionment was all the more pronounced when compared to the German nation, which had gone through a similar painful process of unification. Bismarck's Second Reich was everything Italy was not. Centralization of political power was achieved while maintaining many of the outward forms of the old rule and allowing the disparate regions to maintain at least the fiction of some autonomy. Industrialization was vast and produced great wealth, and if Berlin was even uglier than the new Rome and Milan, the loss was considerably less since Berlin had never been Rome or Milan.

In short, the only thing that was right about Italy was Verdi, and Verdi was gloriously right in a specifically Italian way. As a citizen, he was flawless. When he left parliament in the 1860s, he worked in his farm at Sant'Agata, improving the land and providing for his district in a sensible, rather than ostentatious, manner. He let it be known that he wanted no honors, and was genuinely horrified when there was talk of giving him a noble title. In his eighties, he set up most of his large fortune as a trust to endow a home for retired singers that he had constructed in Milan, designed by Camillo Boito. He seemed to embody all the manly virtues, real or imagined, of the early Roman Republic. Artistically, his legacy was even more impressive. Many thought his *Requiem* of 1875 was to be the grand finale to a splendid career, but the best was yet to come. *Otello*, which premiered, as we have seen, at La Scala in 1887, was not only an undisputed masterpiece—probably, all things considered, the best Italian opera ever—but it was unmistakably Italian. All the gimmicks of traditional Italian opera that had fallen into disrepute among intellectuals, progressives, and Germanophiles—the Drinking Song, the Oath Duet, the Suicide Finale, even the Mad Scene, in a sense—were present in *Otello*, but they were transformed by Verdi's genius (along with Arrigo Boito's) into new, vibrant entities that even made the avant-garde gasp in wonder. Imagine the significance of this to Italians at the time, paralyzed by the weight of their own cultural history: one school of thought seemed to say Italy must remain fossilized in order to preserve her glories, while the opposite school was striving to erase every memory of the past. *Otello* offered the possibility of sublime progress through tradition. Then his *Falstaff* appeared in 1893. The ingenious score impressed the musical world even more than *Otello* had. While *Falstaff* has always towered just a tad above the public reach of true affection, it proved that *Otello* was no fluke. It also proved that age, whether it was Verdi's chronological age or the ancient span of Italian art, need not be a barrier to innovation or triumph. In 1820, when the Carbonari revolt against the Austrians failed, Lord Byron wrote back to England, "Alas, the Italians must [now] return to writing opera." The condescension was patent. Verdi's career demonstrated that writing operas was not an effete avoidance of political or military imperatives. In his case, it was their apotheosis.

The issue of who would be the Successor to Verdi, therefore, meant much more than who would write the next popular operas. It was a search for someone to justify the Italian national identity, since clearly there would be no such justification from the government.

Later, when Italians ceased looking to opera composers for such inspiration and turned, instead, to the government and the military, the result was the greatest disaster to afflict Italy since the barbarian invasions and the fall of the Roman Empire. But that is a story outside of our own.

The success of *Manon Lescaut*, soon making the international circuit, meant that Puccini was out of debt. He settled into his rented villa in Torre del Lago and began to think of building a home there. The success also meant that the brewing resentments among the artistic community were now in full gale force. Catalani was dying and full of invective about the new trends in opera. His own elegant and refined works were being pushed out of the limelight by these new loud, crass operas. His friend Toscanini kept vigil with the dying man, and the experience made a lasting impression on him. Deep down, Toscanini never loved the verismo movement. He thought Catalani was forging the path that the younger generation should follow and that the composer's early death was nothing short of a disaster for Italian art. Toscanini, who married in 1897, named his daughter and son Wally and Walter respectively, from the lead roles in Catalani's opera *La Wally*. He did conduct the premiere of *I pagliacci*, but the experience wore him out mentally and physically (he fell asleep in his evening dress and shoes that night). His distaste for the genre would color his long operatic career. The man who managed to assimilate both Verdi and Wagner when most people thought those two were polar opposites had serious issues with the genre born under his very nose.

La bohème

Leoncavallo soon had a very direct reason to resent Puccini. The two met one day in the Galleria and discussed their current plans. Puccini casually said he was working on an opera, *La bohème*, based on Henri Mürger's play *Scènes de la vie de bohème*. Leoncavallo's jaw dropped.

But of course Puccini knew he himself was working on the same opera! Hadn't Leoncavallo originally offered the libretto to Puccini? Puccini admitted to nothing, and Leoncavallo left in a huff. He promptly alerted the newspapers that he was writing *La bohème*. None of this bothered Puccini in the least. He had taken on Massenet; now he would take on Leoncavallo. And if the two operas were to be written and produced simultaneously, all the better. The public would decide.

Puccini tortured his librettists Giacosa and especially the rather difficult Illica during the composition of *Bohème*. At a time when many composers were writing their own libretti (after Wagner's fashion), Puccini needed the words to be perfect (in his estimation) before he would be able to set them. Sometimes he would write doggerel verse to his librettists to give them a sense of the meters and rhythms he was seeking. But just as often he would change his mind when he received exactly what he ordered. He was frustrating to work for, but there was never any doubt once he found something appropriate. Then the music would flow, and the results would inevitably prove that his carpings had been correct all along.

He composed at the piano, and usually late at night. The very opposite of the temperamental composer who demanded absolute silence in the house for his creative process, Puccini in fact seemed to enjoy having friends around when he worked. Sometimes he would have cronies from Torre del Lago come over and play cards, and he would simply exit from the table every now and then, go in the next room, bang a few bars on the piano, jot some notes, and then calmly return to the game. Other times he would actually have the card games in the same room as the piano! He arranged a ramshackle hut next to a tavern as the "Club la bohème" where he and his drinking buds could gather free of their womenfolk. There was a piano, and amid the rambunctious gatherings, he would compose. Of course, he did not always compose under such circumstances, and occasionally would seek out even quieter spots than Torre del Lago to work on a given piece, but much of his work was done amid daily life. Critics have abused him for this (many critics find composing at a piano to be inherently unmusical), but then we must also consider that Puccini probably came closer to writing music that appears drawn from real life than any other opera composer. Many contemporary composers of our own time go through great exertions to try to imitate the patterns of daily speech in music. I wonder how many of them ever tried sitting at the piano during a drunken card game.

Illica and Puccini both got personally involved with the rehearsals for the premiere, slated for February 1, 1896, again in Turin. The cast had bright spots and problems, but Toscanini was conducting, which assured a certain level of quality. Ricordi sent frequent instructions from Milan: careful with the tricky crowd scenes, don't make the singers lose their voices in rehearsal, and so forth. The big night came. Act I passed with polite applause. Act II was received with absolute frigidity. Acts III and IV went over rather successfully. But the chatter in the lobby was not favorable. The next day, the papers made Puccini gulp. One local critic famously said the new opera would not last beyond the present performances. Some Milan papers, however, were impressed. Ricordi advised caution to Puccini. He had seen many operas come and go, and *Bohème* was different, unfamiliar. It would yet succeed. He was right, of course, and the opera ran for twenty-four performances in Turin, which is highly respectable.

It's hard to imagine today, when *La bohème* has come to stand for all opera in the popular imagination, how it could have ever been considered difficult to understand. And yet, if we look closely at the work and think of it in the true context of its times, the audience's initial bewilderment is not so far-fetched. It all comes down to the understanding of the term verismo. *Cavalleria* and *Pagliacci* defined the genre when they clobbered the audience over the head with violence and a sort of musical vulgarity: that is, clear, gushing music when unadulterated emotion was being portrayed, and so forth. *La bohème* is definitely verismo but it does not work in the same way. It is not about emotionally extroverted peasants in "those places over there, where they act weird" (Sicily and Calabria, respectively, in the cases of *Cavalleria* and *Pagliacci*). It is about modern, urban people of no particular distinction whatsoever who have real emotions about events and situations any one of us could recognize. There are no knives drawn in *Bohème*, there is no code of honor, and there is no exoticism. It was about the audience, as it still is. This may seem mundane now. It was a lot to comprehend in 1896.

Puccini went to Rome for the premiere in that city on February 23, and the same pattern was repeated, only more intensely. The first two acts failed entirely, and the last two were enthusiastically received. On balance, it was a success. He went to Naples to supervise rehearsals at the venerable Teatro San Carlo in March, but left before the opening night. The Neapolitans were insulted, but Puccini explained he did not want to overdo the publicity. He made a jab at Leoncavallo, who never missed an opportunity for applause, and could not resist saying that Leoncavallo was "playing the clown." Yet Puccini was perfectly willing to attend the important premiere of *La bohème* at Palermo, where he was paraded around town and toasted like a victorious general. The Palermo audience created a frenzy from the very beginning of the opera, perhaps intoxicated with themselves for having landed an important composer in their town. In any case, *Bohème*'s conquest of the world's opera houses was now assured. Leoncavallo's *Bohème*, incidentally, was hardly a flop when it came out the following year. It is a very good, very interesting opera whose chief flaw is that it is not Puccini's *La bohème*. The two cohabitated in Italian opera houses and elsewhere for about a decade, until Leoncavallo's opera faded. It is still to be seen, primarily in Italy, on occasion. The mercurial Gustav Mahler, by now general director of the august Vienna Imperial Opera, took a great dislike to Puccini's work, even though he had conducted *Le villi* in Hamburg in 1892. He championed Leoncavallo's opera for years and stood aloof from all Puccini's work. Puccini and Leoncavallo, who were never especially close to begin with, distinctly disliked each other from then on, Puccini usually writing the name Leonasino (from "Lion-horse" to "Lion-ass") in his letters.

Fin de siècle

After *Bohème*, Puccini set to work rather rapidly on his next project, *Tosca*. It was based on a play by the Frenchman Victorien Sardou, a very popular playwright in his day who never aspired to, nor received, high critical acclaim. *La Tosca*, as the play was called, had in fact been written for no less a stage presence than Sarah Bernhardt. It was violent, raw, and even a tad kinky. In Sardou's version, all the cheesiness of the story is embedded in good French dialogue and excruciating dramatic detail, for Sardou was a proponent of what was long called "the well-made play." Everything had a reason, and all the reasons were spoken out at some length.

Nevertheless, there was an emotional core to the work. Verdi had looked at it and pronounced it stage-worthy, which was nothing short of a message from God for Ricordi. But he would not write it himself: the eighty-one-year-old icon was serious, finally, about not writing any more operas. There was a slight problem: Ricordi had assigned Illica to work on the libretto of *Tosca* for Franchetti, and in fact Franchetti was writing *Tosca* as Puccini was composing *Bohème*. Once *Bohème* was done and launched, and while Franchetti was still dithering over *Tosca*, it became necessary to pull the work out from under Franchetti and give it to Puccini. There are several variations of how this was managed: some say Ricordi used fraud and cheated Franchetti out of the chance at a huge success. Others maintain that Franchetti had never really loved the story and was eager to be rid of it. There is plenty of evidence for both points of view. The upshot, of course, is that it went to Puccini, even if there are more hints of strained relations between the two at this time. Franchetti wasn't the only person with reservations about *Tosca*. Giacosa found the whole thing disgusting, and wasn't afraid to say so. He had to be pulled through the process of working on the libretto. Illica, too, felt that it was coming out all wrong, and complained loudly about it. Puccini even got into quite a row with Ricordi—their first ever—over disagreements about the work. There was something about this opera that simply set people off.

Puccini held his ground, wrote conciliatory letters to "Papa Giulio" saying, "You'll see!" and plans were made for the premiere. The story takes place in Rome, and moreover is, as Sardou kept stressing to Puccini in his input into the opera, a Roman opera in more than the setting. The premiere, therefore, had to take place in Rome, where Puccini had never premiered an opera before. Rome was tense in 1900. Pope Leo XIII had declared 1900 a Jubilee Year, and the city was full of pilgrims and tourists. Of course, Rome is also always full of agitators and revolutionaries as well, and just then the anarchists were making their presence known with no subtlety. All the divergent political and cultural spasms of Italy were shaking Rome at just that time, and many feared the city would explode one way or another that year. The premiere on January 14 was especially tense. Bomb threats were made on the opera house. Ricordi was actually more nervous about the many musical notables present in the audience, including Mascagni, Franchetti, and others who he feared would cause a disturbance. Anarchists he could manage, but composers are unpredictable. . . . Queen Margherita of Italy announced her intention to attend (she was late and missed Act I). A disturbance was heard shortly after the curtain went up, and the conductor, thinking a bomb had gone off, played the national anthem (it was latecomers arguing with ushers). People's nerves were shot, which happens to be an excellent way to enjoy this particular opera. The audience was enthusiastic and the critics the next morning were, in many cases, so outraged and repulsed that Puccini immediately knew he had another big hit.

Later that year, King Umberto was indeed assassinated. Queen Margherita wrote a simple and poignant prayer, published in the newspapers. Verdi, never a Royalist, was moved by the prayer, and attempted to set it to music. He got no further than a few notes, though, and they were his last. The Grand Man died in Milan on January 27, 1901. Three days of national mourning were decreed. Giacosa delivered the funeral oration. In case anyone had any doubts, the old century had passed. Attentions would be focused on Puccini as never before, and he was not one who loved attention.

Returning to Torre del Lago after *Tosca*, Puccini was now in a position to build a house for himself. He had already begun to buy, refurbish, or build small residences, hunting lodges, and summer homes in the hills nearby. Puccini had a case of what the locals called "mal di pietra," "the stone sickness," or what we might call "buildingitis." It is not surprising, given his many years of wandering and his desire to live apart from "the world," that he should have indulged in this vice, and at this point in his life he could well afford it. He built the Villa Puccini in Torre del Lago right by the waters of Lake Massaciuccoli, a pleasant but eminently unpretentious home. It is a museum today, and contains a mausoleum where he, Elvira, and Tonio are buried.

Bumps in the Road

Puccini went to London, the only city he ever really liked, in 1900 to oversee *Tosca*. While there, he attended the theater and saw *Madame Butterfly*, a play by David Belasco about a geisha in (then) present-day Japan who is destroyed by believing that her sham arrangement to an American naval officer is a real marriage. Belasco was in the theater the night Puccini attended. According to Belasco, Puccini accosted him backstage after the performance and, in a flood of tears and Latin cheek-kisses, thanked him for the wonderful experience and declared on the spot that he would write an opera on the subject. At least, that was what Belasco thought Puccini, who was blubbering in Italian, was saying. This may or may not have happened in reality, but Puccini was uncharacteristically clear about his intention to set *Madame Butterfly*. It wouldn't have been the first time the remarkable Belasco adorned the facts.

Belasco was born in San Francisco in 1853 of Sephardic Jewish parents from England who had joined the Gold Rush. Somewhere along the line he attended a seminary school, and throughout his life affected clerical garb à la Franz Liszt. He was eventually nicknamed "the Bishop of Broadway," a paradox he adored. He learned acting and stage management in San Francisco and with traveling troupes throughout California's Gold Country, eventually coming to New York in the 1880s. His plays, mostly adaptations, became tremendously popular for their realistic acting and their staging. In one play, set in a typical diner, he not only re-created every detail of furniture and tableware from a nearby New York establishment, but insisted fresh pots of coffee be brewed onstage nightly during the performance so the audience could recognize the smell. He was also among the first directors to plumb the importance of the new science of lighting, and one of the most impressive features of *Madame Butterfly* was a fourteen-minute-long "vigil" over the city of Nagasaki with no speaking from the actors. The audience (including Puccini) was held enrapt by the effects of nightfall, with the lights of the city appearing in the background, and the subsequent sunrise. Birdsongs were used for the latter part of the scene. Belasco appealed to almost all of the senses but, like Sardou, never attempted to challenge the intellect. He was a well-known figure in New York and London, always recognizable in his curious outfit. He owned several theaters in New York (one of which is now the Belasco Theater and another one, the stunning New Victory on Forty-second Street) and was involved in what would become the American Academy of Dramatic Arts. He acted as theatrical mentor to one of his friend's sons, a certain Cecil B. DeMille.

Back in Torre del Lago, Puccini worked on *Butterfly*, which at this point primarily consisted of wrangling with Illica over the adaptation. He had other diversions as well. By 1900, he had met a young woman from Turin named Corinna. We don't know much about Corinna except that she may have been a teacher, she was single (as was Puccini, according to the law), she was younger, and she felt like a breath of fresh air. Elvira had become increasingly difficult over the years, with scenes of jealousy (not without reason), uncertainty about her own status in society and that of her children, unhappy in the swamps at Torre, and terrified to run into her husband in Lucca. Puccini, besides having a roving eye, was also starting to worry about aging: we read comments in his letters from as early as his mid-thirties about gray hairs, his terror of growing old, and a feeling that life was passing him by. Puccini had one of the longest midlife crises in history.

He and Corinna met in Viareggio, the lovely seaside resort up the coast from Torre. Elvira knew about it in a general way, and there were recriminations, scenes, and even a hunger strike. Puccini confided his feelings of guilt about Elvira to his family but could not stop the affair. Gossip got to Ricordi, who wrote strong letters in a paternal fashion to Puccini. Puccini tried to play all sides and did not entirely neglect his home. One foggy night in the winter of 1903, he drove with Tonio and Elvira to Lucca. Puccini always had an interest in cars and the latest machinery and sometimes attended car shows in Milan (occasionally with the rich and apparently ubiquitous Franchetti, who happened to be the president of the Italian Automobile Club). On this particular night, he and Elvira and Tonio were driven by a chauffeur. The car missed a curve on the ride home and overturned. Elvira and Tonio were shaken but without serious injury. The chauffeur had a broken leg. A nearby physician, fortunately, heard the crash and came running. No one could find Puccini. He was eventually found under the car, trapped in a little hollow that saved his life. He was bleeding and his legs were fractured. He was carted to the villa of an acquaintance and left there to convalesce.

Nobody knows what Puccini and his brood were doing in Lucca that night. Ricordi issued a press release to say they were dining with friends. Local gossip, well substantiated, believed that they had gone to see Elvira's husband, Gemignani, who was dying (some said from injuries sustained from a fight with a jealous husband he, in his turn, had wronged). Elvira was trying to get him to forgive her and die free of the rancor that might imperil his soul and, incidentally, to make sure his will provided for her. There were reports of scenes and harsh words from his relatives as the man lay dying, almost a scene worthy of comic opera. In any case, Gemignani did in fact die the next day while Puccini's life lay in question. We can only imagine the toll these few days took on a nervous constitution such as Elvira's.

Telegrams poured in from around the world to Puccini: from the king of Italy, statesmen of several countries, friends (including Mascagni, who was in San Francisco), and well-wishers, although Franchetti mysteriously sent nothing. Puccini's convalescence was slow. He chain-smoked in bed, alternately lost weight and then gained it, smoked some more, and finally was able to move to a wheelchair. He had a special piano rigged up so he could play from the wheelchair and possibly finish up *Butterfly*, which lay languishing. While he was convalescing, doctors diagnosed him with diabetes.

Puccini was pressured to renounce Corinna and marry Elvira, who, according to law, could now marry him after the passage of ten months. Elvira even recruited Giulio Ricordi into the plan, but Ricordi needed little prodding. He was still writing his ominous letters to Puccini telling him that *l'affaire* Corinna was compromising his art, work, and more. Ricordi did not yet know about the diabetes, and stated bluntly that he was convinced Puccini had syphilis, which was all one could expect from "that sort" of woman. Puccini was offended but the prevailing winds carried the day. He broke off with Corinna, who threatened to sue him. Corinna demanded a personal meeting with Puccini in Switzerland, and Elvira moved heaven and earth to prevent this meeting, all to no avail. Puccini did meet with Corinna, but we do not know what was said. According to Elvira, she and Puccini had a fight when he returned and he actually punched her. (In later incidents, Puccini complained of physical abuse from Elvira.) Yet something had been settled with Corinna, and Elvira was able to announce her engagement. She and Puccini were married by the mayor of Viareggio in a civil ceremony. That night (January 3, 1904), they were married in the parish church at Torre, very late, with only a few witnesses, and curtains thrown up over the windows. The claim was that they did not want publicity, but one is hard-pressed to imagine a less romantic wedding.

The Fiasco: Butterfly *at La Scala*

The day after the wedding, Puccini went to Milan to arrange for the premiere of *Madama Butterfly*. He was bubbling with confidence. His life, albeit not perfect, was at least normalized after the accident and the sorting out of his messy domestic situation. He knew he had written his best opera to date. The soprano, Rosina Storchio, was managing the demanding lead role with aplomb. The costumes and the sets were gorgeous, under the direction of Tito Ricordi Jr., Giulio's son, who was being groomed to take over the firm, and the orchestra was well rehearsed under Cleofonte Campanini. For the first time in his life, Puccini arranged for his family to attend the premiere.

La Scala has seen—and created—its share of disasters over the years. Verdi's second opera, *Un giorno di regno*, was a failure that sent the young man into a tailspin and almost (so he claimed) cured him of the compulsion to write operas. Boito's *Mefistofele* was booed off the stage. But both of those nights would seem models of decorum compared to the premiere of *Madama Butterfly* on February 17, 1904. The audience was cold or worse to Act I. Butterfly's entrance was jeered with shouts of *"Bohème!"* from audience members who thought Puccini was recycling material from his biggest hit (and in this first version, a case could have been made for these comments). The applause for the love duet at the end of the act was, hard to believe today, subdued. There were boos and shouts at the curtain. In Act II, all hell broke loose. Storchio's kimono billowed and people shouted that she was pregnant. "From Toscanini!" chimed in others, eager to show that they were in on (true in this case) backstage gossip. When Butterfly subsequently showed her child by Pinkerton to the American consul, the audience fell into a fit of derision and laughter. In the now-celebrated vigil and sunrise scene, which had so impressed Puccini when he saw Belasco's play staged, Tito had arranged for birdsong to accompany the orchestral interlude. The audience answered with its own birdcalls, rooster crows, and eventually, mooing. Giulio Ricordi wrote that the audience, after shouting and screaming for the final curtain, left the theater in a festive mood and quite pleased with itself. Some newspapers attempted a judicious critique of the new work but others fell in with the mob mentality and castigated Puccini. One went so far as to call it a "diabetic opera" and the "result of an accident" in its headline. The Milanese smelled blood and fell into a feeding frenzy.

What could possibly explain the disaster? Sr. Giulio was convinced there was a plot afoot, set in motion by jealous rivals. He squarely blamed Mascagni, even though Mascagni had attended and even stood in his box berating the crowd for its boorishness. Sr. Giulio coldly dismissed this as "crocodile tears." Puccini never made direct reference to Mascagni in this regard but did assent to the idea of jealous rivals and a conspiracy. Indeed, the idea is not implausible, and the butt of the reaction was not merely Puccini but the House of Ricordi and the whole of the Italian musical establishment it represented. The rival House of Sonzogno billed itself as the music of the future, and blamed the problems other composers were having on Ricordi's firm grip on the Italian music scene. Furthermore, Puccini's "little operas" about ordinary people were not satisfying the national craving for something epic that would command the respect of the rest of the world. Puccini wasn't even trying to grow, as they saw it. Another opera about a sad heroine! Just what Italians needed! As if the world didn't already see them as a nation of emotional, teary lightweights with soft, gooey centers! They, or at least a vociferous portion of them, wanted more muscle on their stages to represent the new Italy, a player on the world stage.

Puccini was predictably distraught, but managed to attend a damage-control meeting early the next day with Tito, Giacosa, and Illica. Tito believed in the opera even more than his father, who, despite his spirited defense of *Butterfly* in print, deep down in his heart also wanted something of a larger scale from Puccini. Giacosa felt that his original idea of three acts instead of two would make the opera irresistible. Puccini did not need much encouragement to try again with *Butterfly*: he knew it was his best work, and throughout his life maintained that it was the only opera of his he could bear to hear over and over. Ricordi sprang into action, instructing La Scala to cancel all further performances immediately and refunding them a sack of money for their troubles. He sent agents around to the music stores in Milan to buy up all copies of the piano-vocal score. The creators of the work got to work snipping here and tucking there and made plans for the premiere of the revised work. But where would they give this reborn *Butterfly*? Milan was out of the question. Rome, perhaps? Turin? Forward-looking Bologna? Tito lobbied for Brescia, with a smaller theater and temptingly—even tauntingly—close to Milan. *Madama Butterfly* was given there in three acts and with some small but important other revisions on May 29, 1904. It was a triumph, and Puccini was vindicated. He now needed to conquer (or reconquer) a large city. With a few more revisions, *Butterfly* was staged in Paris, and so began its triumphal tour of the world.

New Directions and New Worlds

Puccini now had an arsenal of four surefire international hits to his name, and took some time to oversee productions and promote his work. On a trip to London in the autumn of 1904, he met the beguiling Sybil Seligman, who was to become his greatest and in many ways his most important friend. Sybil was beautiful, filthy rich, educated, and refined beyond the bounds of civilization. She came from a wealthy background of Jewish banking families that placed high emphasis on cultural achievement. According to later reminiscences from her sister, Sybil and Puccini did begin their relationship as lovers but settled into a much deeper friendship. Others doubt they ever were lovers. Whatever the clinical definition of their relationship, we have many of their letters, and it is clear that Puccini was open and honest with her and held her opinions in the highest regard. The two families became close, the Seligmans passing many summer vacations at the Puccinis' several homes or in nearby Viareggio and the Puccinis meeting up with the Seligmans at every opportunity in London or Monte Carlo. Much information was related by the son, Vincent Seligman, in his book *Puccini Among Friends*, where his memories of the private Puccini add considerably to our knowledge of the man.

After London, the Puccinis sailed for Montevideo and Buenos Aires to attend a series of performances. Toscanini had already introduced Puccini to audiences in those cities, and a special season of Puccini's operas, including *Edgar*, was arranged for his visit to Buenos Aires. Elvira got seasick halfway up the gangplank and retired to her room for the entire trip. On arrival, Puccini was feted, toasted, and celebrated, all of which was difficult for him. The operas were a tremendous success (except for the exhausting *Edgar*, which was now finally retired), and the Puccinis returned to Italy.

But what to do next? Ricordi wanted something very grand. Franchetti had obliged him with the large-scaled *Germania* in 1902, which showed every indication of remaining in the repertory (it didn't). Leoncavallo was writing everything from popular songs (including the still-ubiquitous *Mattinata*, recorded by the tenor Enrico Caruso and then playing in living rooms around the world) to an epic celebration of the Hohenzollern dynasty written at the kaiser's request. The French were churning out everything from the light and lively to poetic grandeur, as witnessed by the surprising popular success of Claude Debussy's *Pelléas et Mélisande* in 1902. Everybody in the world seemed to be writing operas in that decade: Czechs, Russians, Norwegians, even Americans, of all people. New and magnificent opera houses were springing up from San Francisco to Buenos Aires to Sofia. And the Germans, after a post-Wagner hangover, were making noises again. Richard Strauss, a successful composer of orchestral music, was now concentrating on opera. After two misfires, he hit the world on the head with *Salome*, a scandalous shocker an hour and a half long. The Italians needed something big.

Puccini and Strauss paralleled each other for many years. Strauss labored under the burden of being the Successor to Wagner as Puccini struggled with his own expectations. The two composers appear entirely different, at least according to their various partisans, yet time has shown them to have had many similar goals. And they both concentrated on the soprano voice like no previous composers. Puccini was always puzzled by *Salome* but remained fascinated by it and was not afraid to say so publicly. The affable Strauss made some derisive comments about Puccini here and there but also praised him. He once explained to a journalist that he never said he disliked Puccini's music. He simply needed to avoid it because he couldn't get the melodies out of his head and feared that he would write Puccinian Strauss. It's hard to imagine a higher backhanded compliment. The two occasionally met and pointedly avoided discussing music theory, which neither of them enjoyed anyway. They were both happier playing cards.

The remnants of the Old Guard clucked in disapproval at the new popular composers. Boito said he felt the sadness of being trapped between *Butterfly* and *Salome*: the first was a glass of tepid water, but the second an ocean of ennui. Boito returned, depressed, to his literary articles and desultory glances at his still-unfinished *Nerone*. Boito had long since given up his hashish but he retained his melancholy and his abstract musings until the very end. Similar to young radicals everywhere, he had developed into a reactionary.

After the exciting but nervewracking experience of *Butterfly*, Puccini was truly at a loss for his next project. The problem was an overabundance of ideas rather than a lack of them. Giacosa died in 1906, a great loss to Puccini. He and Illica would never produce another opera together, although this was not yet apparent. He set Illica to work on a project that had the full backing of Giulio Ricordi: an opera based on the trial and execution of Marie Antoinette. It would have historical spectacle and opportunities for great, larger-than-life soprano antics, and, most important of all to the Ricordis, it would be about something other than trivial people. Puccini ran hot and cold on the idea. First of all, he did not want to look as if he were capitalizing on Umberto Giordano's success with *Andrea Chénier*, an opera that combined verismo with history and spectacle. Then other times he was excited about it, and allowed Ricordi to publish reports that he was definitely working on the project and it would be his next opera. The one who paid for all this ambivalence was, of course, Illica. Puccini's constant rejections of his written scenes must have told him deep down that the opera would never happen, yet it was not officially put to rest for many years.

Puccini also combed the short stories of the radical Russian author Maxim Gorky for ideas, and again found one or two that sparked his imagination. His plan was to write a trilogy of one-act operas, thereby combining the best of the original verismo ideal of *Cavalleria* with the demand for epic operas. Giulio Ricordi was fixed against the idea from the start, but this did not stop Puccini from sending out ideas to librettists and poets for them to tinker around with. *Anna Karenina* was briefly considered. For a long time, Puccini diddled with a very unusual story by the French poet Pierre Louÿs entitled *La femme et le pantin* (*The Woman and the Puppet*), which told of a woman who tries to get her lover jealous by making him catch her in flagrante delicto with a young boy. The lover beats her mercilessly, causing the woman to declare her love for him, since she never knew he cared enough to beat her. This certainly would have removed Puccini from the category of "sentimental," and shocking operas were all the rage just then. Didn't Strauss get a ton of publicity when his *Salome* was banned from the Met after a single performance? He set librettists to work on this story, calling the operatic version *Conchita*. It remained on his desk for years, but he never wrote it. Puccini then turned to Gabriele D'Annunzio, whom he had originally contacted (through Ricordi's agent) after *La bohème* and again after *Tosca*. D'Annunzio was making quite a name for himself with his poetry, dramas, articles, and mistresses—the most visible of whom was Eleanora Duse, Italy's most famous actress. (Duse began an affair with D'Annunzio while she was still carrying on an affair with Arrigo Boito. It is a testament to her grace and deep affection for Boito that they remained close friends after the affair and until his death.) By this point, D'Annunzio was being called "The Bard of Italy," and on one hand it was only natural that the leading composer and the leading poet of the country should work together. However, the thought of a Puccini/D'Annunzio collaboration must strike anyone familiar with either of their works as perfect absurdity. They met and exchanged flatteries (D'Annunzio being much more successful at this than Puccini). The poet recommended his historical tales *Parisina* and *The Rose of Cyprus*. Puccini was pushing for something intimate, light, and human-scaled. They lived on different planets. They continued to exchange polite letters for years and each took a long time letting go of the ego-flattering idea of working with the other. Privately, D'Annunzio complained of Puccini's lack of vision on the big scale and said he had failed to mature as an artist. Meanwhile, each shopped for other collaborators.

Puccini was invited to New York in 1907. The financier Otto Kahn had joined the board of the Metropolitan Opera of New York in 1903, stealthily taking over the whole huge operation. His intention was to make the Met the world's Number One Opera House Bar None, and he had the money—his own and other board members' such as J. P. Morgan—to throw around. Not content to hire Gustav Mahler as music director, he also made Toscanini an offer he couldn't refuse. The idea was to have Mahler in charge of German repertory and Toscanini take care of the Italian, although in reality there was a good deal of tense crossing over. He then managed to lure Giulio Gatti-Casazza from La Scala to act as impresario. But before any of these colossi could be nabbed, he insisted on getting Puccini himself to New York to attend a sort of Puccini festival, including Met premieres of *Manon Lescaut* and *Butterfly*.

Kahn gave Puccini the first-class treatment, booking a luxurious suite for him and Elvira aboard the steamship *Kaiserin Auguste Victoria*. Elvira fared little better on this North Atlantic passage in the dead of winter than she had on the voyage to South America, but she managed to get out of the cabin occasionally. Puccini, meanwhile,

had a childlike delight in the ship's amenities, particularly impressed
with the bathroom lighting. Still, the ship was late in arriving in New
York, and then had to clear customs and quarantine in Hoboken.
They did not disembark until five o'clock on the afternoon of January
17, with the Met premiere of *Manon Lescaut* slated for that very
evening. The Puccinis checked into the Hotel Astor amid bustling
Herald Square and hopped into evening clothes just in time for the
opera a few blocks up Broadway.

The performance, needless to say, was a great success, and suddenly Puccini was the toast of the celebrity-crazed town. He already
knew the now-legendary tenor Enrico Caruso, whose appearance in
La bohème had been booed off the Scala stage in 1902, partially due
to illness. (Puccini was in the theater on that painful night.) The fun-
loving, card-playing Caruso acted as Puccini's tour guide in New
York and introduced him to many prominent members of the Italian
community there. They found quiet Italian restaurants near the opera
house and in Little Italy where they could play cards until the wee
hours. New York impressed Puccini, but it was all a bit much for him:
the cold, the expense, the crowds. He admired the tall buildings and
the latest in technology. The Met impressed him. And he liked American women. "They could make the Tower of Pisa stand erect," he
wrote his sister Ramelde. Elvira spied on him as ever but he "got away
with everything," he added in the same letter. The boast was premature: Elvira found a compromising note from a local groupie hidden
in the band of Puccini's top hat, and confronted the poor woman at
the first opportunity. Puccini began to wonder if Elvira possessed
supernatural powers of divination.

Meanwhile, however, he was rumored to be having an affair with
the stunning soprano Lina Cavalieri, who was bringing *Manon Lescaut*
to life onstage. *Butterfly* took more rehearsal. The very beautiful and
popular Geraldine Farrar was given the title role. Farrar took great
pains with it, hiring Japanese actresses with her own money to coach
her in deportment. She was even said to walk around New York in
the dead of winter in wooden sandals to master them. Puccini was

never impressed with Farrar, however, thinking her voice too small for the role, especially at the large Met. Caruso was also to sing in *Butterfly*, which he had already sung in London. Farrar complained of his lack of attention at rehearsals and thought the Italians were in a conspiracy together. She may have been right. The newspapers raved about *Butterfly* and Caruso (as they always raved about Caruso) but said little about Farrar. She persevered, and it soon became her signature role, selling out the house frequently for more than a decade.

Meanwhile, Puccini still needed an opera to compose. Sybil Seligman was set on another Belasco play, *The Girl of the Golden West*, which was in fact Belasco's favorite of his own works. Puccini saw the play in New York, was favorably impressed, and returned to Italy. Sybil got the play translated into Italian for him to read (Puccini never came close to mastering English, and his impressions of plays in English were made without regard to the actual meanings of the words, which is a fascinating point to consider.) Sybil also suggested the work's final operatic title, *La fanciulla del West*. *The Girl* would keep him busy on his return, but it would be interrupted by a great crisis.

Elvira Furiosa: L'affaire *Manfredi*

Life cannot have been easy for Elvira. Because of her precarious position as a woman who had left her husband, she must have had hundreds of daily insults and humiliations that we can only imagine today. And her second husband preferred life in small towns and in the country, where attitudes were even worse than those in the large cities. Puccini gave her plenty of real reasons to be furious, and her own fears and paranoia exacerbated the already precarious situation. In the fall of 1908, she finally snapped.

The event is probably the best-recorded incident in Puccini's life. Their maid, Doria Manfredi, had worked in the Puccini household since shortly after the automobile accident, when she was sixteen years old. All seemed peaceful for more than five years. In September 1908, Elvira began to accuse Manfredi of seducing her husband. Both the girl and Puccini denied the accusations, but Elvira would not be convinced. She insulted Doria and spread rumors about her in the gossip-starved village. In early October, Elvira called the girl a whore and fired her. Not even this was enough. She consistently denounced her to anyone who would listen, and even to many who tried hard to avoid her. Puccini was distraught. He wrote to Sybil of his sadness and mentioned that he had "lovingly fingered his revolver." All work on *Fanciulla* was suspended. Puccini wrote to Doria expressing his regret at Elvira's behavior, and to Doria's mother assuring her of the falseness of the accusations and apologizing profusely. He communicated much the same to her brothers, whom he knew from hunting trips.

Elvira left to visit her mother in Lucca before Christmas, and Puccini might have hoped for some peace, but she was even more worked up on her return. She publicly insulted Doria on Christmas Day, and in January actually threatened her life. Puccini considered abandoning Elvira between thoughts of suicide. Finally, he fled to Rome and checked into the Hotel Quirinale. It was, in retrospect, a cowardly act, but he simply could not endure the situation. Elvira increased her battle stance. She wrote Manfredi's relatives detailed letters of the imagined affair and quoted imaginary love letters she supposedly had found. Doria could not even leave the house for fear of running into Elvira, who was constantly on the prowl in the village for the girl or for anyone who would listen to her tirades before they could escape her. Doria wrote a suicide note in which she protested her innocence and begged her family to take revenge on Elvira but not on Puccini, who had never done anything wrong in any way. According to one account, she bought a toxic disinfectant and swallowed some, lying in agony for five days. The doctors could do nothing. Puccini, in Rome, learned of the incident and was distraught. His pity for the girl was clear, but his letters to Sybil at this time speak more of his own life being in ruins. Doria died on January 28, 1909.

Puccini swore he would never speak to Elvira again, asking Ricordi to manage her affairs for him. Torre del Lago began to question if Elvira had not been right after all. Perhaps Doria really died of a botched abortion? A postmortem was ordered, and Doria was determined to have died a virgin.

It's hard to know which is worse: Elvira's persecution of an innocent girl or the attitudes of a community that demanded clinical proof of "innocence." Had she not been a virgin, would that have justified her death? Still, setting aside this admittedly anachronistic quibble, the inquest should have satisfied the questions current at the time, and one would imagine even such a person as Elvira would have sought a way to de-escalate the situation. Not a chance: she actually continued her tirade. The Manfredis brought legal action against Elvira. The story made international headlines. Puccini lingered in Rome, doing nothing. Elvira fled to Milan with Tonio, since life at Torre del Lago was no longer a viable option for her. Friends urged Puccini to take this opportunity to split with Elvira once and for all. Illica even suggested he move to New York to avoid the possibility of him returning to "his weakness," as he called Elvira. In March, Puccini came down with the flu and summoned his sisters to Rome to care for him, effectively eliminating any severe course of action. After much swearing that he would never see Elvira again, Puccini showed signs of wavering, as Illica feared he would. He went to Milan to see Tonio, still insisting he would not see Elvira. He did, however, and she was hardly repentant. Indeed, she reiterated that it was all his fault, that she knew she was right, and that God would punish him for all the suffering he had brought down on her over the years. Here we have clear evidence that Elvira's vehemence was years in the making.

They met in Milan in June, and although she continued her abuse, they moved toward a rapprochement. He told her plainly that he intended to return to her if he could be assured of the peace and quiet he needed to work. The court reached a verdict in the Manfredis' case against Elvira (she was not present) on July 6. She was found guilty of defamation, libel, and menace to life and limb, sentenced to over five months in prison, given a small fine, and ordered to pay all costs. The international press returned the story to the headlines. Elvira wrote Puccini, castigating him for not doing enough. Did he want to see her in prison? (A rhetorical question, one suspects.) And she added a new leitmotif to her tirade: the Manfredis had misled her, the sisters had gossiped, and the mother, the real culprit, was behind it all. Puccini sent the attorneys to work. Finally, the Manfredis withdrew the suit with a payment of 12,000 lire from Puccini. Elvira met up with Puccini again in Bagni di Lucca, and they resumed their life together, somehow.

We do not know on what terms the Puccinis were reconciled and can only imagine what he had said to her privately. Yet everyone noticed that Elvira was slightly changed by the experience. There would not be any more major public scenes in their life together, let alone international headlines. The obsessive spying on her part dropped dramatically. And if friends and intimates never saw them as particularly close, even in the latter days of their bizarre relationship, they did achieve some sort of entente that allowed for at least the appearance of a reasonably peaceful household. Their great marital crisis had this salutary effect, even if it also had a body count.

Assessing Elvira

Before we completely trash Elvira, we need to pause a moment to reflect that women who have married great musicians invariably have a rough time with public opinion. Kostanze Mozart has been unfairly enshrined as a twit. Giuseppina Strepponi was blamed by the people of Busseto for alienating Verdi's affections from them, even though there never was any affection to alienate. Cosima Wagner (admittedly, a difficult character) is always cited as being even more hateful than her husband, which is simply not within the realm of possibility. Pauline Strauss remains the butt of many jokes. In our own day, Yoko

Ono and Linda Eastman McCartney are somehow both blamed for the demise of the Beatles (and a great deal else besides), while the public is convinced that Courtney Love actually killed Kurt Cobain (who called her a "goddess" in his suicide note). Granted, all these women had or have their faults and shortcomings. Other than Strepponi and Eastman, who patiently withdrew from public view and waited for public opinion to change, the others asserted themselves and have been heavily abused for it.

But whatever their faults, the men in question needed no wives to encourage their dark sides. Mozart was an overgrown brat with some serious developmental issues; Verdi loved humanity best from afar; Wagner has a good claim to be rated as one of the real bastards of all times; Richard Strauss was even dumpier and more conventionally bourgeois than his "scrubbing-brush" Frau; John Lennon was a genius and an inspiration but was also a bitter and angry person; and nothing could have stopped Cobain's self-destructive spiral. It is as if the public must siphon off the sins of the artist and dump them on his wife in order to enjoy his art with a clear conscience. People are afraid that admiring the creations of a flawed man will be seen as an inherent endorsement of that man's character defects: thus the whole debate about Wagner the Man vs. Wagner the Artist. It goes beyond music. The public is still shocked—shocked and appalled— whenever a sports hero is busted for drugs or an American president is caught with his pants down. However, there is a particular problem with this in music history, and, the "great musicians" being disproportionately male, we have gotten into the habit of making their wives out to be albatrosses at best, monsters at worst.

With all this in mind, however, it is still rather difficult to discern the good in Elvira Puccini. That she was a handsome woman we take on the word of her contemporaries, since the photos do not bear this out. No doubt she was attractive when she smiled, but one searches the photo archives in vain for such a moment caught on film. Although she came from a musical family, she had no appreciation for music—Puccini's or anyone else's, and he once complained to her in a letter about the way she sneered whenever he mentioned the subject. In fact, she even met Illica for lunch once in the early days of her liaison with Puccini for the sole purpose of telling him that Puccini was hardly working at all on *La bohème*. But little more harm was done in that direction, since Illica learned to avoid her. Ramelde had long maintained that Elvira would ruin Puccini. Even the charming Vincent Seligman discreetly let it be known that he did not care for her and frankly admitted that he and the other children were afraid of her. He suggested that Elvira must have welcomed her own death the day it came, and one wonders if she was the only person to feel a sense of relief on that day.

Glittering New York

Puccini managed to finish *Fanciulla* despite more than the usual amount of problems with the librettists. Working without Giacosa and Illica for the first time in decades, Puccini was paired with Carlo Zangarini, who was half American and whose mother was from Colorado, no less. Puccini was dissatisfied, predictably, and a second collaborator was brought in, a certain Guelfo Civinini, who would spend many subsequent years complaining of the shoddy treatment his verse got at Puccini's hands. The premiere was slated for the Met, the first ever for that house. Kahn was getting everything he wanted for "his" house: Gatti-Casazza, Toscanini, and Mahler were installed in their various positions, and for the moment everyone managed to get along.

New York was brimming with opera. Caruso, Farrar, and a host of other big names kept audiences enthralled. Oscar Hammerstein had opened the rival Manhattan Opera Company on Twenty-third Street, gathering up all the world's best singers who weren't already under contract to the Mighty Met and specializing in everything that wasn't getting full treatment there: French opera, new works, and many performances of *Salome*, still anathema at the Met (as it would remain until the 1930s). Kahn eventually had to buy out Hammerstein, paying him a fortune not to produce opera in New York (surely the sweetest deal ever for an opera impresario). But for the moment there was a healthy rivalry. All Kahn needed was a first-class world premiere to put the Met at the top of the world's heap.

This happened on December 10, 1910. Puccini sailed to New York with Tonio and Tito Ricordi, and without Elvira, who, it seems, was still being "punished." Toscanini had been working the orchestra through its difficult music for weeks. Belasco himself directed, working himself to the bone to try to teach the mostly Italian choristers how to throw a lasso (and what one wouldn't give to have been a fly on the wall for those sessions!). The Met was festooned with flowers and Italian and American flags for the gala, and (predictably) ticket prices were raised. Scalpers pushed prices up to $150. *La toute* New York was there in all their formidable jewelry. The audience went ballistic, American style. Ovations, flowers, and shouts greeted the singers (the Czech soprano Emmy Destinn taking the difficult role of Minnie, supported by Caruso and the star baritone Pasquale Amato) and Puccini, Toscanini, and Belasco. It was two in the morning before Puccini could sneak away to a quiet Italian restaurant.

The newspapers were mixed, puzzled by the opera's American setting and the unusual score (as they still are), but for the moment Puccini could savor the biggest demonstration of public affection of his career. The Met took *Fanciulla* to Philadelphia and to the Academy of Music in Brooklyn, and the ovations continued. The public had not merely been dazzled by the gala at the Met. *Fanciulla*, with the first-rate cast singing roles especially written for them, Belasco's directing, and Toscanini's conducting, was a hit. It would only fade into the background years later, when people started to believe the notion that Puccini's personal life had interfered with his flow of genius and the giddiness of initial audiences was seen as more symptomatic of American pride than artistic judgment. It has since risen again in public estimation, but now suffers from a dearth of Destinns, Carusos, Amatos, Toscaninis, and Belascos to bring it fully alive. If one could operate an operatic time machine, December 10, 1910, would be as good a night as any in history to return to.

The result on the composer was, predictably, a large creative hangover. Sailing back to Italy on New Year's Eve, he stayed in his luxurious cabin while the rest of the ship partied, and poured out his soul in a sad letter to Sra. Carla Toscanini. If she only knew how unhappy he was and how much he envied her happy life! Since he, Carla, and half the world knew perfectly well about Toscanini's infidelities, and knew that Toscanini was at that moment carrying on a grand, very public affair with no less a personage than Geraldine Farrar, Puccini must have been miserable indeed to write such things to Sra. Toscanini. He returned to Torre and leafed through all the uncompleted ideas on his desk, desperate as ever to find another project. He wrote volumes to Sybil asking for help.

Keeping Up with the Times

Puccini's searches for libretti in many ways reflected the schizophrenia of Italian thought at the time. It was not only a problem for music, but for all art and architecture and everything that could define the national identity. The Englishman John Ruskin, for example, had started an international debate centering on the city of Venice. What was to be done with the crumbling treasure? Should it be repaired? Or rebuilt, but as it was? Or rebuilt with modern amenities? And what about new buildings that were required, such as hospitals? Should they be modern or built in the style of the surrounding structures? The architect Camillo Boito designed buildings for the Venetian lagoon (besides his restoration work, such as on Franchetti's Ca' d'oro) that were modern but created in the style of the neighboring buildings as those styles were understood at the time.

This historicity earned scorn from all sides of the debate, but answered a lot of needs as well. On the extreme end of the spectrum were the Futurists, whose famous Manifesto of 1909 declared war on the past. Museums, they declared, were cemeteries. False historicism was deplorable. Struggle was art, and war beautiful. Some Futurists expressed their desire to fill in and pave the Grand Canal of Venice and turn it into the world's greatest drag strip for racing cars. One is almost smothered by the obvious unresolved Oedipal complexes afoot here ("must . . . obliterate . . . patrimony!!!"), and one is grateful that the aesthetics of the movement were so vaguely stated. Yet the fatigue with museums and historicity was not contemptible— every traveler in Italy has felt it, even if furtively, at one point or another. The Futurists may not have succeeded in paving over the Grand Canal, but they were a symptom of the issues of their times, and their influence pervaded many surprising segments of Italian society.

Puccini represented much of what the Futurists hated, or at least thought they hated at the time. He was the established composer of the nation, and therefore was by definition all wrong. His work, long derided as "effeminate" and "sensitive," lacked the muscularity the new age seemed to demand. (Indeed it did, to Puccini's credit, as history has determined.) The young composer Ildebrando Pizzetti wrote a scathing article in 1910, castigating Puccini's bourgeois tastes. And Pizzetti was no fly-by-night trying to make a name for himself by being controversial: he was clearly a serious composer. Pizzetti's music over his long career was good, although when hearing it one always has the fear that there will be a pop quiz after the concert. His was clearly a very different nature from Puccini's, and while he mellowed considerably in his attitude toward the composer in later life, his youthful fulminations against the previous generation upset the always-sensitive Puccini. Pizzetti's articles were nothing compared to the book-length rodomontade issued by the critic Fausto Torrefranca in 1912. Torrefranca reiterated Pizzetti's gripes and then got personal. Puccini was lazy. He did not venture into new territory. (This is a common invective aimed at artists who do not create what the critic would like them to create: one may like or dislike *Fanciulla*, but no one who had listened carefully to it could have made that claim.) He was in it for the money. In short, he was not an artist and he did not produce music.

Again, Puccini took this jab more seriously than the public did. He was at sea trying to figure out what to do next. Mascagni was able to turn out new works according to the latest ideas: none of them have survived in the repertory, but this was not yet apparent. Mascagni even managed to do what Puccini never did in setting two works of Gabriele D'Annunzio's: *Isabeau* in 1911 and *Parisina* in 1913. Puccini could not adapt to the latest fads. Even the House of Ricordi itself seemed to be turning its back on him. Tito Ricordi pushed Puccini for something he was clearly never going to be able to produce: a huge, epic opera that would satisfy and unify all the various national urges and force the world to acknowledge the supremacy of Italian art. Meanwhile, all Puccini could do was read through plays and stories, write to Sybil asking for more ideas, reject them, and carry on another affair.

This one was with the beautiful German Baroness Josephina von Stängel, the wife, we believe, of an officer in the German army. They met in Viareggio, always popular among fashionable northern tourists, and at some point Puccini rented a house for her there. She seemed to think Puccini would divorce Elvira (in Germany, since divorce was not possible in Italy until very recently) and marry her, and welcomed the prospect. Although Puccini resorted to all his usual tricks to keep the affair quiet, he also took some rather flagrant chances this time. Perhaps he thought Elvira was sufficiently chastened after *l'affaire* Manfredi, or perhaps he was enjoying pushing the limits. Or perhaps he just enjoyed the game as much as Elvira did in her own twisted way. He arranged for letters to be sent to a secret post office box. At one point, when he was on a clandestine visit to Josi, as she was called, he tried to arrange sending his letters home to Elvira through a friend, who would have them postmarked in his village and thus throw Elvira off the scent. Yet he also traveled with Josi, and Puccini knew he was a recognizable face throughout Europe and beyond. He and Josi attended the Bayreuth Festival in 1913, the last, as it would turn out, for eleven years. At the festival, a friend of Puccini's from Milan happened to be the guest of Wagner's widow Cosima, and pointed him out to her. Cosima immediately asked the friend to invite Puccini to her box. The embarrassed Puccini explained that he was with the baroness and could not accept the invitation, and the friend had to return to Cosima and say he was mistaken . . . it was not Puccini after all. Biographers take Puccini's excuse at face value, but I am dubious. Although the mores of 1913 *haute société* could confuse anybody, Cosima Wagner was not in a position to put on airs about respectability. Nor was prudery among her many prejudices. And if Puccini was concerned about gossip regarding his latest affair, I don't see why the most famous composer in the world would have dragged his mistress to the Bayreuth Festival, of all places. I suspect Puccini, who was always tongue-tied around notables and celebrities, was simply terrified to make small talk with the scariest *witwefrau* in the Second Reich. Still, history should note that Cosima had the grace, or curiosity, to extend an invitation to an artist whose work, in and of itself, did not interest her much, while Puccini lacked the grace, or the curiosity, or the courage, to effect that meeting.

Somehow, Puccini survived this little indiscretion intact, but that did not solve the artistic problem. He must have wondered if Tito Ricordi was starting to believe the Pizzettis and the Torrefrancas of Italy, since relations cooled between them at this time. Tito had a new protégé, the thirty-year-old Riccardo Zandonai, a former student of Mascagni's. Zandonai had done what Puccini had said was impossible: he had made an opera out of *Conchita*, the lurid Louÿs-derived story, and had a success at the Teatro dal Verme in Milan in 1911. Zandonai made no secret of his contempt for Puccini, and Zandonai had Tito's ear. His next project was exactly what Tito wanted: *Francesca da Rimini*, produced at Turin in 1914. It was based on a play by D'Annunzio, which was in turn an expansion of the celebrated episode found in Canto V of Dante's *Inferno*. It had big passions with larger-than-life people in it—no commoners leading inconsequential lives on the streets of Paris or in the mountains of California. There was a ripsnorting battle scene, pageantry, and drama. The score owed much to Wagner, a bit to Debussy, and also a thing or two to Mascagni and the Italians. This one had it all. It subsumed French Grand Opéra, Wagner's "Music of the Future," and the blood-gushing of Verdi. Yet it was thoroughly Italian, having a provenance of D'Annunzio and Dante. *Francesca* was a success, and it has always remained popular in Italy, although its scale makes it difficult to perform frequently. But it never quite got off the ground outside of Italy. An important production at the Met in 1982 was received with puzzled interest, and everyone was able to praise its qualities (as Puccini himself had). But if the point of *Francesca* was to kill off *Bohème* once and for all, it must be considered a failure. And Zandonai never repeated this early success.

D'Annunzio seemed to be on the cutting edge of everything, even if Puccini was well aware of the man's greatest talent—self-promotion. D'Annunzio even ventured into the newest of new worlds, cinema, getting paid a fortune merely for writing the screen titles in the epic of ancient Rome, *Cabiria*, in 1914. (Pizzetti made some good money writing the music.) Funny, there was no outcry from the Futurist quarters about the historicity of the film *Cabiria*. Mascagni, always hip to new trends, wrote a sound track for the film *Rapsodia satanica* the following year. Puccini never developed, or pretended to develop, an interest in cinema.

Puccini maintained his correspondence with D'Annunzio and would have been delighted to compose something cutting-edge, provided that it had the human element so crucial to his own artistic process. On a visit to D'Annunzio on the Riviera in 1913, the poet was excited about an opera based on the ill-fated "Children's Crusade." Puccini found the notion grotesque. Clearly, the two were getting nowhere. D'Annunzio was obsessed with war, a subject Puccini could never stomach. Nor did war remain solely a poetic stance: D'Annunzio wrote tomes and made speeches encouraging Italian colonization of Libya in 1912, which turned out to be a thirty-year-long disaster for both countries. He took the Futurists' bellicose stance at face value, and wrote odes urging his countrymen to "hurl our seed from Latin shores to make the desert bloom." (Indeed, there is rather a lot of seed-hurling throughout D'Annunzio's work.)

Puccini never once wrote about war after *Edgar*: this alone must make him unique among opera composers. On a subsequent visit to Paris, Puccini and D'Annunzio were supposed to meet again and find something to work on, but D'Annunzio "got busy" and the meeting never happened. It was their last attempt to collaborate. Puccini finally turned away from the whole D'Annunzio idea and actually welcomed overtures from a theater in Vienna that wanted him to write an operetta. The producers had an eye to the lucrative sheet music market. Imagine, a dozen waltzes and other light tunes by Puccini! Tito Ricordi was disgusted with the idea. This was not what he wanted for his business. Puccini collaborated with the journalist Giuseppe Adami, a very agreeable man quite unlike his temperamental previous librettists, and set him to work on the basic outlines of a romance story he had received from the Viennese producers. It soon became apparent that an operetta was not within Puccini's gifts. "Anything but that!" he eventually wrote.

Adami reworked the story as an opera, but under Puccini's constant micromanagement. He wanted something like Richard Strauss's *Der Rosenkavalier*, only lighter and funnier. And yes, there would be waltzes galore in it. Why not? Never content to have librettists work on merely one project at a time, he also set Adami to work on a ghoulish one-act play he had seen in Paris, *La Houppelande*, by Didier Gold. If this weren't enough, Puccini also focused on a novel that had interested him for some time, *The Two Little Wooden Shoes*, by the famous Victorian "Lady-Novelist" who wrote under the pen name of Ouida. This bit of teary fluff by the authoress of *A Dog of Flanders* continued to gnaw at Puccini, and he finally announced to the newspapers that he was setting it as an opera. Within days, he read that Mascagni, too, was setting *The Two Little Wooden Shoes*. All the better, he thought. It would be like the old days, when he went head-to-head with Leoncavallo over *La bohème* and wrangled with Franchetti over *La Tosca*. Now he and Mascagni would finally duke it out. Puccini was back on track. Only a worldwide cataclysm could distract him.

The War

When the cataclysm came in August 1914, Puccini's powers of imagination did not comprehend its magnitude. Austria-Hungary, Germany, Russia, France, and Great Britain mobilized, and Puccini was not alone in hoping that the war would be a quick exercise followed by a tedious session of diplomatic wrangling. Few could imagine that Europe, as they knew it, would be changed forever. Italy was neutral at the outset of the war, bound by a diplomatic alliance with Austria-Hungary and Germany forged in 1882. The pact was denounced by Verdi at the time, and there were still people alive (Boito among them) who had fought Austria in 1866 to annex Venice and the Trentino Valley to the new Kingdom of Italy. (Venice had been won, but the Trentino remained in Austrian hands in 1914.) There were also the cultural and economic ties with France, which most assumed were Italy's natural ally. But there were ties with Austria and Germany as well, and Puccini had a hard time taking sides. In the summer of 1914, while most of Europe was mobilizing, Puccini was enjoying a seaside idyll with Josi in Viareggio. Toscanini visited, and Puccini was tactless enough to mention that he thought it might be a good thing if the Germans invaded Italy and set all the chaos into some sort of "good German order." Toscanini had a fit and locked himself in his own room for a week, steaming. He refused to see Puccini or receive any word from him for some time, and their relationship was permanently compromised.

Nor was Toscanini the only person Puccini annoyed. The Germans invaded neutral Belgium and bombed civilians and targets of cultural heritage in the French city of Reims. Artists of many nations signed on to a French newspaper ad denouncing the atrocities. Puccini refused to sign, saying he had friends on both sides of the conflict. The French journalists now denounced Puccini, who was absolutely bewildered by the rancor. He compounded the problem by writing a letter explaining that he was obligated, as an Italian subject, to remain neutral in the war. The German papers, meanwhile, reported that Puccini had in fact signed the original protest letter, and his operas were immediately banned in Germany. A pose of neutrality had not helped him any more than it had served Belgium. Now he was a fair target for patriots of all sides. Meanwhile, he continued to meet with agents of the Viennese theater to plan for his projected production there. Even after Italy entered the war on the Allies' (France, Russia, and Great Britain) side, Puccini continued to meet with the Viennese parties in neutral Switzerland. Josi, of course, became an enemy alien when Italy entered the war, but she managed to rent a villa in the Swiss town of Lugano, just across Lago Maggiore from the Italian border. Puccini's little trips to Switzerland therefore served a double purpose, at least for a while.

Puccini's conduct during the war stood in stark contrast to his peers. Mascagni, in his array of official positions in Rome, led all the galas and fund-raisers that were expected of him. Toscanini, an ardent patriot, quit the Metropolitan and returned to Italy. There had been artistic differences with Kahn, and his affair with Farrar had reached a breaking point when she demanded he leave his wife Carla if he wanted to continue with her. How little Farrar understood him: asking an Italian man of that time to keep a mistress was one thing, but to leave his family quite another. In any case, Toscanini would indubitably have returned to Italy in the dire times no matter what temptations remained in New York. Farrar briefly married an actor out of spite (it did not last long) and Toscanini moved up the date of his return to Italy. It was just as well: he had originally been booked to sail on the *Lusitania*'s last voyage. Once back in Italy, he forfeited all fees and salaries to work for the cause. He organized a season at Milan's Teatro dal Verme and persuaded the singers to donate their performances gratis. The season was a great success. He gave a series of concerts in other Italian cities and was finally invited to do the same in Rome. His choice of music for these nonoperatic concerts was interesting, and a harbinger of things to come: he played Beethoven, Wagner, and even a work by a living German composer (albeit of half-Italian ancestry) named Ferruccio Busoni. Many were highly displeased. Toscanini did not want to forfeit the iconic power of German art to the German militaristic cause.

Years later, Toscanini would find himself in exile in New York, taking advantage of the great talent pool to be found there among fellow exiles from the Third Reich, giving performances of Wagner and Beethoven at every conceivable opportunity. Even Winston Churchill, one of the great manipulators of imagery of all times, was impressed, and co-opted the famous four-note introduction to Beethoven's Fifth Symphony as the BBC's theme during the Second World War. But that lay years in the future. During the time of the Third Reich, it would be possible, if tenuous, to separate the idea of Germany from the idea of National Socialism. In the First World War, there was no such possible parsing. There were cases of dachshunds in London being killed. The Germans were the Huns, *les boches*, racially defined as bloodthirsty barbarians. Otherwise, what on earth was this war about? Revenge for the French humiliation of 1871? A strip of mountain valley in the Alps? No one was in the mood, yet, for Toscanini's theories about art.

The city of Rome banned German music for the duration of the war, and Toscanini refused to conduct there again until 1920. But he did not relax his war efforts for a moment. His entire household was mobilized: Signora Carla joined the Red Cross; their fifteen-year-old daughter Wally sewed at home and helped in the hospitals. Their seventeen-year-old son Walter joined the ambulance corps and then enlisted in the artillery at eighteen. Toscanini took a band directly to the bloody Monte Santo front in 1917, the apex of Italy's involvement in the war. His aplomb under fire became legendary, with international reports (verified by numerous eyewitnesses) telling of his conducting during battles. When there was an explosion or a flying piece of shrapnel whizzing by, Toscanini might exclaim, "Viva Italia!" but would otherwise not miss a beat. Once, a shell ripped open the bass drum, but Toscanini continued to lead the band. Elvira read this newspaper account aloud to Puccini, perhaps tweaking him a bit, saying the Lord must have intervened to save "our friend." Puccini, we are told, shook his head and said nothing. After the disastrous defeat at Caporetto in 1917, Toscanini and his band were among the last to quit the battlefield, well after the High Command had fled however they could. Toscanini helped soldiers escape on trains and wagons, and calmly went to the hospital, where Walter was wounded. He returned on a slow train to Milan, along with many other scattered remnants of the army, came home, and broke down sobbing in Carla's arms, crying for Italy.

If Toscanini's efforts during the war were exemplary from a patriotic standpoint, D'Annunzio was in a state bordering on the psychopathic. Even before Italy entered the war, he staged public rallies to encourage involvement on the Allied side, quite grander than his Libyan "seed-hurling" exhortations. The theatricality of these events was notorious, always with D'Annunzio as the centerpiece. His passion was beyond any sense of patriotism—he had assimilated all the Futurists' blather about the sublimity of war and decided he himself would become their long-awaited "man of action." He was probably the Italian most responsible for Italy's entrance in the war (along with some good help from the British Foreign Office). Once Italy entered the war, he jumped in with both feet, first in the army and then in the fledgling air force. He lost an eye in an accident in 1916, but returned to active service by the following year. In 1918, he even flew over Vienna and dropped propaganda leaflets he composed himself.

Puccini could not have been further from all this. While he helped friends and acquaintances with letters, and donated a song or two to fund-raising albums, he never once appeared in public in any patriotic or fund-raising activity. He continued to visit Josi until the Italian consul, wondering if the mistress were not in fact a German spy, canceled his visa and threatened Puccini with arrest if he crossed the border again. (Elvira got wind of this contretemps and fortunately kept whatever she had to say private, thereby avoiding an international incident.) After much wrangling through third parties, Puccini managed to secure the right to supervise the premiere of his new work, now called *La rondine*, in technically neutral Monte Carlo, forfeiting royalties in Austria and Germany. The premiere of the offbeat work there was a success in 1917, but it scored Puccini few points back home. Puccini's enemies had a good case against him. By all appearances, his answer to the Great War was to hide in his swamps, ignore public appeals, stand aloof from fund-raisers and morale-boosters (even of the nonbelligerent, Red Cross variety), annoy the French, fool around with a German woman, and compose Viennese waltzes while expressing more fears about his lost royalties than about the greatest catastrophe to strike Europe since the Black Plague. We know from Puccini's letters that the senseless killing grieved him to the point of near-incapacitation. He simply could not wrap his head around the fact of the war, and this looked a lot like treason in 1917.

He discarded his plans for *The Two Little Wooden Shoes*, allowing Mascagni to do what he would with it. Mascagni's opera, *Lodoletta*, was successfully produced in Rome in 1917, but for all its qualities, has not survived in repertory. (Interestingly, criticism of *Lodoletta* sounds much like the primary complaint about Puccini's *La rondine*: namely, that the first two acts are excellently light and fluffy but are at odds with the final act, which aspires to high drama without quite attaining it. Perhaps the times caused disjointed creativity.) Meanwhile, Puccini did manage to rally enough to complete his most ambitious project to date, a series of three one-act operas titled (after much debate) *Il trittico*. The first opera in *Il trittico* was set to Adami's translation and adaptation of *La Houppelande*, which was the first to be completed. The next two were *Suor Angelica* and the comedy *Gianni Schicchi*, both original creations of the playwright Giovanni Forzano. *Suor Angelica* was a real gamble, telling the story of a nun who committed suicide distraught over the death of the child that had been taken away from her. Puccini visited his last remaining sister, Iginia, now the Mother Superior of her convent, and played the score for the assembled nuns. They were all reduced to tears and pronounced their *nihil obstat* on the work. The honor of the premiere went again to the Metropolitan, although Puccini did not plan to attend. Wartime travel was too dangerous. Indeed, the composer Enrique Granados and his wife, returning from the successful premiere of his opera *Goyescas* at the Met in 1916, died when their ship, the *Sussex*, was torpedoed by a German U-boat in the English Channel.

The war dragged on, and another sad tragedy shook artistic circles in Italy. Boito fell ill in January 1918. Puccini wrote depressed letters but did not visit, as others did. Toscanini was a frequent visitor at Boito's bedside and kept vigil there in his last days. They discussed plans for the still-unfinished opera *Nerone*, and Boito died in July. Peace finally came in November 1918, but there could be little rejoicing. Too much had been lost.

Peace and Disillusionment

Il trittico was going nowhere, fast. There was a great success in London, where Puccini was cheered to the rafters at the premiere and received and congratulated by the king and queen. He was surprised, then, to learn of Covent Garden's almost immediate subsequent plans to dismantle the work. Puccini engaged Sybil to lobby for him at the house, and especially for his poor, neglected *Angelica*. It was no use. The Royal Opera was under the direction of a Mr. Henry Higgins, who was an iron-willed impresario. (Once, when receiving a foreign diva's exorbitant salary demands, Higgins told her agent,

"Please inform the good lady that we are only engaging her to *sing*!")
Trittico got chopped up in London, despite all of Sybil's best efforts.
This is better than it fared in Cologne, where it simply flopped. Puccini needed Toscanini's help in bringing the difficult work to life, but
that help was not forthcoming. Besides their usual personality problems, Toscanini simply did not like *Trittico*, and said so publicly. Only
Vienna managed to make a hit out of it, with Lotte Lehmann interpreting the role of Suor Angelica. The trip to Vienna was rewarding
for Puccini, and he was glad to visit the grand old city again in peace-
time. It was changed, of course, shorn of the empire that was its rai-
son d'être. Yet the soul of the city survived intact, and Puccini noted
that the musical life was in fact better than ever.

It was hard to say the same about his own country. The sense of
disappointment in *Trittico*'s fortunes mirrored the malaise of Italy
after the war. Six hundred thousand dead soldiers, many, many
more maimed and wounded, unemployment, Communist agitation,
strikes . . . and for what? The Trentino Valley? A slightly better-looking
map of Italy? Puccini went into another depression. D'Annunzio, for
contrast, went into action, even if it was insane action. Rallying a band
of black-shirted disillusioned "patriots," D'Annunzio decided to cir-
cumvent the peace negotiations at Versailles and annexed the city of
Fiume (over the northeastern border) to Italy. When Italy disavowed
D'Annunzio's action, he set himself up as a sort of "philosopher-
king" of the city, writing a poetic constitution and staging pageants
for the New Order. He arranged exercises for the soldiers and battle
cries of "Eia! Eia! Eia!" with a separate half crying back "Alala!"
Megalomaniacal foolishness, of course, except that there was inevitable
bloodshed. Not D'Annunzio's, naturally. He escaped the city and
saved his hide. His antics were closely watched by the up-and-
coming man on the political scene, Benito Mussolini, who applied
D'Annunzio's aesthetics exactly but more effectively. This was the
payoff of the cries for muscularity and action demanded by the early
critics who deplored Puccini's sentimentality and feminine sensitivity.

We should remember this when we repeat those comments uncritically today.

The Race Against Time

It was time to get back to work. Puccini had lunch with the agreeable Adami and also their acquaintance Renato Simone, a temperamental sort of litterato in the D'Annunzio mold. He would prove to be a difficult collaborator for Puccini, as Puccini would prove for him. But at this lunch, all lights were green. "What about *Turandotte*?" asked Simone casually. He left Puccini with an outline, and within days Puccini had given the go-ahead on the project.

The story of *Turandot*, as it would come to be called, was a major departure from Puccini's norm. The play was written by Carlo Gozzi in 1762 as a reaction to the "realism" of his rival, Carlo Goldoni. Gozzi's play reverted to the Italian tradition of commedia dell'arte and had the familiar clowns of that tradition wander into legendary China. The play was full of topical references made comic by their context. For Puccini, working on this story would be a final break with verismo, although certainly his last few works pushed the narrow limits of that genre almost beyond recognition. He knew it would challenge him deeply. He was also interested in a symbiotic relationship between Italian operatic tradition and Chinese music. Puccini knew nothing of Chinese music, and had no intention of writing an ethnographic essay, but he was delightfully inspired by what he heard on a music box from an acquaintance, the Baron Fassini, who had been in China. Puccini made notes of the music and set to work.

Adami and Simone delivered the first two acts of the three-act opera within a reasonable amount of time and with a relative minimum of rearrangement by Puccini. The third act, however, proved elusive. Either Simone could never get it right or Puccini could never be satisfied. The fact is that Puccini had backed himself into a corner:

Turandot was epic and ambitious. He had beautifully set up the conflict of Male vs. Female. But to resolve that conflict on the stage within a couple of hours, on his own human terms (as opposed to Wagner's very philosophical exploration of the mystical union of opposites in *Tristan und Isolde*) was eluding him. Why wouldn't it, since the conflict itself had never been resolved? Puccini blamed Simone squarely, and complained to all and sundry that his librettists were killing him. (It may have been the other way around. Illica died in 1919.)

So was everything else. Puccini was not feeling well. His diabetes wore him out, and he began to complain of a sore throat that simply would not go away. He continued to smoke two packs of cigarettes a day, however. There was more. Torre del Lago had changed. A peat factory whirred and hummed and stank where there had only been eerie, sea breeze–scented quiet before. It was time to leave. He and Elvira moved permanently to Viareggio. That was hardly a step down, and Elvira must have been overjoyed that her thirty-year purgatory in the swamps was finally at an end, but for Puccini it represented another break with his treasured past. His sister Iginia died in late 1922, praying for the soul of her errant brother until the end. He was the only Puccini left of his generation.

A bright spot, and a sparkle from the past, came that year. Toscanini had taken over La Scala in 1921 and turned the place upside down with positive reforms. In fact, the 1920s, his span of rule there, may well have been the apex of that venerable house's distinguished history. A gala production of *Manon Lescaut* was planned for the 1922–23 season to mark the opera's thirtieth anniversary. Thirty, of course, is a random number to pick as important, but the twenty-fifth anniversary fell during the war and there was no time for galas then at La Scala. It had more significance beyond the thirty years. The production was meant to be an acknowledgment of Puccini's long career, a sort of "lifetime achievement award," and perhaps a token of apology for the fiasco of the *Butterfly* premiere. And it was to solidify the rocky, tenuous relationship between Italy's leading composer and her leading conductor, so injured by the war, their disagreements over *Il trittico*, and their divergent personalities.

The night of December 26 was a tremendous success for Puccini on almost all these levels. No one present had ever heard such a performance of *Manon Lescaut*, not even Puccini. It caused a great deal of reconsideration of Puccini's whole output. *Manon Lescaut* had put him ahead of a very large pack in 1893. Thirty years later, a production that gave the opera the respect it deserved made it clear that Puccini was on an entirely separate plane from the other composers with whom he was invariably grouped. Mascagni may have had the edge on officialdom in Rome, and there would always be *Cavalleria*, but Puccini ruled the opera house. As far as being an official act of reconciliation with Toscanini, however, the night had only a temporary healing effect.

Puccini struck up another affair, his last. This was Rose Ader, a light soprano who (somehow) had premiered the role of Suor Angelica in Hamburg in 1921. The relationship was quite passionate and remarkably free of drama, considering Puccini's track record. Puccini tried to get her hired at the Met, but they replied that they already had plenty of voices of "that type" from within their own country and did not need to import any. Some scholars think the second soprano role of Liù in *Turandot* was written with Rose in mind, although she did not sing it. Rose, who was Jewish, emigrated to the Americas with the advent of the Third Reich and settled in Buenos Aires as a music teacher.

Puccini managed to play what he had of *Turandot* (all but that damned Act III) for Toscanini and told him of his plans for completing the opera. Toscanini had other priorities. The premiere of Boito's *Nerone* was slated for May 1924. Toscanini worked with several others to complete the work, according to what he and Boito discussed in the latter's last days. It was more than a premiere for Toscanini—it was a point of national honor. Puccini, naturally, was curious, if a bit skeptical. Privately he complained about "that God" Toscanini and casually referred to Toscanini's "manipulations" of Boito's score. This got back to Toscanini, who was not pleased. Toscanini closed all rehearsals at La Scala to the public. Puccini snuck in and was discovered, and was unceremoniously tossed out of the theater by Toscanini. Puccini shrugged. "That's the way he is," he muttered to Rosa Raisa, the prima donna, on his way out. The final dress rehearsal was open to a few invited colleagues and musical notables, but Toscanini ordered Puccini to be barred from the theater. Puccini showed up and was forbidden entrance. It was an unnecessary humiliation from Toscanini, based purely on personal rancor. It also demonstrated that in the new era, the conductor held all the power, even over the composer. Toscanini's dictatorial personality, which had so much impact on his ability to yank great performances from musicians, and which would one day face off without flinching against Mussolini and Hitler, simply crushed the gentle Puccini. He retreated from Milan, and *Nerone* was premiered without his attendance. Toscanini got his victorious night of national honor, but the opera did not last in the repertory. Puccini's doubts were not unfounded after all.

Death

It would not matter for long. Puccini was terminally ill. The nagging sore throat he had suffered for some time turned out to be cancer, although Tonio withheld this diagnosis from his father for some time. Doctors were consulted, tried, and dismissed. Finally, a specialist was recommended in Brussels who used a technique of inserting radium needles directly into the tumor. The operation would be grueling and painful, but Puccini agreed to it. Tonio took him to Brussels on November 4, 1924. Elvira was ill and being cared for by Fosca. Both intended to join Puccini in Brussels. Puccini took along sketches for the second part of Act III of *Turandot*, intending to work on it during his convalescence. External treatments were applied for ten days. Fosca arrived with her best friend Carla Toscanini, though Elvira, still unwell, went to Milan. The grueling second phase of the treatment, with a tracheotomy and the insertion of radium needles, began on November 24 and was deemed successful. Puccini showed signs of recovery, but then suffered heart failure. The papal nuncio in Brussels administered the last rites. Puccini died on November 29, 1924.

Before the news hit the papers, Adami was informed. He rushed to La Scala to tell Toscanini, who broke down and sobbed before he assigned himself the unenviable task of informing Elvira. The newspapers told the world that evening. Condolences came from the Italian government, several foreign heads of state, the king, and the pope. For a moment, many factions paused in their rivalries to consider what had been lost to the world.

There was an official funeral in Brussels, paid for by the Italian government. Puccini never attended Mass, but neither had he criticized his religion, unlike Verdi, and the Church buried him with the highest honors. The coffin was sent to Milan, which had an impressive delegation meet it at the station: Toscanini, the mayor of the city, and delegations of musicians, including Zandonai and Pizzetti. A state funeral was held in the Duomo, with Toscanini playing funeral music from poor, neglected *Edgar*. Puccini was buried in the municipal cemetery and reinterred in the mausoleum at Torre del Lago two years later.

Posthumous Premiere

The House of Ricordi, headed by a coalition of partners since Tito's dismissal for mismanagement in 1921, was eager to mount *Turandot*, and Toscanini, quite naturally, was in charge of the task. It would be harder than completing *Nerone*. The final love duet, which brings the whole piece together, had nothing but a few jotted notes from Puccini's hand, and cryptic notes in the margin. A major composer would be needed. But who? Zandonai was the first suggestion, but Tonio vetoed the idea. Zandonai was too famous in his own right (and no doubt Tonio rankled over Zandonai's disparaging comments over his father's music). Mascagni was considered for a while, but also jettisoned. Finally, the task fell to Franco Alfano, a respectable composer whose last bona fide hit was in 1904. Alfano's work, however, would not be included at the emotional premiere.

Apparently, a few million people must have been inside La Scala the night of the *Turandot* premiere on April 25, 1926, and each one had a different memory of what exactly happened. What we do know is that Toscanini led an excellent cast and chorus through to the point where Puccini had finished (halfway through Act III) and stopped the performance. He turned to the audience and said—the exact accounts vary wildly—words to the effect that this was the spot at which the Maestro laid down his pen. Silence was observed. The rest of the performances were given that season with Alfano's ending, which has never entirely pleased anyone, and the critics were not in the least sentimental. They praised certain aspects and took exceptions with others, just like any other opera being given. *Turandot* was given on the international circuit and was well received in general, although the work was rather challenging and the world did not immediately fall in love with it. It stands today as an acknowledged masterpiece, difficult to cast and perform, and with some rather obvious problems. Moreover, it is a constant reminder that Puccini was an ever-growing, ever-evolving artist. He was castigated in his lifetime for failing in this regard, but in retrospect this seems to have more to do with Puccini's failure to write volumes of theory and publish manifestos than to sit at the piano and grow. Every one of his works, from *Manon Lescaut* through *Turandot*, presents a full and different experience, from the handling of the orchestra to the vocal demands. Each is valid in its own way and each shows a creative hand willing to attempt new things. In this way, Puccini's death at the age of sixty-six is more than premature—it is a tragedy. Certainly other composers had died younger, but we can only imagine what Puccini might have done had he lived longer. We must remember how much of Verdi's critical supremacy rests on his final works. There have been Italian operas written since *Turandot*, and there have been some excellent ones, but there has never been an Italian opera that has found favor in the hearts of millions since then. Italians take their chances to write operas like anyone else since *Turandot*. It is the long-unbroken tradition of Italian opera, from the night in a Florentine conversation circle in 1597 until 1926, which ended on the night of the premiere of *Turandot*.

Survivors and Others

Elvira did not long survive her husband, dying in 1930. Tonio studied engineering and died in 1946. Fosca married first a tenor, by whom she had three children, and then an industrialist. Her second child, Little Elvira, received the nickname Bicchi from her grandfather Puccini. She altered this to Biki in her professional life and became a noted fashion designer in Milan, where she lived until 1999. Zandonai kept composing, expanding into chamber music and even film music before his death in 1944. Leoncavallo predeceased Puccini, dying in 1919 after writing a string of operettas and an unsuccessful patriotic opera in 1916. D'Annunzio took a moment from his conquests to comment that the prolific creator with two beasts for his name must have died of "melodic adiposity." Franchetti taught, which seemed a natural place for him from the beginning, and died during the war in Viareggio in 1942. Pizzetti kept writing operas through the 1960s, including one based on a D'Annunzio play in 1954, years after anyone else thought that would be a good idea. Pizzetti's work always had partisans among the critics but audiences have not (yet) sought them out for repertory. Tito Ricordi moved to Paris after his exit from his family firm and died in obscurity in 1934. D'Annunzio met his match in Mussolini when the latter came to power in 1922. Mussolini co-opted everything about D'Annunzio that manipulated public opinion (without, of course, the poetry) and retired the difficult poet to a villa. He was given the euphonious and empty title Prince of Monte Nevoso ("Snowy Mountain") and kept well supplied with money, drugs, and frolicking virgins for his garden as long as he kept his mouth shut. The villa can be visited and is one of Italy's most bizarre niches. He died, subservient to Mussolini, in 1938. Mascagni, always feeling underappreciated, continued to compose but never recaptured his moment of glory from 1890. He injudiciously allied himself with the Italian government in order to maintain a voice in Italy's musical life, and this has severely compromised his subsequent reputation. While it is difficult to accuse Mascagni of having been an ardent Fascist by conviction, the fact is that Italians have been slow to explore his less-known operas because of his work with the regime. The memory of collaborationism is still too painful, even sixty years after the end of the Second World War. Memory lasts longer in Italy than in America. Mascagni died in a hotel in Rome in 1945, having lived long enough to see peace restored. He was a recluse for his last few years.

The survivor was, of course, Toscanini, who had another three decades of conducting in him after the *Turandot* premiere. Toscanini's role in the formation of American attitudes on classical music, for better and for worse, cannot be underestimated. Conductor of the New York Philharmonic in the 1930s, political symbol, the man who made the classics a mass-market commodity in the United States, leader of the NBC Symphony of the Air, familiar figure on the cover of *Life* magazine, and so much more, Toscanini is crucial to study for any understanding of music in the twentieth century. It is interesting to ponder how many of our assumptions in America were influenced, directly or indirectly, by the Toscanini experience, especially regarding Puccini. Toscanini did not conduct at the Met in the later part of his career, but he made opera recordings and performed radio concerts of operas. His idols in his fixed canon remained, as always, Wagner and Verdi. For all his friendship with Puccini, and the important role he played in Puccini's career, from *La bohème* to *Turandot*, he always maintained a certain condescension toward his works. "Puccini was really very good," he once said, "but only very good." That Puccini was neither Verdi nor Wagner cannot be argued, but it shouldn't count against him. Whatever problems the two "friends" had with each other should not color our impressions of Puccini's work (or, for that matter, of Toscanini's legacy). At the very end of his life, the eighty-seven-year-old Toscanini went to the piano and played a beautiful little piece. It was something Catalani had composed during his final illness. Toscanini had never seen the written music, and had not heard it played in sixty years, but that didn't prevent him from remembering it exactly. Toscanini never forgot anything.

Assessing Puccini

Puccini attained a level of popularity in his own lifetime that very, very few music professionals ever achieve. His operas made him independently wealthy from the age of thirty-four on, and he never once, after his student days, had to work at anything uncongenial to him. He was celebrated in person on three continents and his music has been heard and appreciated in every corner of the globe, even by many who would not recognize his name. He is part of the world's subconscious.

Naturally, anyone with this level of popularity will meet some criticism. There were several complaints about him during his lifetime. His art was thought to be trivial, uncommitted to ideology, and lacking in a certain vigor that many wanted at the time. No artist is above criticism, and Puccini had his share of shortcomings. We should not, however, make the same complaints about him that were made at the turn of the last century. Our issues are different from theirs, and it says nothing to repeat what was said then and try to pass it off as critical thinking now. Puccini was trivial if, by trivial, we mean that he placed more importance on the concerns of common individuals than on ideologies. The people he focused on, generally speaking, were of no major consequence. This predilection flew in the face of everything that was considered progressive in 1910, after the brief fluorescence of the verismo movement in its purist form two decades previously. This cannot remain a valid complaint about Puccini's art, although one reads echoes of this same attitude whenever experts want to minimize his art. If the whole rotten, miserable history of the twentieth century has taught us anything, it is that we must trust no ideology that values anything above the needs of the humblest individual. If such a stance as Puccini's was a shortcoming eighty years ago, it looks a lot like hope now.

Virgil Thompson maintained that Wagner was the most intellectual composer and Puccini the least. Thompson knew what he was talking about, but his comment must not be taken as a format for appreciating or disdaining either. Wagner has not survived because of his intellectual accomplishments. Indeed, far better for the world had his intellectual pretensions been forgotten early on. Wagner, as it turns out, has survived for the same reason Puccini has—because somewhere amid the blather about racial destiny and salvation through purity was a thoroughly human artistic core that continues to speak to people's feelings. That same core in Puccini takes second place to no one. If his passion and compassion did not—and could not— disguise themselves behind an ideological framework, so much the better. Puccini's operas stand as naked as anything in art. This is, I believe, what many have mistaken for sentimentality in his work. Couldn't the label of sentimental be a defensive response to the feeling of discomfort that the nakedness of these works elicits in the viewer?

Puccini was entirely aware of all the trends going on around him in the world of music during his lifetime. The most challenging of these trends, paralleled by revolutions in the other arts, are scarcely comprehended by the public (or, if truth be told, by musicians) even today. Puccini understood and even appreciated these innovations in his time, and, when appropriate, he learned from them and applied them in his own work. However, he never once tried to be anyone other than himself. This, alone, should command our artistic respect. He had a mandate (from God, as he understood it) to adhere to his inner dicta. As popular as he was, he never once (despite some rather superficial comments from his contemporary journalists) altered his vision to gain an even wider popularity. How different, how richer, and how truer the world of music would be if other composers had emulated this aspect of Puccini. With all this in mind, and with all the advantages of hindsight, we may well be approaching a time when the intellectuals, the professional musicians, the existing operatic public, and the general public might finally be able to accept their love and need for this man's art without triangulation, without any self-consciousness about susceptibility to so-called sentimentality, and, indeed, without any excuses.

Part Two

THE OPERAS

Manon Lescaut

The Name and How to Pronounce It

The title is French, taken from the source novel by the Abbé Prévost. The actual title of the novel is *Histoire du Chevalier Des Grieux et de Manon Lescaut*, so it shows you where Puccini's priorities were. *Manon Lescaut* is also the name of two other operas based on the same subject: one by Daniel Auber from 1856, which is mostly forgotten, the other the famous opera by Massenet. Therefore, to avoid confusion one must always call the Puccini opera *Manon Lescaut* and the Massenet simply *Manon*. How French one wishes to get with the word "Manon" (that is, how much one wants to swallow the second "n" in the back of the throat) is a matter of personal preference. Lescaut is pronounced "less-co," with a silent "t."

What is Manon Lescaut?

Manon Lescaut is Puccini's first great success, a passionate, romantic opera on a familiar subject that took the world by storm at its premiere in 1893. To depict his tale of the doomed young heroine and her equally impassioned young lover, Puccini employed a full-throttle musical vocabulary for both voices and orchestra, consciously "translating" all the refinement of the French heroine into a more hot-blooded Italian woman. The opera already shows a deft handling of crowd scenes and group dynamics—something that would become a benchmark of his art—right in the first act. Later in the opera, he takes the operatic examination of group dynamics to new heights, heights that would only be surpassed by Puccini himself much later in his career. The core of the opera, however, is the two lovers, and the roles Puccini created for them are perhaps, in their own way, the ultimate operatic incarnations of young, impetuous, erotic love. It is not an easy opera to produce, but it is remarkably easy to enjoy, and a good performance of *Manon Lescaut* can rank with anything in the operatic repertory.

Manon Lescaut*'s Place in the Repertory*

Just under the top tier, but not obscure enough to be a rarity. *Manon Lescaut* is a weightier undertaking than many surefire Puccini operas, requiring a large orchestra and a true spinto tenor who has to work for his paycheck. The lead role, too, requires a certain youth and grace, or at least operatic analogs of youth and grace. While Tosca and Butterfly can both be padded out in outrageous period drag, Manon really must be convincing as a vehicle and inspiration of young love or there's not much point to this opera. And the expense of a period production with crinolines and perukes must be considered. (There are, of course, options to the rococo setting, but they are very rare. This opera is firmly rooted in a distinct social-historical milieu both musically and dramatically.) Unlike *Bohème*, this opera's charms will not carry the work even through a second-rate performance or production. Generally, *Manon Lescaut* is reserved for a star tenor and soprano who can create magic together. When that occurs, audiences eat up *Manon Lescaut* as voraciously as any other Puccini opera.

Cast of Characters

MANON LESCAUT (*soprano*): A sixteen-year-old girl. Beautiful, charming, irresistible to men, and destined for love and luxury. She is both an archetype and a very real, flesh-and-blood woman. It is a tall order for any performer to fill, even compared to the rest of the operatic canon.

LESCAUT (*baritone*): A sergeant in the King's Guards, Manon's older brother. Lescaut is quite an ambiguous character—part loving older brother, part pimp, and part intriguer for the fun of it. It is a frustrating role in that he has much to sing without any particular highlights to let the audience know how hard he's working.

THE CHEVALIER RENATO DES GRIEUX (*tenor*): A student. A passionate and impetuous bag of hormones, like any other tenor in Italian opera, Des Grieux also has a tinge of fatalism to his character (something we encounter frequently in Puccini's works) that adds a level of depth to him.

EDMONDO (*tenor*): A student. This is one of those "second tenor" roles that make budget-conscious producers pull out their hair ("as if ONE tenor isn't hard enough to find these days!"). Edmondo has some pretty music to sing in his single act, the first. It is usually sung by an up-and-coming, eager-beaver tenor trying to attract attention to his budding career. He will generally prance, mug, and do backflips in his attempt to portray some operatic equivalent of youthful bumptiousness. Listen to his voice anyway: he may well be singing Rodolfo in *Bohème*, if not Des Grieux, the next season.

GERONTE DI RAVOIR (*bass*): The Treasurer-General of France. A rich courtier and a dirty old goat. Archetypically speaking, he is the polar opposite on the male spectrum from Des Grieux, although a feminist could argue the point.

AN INNKEEPER (*bass*): His primary job is to bow to Geronte and wipe tables.

A DANCE MASTER (*tenor*): Look for an aging character tenor of yesteryear in this part, which is half prancing in a wig, and half complicated ensemble singing.

A SINGER (*mezzo-soprano*): In the libretto, the singer is listed as "un musico," which was the standard eighteenth-century appellation for a castrato. Making "musician" synonymous with "un musico" demonstrates the primacy of the castrati at one time.

A SERGEANT-AT-ARMS (*bass*): A grumbly sort who orders prostitutes about.

A LAMPLIGHTER (*tenor*): He walks across the stage, singing a supposedly irrelevant song about love. Puccini used this trope, which contributes to his reputation as an artist of realism, to great effect throughout his career.

A SHIP'S CAPTAIN (*bass*): He gets one punch line, nothing more.

A HAIRDRESSER (*mime*): Count on this silent role to camp it up beyond the dreams of Wigstock.

The Opera

Act I

Setting: A courtyard of an inn at Amiens.

Townspeople and students are enjoying the pleasant evening, drinking in the square in front of the inn. Edmondo, a student, leads a madrigal in praise of youth and its pleasures, and encourages the crowd to drink. The students flirt with the girls of the town. They are joined by another student, the Chevalier Des Grieux, who gets taunted for being scarce lately. Is he, perhaps, in love? Des Grieux balks. Not yet, not when there are so many beauties to choose from. He turns to the young ladies: among these beauties, blondes, brunettes, redheads, which one will give her love to him and reveal his destiny in her beautiful face? The crowd laughs with Des Grieux.

Comment, opening and arietta, "Tra voi belle": Puccini eases us gently into the milieu of Manon Lescaut, *with townspeople singing light music in the soft summer air, led by Edmondo. This lyric tenor role has a lot of running around to do in the act and then disappears. Puccini would learn to minimize such roles in subsequent works. The choral background is superb throughout the act. Grouped voices flow in and out of the narrative line with ease and naturalness. Verdi strove his whole career to achieve this sort of organic portrayal of crowd scenes. Puccini had it from the start (or near the start: neither* Le villi *nor* Edgar *were conducive to this sort of naturalism) and developed it with stunning success throughout his career. Our introduction to the hero Des Grieux is likewise subtle and understated. His solo "Tra voi belle" is a bouncy little bagatelle, marked "con grazia" as he sings, almost literally, "I like blondes, I like brunettes." A bit of latent morbidity is revealed in the lyrics, if not the tune, when he*

*equates attraction with destiny. This will become a larger motif in the
subsequent story.*

The flirting and drinking continue. The coach from Arras enters the
square and its passengers come out: Lescaut, Geronte di Ravoir, the
Treasurer-General of France, who chivalrously gives his arm to
Lescaut's little sister Manon, and others. The townspeople remark
on the elegance of the passengers, while the students are completely
stunned by the grace and beauty of young Manon. Des Grieux is especially smitten. Lescaut calls for the inn's host, and Geronte declares
he will stay at the inn that night. Manon sits on a bench as much of
the crowd disperses. Some students remain to play cards here and
there. Des Grieux approaches Manon while Edmondo watches from
a little distance. Des Grieux tells her how beautiful she is, and asks her
name. "My name is Manon Lescaut," she tells him. She is demure . . .
she cannot offer him much, since she is being taken to a convent.
Her star is setting. Des Grieux insists another destiny awaits her, but
they cannot talk right there. She must meet him again in an hour. He
gives his name as her brother calls her from inside the inn. She
protests that she cannot meet Des Grieux again. He insists. She
agrees, and leaves. Alone, Des Grieux realizes he has never seen a
woman like her. "My name is Manon Lescaut. . . ." How those words
caress his spirit! Oh, may they never stop their gentle murmur!

Comment, scene and aria, "Donna non vidi mai"*: Bringing a horse and
carriage onstage is a big nightmare for producers but always captures the
attention of that part of the audience who is bored by mere singing. After
such an arresting theatrical hoo-ha, Manon's entrance is very quiet.
Unlike most operas, the tenor is still the center of the scene, and the
soprano, instead of making a grand vocal entrance, is a mystery that needs
to be explored. Her first line, where she gives her name,* "Manon Lescaut
mi chiamo,"* is a graceful cascading trip down the scale that will become a
central motif of the whole opera. Des Grieux's aria,* "Donna non vidi
mai,"* is the first of many short and shamelessly passionate arias that will*

become one of the hallmarks of Puccini's enduring popularity. The line "Manon Lescaut mi chiamo" is in fact the slancio *of the aria: that is, the single line of gushing romance that people will be whistling on their way out of the theater. Using that line as the* slancio *weaves this discrete set piece (indeed, it is often heard on recital programs) into the fabric of the larger narrative.*

Edmondo and some other students taunt Des Grieux again for his passions, and he angrily walks away. Geronte and Lescaut take a table in front of the inn while students and young ladies continue to flirt. The two older men discuss Manon, in whom Geronte is most interested. Lescaut informs Geronte that Manon is being taken to a convent, and he leaves to play cards with some students. Geronte quietly tells the innkeeper to arrange for a carriage to take him and a lady to Paris. Edmondo overhears and rushes to tell Des Grieux. Manon meets Des Grieux in a dark corner of the square while Lescaut plays cards. He tells her plainly that he loves her. She should run off with him! She hesitates. There is the convent tomorrow. . . . Des Grieux tells her she is about to be kidnapped by the old man. She should run off with Des Grieux instead! She hesitates again, but as the carriage is brought into the square, she agrees. They jump in the carriage and run off.

Geronte comes looking for Manon. Edmondo points to the carriage, now in the distance. Geronte is furious and calls for horses, but allows himself to be calmed. Perhaps restraint is called for. Lescaut assures him that Manon is not the sort of woman who can stay amused with a penniless student for very long. Once the kisses die down, Manon will be extremely grateful for Geronte's fatherly affection before long. Geronte agrees as the students and townspeople gently laugh at the old man's misadventures.

Comment: We hear Des Grieux's passion in urging Manon to run off with him. Manon's state of mind is present as well, but much more subtly. She is ambivalent; she wants two things at once. It reads as if she is merely ditzy and not especially involved in her own future, but listen carefully. It is a setup for the next act, in which her conflicting desires cause the crisis and give her opportunities for full vocal expression. Puccini was bold to make her part here so subdued, as it was bold of him to end this first act on a denouement. Many other composers of that time would have the characters throwing off big notes, even though it would not be dramatically accurate. Note the subtlety of the townspeople's laughter at Geronte and the organic return of snippets of their original music as they return to their pleasures.

Act II

Setting: Manon's apartments in Geronte's palace in Paris.

True to Lescaut's predictions, Manon has left Des Grieux and is now installed as Geronte's official mistress. She is giving orders to her hairdresser and choosing the day's outfits. Lescaut shows up and congratulates Manon on her success in life. What an improvement this palace is over that little cottage she escaped from! She asks about Des Grieux—she left him without a word. These soft, lacy chambers seem cold to her now. The silence is numbing, hopeless. She longs for Des Grieux's passion in the little shack they shared.

Comment, scene and aria, "In quelle trine morbide": Massenet's opera had an important act showing us Manon and Des Grieux in their humble love nest, and Manon's flight from it to live as the rich man's mistress. Puccini and his several librettists realized they had to jettison the entire act, and much was lost in the streamlining. Two of Massenet's opera's most noted solos, "Le rêve" for the tenor and "Adieu, notre petite table" for the soprano, are in this scene, delicate, diaphanous arias that are two of the finest examples of refined and elegant understatement in French opera. There is also much in that scene that reveals some of Manon's ambiguous character—her gentle expression of pity for poor Des Grieux's plight even though it is she who is ditching him, for example, can be perfectly convincing and quite striking if done right. Puccini did not find any of this consonant with the full-blooded Italian woman he envisioned for Manon. Instead, she must communicate all of this—her nostalgia for love, her inability to be content with compromise—in the beginning of this act, and particularly in her beautiful aria "In quelle trine morbide." *She may have ruined Des Grieux's life by leaving him, but she thinks fondly of him and had no intention of hurting him. She has no venality—she simply must have what she requires to live. It is quite a challenge, and most sopranos are content to sing a pretty aria and leave it at that. The great ones will communicate all the ambiguities of the heroine here in her only aria until the fourth act.*

Lescaut admits he sees Des Grieux often. He's teaching the student how to gamble—and cheat. Perhaps he will win enough to take back Manon, but she does not listen to Lescaut. She is only wishing Love would carry her back to the past. A group of singers enters to perform a madrigal for Manon, composed especially for her by Geronte. Manon is bored by it. When they finish, she hands Lescaut some money to give to the singers, but he pockets the money and sends the singers out. The commercialization of Art is an offense! A dance master enters, followed by Geronte and several of his elegant friends. Manon takes her minuet lesson as the friends congratulate Geronte on her charm and beauty. Lescaut notices her lack of interest. A bored woman is a dangerous thing, he muses. He hurries off to find Des Grieux. Manon sings a verse of the minuet and, dancing a bit with Geronte, spins him about playfully. Unruffled, he dismisses the crowd and urges Manon not to linger over her preparations too long. He is eager to promenade with her on the Boulevard with all the most fashionable of Paris. He leaves.

Comment: Puccini had a risky challenge in this scene—portraying Manon's boredom without making the opera boring. The madrigal is a lovely retread: the tune comes from Puccini's Mass of 1880. The lead singer (she's supposed to represent a castrato) is often sung by a lead mezzo or by one who is hoping to become a star. Listen carefully to her, since one way or another she will be the subject of much chatter in the lobby at intermission. The dance lesson is a great deal of phoof and perukes, accompanied by the onlookers, who are invariably decked out in full rococo drag and acting as effete as possible. It can be a bit of a trial. If your attention wanders, admire the wigs. Manon chimes in on the second verse of the minuet she is supposed to be dancing to, and this livens things up. Puccini cut the soprano no slack even in this dainty morsel. Her line rises to a high C, which demonstrates the demanding nature of this score. Of course, it's an optional high C, but all optional notes are expected by audiences in familiar operas. No diva would dare leave it out.

"Ah, I will be the most beautiful woman there!" Manon reflects. Des Grieux bursts into the chamber. "You! My love!" she exclaims, but he rebuffs her. "Don't you love me anymore?" she asks. But he used to love her so much! So much! He orders her to be quiet—she broke his heart. She doesn't know how he's suffered. She tells him to look at all the riches—she did it for him! And now Love brought him here to her. She falls at his feet and begs him to forgive her. Is she no longer beautiful? He calls her a temptress. . . . He cannot resist her. The old bonds still tie him. Those bonds are love, she tells him. He admits defeat and takes her in his arms. In her deep eyes, he can read his own destiny. She kisses him, craving only him. They savor the inebriation and the sweet suffering of love as they fall together onto the sofa.

Comment, duet, "Tu! tu! amore, tu!": Okay, if you can't identify a love duet from a synopsis like that, perhaps Italian opera isn't for you after all. This is one of the great love duets. In fact, this duet is the apex of the genre in one respect: that is, expressing the idea of sheer, youthful "You are so beautiful that I have to have you right here, right now, no matter what the consequences!" No one else ever came close to the real human passion of such a moment as here, and even Puccini's subsequent operas explore other, more nuanced aspects of erotic passion. Only a younger man could have written this, and only if he is lucky enough to experience that brief, golden moment when all the sexual impetuosity of youth intersects the mastery of a mature artist. For all the deftness of Act I and the passion of "Donna non vidi mai," and all the grace of the first part of Act II, there is an abrupt and obvious shift into "high gear" as soon as Des Grieux walks right here. It is not only the turning point of the opera, but might even be the turning point of Puccini's career, since the confident Puccini we know and love seems almost to be born in this moment.

The orchestra forms the melodic core of the duet (a fact that annoyed some conservative critics) while the very difficult vocal lines—often in the lower and middle ranges against a completely unleashed orchestra— "surf" off of the waves of sound. The rolling, self-perpetuating form of the orchestral melody is a very blatant allusion to the score of Wagner's Tristan und Isolde, *and yet there are important differences as well. Wagner's celebrated masterpiece is transcendental and metaphysical. The lovers are commenting on the nature of life and death and the cosmos. The only philosophy in* Manon Lescaut *is purely hormonal. It stays firmly below the belt, and not every tenor and soprano can convince you of this in a live performance. If we do not firmly believe that these are two young people who are viscerally bound to each other, the whole opera becomes nothing more than a messy study for* La bohème.

Des Grieux's outburst about reading his destiny in her eyes, "Nell'occhio tuo profondo," is a jarringly martial piece of music, something you might expect a tenor to sing on his way to a firing squad—which may approximate the actual situation. Des Grieux is abandoning himself to follow Manon, and it is clear that they will not live happily ever after. The theme—let's call it the Destiny Theme—will appear again.

Geronte bursts in on the lovers. Well, no one is perfect. . . . He is prepared to overlook this breach of manners. Manon laughs at him, and holds a mirror up to his face. Look, she tells him. She goes to Des Grieux. "Now look at us. Need I say more?" Geronte withdraws with exaggerated courtesy and promises that they will meet again, very shortly! Manon laughs again. They are free now! Des Grieux tells her they have to leave the palace immediately. "What a pity," she cries, depressed to leave all this luxury. Des Grieux breaks down. How can she be so loving and faithful one moment and then blinded by luxury the next? And he is nothing more than her slave, her victim, gambling for her, disgracing himself. What will become of him in the bleak future? She asks his pardon once again. Lescaut bursts in— Geronte has denounced Manon to the police! They must all leave immediately or she will be exiled as a prostitute! Manon hurries around the room, trying to collect jewels, as the men urge her to leave. Why should she leave these jewels and fineries that she loves? she asks. Des Grieux grabs her. "Bring your heart, only your heart!" He leads her toward the door, but it is too late. Armed soldiers come into the room and the captain orders everyone to stand still. Geronte laughs cruelly. Lescaut restrains Des Grieux, explaining that if they get arrested now, who will save Manon? Manon is led out by the police.

Comment: The balance of the act after the love duet is perhaps even more exciting. After the amusing, if ominous, interlude with Geronte, Manon utters a little laugh. It is, in fact, a version of the line "Manon Lescaut mi chiamo," and it's a cunning and economical way to explain that Manon's careless frivolity is as much a part of her core being as her name. Des Grieux's subsequent outburst is one of his most difficult passages. It doesn't quite amount to an aria—the discernment of what is and what is not an aria becomes a great mystery at this point in the development of Italian opera—but he must again battle the full orchestra in the lowest passages of his register. This sort of exercise can end a tenor's career on the spot without excellent technique. The running-around music (a fugue in the orchestra) builds almost imperceptibly to Manon's loud outburst when she protests that she does not want to leave all this luxury. This in turn elicits another heroic exclamation from Des Grieux when he tells her to bring herself and her love, nothing more. This line also reaches up to a high C (again optional, but, you know . . .) and therefore it makes the opposite demands on the tenor from his previous music. The effect is as if he had just slapped Manon, hard, across the face, which in fact would not be inappropriate under the circumstances. We in the audience should also feel a sort of slap across the face. No doubt some directors will have Des Grieux actually slap her, but that's way too easy. The glory of Italian opera consists in making us think he has done such a thing by the suggestive power of the voice. Manon's apology is yet another variant on the "Manon Lescaut mi chiamo" *motif, although that might not be immediately apparent to the casual listener. The act ends with Des Grieux crying out* "O Manon!" *and a rapid curtain.*

Act III

Intermezzo: The Imprisonment, Journey to Le Havre.

Comment: No, it isn't the imprisonment and the journey to Le Havre, even though the notes say it is. Marking the intermezzo as a narrative piece of music was Puccini's concession to the gaps in the libretto. In fact, the intermezzo was a stock-in-trade of the verismo school, made indispensable by the success of the intermezzo in I pagliacci *and the wildly popular one in* Cavalleria rusticana. *The idea of "pure music" was understood as a component of dramatic truth, another chance for "modern" Italian composers to distance themselves from the conventions of bel canto, and even perhaps a nod to the French and German trends in opera at the time. The music itself is not new. We heard it as the orchestral accompaniment to the love duet. It is built around a series of ascending phrases, sounding like quick, battering waves and very erotic in its implications. It is also a type of "endless melody," a self-propelling theme with no logical conclusion, inspired, as we saw, by Wagner's* Tristan und Isolde, *which also plays the self-propelling theme in both orchestral solo and vocal background forms. Part of the reason for* Manon Lescaut's *tumultuous reception was the feeling among the audience that Puccini had modernized Italian opera with ideas imported from Wagner without compromising the Italian*

melodic birthright. We need not be concerned today about the implica-
tions for Italian musical identity, but the effect still works. The intermezzo
ends with another Wagnerian gesture. The Destiny Theme is played once,
repeated in a minor key (think "doom"), and then moved up the scale for
one ethereal moment of resolution. Redemption in two measures.

Setting: The docks at Le Havre, with a prison on one side and a ship on the other.

Lescaut explains to Des Grieux that he has bribed a guard. All is set to spring Manon from the prison before the arrested women are embarked on the ship to America. Des Grieux muses on the miseries of his life. At a signal from Lescaut, the guard walks off as if on patrol, and Des Grieux knocks on the small, barred window of the prison. Manon appears, touched that he has not abandoned her in her disgrace. She will be his forever, soon. A lamplighter appears away from the jail cell, singing of a king who wooed a simple girl. He passes. Des Grieux urges Manon to run with him. She hesitates, then agrees. A shot is heard, and Lescaut appears. The plot is foiled! He and Manon urge Des Grieux to escape, but he refuses.

Comment: The scene is bathed in murky orchestral tones matching the
darkness onstage, with only a glimmer of light when Des Grieux sees
Manon again. The passing lamplighter is a marvelous gesture, one that
Puccini would repeat at various points throughout his career (Tosca and
Tabarro, especially, have poignant and dramatically ironic passing snip-
pets of song to frame the singing onstage).

The townspeople rush into the square, chattering. What was the shot? A revolt? A woman tried to escape? There is a drumroll, and a sergeant and soldiers bring the women, including Manon, from the prison into the square. The sergeant begins the roll call for the embarkation to exile. "Rosetta!" The named woman approaches the gangplank, defiantly. Townspeople comment on her air. "Madelon!"

She laughs at the crowd insolently. "Manon!" Manon hides her face, and the crowd pities her. Who is she? A seduced woman? She is so beautiful. Lescaut scurries among the crowd, fomenting questions. This one, he says, was abducted from the love of a handsome young man! "Ninetta!" Ninetta crosses the square with great dignity. The people comment on the sadness of Manon's plight. "Caton!" Manon bemoans her fate, as Lescaut embellishes the story to the crowd, which pities her. "Regina!" Manon tells Des Grieux he must forget her and return to his father. He admits how shaken he is, and Lescaut points him out to the crowd as the bereaved bridegroom who had his beloved stolen from him on his wedding day by a filthy old man. "Nerina! Elisa! Nino! Georgette!" The sergeant orders the women in line, and seeing Manon lingering, grabs her. Des Grieux seizes her from him, and the crowd approves his gallantry. The ship's captain appears, demanding to know what is going on, and Des Grieux swears that no one shall touch Manon as long as he lives. He sees the captain and the armed men, and admits he is seized by madness. "Look at me!" he tells the captain. He is begging, pleading . . . let him sail with the ship! He will take any task, do the meanest work, whatever it takes. The captain looks kindly at the kneeling young man. "So you want to populate America?" he asks. "Very good, cabin boy, hurry on board!" Des Grieux kisses the captain's hand before rushing up the plank to the arms of Manon. Lescaut leaves, shaking his head.

Comment, scene and solo, "No! pazzo son! guardate!": *The roll call of the prostitutes is one of the best scenes in opera. Waves of sound, suggesting the long sea journey to come but also spasms of emotion, are the background for solo interjections. There are individuals, groups, and an overview of the situation working simultaneously. Some deride the fallen women while others express pity, some joke about what a fun voyage this will be, and so forth. It is both thoroughly ritualistic and utterly natural at the same time. As the women are lined up and begin boarding, the orchestra plays a low, swaying theme, appropriate to the rocking ship in the background but also forming a basis for Des Grieux's lurching outburst. This is capped by his solo "No! pazzo son! guardate!" (which is a bit too fragmented and brief to be classified as an aria). It requires everything a tenor can muster. Its one minute is as challenging as the entire previous act, cutting through the* passaggio *and sounding like a huge sob. There is even an opportunity for some actual sobbing, when the strings restate the big opening theme unaccompanied by the singer. This technique— restating the big theme in a thunderous orchestral refrain and having the soloist join in later—was considered old-fashioned even thirty years before this opera. It was thought to be heart-tugging and theatrical. The verismo composers used it in defiance of this perception. It was their way of saying, "But I really mean it!" and drawing attention to the gut-level emotionality of a given moment. Puccini maintained this usage through-out his career: in the big (and only) tenor aria in* Fanciulla, *in the ubiq-uitous soprano aria in* Gianni Schicchi, *and even up to the celebrated tenor aria "Nessun dorma" in* Turandot. *Broadway composers have since hammered the idea to death, but paradoxically it still holds up in Puccini's work. The secret is in having a great first line of the melody for the orchestra to restate, but also in having more melodic tricks up one's sleeve for later, when the singer joins in again. This is generally what eludes the Broadway composers, who tend to use up their entire melodic vein in the first line and then leave it to the singer to "wrap up" the tune. The effect is always anticlimactic. No chance of that here. This solo shows off the tenor's abilities (or lack of them) even better at the end than at the beginning of the solo. Tenors can soar into legendary status depending on their handling of this passage. The audience will try to applaud at the end of it (one hopes), but a thump in the bass drum moves the music along to the captain's interjection. (His marvelous line about populating the Americas was actually supplied by Giulio Ricordi—as if this libretto needed any more contributors.) Des Grieux and Manon embrace to an orgasmic restatement of the Destiny Theme, here a sign of good fortune, and cheers (or analogous gestures) from the chorus. Then let the ovation begin—for the tenor, the ensemble, and most definitely for Puccini (whether the audience is aware of this or not) for having created this unique and magnificent scene.*

Act IV

Setting: In the wastelands of Louisiana.

Comment: Okay, stop the laughing right now. This is 1720, and Louisiana refers to the Territory, not the state as we know it now. I'm sure there were plenty of tracts of arid land there in 1720 (Kansas, perhaps?) where a French lady might have died from thirst and exhaustion. Yet one still reads commentaries about this opera complaining of the unreality in showing someone dying of thirst in Louisiana. Amazing.

Manon and Des Grieux stagger across the American wastelands. Manon tries to rally, but she is unable to continue. Des Grieux goes to search for water. Alone, Manon gives way to her fears. . . . Alone, lost, abandoned. But she does not want to die. It is her beauty that has caused all these problems. Even in America, which she thought would be a peaceful haven, her beauty brought new torments, and almost made her lose Des Grieux again. Only the tomb can release her, but she does not want to die! Des Grieux returns, having found nothing but wasteland. He tries to comfort Manon, but falls into tears. She asks him to kiss her rather than cry for her—there is so little time left. She can feel the chill of death already. No longer able to hear him, Manon asks him to remember her youthful beauty. Time will obliterate her faults, but her love will live on.

Comment: Everyone agrees that the final act is something of an anticlimax. Manon staggers on, stumbles, and dies while Des Grieux sobs. One high point of this act is Manon's aria "Sola, perduta, abbandonata," which is rich fodder for divas who know how to wrench sympathy from an audience. The declamatory lines where she says she does not want to die, "No! non voglio morir!" really separate the divas from the mere tune-spinners. It's a unique moment, if you think about it. Opera heroines are supposed to say things like "Kill me, but spare my honor!" Manon has none of that affectation . . . she wants to live, just as she wanted luxury and passionate sex with her young lover. (She wants, in a word, life and all its pleasures. This is the secret of her appeal to men: she represents the Life Force. The fact that she is doomed in this world is more an indict-ment of the world than her morals.) Surprisingly enough, this aria was cut by Puccini for some productions after the initial run. The thinking was that the aria "stopped the action," which was thought for a long time to be the greatest sin an opera composer could commit. When the aria was cut, Act IV actually seemed longer—a phenomenon familiar to many musical editors. Toscanini insisted on replacing it for the famous 1923 La Scala production and it has remained there ever since. Perhaps Toscanini was among those who realized that this act contains no action to stop, so the argument was pointless. In any case, the act can be successful if the two protagonists have won over our sympathies in the previous acts and are capable of vocal "acting." If we can hear the life literally ebbing out of Manon, then the opera will have taken us on a full-circle journey—innocence, the dawn of love in Act I, material concerns and the compli-cations of love in Act II, crisis in Act III, and the slow sunset of death here. Manon's final, breathy words about her love living on must there-fore come across with conviction, since they are the only message of hope in this drama: love endures.

La bohème

The Name and How to Pronounce It

La bohème means "bohemian girl," in the sense of a free-and-easy, unconventional type, rather than referring to any nationality. It refers to the main character, or one of them, in the opera. It is never translated into English, partly because there happens to be another opera, now quite forgotten but once a mainstay, called *The Bohemian Girl*. If you only know one thing about opera—in fact, if you only know one thing at all—make sure you know that the "h" in *bohème* is silent.

What is *La bohème?*

La bohème is a tale of young love and loss. At first glance, *Bohème* could not be simpler in its scope: boy meets girl, girl dies. (Sorry to give away the ending, but the plot isn't really the point of the work.) Their doomed affair happens in the colorful milieu of starving artists in nineteenth-century Paris, self-consciously flouting convention, rejecting bourgeois comforts, and pursuing pleasures while trying to survive life's trials large and small. The hero and heroine are shadowed by another couple, whose differing dynamic provides contrast and context.

To portray these rather ordinary people and their world, Puccini used a musical vocabulary so aptly suited to the characters and the dramatic situation that *Bohème* is, on its own terms, absolutely perfect. In this, he was aided by one of opera's best libretti. Then there is the melodic wealth. Many composers have come up with great melodies, of course, but there is often the feeling that those melodies have come from some great Beyond and we are getting only a momentary auditory glimpse of something sublime. The melodic vein in *Bohème* is uniquely immediate. It seems as if these melodies are the ones we ourselves would express for our own life experiences if we only had the capacity to do so. The lyric infectiousness of *Bohème* is a ruse to bring home the story to us in the audience. This is not a drama of great lords and ladies of yore. *Bohème* is about us, even if the "us" in question is only a representation of our emotional lives rather than our autobiographies.

It's only after repeated exposure to *Bohème* that one realizes the superb craftsmanship beyond the big tunes. There is an amazing economy of expression used to cover a full and authentic drama. The whole work is barely over two hours, because that's all Puccini needed to say what he had to say. There is not a single "extra" note in it—and how many operas, really, can claim that? The seamless balance of recitative, aria, ensemble, and chorus is remarkable: Puccini did not dispense with those forms, but rather made an organic whole out of them. One is hardly aware of them as the work progresses. The moods change as often and as quickly in this work as they do in reality: there is boisterousness, sarcasm, anger, guilt, arousal, self-aggrandizement, resentment, and compassion as well as honest grief. The use of foreshadowing, reminiscence, and allusion is astounding and, again, seems like a true representation of the emotional life. Puccini's light touch—misconstrued by many in his day (and since) as triviality—is perfectly suited to this story of common things and common people. The score of *Bohème* tends to run up and down the scales without huge jumps. The "big phrases" are built incrementally and are therefore coherent and believable.

I have given more attention than usual to detail in my "synopsis" below, since *Bohème* is about little things. This work covers much of the same ground (albeit in a more extremely economical manner) as Proust's *Remembrance of Things Past*. It is, I'm told, a prop master's nightmare: there are, for example, pens, brushes, a stove, loaves of bread, bottles of wine, a key, a candle, a bonnet, a coral necklace, a horn, carrots, toys, a custard, a stuffed turkey, a herring, a muff, a torn old overcoat, and so on. Like Rodolfo's and Mimì's loves, the objects come and go. You never know which one will turn out to have unforeseen significance. In short, you never know which will break your heart. God is in the details. The events, characters, musical constructions, and objects of *Bohème* are all mere details. But life, and the world's most popular and enduring opera, is made of such details.

Bohème's *Place in the Repertory*

The top, the apex, the very pinnacle, which is ironic for such a "humble" work. *Bohème* is the world's most popular, most performed, and most easily identifiable opera. No opera company can, or has attempted to, survive without it. The score has the reputation of being agreeable to a wide variety of voices and is, all things considered, a relatively easy opera to produce. Conversely, it affords even the largest companies an opportunity to show off some magic in one crowd scene that can be as big as all Paris. *Bohème* always works.

It works too well for its own good, in some respects. The fact that *Bohème* can be (and has often been) produced in a barn or a garage means that there are a lot of second-rate *Bohème*s in the world. And having a score that is agreeable to a wide variety of voice types is not the same thing as being easy to sing—or at least easy to sing well and with feeling and nuance. Nor are amateurs and backyard companies exclusively to blame. The world's opera houses have been surviving on *Bohème* for generations, knowing they can sell seats to performances of this work to pay for other, more recherché operas that audiences shun. That's all good and well, except the *Bohème*s one sees in the world's major houses are usually underrehearsed, under-directed, and, with rare exceptions, cast with less-than-stellar leads. The ensemble effect that is at the core of this work rarely gets the respect it deserves in terms of vocal and musical resources. And the audience, whether in a summer stock tent or at the Mighty Met, also becomes part of the familiarity/contempt continuum. Many have seen it before and think they know it when they don't—ask any con-ductor or repetiteur if the details of *Bohème* are evident after one or two hearings. Rare are the smart operagoers who mentally prepare themselves for a performance of *Bohème* the way they would for, say, *Moses und Aron*. But in all fairness, rare are the opera companies who present the opera as what it is: a fresh, ever-astounding masterpiece with an endless capacity to downright rock an audience.

Cast of Characters

MIMÌ (*soprano*): A young woman of Paris, a maker of silk flowers. The role is amenable to light lyric voices, although she must have the ability to convey heft of sound at key moments. A good artist can do this without having to be an actual Valkyrie type, but the role suffers if assigned to canaries.

RODOLFO (*tenor*): An impecunious poet. Although nothing is ever said explicitly, we immediately get the feeling that Rodolfo is hand-some and very popular with the ladies. The role is written in a man-ner agreeable to lyrical voices, although, like Mimì, he should be capable of projecting some heft at various points in the score.

MARCELLO (*baritone*): An equally impecunious and not yet (if ever) successful painter. He shares Rodolfo's attic apartment in the Latin

Quarter of Paris. Lyricism and an ability to blend are the most important qualities in casting a Marcello.

MUSETTA (*soprano*): A Parisienne-about-town, on-again, off-again girlfriend of Marcello. The role is an anomaly—many sopranos who sing Musetta can and do sing Mimì at other times. The same vocal qualities work for both. Yet their personalities are utterly different. Musetta is brash and loves attention. But she is best when not played as an out-and-out harpy. Her appearance in Act IV makes it clear that she is a genuine and loving woman.

SCHAUNARD (*baritone*): A musician and musicologist, sharing the attic.

COLLINE (*bass*): An amateur philosopher, and the last roommate.

BENOIT (*bass*): The landlord. A comic part.

ALCINDORO (*bass*): A rich bourgeois. Alcindoro and Benoit are usually doubled by the same bass, who is often more noted as a character actor and mime than a robust bass in his prime.

The Opera

Setting: Paris, around 1830.

Comment: . . . or wherever the production you see decides to set it (see the chapter "Productions," below). There are specific allusions to the Paris of King Louis-Philippe throughout the libretto, but few people worry about that nowadays. The importance of the setting is in the artistic milieu. Artists who had previously found royal, aristocratic, and church patronage suddenly found themselves severely unemployed after the

*French Revolution and the Napoleonic upheavals. Even the restoration
of the old regime in 1815 did little to alleviate the situation. The only
chance for artists to find any support was in the newly all-powerful
bourgeoisie, the bankers and industrialists who defined the new era. These
bourgeois and everything they stood for, therefore, were most heartily
despised by the artists who suddenly had to cater to them. In this sense,
little has changed since 1830.* Bohème *can work anywhere as long as
there is some sensitivity to the issues that spawned this movement. Otherwise, the characters are merely poseurs acting as if they have invented
art and extramarital sex (which indeed they are at first, even if we can
assume this was less hackneyed in 1830 than it is almost two centuries
later).*

Act I

Setting: The garret apartment of four "bohemians" on the Left Bank.
Evening, December.

Marcello the painter and Rodolfo the poet complain of the cold in
their run-down Parisian garret. Marcello, at work on a painting, *The
Crossing of the Red Sea*, is too cold to work properly. For revenge
against the elements, he decides to make "another Pharaoh" drown
in the waves. Rodolfo stares out at the gray skies of Paris, noting the
many smoking chimneys, while their own lazy, empty stove sits idle
like a great lord. Marcello discloses a profound thought—it is cold!
Cold as the heart of Musetta, his fickle girlfriend. . . . They exchange
aperçus on the nature of love until Marcello decides to sacrifice one
of their four chairs to the stove for a few minutes of warmth. Rodolfo
stops him from this rash act. He offers instead the manuscript of his
tragedy. They tear it up greedily and light it. Their philosopher friend
Colline, a bearded and unkempt fellow, enters. He has been trying to
pawn some books but the pawnshops are closed. It is Christmas Eve.
He approaches the stove, discovers the nature of the fuel being used,

and pronounces the drama "scintillating." Rodolfo offers one act after another to the flame, but soon it is gone and the fire dies down. "Down with the author!" Marcello and Colline exclaim.

The musician Schaunard bursts into the room laden with wood, cigars, bordeaux, and a basket of food, even scattering some real silver coins on the floor. A feast! The friends greedily unpack the goodies. Schaunard is eager to tell how he came by such abundance, but no one listens—they are too much in awe of the unexpected windfall. He continues anyway: he met an Englishman, some lord or milord or whatever, and offered him music lessons. The Englishman sat Schaunard at a piano, pointed to a caged parrot outside the window, and ordered the musician to play until the parrot dropped dead. For three days, Schaunard played, but the parrot was still hale and hearty. Finally he befriended the maid, who found him cute, and they poisoned some parsley and fed it to the bird, which died like Socrates. "Who did?" asks Colline. "To hell with all of you," Schaunard says, packing up the food. He tells them they can drink now but save the food for the dark days ahead. They must dine out in the Latin Quarter, where the streets are lined with sausages and delicacies, where young men are strolling and girls are singing. All agree—it's Christmas Eve! To stay in would be irreligious.

There is a knock at the door. Monsieur Benoit, the landlord! "No one's home!" Colline blurts out. He insists on a word. "One only!" They hide their cache of food and treats and let him in. "Rent!" he demands. "Oh, that!" they laugh, letting him in and producing all their wealth. They'll pay him, but first he should have a glass of fine wine with them, then another. They flatter the old man as a rake about town like themselves. Why, didn't they recently see him at the Bal Mabille with a hot young thing? What a stud! An oak! A big old cannon! Well, admits Benoit, he's old but not dead. . . . And he likes women with a little something on their bones, not fussy, complaining skinny women such as . . . his wife. "Your wife!" the friends cry in righteous indignation. How dare this reprobate pollute a respectable home with his foul desires! They toss him out the door, unpaid, of course, and bid good night to his lordship. They laugh.

They divide Schaunard's money and agree to go to the Café Momus, after they get scruffy Colline a haircut. Rodolfo tells them to go on ahead. He has to finish writing his article for *The Beaver*. Well, cut your beaver's tale short, they tell him, and leave down the dark dilapidated staircase. Colline trips and tumbles down. "Are you dead?" asks Rodolfo from upstairs. "Not yet," Colline replies from below. Rodolfo sits to work but nothing happens. He's not in the mood.

Comment: The opening scene introduces breezy musical themes appropriate to the characters and their unstructured lives. There is even a touch of nihilism in the characters' actions—drowning the Pharaoh, burning the manuscript, killing the bird—that is reflected in the music's seemingly careless tossing off of themes. Listen carefully to the orchestra, though. You'll hear a lot of these later, and the music's transformations will match the character development magnificently. The mock-heroic phrases the characters use are an important aspect of their self-consciousness, and rarely make it through the in-house translations intact. It's even more important later in the story, when they occasionally drop their affected speech patterns and "get real." We have to go to the novel to make sense out of Schaunard's story. There, the parrot belongs to the Englishman's mistress, a young lady with many other admirers. In fact, she is in the habit of entertaining gentlemen of the legislature—all of them. The parrot has therefore memorized the parliamentary debates and recites them without stopping, and shows a particular interest in the Sugar Question currently dividing French politics. Driven to distraction by the chattering bird (and presumably by the reminders of his own cuckoldry), he pays Schaunard to play one chord—an inharmonious one—over and over. The gentleman claims to know something about medicine and is sure this will cause the bird's demise without making him guilty of actual murder (or even ornithicide).

A neighbor knocks on the door. "A lady!" Rodolfo notes, excitedly, opening the door to find a lovely but exhausted young woman whose candle has gone out and who needs a light. She tries to catch her breath—the stairs winded her. He invites her in, and she faints. She revives as he sprinkles her face with water, and he invites her to sit by the fire, offering her some wine. "She's so beautiful!" he says to himself. She thanks him for the wine and lights her candle, saying good night. "Leaving so soon?" he asks. Yes, she answers, but she can't find her key. She must have dropped it when she fainted. The draft blows out her candle, and then Rodolfo's. Oh, now what's she going to do? What a bothersome neighbor she is! They have to look for the key in total darkness. They paw the floor. Rodolfo finds her key and pockets it, denying it when she asks him. He pretends to keep looking as their hands touch. . . .

Comment: Most of this scene is marked pianissimo, with short, broken vocal phrases of one or two words. Even the orchestra, which might be expected to gush forth what is unspoken (yet apparent to anyone who has ever been to a movie, let alone an opera) is remarkably restrained. It vanishes to merely a few "plunks" as their hands paw the floor in search of the key. The "plunks" land on a B-flat, marked sforzando (which is a sudden decrescendo), like a little adrenaline rush, just as their hands touch. The economy of the scene is admirable from a musical point of view; the magic is obvious to anyone. The B-flat is held and becomes the basis for . . .

Your hand is so cold, he says. Leave it in mine so I can warm it. No use looking for the key in the dark: soon the moon will reappear and they can look then. Meanwhile, he asks if he may tell her a few things about himself. Is that all right? "Who am I? A poet. I write. And I live . . . as I live." In careless poverty he squanders poems like a great lord, and in hopes and fantasies he has the spirit of a millionaire. But sometimes all his treasure of dreams is robbed by two thieves—a pair of lovely eyes like hers. This does not bother him, though, since in place of the stolen dreams, hope fills the vacuum. Now she knows something about him: it's her turn. Wouldn't she like to tell him something about herself?

Comment, aria, "Che gelida manina": It is a testament to Puccini's genius, and to the resilience of this score in particular, that the public can retain affection for this most famous love aria of the repertory even after a century of abuse at amateur tenor recitals and tacky Italian-restaurants-with-pianos. Closer inspection reveals the aria's untarnishable originality. It isn't really an aria at all: it is three completely separate exclamations with a near-monotone introduction and denouement. In other words, the lyrical outbursts jump organically out of a sort of typical conversational tone. The effect is that Rodolfo articulates for all of us those feelings that we can never quite manage to express ourselves. He begins carefully, with nine repetitions of one note, expanding into some modest lyricism as he mentions the moon, and persuades her to join him by the fire to "warm up" and have a little chat. He then resorts to a sort of exclamatory (mock-heroic, perhaps?) recitative when telling her about himself. He hits his lyric stride describing his "happy poverty" and the poems he squanders, using the first music he sang when the curtain came up, which will serve as a sort of identifying "Rodolfo theme." There it was in a bouncy 6/8 rhythm ("clip-clop") while here it is a more dignified 4/4 beat. The melodic explosion comes when he tells her that he is sometimes robbed by a pair of bandits, "Talor del mio forziere." This is the slancio, *the big, gushing theme that half the audience will be whistling on the way home. The first phrase of the* slancio *is repeated by the strings, which was a practice much used and even abused by the verismo composers, and subsequently hammered to death by Broadway composers. Here, it is irresistible. It serves the multiple purposes of driving home the big theme and allowing the tenor to collect himself for the final outburst, a run up to high C. Perhaps the most inspired aspect of "Che gelida manina" is that the tenor continues after his climax, returning to a conversational tone in a higher key and suggesting that he is now leaning in toward Mimì. It's as if he's saying, "No, really, I do want to hear all about you now!"*

The problem here has always been how to make it believable that Rodolfo is so in love at first sight. Even with the most ardent music ever written, the illusion does not always come off. Nor does it have to. Rodolfo does not need to be in love at all, in any contemporary definition of the phrase. He is, first off, aroused, and secondly, infatuated with the idea of being a poet in love. "Non son in vena" (I'm not in "the groove"), he mutters when he's alone. The friends aptly chatter "Trovò la poesia" when they understand he has a young lady in the apartment. Mimì is an abstract concept to Rodolfo at this point. Puccini excelled at characters who are aware of how they appear to others: Manon the Coquette, Tosca the Diva, Butterfly the Geisha. Rodolfo is the only male he wrote with the same level of coquetry. (A further hint that we are meant to see Rodolfo in this light might be found in Schaunard's allusion to a pappagallo, a parrot, even though the rest of his tale makes no sense in context. A pappagallo is the Italian term for a young man who makes comments to young ladies on the street.) In opera, however, librettos only direct us: proof of an idea must always be sought in the score, and here we find an interesting idea. Rodolfo, as we saw, mentions, "I squander like a great lord," with the same theme as the first music we heard him sing, culminating in the phrase where he said the stove sat idle "like a great lord." Even with the slight change in beat, we get the sense that this is a little speech he has rehearsed in the past. Or perhaps he introduced himself to us in the audience, in a sense, with the same flirty sense of "Aren't I charming?" that he is now using on Mimì. It does not diminish these characters to define them so—indeed, it is Puccini's genius to bring out their humanity latent under their facades.

Like most countercultural poseurs, Rodolfo and Marcello are really rather morally conventional at base. They want what everybody else wants, without having to "pay the rent," literally and figuratively, for it. This is why the vaunted speech patterns of the previous scene are so important in understanding Rodolfo in this scene. He would not be able to say, "This girl is hot and I want her, now!" Some operatic characters manage to say that sort of thing in one form or another, but they are usually baritones and always bad guys. Rodolfo's self-delusion is part of his youthful

*charm. Real love does come to Rodolfo, later, and he will have to pay an
exorbitant rent for it. For now, it is sufficient if he is merely every cocky
guy in the world giving a "line" to a hot dish—albeit giving the line with
an eloquence and lyricism none of us in real life will ever equal.*

Yes, she replies. They call her Mimì, but her name is Lucia. Her story
is brief. She embroiders silk and satin, at home and out, and her
hobby is making artificial flowers, since she loves all things with gentle magic—the things they call poetry. Does he understand? "Yes."
They call her Mimì, but she doesn't know why. She doesn't always go
to Mass but she likes to pray. She lives alone, all alone, in a small
room looking out over the rooftops of the city. But when the spring
thaw comes, the first rays of sun are hers! April's first embrace is
hers! Then she finds a rose for her vase and breathes in the perfume,
petal by petal, because the flowers she makes, alas, have no scent.
What else can she say? She's just a neighbor bothering him at this
inconvenient hour.

*Comment, aria, "Sì, mi chiamano Mimì": Mimì's character and her sit-
uation in life are marvelously revealed in this aria, if the soprano knows
what she is doing. Like Rodolfo's aria, this one has suffered greatly at the
hands of amateurs and even some professionals who think displaying a
pretty voice is more important than making the character compelling. Too
bad, because this solo reveals as much of a fully realized, authentic woman
as Norma and Isolde display in their respective works. Mimì, like
Rodolfo, begins quite conversationally, with a certain flirty chirpiness that
becomes subdued at the ends of the phrases, suggesting she is catching herself from saying too much. When she tells us she doesn't always go to Mass
but rather prays to the Lord, she is saying that though she may not be conventional, yet she has a soul and Rodolfo had better respect that. Her
explosion of lyricism comes with the line "Ma quando vien lo sgelo" (But
when spring comes . . .), another Puccinian use of the falling phrases
stacked in an ascending order. Musically, it depicts the sun bursting out
from behind clouds, but it shows even more emotionally. For this part, it*

*is best if we hear a tinge of desperation in the soprano's voice. She knows
she is ill—perhaps terminally. She needs the sunlight like any flower does
or she will die, and we must know that she seizes those first rays of sun like
a starving person will grab food. And she needs love for the same reason.
The libretto uses the word "sgelo" (meaning "thaw," and, incidentally, a
real bitch to enunciate) for "spring," and the erotic implications are clear.
Rodolfo, who has already offered to warm up her little hand, must love
her the right way or he will lose her, one way or another. The solo also
ends on a conversational tone, a few notes of quasi recitative returning to
the idea of "Oh, I've blabbed on again." Note how many sopranos will
instinctively fold their hands and look down at the floor at this moment,
trying to look demure even amid torrents (on a good night) of applause.*

Marcello, Schaunard, and Colline call up from the street. What's
Rodolfo doing up there alone? "I'm not alone—there are two of us
here," says Rodolfo. The friends take the hint and go off to the Café
Momus, congratulating Rodolfo on "finding his poetry." Rodolfo
turns to Mimì, his "tender girl," saying she is a dream he could dream
forever. She agrees that Love rules all. She hesitates to ask what she
would really like, but finally dares: Can he take her out, with his
friends? Yes, if she likes, but what about afterward, when they come
back to Rodolfo's . . . ? "Curious!" she chides him coquettishly. He
offers his arm, and she takes it humbly. They leave, saying nothing
more than "Love, love, love. . . ."

*Comment, scene and duet, "O soave fanciulla": The interjection of the
friends' comments from the street level is amusing even if it is usually
camped up a bit: expect some wolf whistles at this point to show us that
they are "regular guys." (The score makes no such indication. It is a tradition.) It also reminds us that the opera is making no claims for this as
Rodolfo's first amorous encounter: whether or not this affair is serious, we
shall see in the subsequent development. When the friends (or their
voices) are dispatched, one might expect a very grand and prolonged love
duet, but Puccini did not find such an encumbrance necessary and sums*

up the situation succinctly. Rodolfo utters a few upward phrases (always a good indicator of a tenor in heat) and the two join for a restatement of the big slancio *from his aria. It is such a good "tune" that it makes any further development superfluous. (Also, notice how the tenor always sounds more secure here than when he sang the same line moments before. Perhaps the support of the soprano helps him, or perhaps it arouses their competitive spirit. It is also, mercifully, a half-step lower here.) After this, the tone is again conversational, although more tenderly now. We get a restatement of the first phrases of Rodolfo's love music, when he mentioned there was no use looking for the key in the dark and they had better just talk for a bit. Interesting: the lovers are already nostalgic about their initial moments together. For the "big finale," Puccini composed one of the most "tingly" moments in all theater. The lovers walk out of the apartment and we should be looking at nothing but the empty apartment and some moonlight. (Directors are always fiddling around with this, and their "improvements" never work.) From offstage, they sing "Amor! Amor! Amor!" The musical direction is "perdendo," meaning "getting lost." This is a difficult effect to achieve with the voice in any sort of pleasing way and without literally getting lost. When it is done well, the audience will heave a collective, amorous sigh. Half the time, the tenor will be eager to show off a high C for the final note, especially if he flubbed the high C in the aria. It isn't written for the tenor: only the soprano gets the high C at the end, and Puccini's instincts were, as usual, right. A soprano can float such a high note sweetly and from afar: it will carry out to the audience. If any of you know where to find a tenor who can do the same, by all means alert the managements of opera companies. Generally they just sound like oafs. The written note is an E, way down south from a high C. The effect suggests him leaning his head down toward hers as they walk down the street, which is much lovelier.*

The scene as a whole, then, has a symmetrical structure as formal as any analogous scene from any opera seria of the baroque era: he sings, she sings, they sing, curtain and applause. The miracle is in the entirely natural way these expressions arise out of the situation onstage.

Act II

Setting: On the streets of the Left Bank of Paris, later that evening.

Schaunard, Colline, and Marcello wend their way through the packed streets of the Latin Quarter as hawkers sell treats and gifts. Schaunard buys an out-of-tune trumpet, Colline a beat-up overcoat and a runic grammar book. Marcello flirts ostentatiously with all the pretty girls but with no success. Rodolfo and Mimì are elsewhere in the crowd; he buys her a pink bonnet. She looks into a shop window, eyeing a coral necklace. Rodolfo says he has a millionaire uncle and will buy her a really special necklace some other day but not now. Colline complains about the vulgar crowd. Rodolfo accuses Mimì of looking at someone. Is he jealous? she asks. Happy men are always jealous. So then he is happy? Oh yes, very. And she? Very! Marcello, Schaunard, and Colline take a table on the sidewalk in front of the Café Momus. Rodolfo introduces Mimì to them. She makes their company complete, since he is a poet, and she is poetry itself! The friends applaud Rodolfo's turns of phrase. Parpignol the Toy Seller hawks his wares to enthused children, who ask for drums, tambourines, and toy soldiers. The friends order large plates of food: venison, a turkey, wine, shelled lobster. Mothers arrive scolding the children around Parpignol's cart. Mimì orders a custard, showing her new bonnet to Marcello. The friends exchange pithy comments on the nature of love, but Mimì is straightforward: Loving is sweeter than honey! Depending on one's palate, interjects Marcello, it can be honey or gall. Mimì wonders if she has offended Marcello. No, the others explain. The painter is merely mourning his latest breakup.

Comment: The Latin Quarter scene is a dazzling achievement in portraying individuals in a crowd. From early on, critics complained of the illogic of the situation: why would people who were freezing to death in a garret choose to sit at an outside café? But Puccini insisted even when his librettists mentioned the incongruity, and he was right. The point of this scene is not to advance the plot—that could have been handled with a few lines farther along. The point was to look at individuals within a group context. And Puccini handled it masterfully. The chorus is divided into multiple parts: hawkers, students, citizens, children, all clamoring one against the other. When it is time for a soloist to be heard, the score thins out miraculously, giving the audio analogy of a "close-up." Puccini did not invent this technique: Verdi used it effectively, especially in La traviata *(which is a sort of operatic godmother to* La bohème*), and Wagner used it most impressively in* Die Meistersinger. *But not even Wagner or Verdi—scandalous to say—managed a crowd scene with such deft subtlety as Puccini achieves here. There is the shortest introduction: a horn fanfare playing a full-throated variation of the tune Schaunard had sung when convincing his friends to go out with him to the bustling streets. The curtain rises on a wall of sound: the hawkers crying out their various, and utterly typical, wares—oranges, carrots, cookies, pies—while the balance of the chorus interjects with comments such as "Hold my hand!" and "Please step aside!" The phrases seem randomly timed: of course, they are not. Schaunard toots on his horn, complaining of the out-of-tune note of D (represented in the orchestra by horns playing the clashing notes of D-flat and E-flat). Right away, you can see and hear a soloist within the scene, even as half the audience is still applauding the set designer and half the chorus is tripping over their hoopskirts.*

It is the relationship of the soloists to each other and to the group dynamic of the crowd that is most interesting. Here we see the π *formula in action. Thus there is a curious impression made when Mimì asks Rodolfo if he is jealous at the same time Colline is expressing his distaste for crowds. Colline also buys his torn overcoat just as Rodolfo buys the pretty bonnet for Mimì. Later these two items will cross paths again. An even greater insight is achieved when the friends order the most expensive dinners on the menu* while *the children are clamoring for toy cannons and hobbyhorses off Parpignol's cart. (And at that moment, please pause to give a thought to the poor assistant chorus director who must somehow*

make a pack of ten-year-olds repeat "Parpignol!" three times in very rapid
succession, exactly on cue.) The implications of such a juxtaposition are
a large part of what keeps both musicians and audiences coming back
to Bohème *time and again. No one—not even the conductor, half the*
time—has exhausted this seemingly simple score. It is also a large reason
why we can apply the apparently incongruous term "realism" to opera. In
life, people say things while other things are happening—the thing that is
said therefore has a relationship to all the other things going on. Yet only
opera, of the performing arts, can re-create this phenomenon in a compre-
hensible way and therefore show the bigger picture of life.

They fill their glasses, but, just then, Musetta (Marcello's ex) arrives,
overdressed and laughing up a storm. He puts down his glass, saying
he'd prefer some poison. All the crowd notices Musetta and her new-
found fortune, the source of which, an old, unattractive, and pompous
bourgeois named Alcindoro, presently appears. He is laden with the
by-products of his mistress's shopping spree, begging her lamely to
be quiet and more decorous. Not a chance. She takes a sidewalk
table at the Momus and loudly orders "Lulu," her pet name for the
old man, to sit, much to his embarrassment. Musetta sees Marcello
immediately and is annoyed that he refuses to look at her. Mimì
admires Musetta's outfit. Do the friends know her? Her name is
Musetta, explains Marcello, but her last name is Temptation! She is a
fickle carnivorous bird whose preferred diet is the hearts of men,
which is why he has no heart left. Musetta notices the gang and is
furious that Schaunard is laughing and Marcello still will not look at
her. But what is she to do with this old pelican on her hands? Marcello calmly asks for someone to pass the stew. Musetta screams to
the waiter that her plate smells greasy, and smashes it on the ground.
Alcindoro begs her to consider his reputation, while Schaunard and
Colline comment that the comedy is stupendous. Rodolfo warns
Mimì that he would never, ever forgive such trashy behavior in a girlfriend. Why speak of forgiveness? she asks. She loves him, she is his,
there is nothing to forgive. Musetta speaks, as if to Alcindoro but

knowing Marcello (and all of Paris) can hear her, that his heart beats like a hammer. Alcindoro commands her to be quiet, so she gets up to sing. When she walks down the street, she croons; everyone admires her beauty. Marcello begs to be tied to his chair. Musetta continues: how she savors the longing her visible charms create for her hidden charms! It delights her. And those who know, who struggle with the memories, how can they escape? You won't admit it, but it's killing you! Mimì says it is obvious that the poor girl is madly in love with Marcello. She feels sorry for her. Everyone comments at once. Alcindoro worries about the gossip. Schaunard bets that Marcello will give in. Colline pronounces himself above such silly behavior, but Schaunard tells him no such pretty creature ever talks to him on the street. If she did, he'd send his philosophy to Beelzebub! Mimì thinks it prudent to tell Rodolfo she loves him, and again expresses pity for Musetta and her cold heart. Musetta tells Alcindoro that she will do whatever she pleases whenever she pleases, making sure Marcello hears her. In the confusion, Musetta cries out as if in great pain. Her shoe! How it pinches! Alcindoro must run and get her a new pair! Marcello concedes to himself that his youth and memory are still alive. Alcindoro runs off to the shoemaker. Musetta and Marcello embrace fervently.

Comment, scene and aria, "Quando m'en vo" *("Musetta's Waltz"): Musetta enters the scene like charging cavalry: her first lines are sung against mixed chorus and plenty of interjections from the other soloists. Often, the soprano pushes for effect, intimidated by the surrounding chorus and soloists. Big mistake and totally unnecessary: Puccini wrote her line to skim effortlessly above the crowd. Musetta may be a gold-digging floozy, but that's no reason for her to sound like a yapping bull terrier. She sings the first stanza of the waltz as a solo. In its reprise, it is an elaborate concertato, and if Musetta has made enough of an impression, few will remember that Marcello actually sings the big theme here, with Musetta singing a decorative descant. (She has "gotten to him," we might say.) Framing this aria as a "song," then elaborating it as a concertato, effectively erases the boundaries between spoken drama (the previous recitative), song, and operatic technique. The jaded may carp that it is a trivial piece of music (and yes, it is true that Puccini originally composed this tune to commemorate the launching of a battleship), but it is triumphantly successful within context and brings the rest of the score to life in a unique way.*

The waiter brings the bill. Everyone checks their pockets. Drums are heard approaching, announcing the parade. The friends have spent all of Schaunard's original loot. Children run up and down the street waiting for the soldiers to march by. Musetta takes their bill and adds it to her own, explaining to the waiter that the old man will pay for both when he returns. This will be her farewell gift to him! The six friends agree to run off through the crowd, now even thicker than before. Alcindoro returns to the café, only to find the huge bill. The soldiers march on, led by the drum major, who dazzles the crowd.

Comment: Puccini racked his brains trying to figure out how to bring the curtain down on this act, and the parade seems as good a solution as possible. Primarily, by projecting the lovers' joy onto the giddy citizenry of Paris, it emphasizes the city itself as a living, breathing character in this story. Paris is as beautiful and as toxic as love itself, and a crucial element, rather than a picturesque backdrop, in this story.

Act III

Setting: Morning at the Tollgate at the Barrière d'Enfer, on the outskirts of Paris. February.

Sweepers try to clear the streets, although the snow keeps falling. The sounds of Musetta singing are heard from a nearby tavern. Customs officers attend the gate, while women on their way to the market declare their goods and chatter with each other. They pass.

Comment: This is a superb exercise in scene-painting. The curtain rises with two ascending chords—a sort of "Ta-dah!" effect that seems the equivalent of certain Italian hand gestures. Once this has, hopefully, shut up all the whisperers and candy-unwrappers in the audience, everything becomes ethereally quiet. A staccato, downward theme chirped by the flutes, divided into thirds, over shimmering strings depicts the icy chill of a winter morning. It doesn't take a musicologist to notice—although it's surprising how many of them seem to have missed it in their commentaries—that this theme is simply the great fanfare we heard at the beginning of Act II slowed down to a biting trickle and played by the piercing flutes. It is the third time we have heard the theme, therefore: the first was in "anticipation" when Schaunard was describing the joys of the Latin Quarter sidewalks to his friends, next was in full bloom in the fortissimo brass when we were experiencing the crowds, and now it is a memory, changed by time and context. As in Manon Lescaut *("there is no greater sadness than to remember happy times in misery"), Puccini has used the Dantean idea of "Nessun maggior dolor" to create a scene of sadness, but began the process one step previous to the happiness itself. It is augmented by the snippets of "Musetta's Waltz" floating out from the tavern—contained, that is, in a box, limited, and reverberating like a memory. This is Puccini's genius for showing a mutable thought or feeling as the background to all action, a lesson subsequent opera composers would do well to note. A few changes in tempo and instrumentation, and he has created a unique portrait of desolation.*

It is a desolation firmly rooted in daily reality, however, and all the more effective for that. Opera composers have always excelled in raising the curtain onto scenes of barren suffering: the haunting English horn solo in Act III of Wagner's Tristan und Isolde and the devastating orchestral introductions to six of the nine scenes in Verdi's Don Carlos jump to mind. And there are certainly choruses depicting the misery of the people in general, the prime example of which might be "Patria oppressa" from Verdi's Macbeth. Here, we have neither war nor evil curses afoot; merely people trudging their way to work on a snowy morning. They even manage a modicum of cheerfulness amid life's cussedness: "Good morning!"

and "We'll meet up later at noon." They are dealing with life's harshness
in a way Mimì no longer can.

Mimì appears, asking for the tavern where there is a painter working.
The officer points the way. Marcello comes out of the tavern, surprised to see Mimì wandering in the snow. He explains that he and
Musetta have been living at the tavern for a month—he earning his
room and board by painting figures on the tavern wall, she by teaching songs to the patrons. He invites her inside, out of the cold, but
when she learns that Rodolfo is inside, she insists on remaining outside. She can't see him. His jealousy is killing their relationship. At
night, when she sleeps, she can feel him staring at her, trying to pry
into her dreams. Then he becomes abusive. What can she do? Marcello advises that they separate, since they cannot live carefree, like
he and Musetta do. Mimì agrees. She coughs violently. Rodolfo is
waking up, and Marcello urges Mimì to leave and avoid a scene. She
agrees, but only withdraws to eavesdrop. Rodolfo bounds out of the
tavern and tells Marcello he is leaving Mimì. She is a flirt. That viscount is always looking at her and she leads him on. Marcello tells
Rodolfo he is a jealous boor and is lying. Rodolfo admits the truth.
The truth is that Mimì is truly ill, getting weaker all the time. His cold
apartment is killing her. Mimì hears them and wonders if she really is
dying. She coughs violently, and Rodolfo is surprised to find that she
is there. He claims he didn't mean it. He was just all excited. Musetta
laughs from inside the tavern, and Marcello rushes in to stop her flirting. "Good-bye," says Mimì to Rodolfo. But where is she going?
Back to the place she left, gladly, when his love first called her. Good-
bye, she says, without any bad feelings. She asks him to wrap up her
few things so she can send someone to fetch them. All except the
bonnet, though. That he should keep as a souvenir of their happy
times. Good-bye, with no hard feelings.

Comment, scene and aria, "Donde lieta uscì" ("Addio, senza rancor")*:*
The business between Mimì and Marcello, and then between Rodolfo

and Marcello, is handled briskly and conversationally. The music coheres into a trio when Rodolfo begins to describe Mimì's illness in less than poetic terms ("a terrible cough strikes her fragile chest"). His music is halting and rising, like he is sobbing. Mimì, although theoretically hidden behind a tree or some such nonsense, sings a longer legato line whose words say very little ("ah! poor me!") but whose music, doubled by the cellos, reveals new depths to her character. She is undergoing an acceptance of her own death, and it is a challenge to the artistic capabilities of the soprano to be able to convey this in an ensemble moment, literally out of the spotlight. Her subsequent solo is one of the many "hits" of the opera. Again we have the pattern that we have seen throughout this opera: the beginning and end are understated, almost conversational, while the only opportunity for unleashed expression is in the middle when she tells Rodolfo to keep the bonnet. If the tenor cannot mime some gesture of anguished guilt at this moment, he had better have a glorious voice to justify his presence on the stage in this opera.

The word "civetta," usually translated as "flirt," literally means "owl." Rodolfo uses it to describe Mimì, and then Marcello uses it again for Musetta, which is another sly invitation to see these two couples as different aspects of one couple. This idea will be flushed out in the subsequent quartet. "Civetta," incidentally, is considerably stronger in common Italian usage than "flirt" and only slightly less insulting than "slut." It has no equivalent in English. In any case, be careful using it in casual conversations in Italy. This I tell you from hard experience. Such are the pitfalls of attempting to learn real Italian from translated libretti.

So it's over, then? asks Rodolfo. The kisses, the sweetness? Yes, she answers, and the jealousies, the fights. But being alone in winter is like death. In the spring, they could each survive apart. Musetta and Marcello come out of the tavern, fighting. What was she doing with that man? Dancing, that's all! How dare she flirt! No horns will grow under his hat! She, for her part, despises lovers who act like husbands. Rodolfo and Mimì agree to separate when the flowers bloom.

Musetta charges off, hurling abuse at Marcello. "Housepainter!" "Viper!" he tosses back. "Toad!" "Witch!" Mimì hopes the winter will never end. She and Rodolfo will part when the flowers bloom.

Comment, "Quartet": I put quartet in quotation marks because a music student would be hard-pressed to recognize this scene as such. It is a continuation of Mimì's and Rodolfo's duet with decorative or strident interjections from Musetta and Marcello. Mimì and Rodolfo sing a beautiful line (it was a retread from one of Puccini's early songs, and inconceivable that a melody of such beauty could have been consigned to Puccini's "miscellany" file had he been more scrupulous about borrowing from himself) and they speak only the most tender words to each other. All their potential resentment and anger is placed in the mouths, so to speak, of Marcello and Musetta, who literally scream invectives at each other. Expect a lot of broken glass at the beginning of Marcello and Musetta's fight. It has become a tradition. Some musicological critics have complained that this quartet does not rank with the masterpieces of the form, since it is basically a song (and an unoriginal one at that) tricked out among four singers. Perhaps, but seen in dramatic terms, this is perhaps the supreme quartet of opera. The notion that the two men and the two women are, respectively, mirror images of each other comes to full flower here. As we use stereo to create an infinity of sound, so here the contrast of the two couples shows the full range of the pain of breaking up. This effect has been tried in spoken drama: Angels in America *even attempted a simultaneous breakup of two couples on two sides of the stage, one couple tenderly, the other screaming, as here. I don't know, but it is inconceivable to me that Tony Kushner did not have this scene in* Bohème *firmly in mind when he penned that scene. While it made sense within the many contrivances of that vast epic, the effect was of a self-conscious tour de force, while in* Bohème *it unravels with the organic inevitability that is this work's essence. If any still doubt opera's ability to render reality on a deeper level than other art forms, let them spend a few years pondering this moment.*

Musically, Rodolfo and Mimì are given the lushest music of the score at this point. The orchestra comes in at full force and then vanishes with equal ease, like spasms of emotion. At times, the two lovers are singing against extremely dense orchestration, including trumpets and trombones. Plácido Domingo once claimed that the orchestration is thicker and more challenging here even than in Verdi's Otello, *the official ballbuster Italian opera. That aperçu has raised many an eyebrow, but who are we to argue? The climax, in terms of volume, comes in the middle of the quartet, as it has in the two first-act arias and in* "Donde lieta uscì." *The contrast is made explicit by having Mimì and Rodolfo sing their last lines offstage and dying away, as a clear and poignant reference to their meeting and love duet in* "O soave fanciulla" *in Act I. The stage is empty for a moment (expect much snow falling). The curtain comes down with a reversal of the opening two chords, this time ascending, marked fortississimo for full orchestra, an emphatic end to one of the most perfectly drawn scenes in all theater.*

Act IV

Setting: The garret. April.

Rodolfo and Marcello taunt each other about their lost loves: each has seen the other's well dressed in a carriage, obviously kept by other men. They each feign indifference and try to return to work. It's no use. The pens and brushes aren't cooperating. Each reflects to himself how much he misses his ex.

Comment, duet, "O Mimì tu più non torni": *It becomes apparent pretty quickly that Act IV is a sort of mirror image of Act I, although in this act nothing quite works the way it once had. In Act I, Rodolfo could not write until he met Mimì, when he "found poetry." Now that she has left him, his pen doesn't work. It's in the score, too. Almost the entire fourth act is composed of reworked themes from the earlier acts, although you might have to listen a few times to identify exactly which. The actual duet is a short but moving piece, and a test of a tenor and baritone's ability to blend their voices. It takes a moment to realize that the primary material in the duet is the central part of "Musetta's Waltz," evocative of happier times rather than a specific reference to Musetta.*

Schaunard and Colline burst in with dinner—four rolls and a single herring. They try to wax poetic over the feast, but it's no use. Schaunard wants to recite a poem but is shouted down. Instead, they dance a quadrille, Marcello as the damsel, Rodolfo the gallant, Schaunard singing, and Colline calling the steps. Schaunard and Colline bicker over the proper order, and with great vaunting go at each other in a mock sword fight. Musetta bursts in—she found Mimì wandering the streets in a stupor and near death, and has brought her back.

Comment: Here again the contrast with Act I is marked. The gaiety is forced, and the fact of the single herring remains on the table like a sobering reality check. Schaunard's attempt at a poem was actually Puccini's attempt at an aria for the second baritone. He never could land on quite the right music to give him, and finally in frustration ordered Giacosa and Illica to alter the libretto and have the friends shout him down. Perhaps Puccini's "failure" was correct in dramatic terms . . . the time for a vaunting, self-conscious poem among the bohemians has passed, and one gets the feeling that they will all soon be getting jobs. (In the novel, that's exactly what happens.) Still, Schaunard is the only one of the bohemians who never gets a solo, and baritones rightly complain about it.

Rodolfo helps Mimì up the last stairs and puts her into bed, assuring her she is welcome in his home. Musetta tells the others how she found Mimì after she fled the viscount, and how Mimì wanted to return to Rodolfo to die. She asks if there is anything in the house. No coffee? No wine? Nothing but poverty, Marcello assures her. Schaunard notes that Mimì will die within a half hour. Mimì complains of the cold. Her hands are frozen. If only she had a muff, maybe they'd be warm again for a while. She greets the other friends, and tells Marcello how good Musetta is. Marcello agrees. Musetta pulls him aside and gives him her earrings, telling him to sell them and get Mimì some medicine and a doctor. She herself will find her a muff—it's the girl's last request. They leave. Colline takes off his overcoat and says farewell to it. It never bowed to the rich or powerful, and it kept poets and philosophers in its pockets. And now, as a faithful old friend, he takes his leave of it.

Comment, scene and aria, "Vecchia zimarra": The sudden change of mood from the mock duel to Musetta's entrance is instantly apparent in the score. All the "fun" music simply vanishes. Things get "real," and this is reflected in the words as well. The poetic phrases of the friends while goofing off (Schaunard pouring a glass of water: "Pass me the goblet, by the leave of this noble company") shorten into blunt statements (Marcello: "Nothing but poverty"). Musetta's fussing and exit with Marcello are quick and brief. Literalists are always stumped by Colline's solo "Vecchia zimarra." Commentators can approach the loopy when trying to explain why Colline would get so emotional about a secondhand coat (especially now that it's spring) and why Puccini would squander one of his most affecting melodies on this moment. Others carp that the inevitable applause after the brief (about one minute) aria interrupts the flow of the drama. Philistines. First of all, it isn't about an overcoat at all, of course, anymore than Proust's madeleines are about cookies. It's the coat—one of life's details—that triggers a rush of emotion about the wretchedness of life in general from this otherwise stoic philosopher. And giving a solo to the bass in this moment was dead-on. If one separates the acoustical impression from the syntactical meaning (often a good exercise in opera), then clearly Colline sounds like a priest saying prayers for the dying. There is no better dirge in vocal music. The fact that it's dressed in a ratty old coat, so to speak, is the genius of the verismo genre. The ancient ways have not disappeared—they are embedded in the trivialities of modern life, if we know how to see (or hear) them.

Alone with Rodolfo, Mimì asks if the others are gone. She was only pretending to be asleep so she could be alone with him. They reminisce about their meeting, and he gives her back her bonnet. She has a coughing spasm, and Schaunard runs into the room. Is everything all right? Yes, Mimì assures him. She will be good and not talk anymore. Musetta and Marcello return, followed by Colline. Musetta gives Mimì the muff, telling her it is a gift from Rodolfo. Mimì sleeps. Musetta prays to the Virgin that she spare Mimì. She assures Rodolfo that it is not serious. Schaunard approaches the bed, and tells Marcello that Mimì has died. Colline gives money to Musetta. The friends signal each other behind Rodolfo's back, but he asks them what all their running around means. Why are they looking at him like that? "Courage!" Marcello tells him. He calls out for Mimì and falls sobbing on her lifeless body.

Comment, scene and aria, "Sono andati?": Mimì's solo in this scene is the only music that is not composed of reminiscences of previous material. The melody itself is a bit like "No! pazzo son! guardate!" from Manon Lescaut, *and a comparison shows how economical Puccini was with the vocabulary of* Bohème. *The balance of the scene is even more austere, solo violin parts taking much of the musical load as the texture becomes quieter and quieter. Musetta's prayer to the Madonna, which might have been a grand scena in another composer's hand, is almost a monotone and has the ring of authenticity to it. This is not pious grandstanding. This one comes from the heart. The orchestra moves into a minor mode as Schaunard realizes Mimì has died, but quietly. (It is traditional at this point for the muff to drop out of the lifeless hand.) No thunderous chords, no shouts of "Gran Dio!" from Schaunard. It is only when Rodolfo grasps that Mimì has died that the orchestra blares forth the repeated E major chords from "Sono andati?" fortissimo in the orchestra. They die away again, as so many of the powerful orchestral outbursts in this score do, like a punch to the gut. Death itself is the quiet part of the tragedy, while Loss becomes the new tragic focus. Loss becomes general, too, because when*

Rodolfo realizes Mimì is dead, we can logically and emotionally extrapolate that much else is gone besides. All the delusions of youth—that there is anything romantic or defiant about poverty, that art and love can provide sufficient nourishment in the modern world, that one can create one's own reality within the realities of life—die simultaneously. Plenty of plays, movies, and operas kill off the ingenue in the end and leave the audience much the same as they were before they attended, but Bohème's tragedy is everybody's tragedy. Small wonder that it has, in defiance of all logic, become the opera that stands for all opera.

Tosca

The Name and How to Pronounce It

Not very challenging here: accent on the first syllable.

What is Tosca?

Tosca is one of a handful of operas that define the medium. It is the pinnacle of the verismo style, even if it does not conform verbatim to many of the supposed qualifications of that style. It is also Puccini's most extreme opera, in terms of story, situation, and score. The story is based on a historical play, *La Tosca*, by Victorien Sardou, a popular Parisian playwright. Sardou wrote his play as a vehicle for Sarah Bernhardt, the definitive exponent of the no-holds-barred school of acting. Sardou obliged his star with a play that included a torture scene, a prolonged attempted rape, love scenes, and an absolutely smashing suicide finale. Knowing all this, Puccini pushed his librettists to ratchet up, rather than tone down, all the most sensational aspects of the play when constructing the opera. Even Giacosa found the story repellant and tried time and again to mitigate the tale's perceived excesses. But Sardou, who kept in touch with Puccini throughout the process, urged the composer to follow his instincts. Puccini then matched this story with a score that is brash, abrasive, and distinctly "in your face." There are crashing dissonant chords, lush, heart-tugging cello passages, a church procession Cecil B. DeMille could hardly have imagined, and at least two of the most irresistible tragic arias in the repertory. Not even the definitive verismo opera, Mascagni's *Cavalleria rusticana*, with its battered pregnant woman and hysterical death-shriek at the finale, beats *Tosca* for sheer emotional volume.

Imagine, then, what scorn this has earned *Tosca* from many quarters. Since its premiere, critics have accused Puccini of using mere shock effect. Act II, Tosca's great confrontation with Scarpia that includes the attempted rape and a murder, is singled out for wallowing in sadistic depravity. (It's hard to imagine which composer's well-adjusted, psychosexual operatic ethos they are comparing this to.) After *Tosca*'s premiere at Covent Garden in 1900, a London newspaper carped, "The alliance of a pure art form [opera?!?] with scenes so essentially brutal and demoralizing . . . produced a feeling of nausea." And so forth, throughout the years. The definitive *Tosca* putdown came from Joseph Kerman in his otherwise lucid book *Opera as Drama,* where he calls *Tosca* a "shabby little shocker." Shabby, in a sense. Shocker, yes indeed. Little? Not on your life.

Tosca's *Place in the Repertory*

At the top, if not quite sitting atop the summit like *Bohème*. *Tosca* is indispensable to every company in the world, and performances keep selling. This despite the purists' and naysayers' complaints that *Tosca* is not "really a great opera." (The same thing is often said about Gounod's *Faust*: God save us, then, from "great" opera.) *Tosca* is dependent on the diva, of course, as is nearly every Puccini opera, but the role can be successfully delivered by many varying vocal types. It can also succeed with many different character interpretations. Leontyne Price, for example, was close to the edge from her entrance, while Montserrat Caballé moved hardly at all and merely walked off the stage at the end. Both were unforgettable. The tenor role, likewise, can be convincingly delivered by a great many different qualities of voice. That's the good news for producers. The staging can be very expensive, unless one finds a creative way to get around the Te Deum scene at the end of Act I, which is not easy to do. Yet somehow every company manages to find a way to produce *Tosca*. They can hardly afford not to.

Tosca is also, curiously, known as the *Macbeth* of operas—that is, if your opera house is going to burn down, it will most likely be during a run of this opera. One would think Verdi's *Macbeth* would be the *Macbeth* of operas, but no. It's *Tosca*. A quick outline of some of the most notorious: underrehearsed extras for the firing squad in Act III getting cues mixed up and firing at Tosca; a trampoline substituted for a mattress for the finale, with the predictable result that Tosca came flying back up, skirts over head, at the finale (these two and some other escapades are outlined in Hugh Vickers's amusing book *Great Operatic Disasters*); Eva Marton and Juan Pons getting a little too rowdy in the scuffle in Act II and Pons dislocating Marton's jaw directly before she had to sing "Vissi d'arte" at the Met in 1987; Maria Callas's hair catching fire as it came too close to the candle in the same act (and such was Callas's legendary concentration that she didn't flinch or break character, but waited for baritone Tito Gobbi to extinguish the smoldering locks as part of his "copping a feel" act). The list goes on. There is inarguably something a bit cursed about this opera, which of course only adds to its popularity among fans.

Cast of Characters

FLORIA TOSCA (*soprano*): An opera singer. In the Sardou play, we learn much about Tosca's background: She was actually a native of the Veneto region, reared in a convent and in fact destined for the cloistered life until the pope heard her sing and released her from her vows. She is currently singing in an opera by Giovanni Paisiello at the

Teatro Argentina in Rome. Puccini, with Sardou's consent, jettisoned all this information, and our heroine takes on a much more native Roman persona (think Anna Magnani in *Open City*). She is also notable in that she is not an ingenue, a naive young girl (as are most of Puccini's heroines), but rather a mature woman with a life of her own.

The Cavaliere Mario Cavaradossi (*tenor*): A painter, and Tosca's lover. Cavaradossi is a man of revolutionary sympathies, little patience for church authorities or religion in general, and a taste for reading Voltaire, of all radicals. In *La Tosca*, he is actually a Parisian, born of an exiled Roman noble and a French mother. The notion was that of course a liberal would be Parisian, whatever his ancestry. Again, Puccini urged his librettist to dump these details. The role itself calls for the ability to communicate great ardor both in love and in politics.

The Baron Scarpia (*baritone*): The despised police chief of Rome, a reactionary bigot, a hypocrite, and a sadistic pervert, to boot.

Cesare Angelotti (*bass*): The deposed tribune of the late, lamented Roman Republic.

A Sacristan (*bass*): A rather comic character fussing about the Church of Sant'Andrea della Valle.

Sciarrone (*bass*): One of Scarpia's henchmen.

Spoletta (*tenor*): Another of Scarpia's henchmen.

A Shepherd Boy (*boy alto or soprano*): An offstage role (hence one can "cheat" by casting a woman in the part), and one of Puccini's most effective "passing moments of song."

A Jailer (*bass*): His main job is to mutter one line and get out of the way while the tenor prepares himself and primps for the big aria.

The Opera

Setting: Rome, on the afternoon of June 17, 1800.

Historical note: Any libretto that tells us a specific afternoon in history is drawing attention to historicity. Here's some of what we need to know: The French armies fought back against the "Allies" (virtually every other nation in Europe at this point) with great initial success, setting up local republics wherever they could. In Naples, there was the Parthenopean Republic, established with some degree of local support. Indeed, events throughout Tosca *seem to recall actual events in Naples of that time rather than in Rome. Nobody "lamented" the passing of the Roman Republic, except perhaps the curator of the Louvre Museum. Rather than bringing freedom to the people of Rome, the French-backed republic achieved nothing except the systematic looting of Rome's treasures. The Bourbon king of Naples finally managed to evict the French and crush the republic by 1799, occupying Rome with the help of Austrian troops. In June 1800, the French were again on the march, this time led by Napoleon Bonaparte and more interested in securing military victory than in setting up Liberty Trees. A thorough outline of the actual situation in Rome at this time is to be found in Susan Vandiver Nicassio's invaluable book* Tosca's Rome. *Readers are urged to buy this book immediately. You will even learn that there was only a quarter moon on the night of the seventeenth, although the love duet would have us believe there was a full moon!*

Act I

Setting: The inside of the Church of Sant'Andrea della Valle.

Angelotti, a political prisoner just escaped from the Castel Sant'Angelo, runs breathless into the church. His sister, the Marchese Attavanti, promised to leave him a disguise inside the family chapel off the nave of the church so he could flee Rome. He searches for the key and hides in the chapel.

A silly old sacristan with a nervous tic wanders on. He was supposed to be helping the painter, Cavaliere Mario Cavaradossi, who is painting a portrait of Mary Magdalene on one of the church walls. The sacristan apologizes for being late, but the painter is not there. Funny, he is sure he heard footsteps. . . . No, he must have been mistaken. The basket of food he left for the painter has not been touched. The bell rings announcing the time for reciting the Angelus, which the sacristan obediently utters. Cavaradossi enters and interrupts the prayer gruffly. He mounts the scaffold, unveiling the portrait of the Magdalene he is working on. The sacristan recognizes the face. It is a woman who has been coming to the church to pray. Such devotion and piety! Yes, says Mario. While she prayed, she did not notice him observing her and using her features as a model for the saint. "Away, Satan!" grunts the sacristan.

Comment: The Three Big Chords that bring us directly into the action are loud (fortissimo), menacing, and unresolved (that is, they include almost all the notes of an octave, natural, sharp, and flat, with no hint of an aural "resting place"). They represent Scarpia and his terrifying presence, seen and unseen, throughout Rome. Musically, they also telegraph to the audience what sort of a musical vocabulary to expect from this opera. Bohème, it isn't going to be. . . . The orchestra then shifts to the comical dum-dee-dum music of the blubbering sacristan. The shift is abrupt, yet seamless, accomplished with the deftness that came so naturally to Puccini and that his musicological detractors would do well to note, if not emulate. The sacristan is invariably played by an aging baritone in the golden sunset (if you're lucky) of his career. Expect him to make the most of his short time left onstage, endlessly fussing and making the sign of the cross more frequently than St. Teresa in ecstasy.

Mario asks for his paints. He looks at the painted face while mixing colors on the palette, then stops to look at a miniature in his pocket.

How strange, this harmony of different feminine beauties! Tosca, his lover (and the portrait in the miniature), has brown hair and her eyes are black, while this unknown beauty is blonde and blue-eyed. "Play with toys but leave the saints alone!" warns the sacristan. Art blends all beauties, but while painting that one, Mario's only thoughts are with Tosca. The sacristan continues to mutter his warning not to mix the sacred and the profane.

Comment, scene and aria, "Recondita armonia": This aria is one of the staples of the repertory, but it's much more than a (very) beautiful solo. All of Puccini's economy and mastery is there. In one brief minute, hardly three minutes after the last members of the audience have taken off their coats, we learn most of what we need to know about the character, much of what we need to know about the opera, and everything we need to know about the tenor. The orchestra sets the scene superbly: the flutes play parallel fifths (a note accompanied by the one four notes away) followed by parallel fourths (do the math) as Cavaradossi "blends" the paints on his palette. Get it? It's this specificity of action in the score that helps Tosca *earn the classification of verismo, despite the absence of scruffy, knife-wielding peasants and unemployed workers. Characterwise, we learn that Cavaradossi is passionate and genuinely in love with Tosca. (The pronoun he uses for the Attavanti woman, costei, "that one," has a pejorative tone in Italian.) Musically, we learn even more. The big theme, stated at the beginning and repeated at the end, is built on two notes, E and F. This is the celebrated and dreaded* passaggio *of the tenor voice, which only the best vocal composers knew how to manage. The voice sounds inherently emotional in this range. If the tenor's technique and pitch are secure, he will simultaneously convey manliness and expressive sensitivity right here—two necessary traits for Cavaradossi. You're lucky if the tenor you hear has either aspect, let alone both. If his technique is flawed, he'll sound like an unfixed tomcat in the moonlight. There's no way to fake it.*

This moment also presents a problem in staging. The painting is usually conceived as a wall painting, typical of Roman churches. The poor tenor must therefore abandon all reason and turn to the audience while

*theoretically meditating on his artwork. Some productions put the paint-
ing on an easel, unseen by the audience. Worse. Having the tenor pop his
head out from behind the canvas reads like Bugs Bunny's assays into
opera. Better to forget logic for the moment, verismo though this may be,
and count on the luscious flow of voice to distract us.*

The sacristan reminds Cavaradossi of the basket of food. Is the
painter perhaps fasting in penance? "I'm not hungry," grunts Mario.
The sacristan suppresses a giggle. May he be excused? "As you like."
"Don't forget to lock up." "Go," says Mario. "I'm going," is the reply.
He leaves, crossing himself. Angelotti, thinking the church is empty,
comes out of the chapel, and is startled but thrilled to find Cavaradossi. Doesn't the painter recognize his old friend? Has prison
changed him that much? Mario recognizes the tribune of the fallen
Roman Republic, and places himself at his service. Just then, a woman's
voice crying out Mario's name is heard in the distance. He rushes
Angelotti back into the chapel, telling him to hide there. It is nothing,
just a jealous woman. He will get rid of her quickly. "Mario! Mario!
Mario!" repeats as Angelotti hides in the chapel. At last, Cavaradossi
unlocks the door and lets in his lover, Tosca.

"Where is she?" Tosca demands. "I heard you whispering! I heard
the rustling of a dress! Do you deny it?" "I deny it and I love you,"
says Mario, attempting to kiss Tosca. "Not in front of the Madonna!"
says Tosca, demurely, then arranging flowers she has brought before
the statue of the Virgin and praying. When she has finished her
prayers, she tells Mario that she will be singing at the theater, but the
performance will not be long. He can wait for her at the stage door
and together they can go to his villa. "Tonight?" he asks, distracted.
"Yes," she answers. There will be a full moon . . . isn't he happy?
"Very!" he answers. She is unconvinced. He asks her to leave and let
him work. She is being dismissed? Fine, she begins to go, but staring
at the painting, wonders who that woman is. Wait a minute . . . wait a
minute. . . . It's the Attavanti! That slut! Is Mario seeing her? Does

he love her? Does she love him? Oh, betrayed! "Against me! Me!" she wails. Mario swears he doesn't know the woman. He merely saw her praying and thought she would be a good model. How foolish and jealous Tosca is! What eyes in the world could compare to Tosca's own? His whole being is entwined in them! How well he knows the right words to soothe a woman, she says, won over. "But," she adds, "paint her eyes black!" He assures her of his love, and finally insists she leave and let him work. Yes, she will leave, but he must promise to meet her at the theater, and that there will be no women praying at the church that afternoon, blonde or otherwise, and then he may kiss her. "In front of the Madonna?" he chides. Tosca points to the painting. "Paint her eyes black," she whispers, leaving.

Comment, scene and duet: Angelotti barely has time to pop his head out of the chapel and hide again before Tosca makes one of the notorious entrances in all opera. Her repeated shouts of "Mario! Mario!" from outside establish her character before we even see her. The same is true for Mimì and Butterfly in their respective operas, but those two lovely ladies could not be more different from this battleship in war mode. Traditionally, Tosca always carried a sort of decorated walking stick, a bunch of flowers for the Madonna, and the world's widest-brimmed hat. The stick and the Queen Mother–sized hats are generally gone these days, but the flowers are essential. If she seems ridiculous, running around ready to "scratch the eyes out" of her rival, no matter. A little comedy in this moment is no barrier to an effective performance, but with luck the soprano will not lose sight of the real characterization at stake here. Her jealousy is more than theatrical, as it is usually called. It is epic, like that of Juno in the Aeneid. *"A me! A me!" she says, enigmatically. Clearly, this is not the Girl Next Door. As far as what she is, we shall need a whole subsequent chapter to begin to explore.*

The business about the Attavanti woman is recitative, and the duet proper begins with Mario reassuring her of his love. This duet is popular in concerts but is not quite in the same league as those in Puccini's other operas for the simple reason that there is very little at stake. In other operas, Puccini presents lovers meeting (Bohème, Butterfly), having a torrid, illicit relationship (Tabarro, Schicchi), or in the midst of a great argument of some sort (Manon Lescaut, Fanciulla). Here, the lovers are in the middle of their affair and quite comfortable with their appointed roles. Sure, they had a little spat, but you get the feeling that this level of argument is nothing more than foreplay for them. The purpose of the duet is to show us their passionate natures, their genuine affection, and to provide a gold mine of themes for later reminiscences.

Cavaradossi locks the door behind Tosca and fetches Angelotti from the chapel. The ragged man ate the food and drank the wine in the basket. He explains that his sister, the Marchese Attavanti, arranged for his escape from the *castello* and his women's clothes in the family chapel in order to save his life from the evil Baron Scarpia. Cavaradossi sneers at the name, calling him a bigoted satyr who uses religion as a tool for his perverted lust. Mario tells Angelotti to follow a path from the back of the chapel out to his own villa in the suburbs. He may hide there. If there is trouble, there is a chamber halfway down the well in the garden where he can hide and will never be found. A cannon shot is heard, announcing that a prisoner has escaped. No time to lose. Mario will flee with Angelotti to the villa, and, if necessary, fight to the death. They run out.

Comment: Poor Angelotti—so much plot, so little music. This brief scene does serve to show us Cavaradossi's heroic aspects. The tessitura of this scene between tenor and bass lies very high for both, and they tend to speak in hurried phrases, but Cavaradossi gets to toss off a couple of high A's and a B-flat when swearing to protect Angelotti. (The B-flat has a "fermata" over it, meaning the tenor is expected to hold the note and impress us with his virility.) Beyond this, Angelotti's appearance is purely a plot function.

And a much-simplified plot function compared to the play. Sardou gave his characters reasons for their motivations, and in excruciating detail. The opera preserves his status as the fallen tribune of the defunct Roman Republic, but the play had more reason for him to fear for his life. Apparently, Angelotti had spent some exile years in London. While there, he secured the attentions of a young lady of easy virtue for a slight fee one night in the Vauxhall Gardens. The floozy had some success later in life, for by 1800 she was none other than the celebrated and somewhat notorious Lady Emma Hamilton, wife of the British ambassador to Naples, best friend and confidante of the Neapolitan Queen Carolina, and eventual mistress of Admiral Nelson. Lady Hamilton is determined to have Angelotti killed and silenced, thereby protecting her secret past. More historical revisionism: Lady Hamilton's past was never secret, and, if legend is to be believed, the combined secret police forces of all Europe would have had to commit near-genocide to silence her past liaisons. No matter. Sardou, the good French dramatist, required solid reasons for his characters to act as they did, and he has Queen Carolina, prompted by La Hamilton, make it clear to Scarpia that he either find and kill Angelotti or he himself will be killed. That Puccini dispenses with all this is another indication of how we are to read the opera: here, the conflict is not "situational" ("You did this to me so now I will do this to you"), but one of opposing natures—specifically Tosca and Scarpia, whose antipathy cannot be explained by mere human causes.

The sacristan rushes in to annoy Cavaradossi with some news, but he finds the church empty. Too bad. It earns an indulgence to annoy a nonbeliever. Students, choirboys, and priests come rushing in. The sacristan tells them the big news: Napoleon's forces have been decisively defeated by the Allies at Marengo. Italy is saved from the revolutionary heresy. The queen of Naples will host a gala at the Palazzo Farnese to celebrate, and a new cantata will be performed by the celebrated Floria Tosca. All sigh in recognition of the diva's name. Furthermore, there will be great celebrations in the churches. The choristers rejoice. A Te Deum! Double pay! They sing, laugh, and dance around the sacristan.

Baron Scarpia enters, followed by several policemen. All freeze in terror. "What a bacchanalia in church!" he sneers. "Fine manners!" "Excellency, the excitement, the victory . . ." stammers the sacristan. "Prepare for the Te Deum," orders Scarpia. The sacristan tries to sneak away but is ordered to remain by Scarpia. "I'm not moving," he mutters. Scarpia sends his henchman Sciarrone to search the Attavanti chapel, and the fan of the marchese is found. Scarpia asks who is painting the Magdalene. "Cavaradossi." "A suspicious character! A Voltairean!" And then to himself, "and Tosca's lover!" The sacristan is surprised to find the food basket empty. He begins to understand what has happened. Tosca is heard from outside shouting for Mario. Perfect, surmises Scarpia. Iago had a handkerchief, he has a fan. She rushes in. The sacristan does not know where Cavaradossi is. Vanished, perhaps, using his witchcraft. No, she hisses. He can't have betrayed me! Scarpia steps out and offers her holy water. She accepts, composing herself before the police chief. He praises her piety— unlike some hussies, who pretend to come to church to pray but are actually meeting their lovers! He shows Tosca the Marchese Attavanti's fan. Tosca becomes furious immediately. Betrayed by Mario! She knew it! She had come to the church to tell Mario she would not be able to meet him that night since suddenly she had to sing at the queen's gala. And he is running off with the Attavanti, even now, the two of them laughing at Tosca! Scarpia gloats to himself. Tosca swears to catch the "lovers" at the villa and runs off.

Comment, scene: Scarpia's entrance is one of the most impressive in all opera, with the "Scarpia Chords" slamming down on the dance rhythms and boyish laughter of the choristers like marble over a tomb. It is absolutely essential that the baritone have a palpable presence, vocal and physical, someone before whom "all Rome trembles." After he takes care of his police business with Sciarrone, he has some excellent "thinking music." This morphs elegantly into the slimy, insinuating music he has while inciting Tosca's jealousy. This man is sly and slick—not the drooling pig that we sometimes see onstage from baritones with no nuance. Listen for the vocal colors as he works Tosca: if he can convey charm, con-

fidence, and manipulation without resorting to crooning, he is an excellent Scarpia. It also does not harm the tension in the opera in any way if there is a touch of erotic attraction, or at least the possibility of some, between Tosca and Scarpia.

Scarpia orders his other henchman Spoletta to follow Tosca, knowing this will lead to Angelotti. The procession for the Te Deum begins as the church fills with participants. A cardinal passes, the congregation prays aloud, and Scarpia kneels. He becomes excited thinking of his double quarry: the prisoner hanging from the gallows and Tosca writhing in his arms! The chant of the Te Deum disturbs his thoughts and he crosses himself. "Tosca!" he cries. "You make me forget God!" He prays as the Te Deum comes to a climax.

Comment, Te Deum: *This is the "production number" of* Tosca, *and true to the extravagant nature of the opera, it is gargantuan in scale. The score calls for auxiliary choruses, organ, three horns and four trombones onstage, a cannon (!), and half the bells of Rome (some real bells, some effected by the orchestra). Conductors have told me they dread this moment as much as any other in opera. And that's just the music. Stage directors earn their pay here as well, with a huge procession of church officials specified in the production notes (all in full ecclesiastic finery), Swiss Guards, and a bevy of congregants rich and poor. Some productions even throw in the pope for good measure. (The pope? Had there been a pope in Rome in June 1800, he wouldn't have been at Sant'Andrea della Valle, the queen of Naples wouldn't have moved into the Palazzo Farnese, and no woman [e.g., Tosca] would have been singing at the Teatro Argentina. But who can resist a little gold trim amid all the splendor of this scene?) Of course, anyone can order up a huge spectacle onstage, but we also get Puccini's genius to make this something more. There is a tremendous eroticism to the music in this scene. The intrusion of the spoken prayer—first the basses, then the rest—propel his line with a startling breathiness. The bells, building off of the pretty little four-note theme that played when Scarpia was "moving in" on Tosca, have now become a rather menacing choir of lower bells: listen for the lowest bell tolling a sustained F–B for seventy-three bars, creating a sort of scary trance. Scarpia's comments are punctuated by shots of the cannon—hey, no one said this was subtle. His vocal line climbs up the scale culminating into a frenzy ("wildly" is the musical instruction) when he drools over the idea of torturing Mario while raping Tosca, just as half the congregation kneels. The sung* Te Deum *itself, a mere eighteen measures long, is genuinely orgasmic: all orchestral accompaniment stops except for the onstage trombones. Scarpia is directed to sing along with the congregation after his outburst about forgetting God. In theory, we should be able to discern his voice clearly amid the trombones and chorus of, say, one or two hundred. Don't count on that, but if he can manage it somehow, the effect is astounding. Nowhere in opera is the contrast between inner and outer impressions—and the possible relation between the two—portrayed more stunningly than here. If you haven't broken out in a sweat by the time of the final chords (the same "Scarpia Chords" that began the act), hold your applause. Something has gone seriously wrong.*

Act II

Setting: Scarpia's apartment on the upper floor of the Palazzo Farnese, Rome, on the evening of June 17, 1800. He is having supper, alone.

Scarpia muses how Tosca, a good "falcon," will capture both Angelotti and Cavaradossi for him. He summons Sciarrone, who opens a window. Sounds of an orchestra playing a gavotte are heard from the queen of Naples's rooms below. Tosca has not yet arrived at the palace to perform the cantata in honor of the supposed Allied victory at Marengo. Scarpia gives Sciarrone a note summoning Tosca to see him immediately after her performance. Sciarrone leaves, and Scarpia returns to his dinner. He muses on his plan to force Tosca to submit to him. Romantic love does not interest him—violence is what excites him. God made different kinds of beauties and different kinds of love just like He made different wines, and Scarpia intends to taste them all. He sips his wine.

Comment, scene: The gimmick of opening the window to let in the music from "downstairs" is an excellent, precinematic technique of juxtapositions, setting the elegant gavotte (a court dance) against Scarpia's perversions. The effect suggests that all the elegance and phoof of the ancien régime not only fails to cover ("drown out") the inner corruption, but is in fact an integral part of the rot. This also sheds light, retroactively, on the previous Te Deum *scene, where Scarpia likewise becomes aroused (so say the stage directions) during the liturgy. Critics have faulted Puccini for failing to portray a convincing tension between Scarpia and the church procession—Carner says only a Verdi or a Wagner could have done that. But here we realize that there isn't a disconnect between Scarpia and his "background" music; there is actually a parallel. The trappings of power of both the church and the state literally make him a sadistic monster. His little solo here is a rare example of a Puccini aria for baritone. It is a good piece of music but is dramatically problematic. Having people onstage alone expounding their character belongs to an earlier tradition than verismo, and it seems inspired by Iago in Verdi's* Otello.

Spoletta enters to report on his assignment at the villa. He begs Saint Ignatius to protect him, and reports that they could not find Angelotti. Scarpia is furious and threatens him. Spoletta says that Cavaradossi, however, was so arrogant and defiant of the police authority that they arrested him and brought him to the Palazzo Farnese. This mollifies Scarpia, and Cavaradossi is brought in with a judge, an executioner, and four bailiffs. The cantata, with Tosca as the soloist, is heard from below.

Scarpia, formal and officious, questions Cavaradossi, who denies everything. He knows nothing about an escaped prisoner, an empty food basket, an outfit of clothes. Lies! He laughs at the police. Scarpia warns him that this is a place of tears, not laughter. Tosca rushes in, breathless. Mario whispers to her to keep silent, or she will kill him. He is led off to an adjacent torture chamber. Scarpia resumes his chivalric tone with Tosca. So there was nothing at the villa? No lover? No one? No, Tosca assures him. Mario was alone. A jealous eye sees everything. Sciarrone appears at the door: Cavaradossi denies everything. Scarpia orders the torture increased, describing it in detail to Tosca. Groans are heard. Tosca begs Scarpia to stop. She calls out to Mario, who admonishes her to remain strong. The torture resumes. She pleads again but Scarpia laughs. Tosca on the stage was never more tragic than now! He orders the torture increased. She begs Mario to let her speak, but he calls her a fool and insists she knows nothing anyway. She turns on Scarpia. It is she he is torturing! Her spirit! Why? Spoletta utters a prayer, "Nil inultum remanebit." A piercing cry is heard from the torture chamber, and Tosca blurts out to Scarpia, "In the well, in the garden!" She demands to see Mario. He is dragged in, bleeding, half-unconscious. She assures him she remained strong. Just then, Scarpia orders Spoletta to the well in the garden. Furious, Mario turns on Tosca as she begs him to forgive her—she could stand no more. He repulses her embraces. Sciarrone bursts in with urgent news. The report from Marengo was premature! Bonaparte has destroyed the Allied forces entirely and Italy awaits his occupation. "Victory!" exults Mario. Tosca begs him to be silent, but he continues. The dawn now breaks, and tyrants tremble! With this outburst, Scarpia orders him removed for execution.

Comment, scene: Spoletta's quick prayer to St. Ignatius demonstrates the tortured historicity of the Sardou play—exact specificity of historical time and place combined with curious manipulations of history. The prayer identifies Spoletta as a Jesuit, or at least a Jesuit sympathizer. The Jesuits were the mortal enemies of the Bourbons. There weren't any in Rome in 1800, least of all working with the secret police. However, by Sardou's time the Jesuits were associated with reaction and with all sorts of nefarious activities, real and imagined, in support of the Papal State. It is a little glimpse into the workings of this story, which aspires to inhabit several periods of time at once.

The cantata heard from "below" is an elaboration of the previous gavotte music floating in the window. It is superbly handled, with swells from the chorus and Tosca's lines twining in and out of Scarpia's and Cavaradossi's brief, clipped snarls at each other. Structurally, it forms a trio with an elegant choral accompaniment simultaneously uniting the vocal action and increasing the tension with contrapuntal "tics." The earlier Italian opera would have had the chorus standing in a semicircle around the soloists, who would be lined up at the footlights like "a row of artichokes" (in Rossini's phrase).

The torture scene is placed in the adjoining room, unless one of our more graphic directors gets a hold of it. Mario's "cries of pain" are sung— singers can't scream and then still sing. The artistry comes from making you think they're screamed. His cry of "Vittoria!" is a grand scena compacted into a few seconds. He cries out "Vittoria!" on an F-sharp—in the passaggio—*as if choked and incredulous at the enormity of the news. He repeats it on an A-sharp, a cappella, in triumph. There is no fermata over the notes, but expect any good tenor to hold the note until the audience is ready to explode. It is the aural equivalent of the classic spit in the eye the tortured man in movies delivers to his tormentor. The subsequent denunciation of tyranny is very brief and equally impassioned. He knows his "rebirth" is his death warrant, which is a microcosm of his situation in the following act. Even more than his two arias, the tenor is made or broken by "Vittoria!"*

Tosca is ordered to remain. "Save him!" she tells Scarpia. "I?" he asks. "No, you!" He sits calmly at his table and comments that his poor little supper was interrupted. With utmost gallantry, he invites Tosca to his table and offers her a glass of good wine from Spain to help her nerves. Let them see if they can discuss a way out of this unpleasantness. She approaches the table and with utter contempt asks him, "How much?" "How much?" he laughs. "The price!" she demands. Yes, he says philosophically, he knows people consider him venal, but he's not so cheap that he would betray his duties for mere money. But tonight, when he saw the hatred in Tosca's eyes, he vowed he would have her! She runs to the window and threatens to jump out. That would hardly save Mario, he sneers. She makes for the door, but he reads her thoughts. There is no need to sneak around. She is perfectly at liberty to leave. However, she had better forget about begging the queen for mercy. By the time she reached the queen, Mario would be dead. Ah, how Tosca detests him! All the better. Spasms of love, spasms of hate . . . what's the difference? She cries for help, but then she hears the drums rolling for Mario's march to the executioner. Scarpia warns her they are building the gallows even now.

She says she has lived for art and for love, never hurting anyone, being kind to children, and never forgetting to bring flowers to the Madonna and jewels for her robe. "Why, Lord, do You repay me like this?"

Comment, scene and aria, "Vissi d'arte": The soprano's only aria of the opera is a diva moment in every sense of the term. Critics complain that it stops the action, which is exactly what Puccini must have wanted: to break up the unrelenting depravity of the torture/abuse. Besides, it is more dramatically apt than most would admit. Tosca is a diva. What else would she have here but a diva moment? And like it or not, a big diva moment means an aria. Scarpia had already given the cue when he said, "Tosca on the stage was never more tragic!" Her whole life has been performance art. It takes away none of the sincerity of her prayer to God to suggest she is also trying to get a reaction out of Scarpia here, and in fact it adds an interesting dimension. It could well be understood as early metatheater. The tradition has long been for the soprano to deliver the aria from the floor, where she has fallen in her scuffle with Scarpia. This was "invented" by Maria Jeritza during the triumphal miniature Puccini-fest at the Vienna State Opera in 1920, which Puccini attended and applauded enthusiastically. The legend grew that Jeritza had actually fallen unintentionally and found herself on the floor as the conductor picked up the baton for the aria. Jeritza denied that, and others claim they saw her rehearsing the fall for hours on end before the first performance, even to the point of releasing a small thread in her tresses and causing her long, luxurious red hair to fall loose at exactly the right moment. Little wonder legends grow around such women. Whatever the truth, it has remained traditional ever since. Callas, who rethought every movement onstage as if the role had been written by her, sometimes sang the aria à la Jeritza, but, when she was so inclined, stood upright on center stage and let it be known she would not borrow gestures from her predecessors—a case of the diva as diva playing the diva. It always created an impression. The aria itself begins in falling, plaintive phrases that Girardi finds "liturgical," and builds around phrases we heard when Tosca made her entrance in Act I. It underscores a genuine piety amid whatever "theatrics" might be going on. This expansive lyrical section demands a long legato and an emotional vulnerability that allows the great sopranos to transcend self-pity and express an existential sorrow. It has become the diva's "national anthem."

Scarpia is unimpressed. Such a cheap bargain: a whole life in exchange for a mere instant. Spoletta bursts in. Angelotti killed himself when he was discovered. Scarpia orders the corpse hanged as an example. And Cavaradossi? All is ready. He looks at Tosca. "Well?" She nods in assent, demanding that Cavaradossi be freed. No, Scarpia corrects. Appearances must be maintained. There will be a mock execution, a firing squad with fake bullets. He gives the order to Spoletta. "Like we did with Palmieri," he says. Spoletta assures him he understands, and leaves. Scarpia goes to his desk to make out the safe conduct pass out of the country for her and the unnamed Cavaliere who accompanies her. She goes to the dinner table to pour herself a glass of wine, and sees a knife. Which route does she prefer? The quickest! Civitavecchia? Fine. As Scarpia writes, she hides the knife behind her back. He seals the passport with wax and approaches her. "Tosca!" he cries. "You're mine at last!" She stabs him in the chest, telling him that this is Tosca's kiss! He cries for help, choking, falling to the floor and writhing. She stands over him. "Are you chok-ing on your blood? And killed by a woman! Did you torture me enough? Can you still hear? Look at me! It's me, Tosca!" He cries for help again as she screams for him to die. Finally he is still. "Now I forgive him!" she says. She pours water from a pitcher and washes the blood off her hands and arranges her hair before a mirror. She looks for the passport but cannot find it. At last she sees it clasped in Scarpia's now-stiff hand, and pries it out. About to leave, she returns to Scarpia's body, placing a candle on either side of his head and finally a crucifix from the wall on his chest, and prays. A drum is heard from outside as Cavaradossi is marched to the Castel Sant'Angelo, rousing Tosca. She rises and looks at the corpse. "And before him, all Rome trembled!" She leaves the room.

Comment: Most of the music is in the orchestra throughout this scene, led by a trembling theme in the cellos (an effect since overused in B movies). Scarpia's murder and Tosca's exit demand the ultimate in acting from the soprano. Remember, this was originally conceived for Sarah Bernhardt, so it can't be overdone. The important thing, as always with Puccini, is attention to the details: the knife, the passport, the crucifix. Tosca's lines while Scarpia is dying can be sung, rasped, or screamed. It always works as long as the soprano is convinced of what she's doing. Note the full range of action here: prayer, bloody murder, fixing her hair. . . . A wide range of the possibilities of womanhood must be conveyed in a short time, and with little singing to carry it. It is perplexing, annoying, vulgar, "stagy," melodramatic, and, given the right soprano, absolutely thrilling.

Act III

Setting: Atop the Castel Sant'Angelo, later that night toward dawn.

A shepherd boy is heard singing a love song in the Roman dialect, accompanied by the bells of his scurrying sheep. Dawn begins to break over the Eternal City. The church bells of Rome announce the sunrise.

Comment: This opening scene, about five minutes long, is a superb mood piece. A forthright trombone fanfare, whose tune is heard again later, opens the curtain on an ominous, Wagnerian note. This gives way to the very striking, pentatonic ("primitive-sounding") shepherd's song, sung in the Roman dialect by an offstage boy alto (if one can be found). The bells of Rome sound one by one at various volumes and pitches, sometimes overlapping but never more than three at a time. The strings play low while the bells toll. The effect is both of the passing of time and the timelessness of Rome itself, whose full stature as a main character, so to speak, in this drama is revealed here.

A jailer brings Cavaradossi out of the cell. A priest is waiting to hear the condemned man's confession, but Mario declines. He requests a favor. There is someone special he is leaving behind. If he could just write her a letter. He offers the jailer a ring, all he has left. The jailer gives him paper and pen and leaves him. Mario muses as he writes. . . . The stars were shining, she entered the garden, and fell into his arms. He remembers the sweet kisses and caresses and how he trembled while she shed her clothes and revealed the beauty of her body. And now that dream is gone forever, and he dies, hopeless. And he had never loved life so much before this!

Comment, aria, "E lucevan le stelle": The cellos introduce the big theme of the aria before Mario has his bit of business with the jailer. The final bell to chime is the famous Campanone of St. Peter's, a very low E that rings out just as the cellos begin the theme of the aria. Listen for it—it is a marvelous effect that usually escapes people caught up in the beauty and familiarity of the melody. In fact, it is the tonal base of the aria. This is Puccini's economy at its best. The worlds of love and death, to be sure, intersect here, but so do religion, politics, and art. The theme is then played again by a flute and clarinet, suggestive of memory. The aria begins, as so many of Puccini's best tenor arias do, with monotone lines introducing the theme, which is then basically repeated twice. The whole magnificent scene is constructed around ten measures of melody, repeated and varied in tone and expression. In other words, it is up to the tenor to turn it into art. Some fail through lack of musical taste, others don't have or have lost the technique to make it soar. (I remember one dreadful night in San Francisco a couple of decades back when the once-fine tenor had clearly lost his juice, inspiring one dread-filled member of the audience to yell out, "Shoot him now, before he sings!" Performances of this opera lend themselves to such antics, as we have seen.) However, a tenor in command of his technique can turn this basically simple (albeit ravishing) theme into a heart-wrenching moment. Note the honesty of the thoughts portrayed—no heroic declarations, or tenorial posturing. Just love, passion, and regret at having to die just when life was worth living. The variation of vocal color is what brings this alive, and this is what we mean when we speak of "acting" in regard to opera singers. Singers can't learn that at music school. Puccini demands raw emotion here. As if to bait his critics, who might accuse him of sentimentality, he has here marked the score "con grande sentimento." Furthermore, he has the strings double the final reading of the theme line, in not one, or two, but three octaves! In other words, please don't think you are being profound by saying that you find this aria a trifle sentimental. Puccini has already outlined the sentimentality in neon lights for this moment, perhaps the most shamelessly emotional he ever penned (and he penned a lot). It is up to the tenor to make it convincing. If you are not seized with a sob at the line "e muoio disperato" ("I die without hope"—the line was supplied by Puccini himself), then something is wrong with either you or the tenor.

Spoletta brings Tosca to the rooftop and departs. She goes to the weeping Mario. Astonished to see her, he reads the safe-conduct pass. Free! she tells him. An act of clemency from Scarpia? This was his first. "And his last!" says Tosca. She tells him all that happened, and how she stabbed the monster. He lovingly takes her hands, which were made for kindness and love. These very hands killed? For his love? She tells him what must happen next: a mock execution. Then when the soldiers depart, they can leave, free. They think of their new life together, wandering the world, loving and growing old with one another.

Comment, scene and duet: Tosca rushes onto the stage and then launches into her solo, describing the murder and full of snippets of reminiscences from Act II, with little time lost. Mario's reaction is a very gentle, lovely line while he caresses or kisses her hands: most tenors croon here. A genuine mezza voce (see glossary) will be much more effective. Applaud him generously if he manages it. The balance of the duet is the theme we heard in the trombones at the beginning of the act, a rather martial theme appropriate to the triumph of their love. It is sung a cappella. The orchestra then turns playful when Tosca is "coaching" Mario on how to fall at his mock execution, using snippets from their Act I duet. The tension is tremendous. It is a great example of how opera can use the same music to entirely different ends, depending on the dramatic context. There was originally to have been a "Hymn to Art" at this moment. In fact, it was Giacosa's verse for the "Hymn" that originally impressed Verdi with the libretto of Tosca. Puccini struggled with it until he finally decided he simply couldn't write one, Verdi or no Verdi. Why would they be singing of art at this moment? All they would be thinking about would be getting away from Rome and starting a new life. It is a good thing that Puccini was incapable of much abstract thought. It left him capable of understanding how real people react in given situations.

This brings up an interesting instance of how good acting, in the larger, nonsinging definition, can help an opera. Plácido Domingo played this scene as if he understood the deception and knew he would be shot. I'm not sure if he "invented" this tack, but his rendition was the first time I ever saw it. Perhaps he was just the first tenor who was a good enough actor to convey it. In any case, it was a logical character study of a romantic hero whose courage only fails when it's time to tell his lover they are parting forever, and it made the subsequent duet almost unbearably poignant.

The firing squad enters. Tosca warns Mario to act well, not to move until she gives the signal. Spoletta gives the order to the sergeant as the bells strike four. The sun rises. Mario refuses the blindfold. Tosca grows impatient at the farce. Why do they take so long? Ah, how handsome Mario is! The squad fires, and Mario drops. Ah, what an artist! she exclaims. She tells him not to move as the soldiers file out. Wait, wait. . . . Now! Get up! she says. Mario doesn't move. She realizes in horror that he has been shot dead. Voices are heard below. Scarpia has been stabbed! Sciarrone and Spoletta run on and order the soldiers to get Tosca. She pushes one away and manages to run up to the parapet. "Oh, Scarpia!" she shouts. "Before God!" She leaps off the parapet to her death.

Comment, finale: It all happens rather quickly—her cries of "Mario! Mario!" (on the same notes she always said them, when pounding on the doors of the church in Act I), Spoletta and Sciarrone's entrance, and of course the famous leap. The leap is underscored by the orchestra thundering out the big theme from "E lucevan le stelle," a choice for which Puccini has received a thorough drubbing, but the effect is apt and emotionally cathartic. A lot can go wrong at this moment, but it can be immensely effective. It defines opera as an "over-the-top" form of expression in the best possible way.

Madama Butterfly

The Name and How to Pronounce It

This one is trickier than it looks: Having been based on an American play, the English "Madame Butterfly" has prevailed over the Italian "Madama." Furthermore, it gets the American pronunciation, "Madam." Americans who pronounce it otherwise sound odd, or worse. This is strange considering Puccini's subsequent opera, *La fanciulla del West*, is also based on an American play by the very same author yet is generally called by its Italian name. Opera is odd that way. I'm just reporting the facts, without editorial comment.

What is Madama Butterfly?

Butterfly is a tragedy about a young Japanese girl who believes her arrangement with an American naval officer is something other than what it is. The opera is an undisputed masterpiece, and even critics of it can only complain of its ubiquity and occasionally (although less so recently) take issue with its political content. The "myth" of *Butterfly* seems to reinforce many repugnant Western clichés about Japanese culture, which may be true, but the opera itself is remarkably free of these attitudes. The heroine is a full and complete person, and only a "victim" in the most convincing manner of the greatest tragedies. There is nothing reductive about her. The opera is based on a successful play by the American David Belasco, and manages to confer on the heroine a colossal stature that spoken drama alone could not. Puccini, along with Giacosa and Illica, fashioned a work that utilizes all the power of the verismo genre (exploring the hidden depths in everyday characters) while avoiding many of the pitfalls of that category. There is no gratuitous emotion in this work. In fact, there is nothing gratuitous in it, and it therefore achieves its tragic grandeur with a simplicity and inevitability that is rarely found in opera (or other drama, for that matter). Puccini grew enormously as a musician between the composition of *Tosca* and *Butterfly*, and his increased mastery of orchestral technique allowed him to plumb the greatest feelings and experiences with a remarkable absence of musical excess. It may be Puccini's most compelling work.

Butterfly's *Place in the Repertory*

Butterfly sits at the top of the repertory, one of the "Big Three" of Puccini's corpus along with *Bohème* and *Tosca*. It is in many ways Puccini's most "modern" opera in that it has "worn" extremely well. *Bohème* will always please an audience and *Tosca* will always make some sort of impression or other, but *Butterfly* continues to move audiences. *Manon Lescaut* and *Bohème* make no pretense to dramatic unity: they are vignettes of episodes strung along complex dramatic narratives, offering salient "clips" of a whole story. *Tosca* has an excellent dramatic unity, taking place, as it does, within a single twenty-four-hour period, but there are still offstage events we must imagine. *Tosca* is furthermore, at least in my reading, a portrait of archetypes in conflict. Even though it has a verismo tone, it does not unfold among "real people" as any modern person would understand that term. *Butterfly* supersedes all these issues. The story unfolds in real time. Even though three years elapse between Acts I and II, we have missed nothing we need for the story. More than anything, the character of Butterfly is one of the most finely drawn human beings ever to grace an operatic stage. I cannot think of her equal in the opera world, and must turn to Ibsen or Chekhov to find her equal in the dramatic world. Everything she does makes perfect sense for her, and her fate is thoroughly believable. The descent toward the tragic finale is inexorable, which means she develops before our eyes (and ears) in a way that is rare in opera. Neither Tosca, nor Mimì, nor Manon go through the psychospiritual life journey that Butterfly experiences within the confines of the couple of hours on the stage. (For that matter, neither do Aida, nor Carmen, nor Lulu, nor even, really, Isolde experience the same depths of transformation in their respective operas as Butterfly undergoes in hers.) On first hearing, it packs an undeniable punch, but *Butterfly* holds up magnificently to repeated exposure (and just as well, for those of us who attend operas frequently). We can always experience anew Puccini's deftness in handling the psychological subtleties that make this work so believable. Puccini himself often referred to it as his favorite of his own operas, and, significantly, cited it as the one he could listen to over and over again without ever tiring of it.

I have so far spoken only of the lead character in listing reasons for *Butterfly*'s continued popularity, and not without reason. She is the whole opera, in a manner unique to Puccini's corpus of works. Since she must portray a credible journey from innocent victim to a fully realized woman who takes charge of her own destiny, she must be able to convey every aspect of human emotion in her voice. The score reflects the drama, of course, and our soprano must be convincing as coy, naive, fixated, polite, formidable, vengeful, defeated, and run amok—sometimes simultaneously! Other sopranos have similar tall orders, but the role of Butterfly gets very little help from the others on the stage. The tenor role, rather like male lions in the animal kingdom, serves One Purpose Only, and the story is much more about the soprano's reaction to his sole action than about his actions. The baritone and mezzo are important musically, but always as an adjunct to the soprano. She is on the stage from her entrance early in Act I until (with one short break) the final curtain. Minnie in *La fanciulla del West* has, in many ways, a more difficult musical challenge, but she is supported by the others on the stage and by a thunderous orchestra in a way that Butterfly is not. And she must probe her musical and dramatic abilities all while performing within the extremely rigid confines of her character, who is a geisha, with all the stylized semiology of movement and gesture associated with that unique social construct. A performance of *Butterfly* succeeds or fails entirely because of the soprano. This opera would probably be performed as often as *Bohème* if the lead role were easier to cast.

Cast of Characters

CIO-CIO-SAN, ALSO CALLED MADAME BUTTERFLY (*soprano*): A young girl of fifteen, who has worked as a geisha and is, at the beginning of the opera, contracted into a sort of marriage with an American naval officer. In Acts II and III, she is all of eighteen years old. Cio-Cio-San (the Italian spelling for what we would render and pronounce as Cho-Cho-San), I'm told, means "butterfly" in Japanese.

LIEUTENANT BENJAMIN FRANKLIN PINKERTON, U.S. NAVY (*tenor*): Our romantic lead, although calling him our hero might be overstating the case. Pinkerton is a very curious role in the repertory. Besides his questionable character, he is absent from the stage for much of the opera. However, he must be as attractive, physically and vocally, as any other tenor role in opera, or the story will make very little sense.

SHARPLESS, THE AMERICAN CONSUL AT NAGASAKI (*baritone*): The anchor of common sense and compassion in the story, not unlike Starbuck in *Moby Dick*. Sharpless must have a soothing and authoritative sound, even though he is actually remarkably ineffectual (hence, perhaps, the name). Like many other Puccini baritones, he has a lot of music to sing but no aria where he gets to shine.

Suzuki, Butterfly's Servant (*mezzo-soprano*): The "trusty mezzo-maid" role takes on a greater significance than is usual in opera, with much important music (especially in Act III). Suzuki is also a voice of reason, like Sharpless, and provides a nearly continuous vocal contrast to Butterfly throughout Act II. It is not unusual to see star mezzos in this role.

Kate Pinkerton (*mezzo-soprano*): Poor Kate, alas, does not get to make much of a musical impression on us in her one appearance toward the end of the opera. Her primary purpose is to look compassionate, dignified, and very American.

Goro, a Marriage Broker (*tenor*): A very sleazy role, somewhere between a pimp and a busybody, with a lot of deliberately obnoxious music to sing. Goro always (to my knowledge) appears in Western dress. This is one of many small but important comprimario tenor roles found throughout Puccini's operas.

Prince Yamadori (*baritone*): A lovelorn character with little to do except sigh and walk away in what we are to conceive as a dignified air. The wife of the Japanese ambassador in Rome, who helped Puccini with music and other pointers for this opera, found no fault with the libretto except that she thought Yamadori to be an "effeminate" name. Puccini valued these contributions to his work, but for some reason the name was retained.

The Bonze, Cio-Cio-San's Uncle (*bass*): A cameo appearance that needs to shake the rafters with a sort of "voice of God."

Yakuside, Another Uncle (*baritone*): This baritone is more of a comic character role than a major voice-buster. His "business" is brief and part of the background of the wedding scene at the beginning. It is much reduced from the original version, where Yakuside was stealing drinks and being obnoxious in a way that was deemed offensive by Puccini and his librettists upon further review. Besides racist caricature, he served no purpose and wasted time in his original incarnation.

THE IMPERIAL COMMISSIONER (*bass*): He mutters a few lines of official jargon and departs.

CIO-CIO-SAN'S MOTHER (*mezzo-soprano*): She has two lines and departs with the others in Act I.

AN AUNT (*mezzo-soprano*): A mere few comments in the wedding scene.

A COUSIN (*soprano*): And a single, unflattering comment about Pinkerton in the wedding scene.

SORROW, CIO-CIO-SAN'S CHILD: This character has no spoken or sung lines. He is supposed to be three years old, but is usually portrayed by a girl slightly older.

The Opera

Act I

Setting: The garden terrace of a small house on a hill overlooking Nagasaki harbor, with the house in the background. The year is around 1900.

Comment: All right, let's address one little bit of persistent nonsense right away: Nagasaki was for many years the only port in Japan open to foreign trade, and even after the "opening" of Japan in 1853 was the main customs port for foreign vessels. It is the only logical setting of the story: sufficiently cosmopolitan to have such interactions between foreigners and locals, yet small enough to present a community from which a disowned, disgraced girl could find no practical escape. Director Ken Russell, in explaining the excesses of his 1993 Butterfly production for Spoleto and Houston (which included, as a grand finale, an atomic bomb explosion), found the choice of Nagasaki to be "prophetic." "Why," Russell asked, "would Puccini have chosen Nagasaki of all the cities in Japan?" First of all, Puccini didn't choose it; Belasco did, and secondly, read a history book, Ken. Reducing the history of Nagasaki to its single glaring meaning in the Western mind reeks of the sort of cultural imperialism from which directors are always trying to distance themselves in this opera.

Goro shows Pinkerton around the little house, while Pinkerton is amused by the paper walls. The servants are presented: the cook, the houseboy, and the maid, Suzuki. Suzuki chatters on, quoting platitudes and wisdom, until Goro silences her with a clap of his hands. Pinkerton comments that women everywhere chatter like that. Goro speaks of the upcoming wedding: the bride will come with her relatives, except her uncle the Bonze. He would not deign to come, but no one will miss him. Sharpless, the American consul in Nagasaki, arrives after his ardent climb up the hill. Did Pinkerton buy the house? No, he leased it for 999 years, and can cancel the contract whenever he wished. Houses and contracts appear to be elastic in this country! Anywhere in the world a Yankee trades and enjoys himself, he laughs at the dangers. He offers Sharpless the choice of milk punch or whiskey, pouring two shots. Life isn't profitable for a Yankee, he continues, unless he tastes every pleasure and plucks every flower. A facile gospel, mutters Sharpless, one that jades the heart. And now he is married for 999 years, but can cancel anytime. "America forever!" he toasts. Sharpless repeats the toast. He asks if the bride is beautiful. Goro interrupts to praise her: a garland of fresh flowers, a ray of golden sunshine! And cheap! Only 100 yen! Pinkerton impatiently sends Goro to fetch her, and Goro leaves down the hill. Sharpless asks Pinkerton if he loves the bride. That depends on how you define the term, responds Pinkerton. He is enthralled, and must chase her even if it means breaking her wings, but with luck he will teach her wings to fly. Sharpless is not convinced. He heard the girl's voice at the consulate, and she impressed him—he doesn't know why. He advises Pinkerton to think it over. Pinkerton pours more shots, and Sharpless toasts Pinkerton's parents in Kansas. Pinkerton drinks to the day when he will return to America and marry a real wife.

Comment: The curtain rises on a fugato theme in the orchestra. Commentators remark on how well it describes the running around of Goro and the servants, small, quick phrases reflecting their small, constant movements. To my ears, it also refers to Pinkerton and his squirrely state, as his impatience will soon bear out. Incidentally, you will note how even an American tenor will sing the line "America forever!" (to the strains of "The Star-Spangled Banner's" first line minus the two-note pickup) in an Italian accent, complete with rolled r's. Laugh it off: it is virtually impossible to sing American r's in the European musical tradition. That, of course, is quite unimportant compared to what we are learning about Pinkerton in this scene. We are immediately confronted with the difficulties in his character. I am amazed at how far people go to defend him. Panelists, commentators, and others (notably tenors) have a habit of pointing out that Pinkerton is a flawed person but not actually a bad guy. Rodney Milnes entitled an otherwise lucid essay for liner notes "Butterfly: A Tragedy Without Villains." Certainly Pinkerton is not the moustache-twirling pure evil villain of other operas (think Iago), but this is only part of the opera's modernity. Verismo, I repeat, seeks the ancient archetypes in everyday contemporary people, and Pinkerton is no less a villain simply because he is a plausible modern person. Perhaps people are uncomfortable with the American being the Bad Guy, and Benjamin Franklin Pinkerton is not just an American. He is ur-

American: his name, the ship he sails on, the Lincoln *(in the play it was merely the* USS *Connecticut—presumably this was unsingable in Italian, or perhaps it was not evocative enough). He even has parents in Kansas, the emblematic American locus (cf. Dorothy in* The Wizard of Oz*). As always, we must turn to the score to see how much of a cad Pinkerton is in Puccini's point of view. His breezy aria "Dovunque al mondo" is blustery, affable, and rather hollow. The melodic line jumps fifths effortlessly. This guy is really just a bit full of himself. We all know the type. Not a villain, perhaps, but a type that can cause as much pain and sorrow as any scheming moustache-twirler. This is the beauty of verismo, to show us how bad guys don't always have to wear the emblems of villains. Bad guys don't always wear black. Sometimes they even wear the white dress uniforms of American naval officers.*

Goro reappears, announcing the arrival of the bride and the guests. From down the hill, they hear the voices of the girls and then the voice of Cio-Cio-San. She proclaims herself the happiest woman in Japan. As they appear, Cio-Cio-San, who is called Butterfly, points out Pinkerton to her companions, who genuflect to him. Pinkerton smiles. Did she find the climb up the hill difficult? Waiting is much more difficult than climbing for a young woman who is about to meet her husband, she replies suavely. What a lovely compliment, he counters. Oh, she has many more, she answers. Any sisters? No, but a mother, who is as poor as she is. And her father? "Dead!" she replies bluntly. And is she from Nagasaki? Yes, her family was rather wealthy once. Everybody says so, she knows, but it is true for her, although she and her friends have had to work as geishas. Her friends giggle, and Sharpless laughs. But why laugh? she asks. It's just the way of the world. They ask her age: she tells them to guess. Ten? She giggles. More than that. Twenty? Less than that! She is fifteen. "Fifteen," repeats Sharpless. "Fifteen," repeats Pinkerton. "An age for games!" Sharpless suggests, but Pinkerton thinks it is a good age for marriage. The imperial registrar arrives with more relatives. Pinkerton urges Goro to set up everything quickly. One of the cousins looks at

Pinkerton and declares he is not handsome. Butterfly is offended. He is a prince! Her mother adds that Pinkerton seems like a king. Uncle Yakuside adds that he's worth a Peru, and asks for wine. The relatives chatter. Butterfly counts one, two, three, and all bow deeply to Pinkerton and Sharpless. They all disperse into the garden while Pinkerton brings Butterfly toward the house. She shows her possessions, which she has folded in the sleeves of her gown: kerchiefs, a pipe, a mirror, a fan, some dye. Pinkerton sneers. He doesn't like it? She throws away the dye. She pulls out a wooden box. Pinkerton asks to see the contents. "There are too many people. Excuse me," Butterfly says, running into the house. Goro whispers to Pinkerton that it was a gift to her father from the emperor, who invited her father to kill himself. "And the father?" "He obeyed," Goro answers. Butterfly reappears on the terrace of the house, removing small statues from her sleeves. "What are these puppets?" Pinkerton asks. "The spirits of my ancestors," she replies. She confides in him that she has been to the Mission in town, although her family does not know it. She will bow to her husband's God and be content to forget her own people. Goro opens a screen and announces all is ready. The relatives kneel in the garden as the registrar reads: Lieutenant Benjamin Franklin Pinkerton, serving in the navy of the United States on the gunboat *Lincoln*," and so on. Goro invites him to sign, then Butterfly, and all is done. "Madame Butterfly!" say the guests, but she corrects them: "Madame B. F. Pinkerton!" Sharpless warns Pinkerton again to be careful, and leaves. Pinkerton proposes a toast and all join in.

Comment: Butterfly's entrance is Puccini at his best, both in lyric beauty (for which he is always credited) and for dramatic aptitude (for which he is rarely credited). The sustained lyric pattern is unique in his works and is built around a simple phrase of four chords. These will later become one of the cores of the love duet. (That is, Butterfly is in love with Pinkerton before she even sees him, although this will only become apparent in retrospect.) The phrase rises up the scale, describing the party's ascent up the hill and their approach to the stage as well as the mounting excitement of the two protagonists. The climax effect is not achieved through volume but through tone, no easy accomplishment. At each resolution of the phrase, the female chorus settles on various notes creating a whole-tone scale. The whole-tone scale was not new in Puccini's work here—he had used it in Tosca *to convey a sense of unease at key points. Here, the effect is of doors opening onto new vistas (as is often used in film sound tracks when the camera opens onto a wider shot). The relatives' comments about the expanse of sea and sky from the hilltop adds to the sense of unfolding magic and mystery. The balance of the scene is conversational and built along short phrases and small musical intervals, as befits the shyness, and slyness, of the situation. One interruption in this pattern is the abrupt bass drum thump at the word "Morto" ("dead") when Butterfly mentions her father. It is a musical cue, followed by a forthright statement of a Japanese melody. Throughout the opera, these full-orchestral quotations of Japanese melodies have the effect of reality bursting in on Butterfly's fantasy world.*

Shouting is heard from the hillside path. Butterfly's uncle, the Bonze, appears in a fury, denouncing Cio-Cio-San. Goro complains about the intrusion of these mettlesome uncles. What, the Bonze demands, was she doing at the Mission yesterday? An abomination! The relatives are appalled. He continues: she renounced her people, her ancient religion. She has denounced her people: now let them denounce her! The relatives follow suit. Pinkerton comes between the Bonze and Butterfly and orders him out. He leaves, followed by all the relatives.

Comment: The Bonze is every religious authority in opera crying hellfire and damnation to a terrified protagonist. It's interesting that they are always, always basses in opera, even though the avenging preachers I see on television tend to sound like high, squeaky tenors. It is the bass voice, of course, that resounds with authority, tradition, and the fear of God (or gods, as the case may be). Puccini does not let the case rest with the scary bass voice, however. His statements are punctuated by curious cries from

the sopranos, "O! Cio-Cio-San!" that are meant to be sung as little yelps
starting high and ending low. The effect is of the snapping of a string or a
cable, and indeed Butterfly is being "cut loose" from her moorings at this
point. The cries continue periodically as the chorus departs the stage (walk-
ing down the hill, in theory), like jabs from an ethereal conscience.

Butterfly bursts into tears. Pinkerton comforts her: all the Bonzes in
Japan are not worth one of her tears. What kind words, she says. No
one has ever spoken so nicely to her before. They hear Suzuki chant-
ing her evening prayers from inside the house. Suzuki and Butterfly
go into the house to prepare her night attire and arrange her hair.
Pinkerton watches, aroused. Butterfly appears on the terrace. She
can still hear her relatives disowning her, yet she feels like the moon
goddess, all in white. He moves toward her: with all her kind words,
she still has not told him she loves him. "For fear I might die if I
uttered them!" she replies. He takes her in his arms, but she gets
away. He will always mean everything to her. He is tall and strong and
his smile is so easy. She is content. And he should love her, just a little, like a child. That would suit her. Japanese are people accustomed
to small things, humble and quiet, but it is a gentleness as deep as
heaven and the ocean. He kisses her hands. How well she is named,
Butterfly! Yes, she remarks, but in his country don't they pin butterflies to boards and frame them under glass? Only so they won't get
away. He takes her in his arms again. "Be mine!" "Yes!" she answers
in surrender. "Forever!" "Come! Away from fears and troubles." She
stares into the sky, ecstatic. The night is enchanted, and the stars are
blinking. "Come!" he repeats.

Comment: Puccini's most celebrated love duet is undeniably ravishing,
expressing passion and yearning in its melodic surge. Half the audience
will be humming along, while the other half will whistle its two gorgeous
themes the following day at the office. There's no way around it. How-
ever, this duet is more, in context, than an admittedly beautiful exercise in
romantic music. Puccini uses his lyric powers to force us into believing

that Butterfly is genuinely transported by the promise of love. Otherwise the balance of the story would not make a lot of sense. Yet Puccini has not abandoned the dramatic truth of what is occurring on the stage. When Butterfly sings her lines, they sound yearning, transcendental. When Pinkerton sings his lines—which are louder, less finely harmonized, and more urgent, even though he sings the same notes—what we hear is more blatant horniness. Of course we in the audience have the advantage of having heard his previous digressions on careless pleasure, but his position is affirmed here by his twenty-two repetitions of the word "Vieni!" ("Come," which has the exact same sexual connotations in Italian as it does in English). It is an excellent portrayal of the common ground of separate agendas. This is how opera can be called "subtle," even though few people would readily apply that word to the medium. The fact is that Puccini has written music for Pinkerton that is utterly persuasive. If we knew only what Butterfly knows of him, we, too, might be convinced of the possibility of romantic love with this individual. The net result is one of the supreme love duets in opera, one that acknowledges all the problems inherent in lovemaking while reveling in the irresistible power of erotic/ romantic attraction.

Act II

Setting: The interior of Cio-Cio-San's house, with the garden to one side, three years later. Spring.

Suzuki prays to the gods to relieve Butterfly of her suffering, but Butterfly berates her and her gods. The Japanese gods are fat and lazy, but the American God would hear their prayers if he were not so far away! She asks Suzuki how much money is left. Suzuki produces a few coins. If this husband doesn't return soon, there'll be real trouble. Butterfly says he will return. "Are you sure?" asks Suzuki. Of course! Why would he bother to have the consul pay their rent all this time? Suzuki is still in doubt, but Butterfly becomes irate, and forces her to say, grudgingly, that he will return. Butterfly becomes conciliatory. Suzuki will see. One beautiful day, they'll see his ship coming into the harbor, but she won't run down to meet it. She'll wait in the garden, maybe hide for a bit, because she might die of love if she ran into his arms. He'll call out to her, his little wife, his little flower. That's the way it will be! How can Suzuki doubt it when she herself remains unshaken?

Comment, scene and aria, "Un bel dì": The "big hit" of the opera, as frequently abused in amateur recitals and on television commercials as anything in Puccini, is a masterful microcosm of the character. This is why it is so easily "detached" from its context and remains impressive anywhere, but in context it is truly marvelous. The aria begins high in the register and quietly, like the far-off vision she is describing (or better yet, hallucinating). The extended melody wanders ever downward an octave and a half and settles into a middle section of breathy, broken phrases while she imagines hiding in the garden and playing coy with Pinkerton, exploring the lower vocal range just under the staff. It is impressive if the soprano can change the color of her voice at this point without dipping into the dreaded chest tones. She is quoting Pinkerton here in some of the lowest notes, but that is irrelevant: the wide tonal and dynamic range of this aria tells us that the vision she is describing now encompasses her entire being. She explodes back into fortissimo and a return to the original statement when she speaks of "dying of love." A phrase like that is a none-too-subtle cue that the singer's line should be orgasmic, describing a long-awaited victory that is her only reason for living.

Goro and Sharpless appear in the garden. Sharpless taps on the wall, asking for Madame Butterfly. "Madame Pinkerton," she corrects, but happily welcomes the consul into her "American" home. Sharpless is trying to tell Butterfly something, but she interrupts him repeatedly. Would he care to smoke? How are his ancestors? He manages to say that he has heard from Pinkerton, and this sets Butterfly off into more chatter. She asks a question: in America, when do the robins build their nests? Sharpless is stumped by the question, but she explains that Pinkerton told her he would return when the robins build their nests. The local robins have built their nests three times since she saw Pinkerton, but it occurred to her that perhaps in America they do so less frequently. Sharpless evades the question. He has not studied ornithology. "Orni . . . " she asks, ". . . thology?" Goro laughs from outside, and Butterfly sends him away. He retreats as far as the terrace. Butterfly explains that this nuisance has tried to get her to marry others since the day Pinkerton left. "The wealthy Yamadori," interjects Goro from afar, and this prince appears in the garden, attended by servants. Butterfly kneels to the approaching Yamadori but addresses him sarcastically: Does the prince still sigh for her? He does. But, she says, with all the times he's married, it is getting to be a habit with him. He says he has been given a divorce each time, and with her it would be different. Goro urges her to accept the prince: houses, servants, gold all await her. She protests that she is already married, and Goro says desertion is the same as divorce. "Here perhaps, but not in my country, the United States!" There judges will send men who are bored with their wives to jail. She orders tea for the guests. Sharpless confides to Yamadori how Butterfly's blindness pains him. Pinkerton's ship is approaching Nagasaki, and he does not want to see her. Sharpless came to prepare her. Yamadori takes his leave. If only she wanted . . . "The problem is I don't," she interrupts. Yamadori leaves, followed by Goro and his servants.

Comment: Yamadori gets shortchanged, not only by Butterfly but musically as well. His purpose is to show another aspect of Butterfly. We see here that she is not, in fact, a blushing victim, but can stand up to men quite well. Her little reenactment of American justice is coy and comic, and is nothing short of a miniature mad scene: note how snatches of waltzes and "The Star-Spangled Banner" weave into her fantasies when she speaks of her imaginary America.

Sharpless brings her attention back to the letter he is trying to read, which she kisses. Sharpless tries to read Pinkerton's words, greeting the "fair flower" and suggesting she might not remember him, but Butterfly interrupts continually. "Try to prepare her," read Sharpless, but Butterfly cannot contain herself. "He's coming!" Sharpless can go no further, and puts away the letter. That devil Pinkerton! He asks Butterfly bluntly what she would do if Pinkerton did not return to her. She staggers, and replies distantly that she could do two things: return to singing for people, or better yet, die. Sharpless apologizes for being blunt but advises her to accept Yamadori. Butterfly calls Suzuki to show their guest out, immediately. Sharpless apologizes. Butterfly staggers again and tells him how deeply he has hurt her, but she is better now. So, he has forgotten me? She leaves the room and returns with the child on her shoulder. "And this? Can he forget this?" "Is it his?" asks Sharpless. "Have you ever in all Japan seen a baby with blue eyes and lips and golden hair like his?" Pinkerton does not know. He was in his country when the child came, but Sharpless must write him and tell him, and Pinkerton will come flying back. She kisses the child tenderly, pointing to Sharpless. Does the child know what that man thinks? He thinks his mother should go begging in the streets with him, in wind and rain, singing for people and begging food and money. And the geisha should sing her gay songs again . . . No! Never again! Death, death but never again dancing! Sharpless asks her forgiveness. What a beautiful child. What's his name? "Sorrow, but tell his father that when he returns, his name will change to Joy." Sharpless promises to tell Pinkerton, and leaves rapidly.

Comment: The "Letter Scene" here settles into a formal pattern, with an underlying orchestral pattern, subtle and beguiling, providing the structure over which Sharpless's and Butterfly's comments float. The theme will become the framework for the subsequent "Humming Chorus" that ends the act (in most of the versions performed). The effect here is one of

tension, of people who are using etiquette to avoid saying painful truths.
Butterfly's many interruptions underscore her growing isolation from the
rest of the world: she is "out of sync" with the orchestra. When Sharpless
tries to suggest she forget Pinkerton, there is a "thump" in the orchestra as
Butterfly staggers, but the tone remains repressed. Some see her revulsion
at returning to life as a geisha as part of her process of Americanization, an
assumption of Puritan values. As much as there is a basis for this in the
libretto, since her earlier reference to the life of a geisha was philosophical,
it seems illogical to me. It is her distance from her former life that has led
her to her present realization of its inherent degradation. She does not sing
in loud phrases of denunciation about the evils of being a geisha. She
remains calm and understated throughout this moment. The explosion
comes when she runs back in with the child and asks, "And this?" ("E
questo?"). Here she gives full rein to her voice as the orchestra thunders
out a Japanese theme, although the audience is hard-pressed to identify the
theme as such. Again, the overall idea is "reality" crashing in on Butterfly,
and Puccini uses the Japanese theme orchestrated in a Western manner.
There are no "tweets" on the piccolos here to suggest exoticism. It is a
Japanese melody but a full-blooded Italian expression, and one of the
most heartrending moments in the opera.

Suzuki is heard abusing Goro, who was lurking in the house. This
reptile was telling people all over town that no one knew who the
father of Butterfly's child was. "It's the truth," he defends himself. In
America, a child like that is an outcast. Butterfly pulls a knife on him
and chases him away, calling him a liar. She turns to the child. He'll
see. His father will come and take them away from these people,
back to his country. She knows it. There is a cannon shot in the harbor. A ship has entered. It is a warship . . . white, American . . . she
looks through a telescope to read the name: *Abraham Lincoln.* Everyone has lied; only she, Butterfly, has known the truth. Does Suzuki
now see how foolish her doubts were? But Butterfly never lost her
faith, and now it triumphs. He loves her and he returns!

Comment: The business with Goro is brief, clipped, and angry, with snippets of themes rushing in and out of the orchestra under broken vocal declamations. The point is to raise the emotional volume level, after the repressed "Letter Scene," for what follows. When the "truth" of Pinkerton's return seeps into Butterfly's mind, "He loves me and he returns!" her line explodes onto a high A marked with a fermata on the single word "m'ama" ("he loves me"). Butterfly has had some pretty voluminous moments in this act so far. There was the climax to "Un bel dì" and the bigger moment when she showed the child to Sharpless, "E questo?" Somehow, she must dig into her voice (and soul) and make this "Victory shout" top her previous fortissimo expressions. It's as if she is saying to the world, "You see?" I would never say this in a roomful of serious musicologists, but just between you and me, the most impressive Butterflies will blast this note and hang on to it until they force the audience to burst into applause. Applauding in the middle of the score is, of course, a serious breach of operatic etiquette, and that is precisely why it is effective here. A soprano has one single weapon to wield against the whole world—a voice that, by its very nature, can be heard over an entire orchestra and chorus. It is this voice that allows opera to explore the dignity of the individual who is at odds with "the entire world" (i.e., the chorus and orchestra). Verdi knew how to use this like no one else: think of Violetta in La traviata, *Aida singing against the entire population and government of Egypt, or the soloist in the* Requiem *who even demands to be heard amid God's fulminations on the Last Day. Puccini had not utilized the soprano voice in quite the same way until this moment here, which has much in common with Verdi's cited examples. There is no chorus onstage, of course, but everyone sensible (Sharpless, who represents reason and moderation, along with Suzuki and Yamadori and Butterfly's entire society) has tried to make Butterfly see things a different way. We in the audience are, we might say, lumped along with Sharpless et al, since any audience member who is the least bit engaged in the story must be rooting for Butterfly to do the sensible thing and marry Yamadori or take some such action. Butterfly's outburst must therefore also be a slap at us in the audience, a victory*

of her will over ours. If we are compelled to do the "wrong" thing and
burst into applause, her false victory will be complete and we will be all
the more involved—even implicated—in the ensuing tragedy.

She bids Suzuki join her in taking all the flowers from the garden and
strewing them around the house, to welcome Pinkerton home. They
will make a winter out of spring, shaking all the flowers from the
trees. More, still more! When the inside of the house is covered with
flowers, Butterfly takes the child to dress him, and then prepares herself. Suzuki brushes her hair. What will they all say? muses Butterfly.
That uncle of hers, the Bonze, and Yamadori and his sighs. She
fooled them all. Suzuki prepares her wedding gown for her. Butterfly
adds a poppy in her hair. Night begins to fall. Butterfly leads the child
to the screen and makes three little holes in the screen for each of
them to keep watch from. They will sit there, patiently, quiet as mice,
and watch. The child falls asleep. Suzuki also eventually falls asleep.
Only Butterfly remains awake, watching. . . .

Comment, "Flower Duet" and "Humming Chorus": The popular "Flower
Duet" is pure lyric fancy, with a built-in "swirling" sound that simply
demands the soprano and mezzo twirl in circles strewing flowers on the
stage. It's a giddy moment in the score—the only one, really, the whole
night, and poignant because of it. The business of dressing in the wedding
gown is an opportunity for the general tone to settle into an eerie calm—
Butterfly talks to Suzuki as if she is in a daze during this part. It's an inge-
nious technique for lulling the audience almost—but not quite—to sleep
for the "Humming Chorus." Since it was this analogous moment in the
staged play that caught Puccini's attention first, we can assume he started
at least thinking about this moment from the very beginning of his work
on Butterfly. *There are any number of possibilities for what we might*
actually see on a stage. The three holes in the shoji is a bit out of style just
now, and it really doesn't matter as long as the characters onstage stay still
and allow us to take a little trip during this chorus. The chorus itself is

composed of tenors and sopranos only, singing the same line an octave apart. The singers are distinctly required to hum, not sing pretty with their mouths open (even though many try). It is furthermore marked pianississimo, so really it should be barely audible. In spite of this, one sometimes comes across performances these days where the offstage chorus is miked into the hall. The current craze for amplification is a serious problem, and there ought to be a law against such practices. Another problem with the "Humming Chorus" is pitch: it is an eerie melody covering two octaves and easily gets lost. Puccini arranged for a viola d'amore to play offstage with the chorus to keep them on pitch, and chose that instrument because it would be inaudible in the auditorium. Clearly, the intended effect is one of mystery and diaphanous beauty, not a chance to "sell" a ripsnorting tune to the audience. So what, exactly, is it supposed to signify? Some hear the town of Nagasaki settling into sleep, while others think it is the spirit world consoling Butterfly. There is a lot to say about this second point of view, since the melodic line of the chorus does meander in a way suggestive of the other world. In either case it is cruelly ironic since we know that any consolation is delusional.

In the original version, of course, the opera went directly into the subsequent action with no intermission. Even when the revised editions of the opera are performed (as they are most of the time), it is not unusual to play Acts II and III without a break. Critical opinion prefers it, and it works beautifully. But there is also something to be said about the "suspended in midair" effect of bringing down the curtain directly after the "Humming Chorus." Listen for the audible collective sigh from the audience as the curtain falls.

Act III

Setting: The same as Act II.

The sun rises.

Comment: There is an orchestral interlude of about four minutes, which was originally directly connected to the "Humming Chorus." This is where Tito Ricordi had arranged for actual birdsong to be interpolated into the sunrise depiction, causing a genuine riot of meowing and mooing in the opening night audience. Directors still often feel obligated to "stage" this scene, although it works best if it's either played while the curtain is down or all we see is the lighting crew working its magic on an otherwise still stage. The first part of the interlude is a literal depiction of a sunrise, with rising arpeggios. This expands into a rich melodic fantasy built around a waltz pulse, of all things. Some commentators hear the town of Nagasaki waking up, and there are hints of people at work in the score, but it is inconceivable that the underlying waltz could refer to anything but Butterfly's giddy dreams of Pinkerton's return. Jean-Pierre Ponelle, in his 1974 film of this opera, has Butterfly imagining an American social function, waltzing with Pinkerton as she twirls her beautiful evening gown. Ken Russell, predictably, went much, much further for his 1993 staging of the opera in Spoleto and Houston: he had Butterfly roll around in the emptied contents of a box of Corn Flakes during this interlude. (Hey, he had Ann-Margret wallow in baked beans in Tommy, *so perhaps he was working on a motif.) None of this is remotely necessary, since orchestral interludes are far more powerful in what they suggest rather than in what they depict. Ponelle may be forgiven: his movie is a minor masterpiece and he did have four minutes of screen time to fill in. Russell, conversely, was merely being reductive, and mistakenly so at that. (His goal was to get to "Puccini's real message, the conflict of East and West." Well, it's someone's message, but not Puccini's.) In any case, this inter-lude is part of the verismo tradition:* Cavalleria *had set the tone with its*

famous "Intermezzo," and Pagliacci, Manon Lescaut, Tosca, *and others*
followed suit. The stated goal was an attempt at dramatic truth as it was
understood at the time: that is, pure emotions (the orchestra) unfiltered by
social constraints (the sung line). Puccini has merely taken this a step fur-
ther and added all the possibilities of dreams to the verismo intermezzo.
Dreams, too, remain more evocative when they are not defined.

Suzuki wakes up suddenly. Sunrise! She convinces Butterfly to get
some rest. Butterfly withdraws, urging God to protect the child as he
sleeps. Suzuki is surprised by a light tap at the shoji, and then gasps
when she sees Sharpless and Pinkerton. They ask her to be quiet and
not to wake up Butterfly. Indeed, Suzuki says, she was up all night.
"Didn't I tell you?" Sharpless says to Pinkerton. She shows them the
flowers, strewn around the house for Pinkerton. "Didn't I tell you?"
Sharpless repeats. Pinkerton is ashamed. Suzuki is surprised to see a
lady in the garden. But who is she? Sharpless orders Pinkerton to tell
her the truth, but Pinkerton stammers. The lady came with him. . . .
"She's his wife," blurts out Sharpless. Suzuki cries out to her ancestors. There is no more hope for Butterfly. Sharpless tells her they
want her help to prepare Butterfly for this. She must help Butterfly,
and convince her to give the child to this woman, who will be a good
mother to him. Suzuki is not convinced. To ask a mother to give up
her child is too much. Pinkerton notes the fragrance of the flowers in
this house where he had loved, and now it has the chill of death.
Look! He notices his own portrait, which Butterfly has kept. He cannot stay there any longer. He bids farewell to the flowered refuge of
joy and love, and runs off, calling himself vile. Kate Pinkerton enters
and speaks to Suzuki. Will she tell Butterfly to trust that she will be
like a mother to the child? Yes, Suzuki believes her, but they must
leave now and let her speak to Butterfly alone.

Comment, scene and aria, "Addio, fiorito asil": The meeting between
Suzuki and the Americans is accomplished quietly and in small bits of
recitative, which grow into a rather old-fashioned trio of modest propor-

tions as Sharpless, Suzuki, and Pinkerton reflect on the situation. This was much altered between the various editions, and you might occasionally see a quartet including Kate, which was the original plan. As it generally stands, Kate never quite gets a coalesced musical identity: she is merely a scary phantom hovering in the garden, for all her nice words. Pinkerton's short little aria, "Addio, fiorito asil" was an addition to the Brescia revision of the score. It has caused a bit of controversy from the start. Critics early on complained that Puccini was pulling back from his "biting satire" of American imperialism by trying to make Pinkerton more sympathetic and thereby mollifying his bourgeois audiences who had rejected Butterfly's *radical political stance. This is nonsense, of course, on several levels. First of all, Puccini never intended to compose a biting satire of American imperialism. The man who leafed through stories from both Maxim Gorky and Gabriele D'Annunzio in search of librettos obviously had no single political ax to grind, whatever Belasco's issues were. Puccini, ordained by God (as he said) to work only in the theater, knew that the Scala edition of the opera had dramatic problems, not political problems. It just doesn't make operatic sense for a lead tenor to return to the stage after an absence of over an hour merely to walk off again with a few lines of recitative and a modest contribution to an ensemble. Besides, I'm not the least bit convinced that this aria makes him any more sympathetic, although I seem to hold the minority opinion in this. Carner rightly says that the aria makes the tenor more conspicuous in this scene, but Budden says its "air of sincerity does something to rehabilitate the singer's character," and this is the general consensus. Singing pretty in Italian opera does not necessarily confer virtue on a character, as we might have learned from the Count di Luna in Verdi's* Il trovatore *(not to mention from Pinkerton himself in the Act I duet). One may use the words of romantic love to drive at something very different, and here we see Pinkerton speaking only of flowers and perfumes. He is still thinking with his senses, and the compassion he expresses in the music is only for himself and his lost moment of good sex before he returns to the States. If anything, "Addio, fiorito asil" renders him even more contemptible. One favorite parlor game among opera fans is to imagine what will happen to the characters that are still living at the end of an opera in their later lives. Romantics, optimists, and tenors tend to imagine Pinkerton all reformed by his experience in Japan. I find no evidence of that in the opera. I can only imagine Pinkerton in a few years' time haunting some waterfront bar in San Diego or San Francisco, moralizing on family values until he downs a few beers and begins weepily castigating his own transgressions and calling himself vile. He begins as a cad and ends as a bore, in the manner of locker-room braggarts everywhere. This isn't character development—that belongs only to Butterfly in this opera. So much for the meaning of the aria. Whatever its deeper significance, if any, "Addio, fiorito asil" is a lovely little morsel and was, in fact, one of Caruso's most popular early recordings. It provides a moment of relief for the audience in an act that is otherwise all tragedy, and therefore heightens the tragedy. We are accustomed to the term "comic relief." Perhaps we who attend the opera should also think in terms of "lyric relief" when confronted with such moments as these, rather than seeking literal meanings.*

Butterfly runs in . . . where is he? Suzuki tries to hold her back from the garden, where she has already seen Sharpless and Kate. Calmly, Butterfly demands to know if Pinkerton is still alive. Yes, Suzuki answers. But he will not return? Suzuki is silent until Butterfly harshly demands an answer. No, he will not return. Unmoving, she asks who that woman is in the garden, who fills her with so much dread. Sharpless intervenes, explaining that she is the innocent cause of Butterfly's pain. Butterfly must forgive her. Ah, his wife, Butterfly understands. All is finished. They want to take everything from her . . . even her son! Sharpless urges her to make the sacrifice for her son's sake. Butterfly is calm: it is the cruelest thing to take a child from its mother, but she must obey the father's will in all things. Kate asks if Butterfly can forgive her, but Butterfly assures her there is no woman in the world happier than Kate. She must not weep for Butterfly. And the child? Butterfly will give him to the father, in half an hour. He should return to get him. Suzuki escorts Kate and Sharpless out of the garden. When she returns, Butterfly orders her to close all the shades—there's too much light, and too much spring in the house. And where is the child? Playing, Suzuki answers. Should she go get him? No, let him play. And go with him. Suzuki wants to stay with Butterfly but is ordered away. Once alone, she kneels before the statue of Buddha until she is struck with an idea. She opens a drawer and removes the box containing her father's hara-kiri sword. She reads the inscription: "Let him die with honor who cannot preserve honor in life." She points the sword toward her neck. Suzuki opens a screen and pushes the child toward his mother. He runs into her arms. You! You! You little god! she cries out. Though he may never know it, his mother died for him, and maybe one day he will remember not that his mother abandoned him, but think of her lovely features. No, go, play! she tells him. She blindfolds the child and places an American flag in one hand and a doll in the other, then goes behind a screen with the knife. The knife falls to the floor. From outside, Pinkerton's voice is heard crying out "Butterfly!" three times. He runs into the room as Butterfly, a white veil tied around her neck, falls from behind the screen, pointing at the child.

Comment: Butterfly's interactions with the others are even more severely understated (and repressed) than her previous exchanges with Sharpless. She is quite catatonic, dead to the world, some would say. The eruption does not come until she is alone onstage, and what an eruption it is: the orchestra blares forth another reworking of a Japanese theme (again, as I read it, signifying "reality"), and there is a special role for the timpani. It pounds forth rather rapid, even quarter notes, dies down quietly without altering rhythm, and crescendos again for several bars. The driving drumbeat is as crass and "artless," in a way, as anything in Tosca*, yet all the more shocking and impressive because of its context in this much more sophisticated score. Butterfly's final solo sung to the child, "Tu! tu! piccolo iddio!" is an arching line demanding great emotion, fine legato, and, frankly, a lot of volume. There is also a huge range of notes to cover. Throughout the opera, we have seen Butterfly's transformation from innocent to something akin to a vengeful fury. This has been reflected in her* music. The intervals in her line, that is, the spaces between her notes, have become increasingly wider as the drama has progressed. On the one hand, this depicts a character "losing" her bearings, while on the other hand it describes a character becoming herself and claiming her humanity. There is only the finest of lines between operatic mad scenes and operatic triumphs (don't we call a truly great performance "demented"?). While Butterfly is not exactly mad here, her solo must subsume all the cathartic power of a mad scene while functioning as a real person in real time. Butterfly's suicide is no mere dramatic device to bring down the curtain. It is the inevitable outcome of everything that has gone before, and remains one of the most effective and affecting moments in theater. The suicide itself, however, is less important than the vocal solo that precedes it and makes it inevitable. The spiritual fact of suicide occurs in the sung line, not the stage directions. There are, however, stage directions to be followed in order to validate for our eyes what our ears have already digested. The orchestra plays another Japanese theme (sounding particularly ominous in this incarnation) while the business is carried out, and that business can vary widely depending on the production. Some directors like to see the suicide on the stage, others keep it tastefully behind the screen as per the libretto. Sometimes Pinkerton appears and sometimes he doesn't. (Of course, the libretto instructs him to appear, but it's difficult to know what to do with him once he's on the stage, beyond looking appropriately horrified.) If Butterfly has sung her final solo well, none of this will matter, and the best idea is to do as little as possible. The tragedy is complete already.

La fanciulla del West

The Name and How to Pronounce It

It is called *La fanciulla del West*, which, after much wrangling, was how Puccini decided to translate the title of the Belasco play *The Girl of the Golden West*. (It was Sybil Seligman's suggestion.) "Golden" got lost somewhere. "Fanciulla" is one of the many Italian words for "girl," and is pronounced "fan-CHOO-lah." Usually, "Fanciulla" alone is enough to designate this opera. If you want to say the full title, be warned that the letter W, where it exists at all in Italian, is pronounced as a V.

What is Fanciulla?

La fanciulla is a tale of redemption and unlikely love in Gold Rush California. Like *Butterfly*, it is based on a play by David Belasco, who worked closely with Puccini on the original production. It is a curious opera with many unusual qualities that keep it on the fringes of the repertory: there is only one female lead role and only two females altogether in the cast. There is a large ensemble of male solo parts, sometimes individuated and sometimes functioning as a chorus. And there is the orchestral texture, which is big, lush, and quite daring. It is a far cry from the world of *Bohème*. One critic after the premiere thought the score more appropriate for the San Francisco earthquake than for a tale of inconsequential little people living outside of civilization.

Fanciulla*'s Place in the Repertory*

As *Tosca* is an "opera-lover's opera," so *Fanciulla* is the Puccini fan's opera par excellence, a fully satisfying helping of everything that is best in this composer's theatrical output. Beyond us afflicted types, however, *Fanciulla* is just outside the standard repertory—not a mainstay of the season, but not rare enough to be a curiosity either. There are a few possible reasons for this.

Most commentators agree that *Fanciulla* represents Puccini at the very pinnacle of his musical powers. Puccini, sensitive as always to criticism, tried to do something a little different in this work. The all-important soprano role, for example, does not have a single aria. Puccini always rankled at the way "Vissi d'arte" in *Tosca* stopped the action, and decided to dispense with such moments. However, the fact remains that depriving a diva of her moment standing (or groveling, as the case may be) at the footlights leaves audiences a bit befuddled, and leaves many sopranos resentful. Critics always fault composers for stringing together a series of hit tunes in an opera, but audiences will rarely buy tickets without them.

Fanciulla, as we have seen, had a dizzying opening night, although this is partly attributed to the Met audience's self-satisfaction at having nabbed a premiere from the world's most popular composer. Indeed, one astute critic friend of mine maintains that a standing ovation in New York invariably means the audience is applauding its own sophistication at having caused such an Important Event. Hard to argue, but in the case of *Fanciulla* we must remember that the *furore* was repeated whenever the opera premiered throughout Italy, in Boston, Philadelphia, and Chicago, and in London, Vienna,

Budapest, and Buenos Aires. The critics in France panned it (as they did reflexively with Puccini's works), but French audiences ate it up. Only the Germans seemed genuinely mystified by it, which is odd considering the work's orchestral and structural qualities. It's also important to remember that Puccini himself maintained detailed directorial and musical control over the productions in those afore-mentioned places where the opera was a wild success, either directly or through close contact with colleagues. This might explain the opera's subsequent neglect. *Fanciulla* took a nosedive in the 1920s and became something of a rarity. It began its climb back into grace in the 1950s and 1960s, with divas such as Renata Tebaldi and Eleanor Steber and tenors like Mario del Monaco and Richard Tucker mining the work (forgive me) for its true glories.

Fanciulla is Puccini's most difficult opera to cast. The title role requires a convincing stage presence, combining feistiness with inno-cence and youth. (One London critic called a production featuring a diva who was past her first flush of youth "Granny Get Your Gun." Tsk tsk.) Then, of course, it requires all the vocal powers of a Butter-fly, and more. Delicately floated pianissimos and important, breathy little utterances alternate with Wagnerian outpourings of sheer sound (e.g., the finale to Act II). Indeed, the great Wagnerian soprano Birgit Nilsson made a notable recording of the role (the cover photo alone is priceless) but avoided it onstage, insisting she simply couldn't get through it. The formidable Leontyne Price took one swipe at the role at the Met, and promptly disappeared after a single performance. And all this without an aria to make sure everyone knows just how incredible you are! It doesn't stop with the soprano role. The role of Dick Johnson is the most demanding role Puccini wrote for tenor, at least since his youthful *Edgar.* A star baritone, someone who could hold the stage as Iago in Verdi's *Otello,* for example, is needed to complete the main protagonists. There is little chorus, and the women's chorus gets the night off, but there are fifteen important compri-mario roles, all but one of them male, who ideally must have voices of sufficient character and color to retain individuality in extraordinary ensembles. A masterful conductor and a full and excellent orchestra are needed. How many houses will hire a great conductor to conduct Puccini? While *Bohème* is still *Bohème* played on two pianos in a barn (I've seen this), only the larger opera houses dare to take on *Fanciulla*. No wonder it remains outside the general repertory. With only half the forces needed to mount *Fanciulla*, you can always throw another *Butterfly* onstage and be sure to sell out the theater.

But there is more to it than casting. *Fanciulla* makes English-speaking audiences uncomfortable. Let's address this foolishness right now. It's all good and well when Chinese or Japanese or Spaniards or whoever sings in Italian, but Americans? It's simply too much for many people. Europeans are not immune to this pose—Stravinsky referred to it as "that horse opera" (this from a man who lived in the Hollywood Hills and was forever doing backflips to wrangle a lucrative contract out of Walt Disney)—but the biggest antagonists are Americans. Critics must always distance themselves from the work with a few caveats about its "problems." Thus Anne Midgette of the *New York Times* as recently as 2004 felt obliged to call it "hokey." Well, perhaps it is, but compared to what repertory opera? *Werther*, maybe? *Fidelio*? And the blogger who calls himself by the apt name of Curmudgeon must explain that he winces at lines such as "Hello, Mr. Ashby, dell'agenzia Wells Fargo." I am racking my brains trying to figure out exactly what is so outrageous about "dell'agenzia Wells Fargo." This, among all the lines in opera, causes our poor friend to wince?

It's all pretty tired. The word "sentimental" gets tossed around a lot, and again one must wonder if it is coincidence that the sole "American" opera by a great European composer gets this categorization. Minnie herself gets a lot of flack. She is called "Bible-thumping," which is utterly unfair. She doesn't come close to thumping the Bible. She reads it with compassion and patience, and as a means of teaching writing while lifting spirits. Some thumper. I've never heard Marie in Berg's *Wozzeck* called a Bible-thumper, and she does a lot more thumping with the Good Book than Minnie (even if it is only on her own head). But, of course, Marie is not meant to be an American. The issue of Minnie's first kiss is often singled out as particularly unbelievable, but is it? Minnie's virginity is what makes her special, and that is hardly a unique trope in opera or anywhere else. The rivalry of the miners for her affection acts as a system of checks and balances, and Minnie is holding out for something better. Or do people rate the allure of men so irresistible that they can't conceive of a virgin "holding out"? In any case, I've never heard the same accusation thrown at Donizetti's *La Fille du régiment*, who finds herself in similar circumstances. Perhaps it's just inconceivable among American girls. As a native Californian and one familiar with the independent women of Calaveras County, I can tell you that Minnie is right on the mark. Belasco knew what he was talking about. I have known many strong women, fiercely independent, totally heterosexual despite their 4 x 4s and their Levi's and flannels, who can slam down whiskey with the boys on the way to teaching a Scripture class, and who are ready to protect their independence or their hoard of gold (hello, metaphor!) with a good right hook or a cocked Smith & Wesson. In fact, a rather militant feminist friend of mine once told me she preferred *Fanciulla* to all the other operas she saw because it was the only one where the prima donna wasn't a monster (*Salome*, *Lulu*, *Macbeth*) or a victim (every other opera ever written). "And she doesn't even get tuberculosis!" added my astonished friend. Minnie's comments reveal that she is not a "goody-goody." "And how many times have you 'died'?" she asks Johnson. She knows men only too well. Hence her virginity, so mystifying to so many. Minnie is a type of priestess. Yes, a priestess. She is the means of salvation for a community. She knows she will lose her "power" if she submits to any of the men around her, and therefore must leave when she chooses her own foreign lover (as in ancient Greece, where exogamy is the rule among the highborn). I believe it is Minnie's power, her real humanity under her relatively modern garb (as compared to, say, Bellini's Norma), and her refusal to be a victim or a monster that alienates many who are not accustomed to facing such an anomaly in the opera house. If *Fanciulla* pushes the boundaries of verismo, it still has at its center that which I believe is the essence of verismo—the search for archetypes among the most commonplace people of the real world. We are used to calling the Old West a "mythic place," but then we balk at the real implications of this appellation. If there is a single place on this planet supremely appropriate for exploring the issues manifest in grand opera, it surely must be California. So let's just stop all the tittering about this.

Cast of Characters

MINNIE (*soprano*): The barmaid of the Polka Saloon. Minnie is a girl of about eighteen or so who lives independently and likes it that way. In the Belasco play, she had no name at all: she was simply "The Girl." If that doesn't signify an archetype, I can't imagine what does. Vocally, Minnie is one of the great challenges of opera. A large spinto or dramatic voice is required to be heard above the thunderous orchestra, although an occasional lyric soprano with tremendous focus and artistry (Dorothy Kirsten, Barbara Daniels) can also make a mark on the role. If vocal prowess and youthful appearance were not demanding enough, Minnie should also, in theory, be able to ride a horse while holding a gun in her teeth (cf. the stage directions), but this detail is often overlooked in casting.

SHERIFF JACK RANCE (*baritone*): The Law in the miner's camp. Rance is an embittered man but is much more nuanced than the average operatic villain. Indeed, he is not really a villain at all, although he makes a lot of base assumptions about the nature of love, is highly jealous, and gets a bit rambunctious with our heroine when he's alone (or so he thinks) with her in her cabin. Still, their dialogue after this little indiscretion indicates that he and Minnie have been playing a sort of cat-and-mouse game for a while, and in their own way have a certain understanding. His music soars into the higher registers and yet must command great authority, so a first-rate baritone is needed to plumb all the aspects of the character beyond the moustache-twirler dressed in black (usually).

DICK JOHNSON (*tenor*): The classic "gentleman-bandit," a holdover from the High Romantic era (cf. *Ernani*). Dick Johnson di Sacramento is, in reality, the dreaded bandit Ramerrez, an evil Mexican! God knows where Belasco came up with the name Ramerrez, and most modern productions will pronounce the name Ramírez, which has the virtue of being an actual Spanish name. The inherent racism in the idea of "Johnson = good, Ramírez [or whatever] = bad" is patent, but getting beyond this problem, it is actually an interesting summation of the man's plight. He is conflicted between his virtuous and demonic aspects and needs the intervention of an angel to conquer his lesser self. Needless to say, one needs a tenor who is capable of more than the traditional stand-and-hit-high-notes variety to bring alive the man's inner drama. Besides this, the vocal line is demanding in the extreme. Great Johnsons are a rarity.

NICK (*tenor*): The bartender of the Polka Saloon, a gruff guy with a soft spot.

ASHBY (*bass*): The Wells Fargo agent. The voice of "civilization" (barely) intruding on the camp, with remarkably lyrical music to sing.

SONORA (*baritone*): Sonora is the quintessential miner: a tough guy who gets into fights easily, and wouldn't dream of line dancing with other men, and yet, wouldn't ya know it, the guy's a big softy deep down. (He gives Minnie a pretty ribbon as a gift, so this tells us something right away.)

TRIN (*tenor*): Another tough miner, who also scoffs at the idea of dancing with men.

SID (*baritone*): A miner, and, as we find out, a cheater at cards (the gravest sin a forty-niner could commit, presumably).

BELLO (*baritone*): Known as Handsome in the play, and sometimes still listed as such in the program of the opera.

HARRY (*tenor*): Another tough miner who gets all squishy around Minnie. He buys her a handkerchief. Harry is also kind of dumb, as we see in the Bible-lesson scene.

JOE (*tenor*): This miner is a softy on the outside as well as on the inside, picking flowers for Minnie and content to have the others see him cry over the news of his dead grandma.

HAPPY (*baritone*): I suppose this miner got his name in a relative sense to the others in the camp, since he doesn't do or say anything to earn the name, but neither does he have any maudlin moments. Interestingly, he is one of the last to be "converted" in the finale. It doesn't help this opera that, through no fault of its own, the miners' names bring to mind the Seven Dwarves in American audiences.

LARKENS (*bass*): The miner who is deeply homesick (for Cornwall, no less!) and dispatched almost immediately.

BILLY JACKRABBIT (*bass*): This Indian has obnoxious ways of saying things but interesting things to say all the same, and very wacky bits of music. Puccini opted to cut a bit of business he originally had of stealing shots of whiskey at the Polka Saloon, thank God.

WOWKLE (*mezzo-soprano*): His squaw, as the libretto states it, and the only other woman in the opera.

JAKE WALLACE (*baritone*): The camp minstrel. A "cameo appearance" with tremendous power to make an impression, Jake Wallace should have a voice of unrelenting beauty. In theory, his voice is what pushes Larkens over the edge.

JOSÉ CASTRO (*bass*): A "dirty, dark, half-breed Mexican," or some other insufferable indication in the libretto.

A PONY EXPRESS RIDER (*tenor*): He comes and goes, appropriately.

The Opera

Act I

Prelude

Comment: This is Puccini's first prelude since Le villi, *a departure from his usual practice of raising the curtain with a few chords. It is very brash and loud, full of noise but also full of information. We sense the grandeur of the local scenery, but we are also told of the expansive musical vocabulary we will hear to depict the issues at stake. It's as if Puccini is saying, "Big Country, Big Feelings, Big Music." We are also given notice to pay attention to the orchestra in this opera as in no other Puccini work. Two major themes emerge from the rush of sound: the main theme of the opera, generally (but not exclusively) used as the lovers' theme, and a rollicking "cakewalk" that is associated primarily (but not exclusively) with the hero Johnson/Ramerrez. It also represents the Wells Fargo agent, Ashby, who is trying to capture Ramerrez. Perhaps we should understand it as a more generic "horseman's" theme. To my ears, it sounds like the celebrated theme music to* The Magnificent Seven.

Setting: The Polka Saloon in a miners' camp in California Gold Country, during the Gold Rush.

Sheriff Jack Rance sits alone, smoking a cigar. Larkens also sits alone, writing a letter. Nick the bartender comes in and lights lamps. The miners are heard singing outside, done with their day's work. Harry, Joe, and Handsome come into the Polka with some other miners, singing and ordering whiskey and cigars. Sid enters the bar and suggests a game of faro. Sonora and Trin enter the bar. Rance asks Nick what's the matter with Larkens. Is he sick? Same old problem, Nick says. Homesickness. Rance notes that Minnie is late tonight. Sid, Happy, Trin, and Joe gamble. Nick announces that the dance hall is open as well, but Sonora and Trin scoff. They don't dance with men! Sonora quietly asks Nick if Minnie has made her choice yet, and Nick suggests that Sonora is her favorite. Sonora buys cigars for all. Trin asks the same question, and Nick answers that he is her favorite. Trin orders whiskey for all.

Comment: The opening scene manages to introduce each of the miners individually while also creating an impression of the communal life, an excellent use of operatic techniques. Detractors object to hearing miners singing "Dooda dooda day," and it always gets a few chuckles, but listen again. It isn't exactly "Camptown Races" (which Belasco had the miners sing onstage), but rather a curiously cryptic gloss in a minor key on that famous theme. It will reappear in Act III, where its hint of underlying malevolence will become patent.

The minstrel Jake Wallace is heard from afar, singing a sad song about the folks back home. He comes into the bar and the miners join in the song. It is too much for Larkens, who breaks down sobbing. He can't stand it anymore. The miners take up a collection and send him back home.

Comment: The minstrel interlude is a superb mood piece, creating a background of loneliness and despair amid all the exuberance of the Gold Rush. Jake Wallace begins offstage and "afar," so he needs a voice of some color and character to bring out the impact of the scene. Indeed, a few star

baritones have begun their careers by making an impact in this small role.
When he enters, the miners join in, and the song becomes a full ensemble
of male voices. For years, commentators and program notes repeated the
error that the tune was Stephen Foster's "Old Dog Tray," although appar-
ently no one ever thought to look at or listen to that song. "Old Dog Tray"
is an upbeat, perky little tune worlds away from what we have here.
Recent scholarship has determined that it is actually a Zuñi Indian tune. I
cannot verify that myself, but everyone agrees that it is.

The miners return to their games. Bello accuses Sid of cheating, and
Sonora pulls his gun. Everyone calls for him to be strung up right
away. Rance intervenes. Why kill Sid? What's death? He knows a
better punishment. Rance pins the two of spades on Sid's chest, over
his cheating heart. If the card is ever removed, then he can be killed.
They kick Sid out. Rance starts a game of poker. Ashby comes into
the bar and approaches Rance, who introduces him as the Wells
Fargo agent. Ashby orders a drink, asks Nick how the girl is ("Fine,
thanks"), and tells Rance he is close to catching the bandit and his
gang of Mexican thieves. Nick brings out a round of drinks, compliments of Minnie. The miners cheer Minnie. "Mrs. Jack Rance, soon
enough," mutters Rance. Sonora insists otherwise—he will marry
Minnie! He and Rance exchange insults and fight. Sonora draws his
gun but Trin grabs his arm. A shot goes off in the air and everyone
ducks for cover. Minnie enters the room and everyone cheers.

Comment: A lot of business is managed here very quickly and efficiently
before Sonora and Rance start brawling. Rance's little business with Sid
is an interesting insight into his character. The sheriff actually is a civiliz-
ing influence on this semibarbaric community, even if he has to disguise it
sometimes to make it comprehensible to the men. The fight itself turns
into a free-for-all, and the orchestra provides plenty of "boffo" effects:
markings such as "con violenza" and "più che fortissimo" abound. It's all
a great setup for Minnie's entrance, which is one of the giddiest in opera,
and never fails to get a reaction out of the audience. Some laughter, usu-

ally, which is fine. It stretches the emotional range of the audience. The best productions embrace this moment, with the miners throwing their hats up in the air and even a couple of pistol shots going off.

Minnie scolds the miners for fighting. As a punishment, she will cancel the school session for the evening. They beg her not to, and each line up to give her little gifts. Joe gives her flowers he picked, Sonora gives her a ribbon he bought from a peddler, and Harry a handkerchief, blue, like her eyes. She thanks them. Ashby buys her a drink, compliments of Wells Fargo. Nick urges Minnie to mingle around the bar. It's good for business. "Fresh!" she tells him. Sonora gives Nick a bag of gold, settling his bar tab. Nick makes notes and drops the gold into the cask used as a safe. Minnie gathers the miners to begin her lesson. Where were they? Ruth? Ezekiel? Ah, Psalm 51. Do the boys remember who David was? Harry pipes up—a hero king in olden days who slew a giant with the jawbone of an ass! "What a mess!" says Minnie, smiling. She reads: "Sprinkle me with hyssop and I shall be clean." "What's this 'hyssop'?" asks Trin. Minnie explains that it's a plant that grows in the East. "And not around here?" Joe asks. Yes, says Minnie. In each of our hearts there grows a little sprig. "In our hearts?" he asks, confused. "In our hearts," she assures him. She reads on, explaining the verse. There's not a sinner in the world who is barred from the path of salvation. Let them each remember this.

Comment: After a bit of business, the mood settles into one of serenity for the Bible lesson, which is also, we can assume, a literacy lesson for the miners. Girardi finds it "sentimental," which seems a random complaint in the context of Italian opera and Puccini, specifically. One recent critic in England (he wasn't the first) called Minnie "Bible-thumping," but there's no thumping in the orchestra or her words here. It is probably one of the best and subtlest uses of religion in opera. Minnie's lighthearted banter with Harry's confused biblical history (listen for the quick "hee-haw" in the orchestra as Harry confuses David with Samson) tells us she doesn't use Scripture as a weapon. The orchestration of the scene contrasts greatly with the previous music, becoming almost eerie with the addition of a celesta and some other "tingly" effects. We hear the curious four-note, whole-tone scale "droop" that we first heard, barely, in the prelude, and now can identify this as a sign of redemption. Forgiving someone who has harmed you is transformative for both parties. Shakespeare required a dozen lines to explain how the "quality of mercy is not strained." Puccini can depict the mystical workings of Grace with a few deft musical touches. The episode ends with a reminiscence of Larkens's song, which is very interesting. It seems to suggest a formula of "Mom—Back home— Primal Innocence" that underlies the camp's sense of exile and separation.

The Pony Express arrives. He has letters for the miners, but warns them to be careful. He saw an ugly half-breed on the trail. Ashby asks the rider if he knows a woman named Nina Micheltorena. Minnie interrupts: "She's a phony Spaniard who uses lampblack and makes eyes at the men. Ask the boys!" Ashby promises to have the bandit Ramerrez that night. Nina will lead him to his quarry. A scorned woman. . . . Rance warns against trusting Nina. The miners read their letters from home. Joe's grandmother died. He orders a whiskey. Nick tells Minnie there's a stranger outside—an odd sort who ordered a whiskey—and water! Minnie laughs. Nick assumes the guy must be from San Francisco. Minnie tells him to invite the stranger in and they'll curl his hair for him.

Rance approaches Minnie. "I love you, Minnie," he says bluntly. She tells him not to talk like that—she's told him she doesn't want to hear it. He offers a thousand dollars for a kiss, and asks her to marry him. "What would your wife say?" she shoots back. He'll never see his wife again if Minnie says the word, but she brushes him off. She prizes her independence, living alone, and, waving a pistol in Rance's face, is prepared to defend it. He continues: when he left home, no one missed him. So he followed the only thing that had never let him down—gold! Now, just for a kiss, he would throw away a fortune! But love is something else, Minnie says. "Poetry!" Rance scoffs. Down in Soledad, she says, when she was small, she remembers how her parents would play footsie under the table in the gambling saloon they ran. They were so in love! That's how she wants to be with her husband, and she would love him just like that.

Comment: Historical inaccuracy here—no Pony Express in the Gold Rush. Blame Belasco. The Italian libretto only specifies a "postilion." Nick's priceless comment about the sort of man who would order a whiskey and water always gets a big laugh in San Francisco but seems to pass flat elsewhere. The scene between Minnie and Rance is excellent. You get the feeling these two have been at this game for a while. Rance's soliloquy ("Minnie, dalla mia casa son partito") is telling. The cellos play a lyrical, expansive melody underneath his comments, suggesting that he is trying to be seen as more cynical and hard-nosed than he actually is. Not many "bad guy baritones" in opera have this much dimension. Minnie counters with her monologue, the closest she gets to an aria, "Laggiù nel Soledad." She floats up to high B-flats describing her parents' love. Hardly the Bible-thumping, repressed virgin she is sometimes called by desultory critics. She just wants something better than what Rance is offering. And something better is about to walk in. . . .

The stranger enters the bar, asking who is going to curl his hair for him. Minnie hides her instant recognition of the stranger, while Rance makes it clear he doesn't like him. What's his name? Johnson. "Just Johnson?" asks Rance. "Johnson from Sacramento." They don't usually allow strangers in the camp, Rance says. Was he lost? Was he looking for Nina Micheltorena? "Rance!" Minnie snarls. She tells Nick to give the man his whiskey however he wants it. She welcomes Johnson and asks if he remembers her, on the road to Monterey. Of course Johnson remembers her. He gave her some jasmine, and they said they'd never forget each other. Rance deliberately spills Johnson's drink, and demands to know his business. The miners gather round, ready to throw him out, but Minnie vouches for him. The miners are happy to see Rance have a little comeuppance. She introduces Johnson to each of the miners. He asks her to dance. She laughs. Funny, but she's never danced in her life! He leads her into the dance hall. The miners hum a waltz.

Castro, one of Ramerrez's gang, is dragged in. He notices Ramerrez's saddle. Rance grabs Castro's hair, and tells the filthy-faced son of a bitch they know he's part of Ramerrez's gang. Castro says he hates Ramerrez and runs off—he will lead Ashby and Rance and everyone to the hideout. Meanwhile, he notices Ramerrez waltzing in the dance hall! The miners prepare to follow Castro. Johnson comes back from the hall, and Castro whispers to him that the gang is just outside in the woods. He'll throw everyone else off the trail and whistle. If the job is on, whistle back! The men leave with Castro. Nick stares at Johnson a moment before leaving also.

Comment: The simple waltz, hummed by the miners, is thoroughly effective. It will morph a few times as a love theme for Minnie and Johnson. Musicians admire the subsequent scene, when Castro is dragged, for its rushing snippets of broken phrases, so typical of this score.

Minnie comes back into the bar. Has Mr. Johnson stayed behind to help her defend the place? Yes, if she'd like. She assures him that she can defend the place herself. But what, he asks, if the thief only tried to steal a kiss? She laughs. Many have tried, but none have succeeded so far. She puts the bar's money in the cask with the gold, and says she feels she can trust Johnson, even though she doesn't know who he is. He admits he is not sure who he is either. Minnie has no idea who she is, just a poor, good-for-nothing girl, but there's something about Johnson that makes her want to rise above herself, up, up to the stars to be by him. He felt her tremble as they danced, and it brought him peace. Nick bursts in—another ugly Mexican has been seen outside the bar. Minnie goes to see, but Johnson stops her. A whistle is heard. What can that be? she wonders. She admits to Johnson that the cask at the bar is full of gold. These poor boys have left everything for a chance to make something of themselves, and, pulling out her gun, she insists that anyone who tries to take the gold will have to do so over her dead body. Johnson promises no one would dare. But he must leave. She invites him to eat at her cabin up the hillside. He is not to expect too much. She's only had thirty dollars' worth of schooling. Had things been different, no telling what she might have been. "What we both might have been," Johnson muses. "Just a good-for-nothin' nobody," she mutters, crying. Johnson tells her she doesn't know her true worth, good, kind, with the face of an angel. He grabs his saddle and rushes out. She is alone. What did he say? "The face of an angel!" She sighs.

Comment: The first love duet of the opera is longer than that in Butterfly, *although most casual opera fans would be hard-pressed to recognize it as a love duet. There are no traditional forms in it. They begin in the whole-tone scale, which is followed by a recap of the waltz. Each has a separate solo (shades of* La bohème!*) that climax on gentle high B-flats: these two are coming from separate places but have the same aspirations. After Nick's interruption, Minnie runs up the scale to a B-flat again, but with an entirely different voice: this is Minnie-with-a-gun, Minnie who defends the pot of gold. It's as if her gentle side and her toughness are fully integrated, and it has an effect on Johnson. The whole-tone theme moves toward the redemption theme, which is a diatonic variation of it. The conclusion is all Minnie, even before she is alone on the stage. The orchestra seems to evanesce as she regards her worth alone, but it only seems to disappear. Actually it is an extremely involved orchestration to get this effect of "not being there." There is a soft chord, and a shadow chorus of fifteen humming tenors offstage. Furthermore, Puccini wanted a new instrument for this moment. He turned to Romeo Orsi, an inventor of musical instruments who in fact had developed the bass xylophone for Engelbert Humperdinck's* Hänsel und Gretel *(and which Puccini would eventually use in* Turandot, *where it quotes Richard Strauss, no less). Orsi came up with the "fonica," a device of metal strips above brass sounding bars. These days, few opera houses bother to come up with a "fonica" and a vibraphone is generally used, but the effect is still marvelously shimmer-*

ing. If we consider Johnson's dual nature as the gentleman and the bandit and think of his internal struggle, then his line about Minnie having the face of an angel is more than a hollow cliché. He has recognized her divine potential before she has, and she responds to him as having turned her into something better than she is. It is a deep portrayal of love, considerably more than standard operatic lyricism.

Act II

Setting: The inside of Minnie's cabin.

Wowkle is singing a lullaby to her baby. Billy Jackrabbit, the baby's father, comes into the cabin, scrounging. They grumble about when they will get married. Billy tells her to sing "Like blades of grass are the days of man" in church in the morning. Minnie enters, and asks Billy when he's marrying Wowkle. "Tomorrow," he grunts. Minnie sends him off.

Comment: Yes, it's true, we really have two Indians who say "ugh" to each other and speak in infinitives. It's pretty damned painful and there's no logical way around it. On the plus side, their music is quite interesting. Wowkle's lullaby is a somewhat nervous theme in a pentatonic scale. It's not your standard, serene lullaby, but the sound of an overworked mother almost desperate to make the little brat fall asleep. Billy Jackrabbit reveals touches of latent philosophy in his little Scripture rumination, a good counterpoise to Minnie's Bible lesson. Throughout Puccini's operas, we get glimpses of characters' hidden insides that are either so subtle that they are missed by audiences, or are perplexing. We will see this shortly in Minnie.

Minnie orders dinner for two. "First time," grunts Wowkle. Minnie gets dressed in her Sunday best. Not so bad-lookin', she considers. Johnson comes in. How pretty Minnie looks! Was she stepping out? He tries to kiss her. Wowkle grunts. Minnie tells him to slow down.

They sit at the table. Johnson compliments the room. Isn't Minnie lonely up here all alone? Oh no, she explains. She rides through the fields of flowers and then up into her mountains, closer to God. And in winter? Then she's busy, with her schooling. He offers to send her some books. She thanks him and suddenly speaks of love. She believes it should be forever. How can some men want a woman for only an hour? Well, Johnson explains, some women are worth dying for even if you only get to spend an hour with them. "Oh really," says Minnie. "And how many times have you 'died'?" She offers him a cigar, "one of our Havanas." He tries to kiss her again, but she backs off. Men often ask for a hand to get a whole arm. Minnie sends Wowkle to sleep in the barn. "Ugh, snow," says Wowkle, leaving. Minnie offers her first kiss to Johnson, who takes her in his arms. The wind blows the door open and snow swirls around the cabin, but the lovers are oblivious until they finally shut the door. They admit they loved each other at first sight, but Johnson says it is hopeless, a vain dream. He tries to leave, but the snow is now a blizzard. It's destiny, Minnie says. He will spend the night with her. Shots are heard in the distance. Is it the bandit Ramerrez? What do they care? They will never leave each other. He can sleep in the bed, and she will sleep on the bearskin by the fire. It's all right; she does that all the time when it's cold. He is charmed by her simple innocence as she prepares for bed and says her prayers. Meanwhile, he furtively checks the window. What was that sound? Wind, she explains. He goes to bed. What's your name? she asks. Dick, he answers. And did you ever know Nina Micheltorena? No, never, he replies. They drift off to sleep.

Comment: The conversation of the first part of this scene is casual in tone, although there are always indications in the orchestra of the emotions—or whatever we should call them—smoldering below the surface. The kiss is a huge buildup, and there is a marvelous touch as the door blows open. Operagoers will of course recognize the idea from Wagner's Die Walküre, *when spring bursts in on the lovers. Here it is no less impressive for being winter, and the orchestra pulls off a fine trick: the whole-tone scale theme blasts out as the door flies open, returning to the diatonic theme when the door is shut. Few film directors, with all their resources, can manage such a convincing statement as Puccini achieves here with eight notes. Something has been untapped in Minnie. It is up to each member of the audience to decide how clinically they wish to understand the moment. Minnie and Johnson then indulge in a full-steam-ahead love duet, as raw as anything in Puccini since* Manon Lescaut. *It apparently wasn't raw enough for Puccini, who added a repetition of the climax for the Rome production in 1919, taking both singers up to a high C. The addition is rarely performed, since most people agree it accomplishes little except wearing out the singers, and they're right. We are either caught up in the moment or we won't be with the repetition and a couple of high C's. The passion winds down of its own accord, quite naturally, and all becomes quiet again, except for a wind machine whirring away in the wings.*

Nick's voice is heard calling from outside. Minnie tells Johnson to be quiet and hide, and opens the door. Rance, Nick, Ashby, and Sonora come in. Ramerrez was seen on the trail and they came to check on her. Ashby tells her that her friend from the Polka Bar, Mr. Johnson, is in fact—Ramerrez! He came to the Polka to rob it. But he didn't! says Minnie. But he could have, says Sonora. And Sid saw him heading this way. Nick sees the ashtray on the mantel. One of their Havanas! So he's here! Minnie glares at Nick. Of course, says the bartender, Sid's a big liar. Rance gloatingly says he can prove it. Nina Micheltorena gave them his picture. Look! She forces a laugh. What's so funny? "Nice company he keeps," she says, blithely. All right, it is getting late. Thanks for the help, boys, she says, shooing them out the door. They warn her to be careful. Nick quietly offers to stay. She sends him out with the others.

A moment passes, and she demands Johnson step out. He came to rob her! He denies it. It looks bad, but when he saw her. . . . He begs to explain, not to defend himself. Yes, he is Ramerrez the bandit. It is his destiny. It's six months now since his father died. He never knew it, but his father was a highwayman, and he had to take his place to support the family. He accepted his fate, knowing he was damned. But then he saw Minnie on the road to Monterey, and he thought maybe it was possible to live a good life and find honest work. That's been his only prayer since they met, and now it was all a vain dream. Minnie says let God forgive him for being a thief, but for stealing her first kiss, when she thought he was hers alone, she cannot forgive. He must leave. They'll kill him, but what's that to her? Go. He walks out the door. There is an immediate gunshot. She has a change of heart and drags him in. He begs her to let him die, but she refuses. She loves him; he cannot die. With great effort, she lowers a ladder to the attic and pushes his bleeding body up. Later, they will escape together. Johnson collapses in the loft.

Comment, scene and aria, "Or son sei mesi": The intrusion of the men is all nuance and understatement, with pianissimo rolls in the percussion. These crescendo when the men leave and Minnie demands Johnson step forward, and if possible Minnie should be able to summon up all the vocal power of a Wagnerian soprano in heat for her line "Vieni fuor!" This is no easy trick after seemingly spending all her resources in the passionate duet, and another reason the addendum to the duet is usually better left out. Johnson's response must also, somehow, reach a new level of vocal substance. Commentators always call "Or son sei mesi" ("It's been six months") a narrative rather than an aria, although it's damned hard to tell the difference sometimes. In any case, it is in many ways his most important music. A rolling, thumping theme in the orchestra hammers out what we imagine to be a heartbeat, or his pangs of conscience, or something, and his phrases are meant to be spit out as if he were hurling out secrets he had never intended to reveal. (Not many tenors can do this without sounding like they're simply gasping from the difficult music.) The full musical microcosm of the opera is finally made clear in this solo as well: he mentions meeting her on the road (whole-tone scale theme) and realized he wanted a different life (transformation) and prayed for this to happen (redemption theme in full statement). It was all for nothing, as was his impassioned solo. She quietly kicks him out and he is shot.

*There are more murmurs from the kettledrums as she wonders what to do,
and another orchestral explosion as she pulls him back in and hides him in
the loft. And since he must be convincingly wounded and staggering
around, have pity on the poor soprano who must shove a tenor up a ladder
as she is singing!*

Minnie removes the ladder as Rance knocks on the door. He enters,
pistol cocked. "What's new, Jack?" Minnie asks blithely. "I'm not
Jack Rance, I'm the sheriff," he snarls. Where is Ramerrez? He can't
have escaped. Minnie says Rance is wearing her out with this Ramerrez of his. Does she swear that he is not there? She tells Rance to
look around if he wants. Rance says he wants her, now. They struggle.
She picks up a bottle and threatens him with it, breaking free.
Strange, says Rance. "There's blood on my hand." Minnie suggests
she might have scratched him while they were tussling, but Rance
pushes her away. No, it's still there, even after he wipes it! He looks
and sees blood dripping from the roof. He's there, in the attic! Minnie tries to stop him but he throws her to the ground, ordering
Ramerrez down. Painfully, Ramerrez climbs down, threatened by
Rance. Minnie helps him to a chair, where he collapses, bleeding and
unconscious. Enough! she tells Rance, suggesting they discuss this.
What are they? Who are they? Thieves, all of them, gamblers and
thieves. Well, tonight Rance demanded a reply from Minnie, so
here's her stake. A life for a life: Ramerrez's for her own. What is she
suggesting? A game of poker, she answers. If she wins, Ramerrez
goes free. If she loses, she will marry Rance. Deal? Rance accepts,
giving his word of honor. She nervously fumbles for a new deck of
cards. To think a man's life depends on a card game. Meanwhile, she
stuffs something into her stocking. Two out of three? Rance shuffles
and deals. How many cards? Two. Rance asks why she loves the bandit. She counters by asking why Rance wants her. They study their
cards. Rance throws down a king, as does Minnie. Next is a jack. She
throws down a queen. She wins the first. Minnie deals. Rance has
two aces and a pair. Minnie, nothing. They're even. Final hand. She

makes small talk, apologizing for her harsh words earlier. She has always thought fondly of Jack Rance and always will. He shows his cards: three kings! He's won! She pretends to swoon, begging Rance for a glass of water. When he gets up, she pulls cards out of her stocking. No, she's won! she tells him when he returns with the glass of water. She shows: three aces and a pair! Rance stares at the cards. "Good night!" he says, and leaves. "He's mine!" she cries out in a burst of ecstasy, running to the collapsed Ramerrez.

Comment: This is one of the great scenes in opera. Minnie must compose herself, vocally as well as physically, when Rance enters. If she manages a modicum of perky humor in her greeting, the audience will be fully on her side and convinced during her subsequent cheating. Rance's rambunctious moment must not read like Scarpia trying to rape Tosca. He is just "making his move," as Johnson had with more success only a few minutes earlier. This is why she can turn so suddenly into concern about the blood on his hand. The orchestra plays a menacing minor ostinato with beats on the side drum that blossoms fully as Rance mutters his eerie line that there is no scratch but still blood on his hand ("No! non c'è graffio! e sangue ancora!"). Imagine the headaches of the poor stage director here who must get a tenor to squirt blood furtively out of a turkey baster, or whatever, from several feet above the stage to land on the baritone's hand with the exact cadences of the ostinato. Pulling Johnson down from the loft, with Minnie tearing at his pants, is always a difficult moment to stage as well. At least the tenor's problems are over once he plops down the ladder and collapses somewhere. Minnie must now change her vocal sound again, perhaps adding a seductive tone, and some genuine affection as well ("Ho sempre pensato bene di voi, Jack Rance"). The poker game returns to the idea of muted rolls in the orchestra led by the percussion. The card requests and declarations are parlato. When Minnie shows her winning full house, the score indicates that she should sing the line, but few American sopranos can resist spitting out the words "Tre assi e un paio!" as a spoken slap in the face worthy of Tosca. The line works in either case. When Rance leaves with admirable dignity, Minnie explodes in a cascade of voice. *"E mio!"* she cries, hovering around a high B-flat, but you're lucky if you hear any words beyond *"Whaaaa!"* This is Minnie's *"Valkyrie"* moment, and no amount of volume is too much for it. The effect is so startling and frankly orgasmic that Ashbrook and others wondered if it didn't betray a touch of latent insanity in Minnie. Opera can show the times when extremes of passion are indistinguishable from insanity (Il trovatore, anyone?) but Puccini's art is uniquely qualified to explore what lies just beneath the social facades of everyday people. We have already seen that Minnie contains a touch of divinity, and now it becomes clear that she likewise harbors an intensely passionate erotic nature as well, so intense as to read as insanity. Perhaps, just perhaps, Puccini is also drawing our attention to the corollaries between divinity and insanity, which is what I believe forms part of the equation in Tosca and which he will explore more fully in Suor Angelica. Yet these extremes are even more powerful, and disturbing, in Minnie, since she is a familiar and very typical real-life person.

Act III

Setting: A clearing in the California forest.

Rance and Nick huddle by the fire while the men search the hills for Ramerrez. Rance resents that he is freezing in the mountains, while Ramerrez is warm somewhere, huddled with Minnie. Nick disgustedly cuts him off. What can Minnie see in that guy? Rance wonders. It's love, explains Nick. The whole damned world falls in love, and now is Minnie's day. Ashby rushes over as voices are heard in the distance. They've caught the bandit! It's a great day for Wells Fargo! After a chase through the hills, the miners drag in Ramerrez, bound. Ashby hands him to Rance for justice. Billy Jackrabbit starts preparing the noose. Nick bribes him to take as long as possible with his task, and disappears. Ramerrez begs them to hurry up with their job. It's all he wants. They taunt him and accuse him of all sorts of crimes.

He admits he is a thief but has never killed anyone. They call him a lying son of a bitch and rough him up. Worse yet, he stole Minnie from them. He defies them. He doesn't fear death, and they all know this. But he demands the right to speak. He has one thing to say, about the woman he loves. The miners shout him down, but Sonora insists they let him speak. It's his right. Ramerrez thanks Sonora. She must never know how he died. One minute, says Rance. Be brief. Johnson asks to let her believe that he is free and far away, on a new path of redemption. She will wait for his return, but the days will pass, and he will never come back. Oh, Minnie, the only flower of his life! Rance slaps him across the face. Anything else to say? Nothing.

Comment, scene and aria, "Ch'ella mi creda": The act opens with a moody meditation as Nick and Rance stare into the fire, each lost in his own thoughts amid the immensity of the Sierras. The chase scene is well handled considering the "stagy" constraints: calls and shouts between groups of the men build up, creating growing waves of tension. It is a case of music as a substitute for what cannot be visually presented, and frankly is a lot more thrilling than another cinematic chase scene, if one is open to the idea of "seeing" with one's ears. It lasts for five minutes and has been dissected by scholars as a symphony in miniature—at least miniature in time if not in volume. The original production demanded eight horses to be ridden on and off in this scene. Few people have horsemanship skills today, and fewer audiences want to see a horse-ballet in this moment, so it is usually dispensed with. The occasional outdoor production in Italy will indulge in some actual horseplay for this scene. When Johnson/Ramerrez is brought onstage, the latent violence of the miners becomes overt. They sing snatches of "Dooda dooda day" among their insults, in the same key as at the beginning of the opera but now sounding much more sinister. It is a difficult scene to stage, and the publicity photo of the premiere perfor-mance at the Met, showing Caruso with a noose around his neck and a facial expression that wouldn't have disgraced Lillian Gish at her most terrified, is hilarious camp. (It's available as an eternally popular post-

card, and not just at opera shops.) Handled well, however, the scene is effective, and serves as a good setup for the only detachable aria of the opera, "Ch'ella mi creda." In a career full of ostentatiously gorgeous melodies, "Ch'ella mi creda" still stands out as uniquely appealing. Predictably, many critics faulted it for its structural naiveté, and some still seem to have missed the point. Like its close relative "O mio babbino caro" in Gianni Schicchi (q.v.), the structure is so conventional and symmetrical and "out of place" with its context that we must pause to wonder what it all means. There are only four lines, albeit of great length. The first (A) is the theme, the second (B) is the countertheme, each rising to a tonal pinnacle about two-thirds through before falling incrementally back down to the starting point. The third line is A repeated by the orchestra alone, and the fourth is B with a protracted climax. That's all there is to it. It is innocent and retrogressive in musical terms. As effective as this aria is on its own (it was one of Caruso's best-selling 78s), we can see how the details of Act I have coalesced for a unified dramatic statement. Innocence equals nostalgia (for home, for Mom, and so forth), which equals redemption. It ought to rip up the audience, and Puccini has forbidden any break for applause with a directness even Wagner could not have imagined— having the baritone slap the tenor across the face and continue singing, as if to add insult to injury by depriving him of a bow at the footlights. (Not that they bow at the footlights after an aria anymore, but you get the idea.) For years, there were stories about Italian soldiers singing "Ch'ella mi creda" as a sort of anthem, but these stories were later denounced as hooey by many who did not want to accord Puccini more sentimental value than he already had. Vincent Seligman, however, wrote that he heard Italian prisoners on the Salonika front singing this aria in perfect unison and giving him a major case of the creeps. Budden has pointed out that nowhere else in all his writings does Seligman appear to tell a "tall tale," and since Seligman spent a good deal of time alone with Puccini, he was well positioned to make up any story he wished. There is no reason to doubt it. Sometimes real life has more honest sentiment in its "theatrical effects" than many are willing to admit.

The miners cast the noose over a tree branch. Minnie's voice is heard from afar. Rance orders them to hurry up and string up Ramerrez, but all ignore him. Minnie rides on and leaps from her horse, in front of Johnson. She tells Rance to back off. He orders her to allow justice to be done, and the miners cry, "Enough! Step aside!" She draws her gun, and threatens to kill both Johnson and herself if they don't back off. Sonora forces his way to Minnie and moves the miners back. Minnie speaks to them. No one ever said "Enough!" when she gave them the best years of her life, sharing their hardships. Now she claims this man for herself and for God, who has decreed a new life for him. The thief is dead. He died in her cabin that night. Sonora protests that Ramerrez stole more than gold, since he stole her. She tells Sonora he will be the first to forgive Ramerrez. First Sonora, and then the others. Sonora agrees that they owe her this much. The others protest. It is too much to ask. No, she insists. They can and they will forgive him. Didn't Joe bring her flowers? Doesn't Harry remember how she stayed up with him when he was sick and his fevered mind thought she was his little sister from back home? And Trin, does he remember how she held his hand and guided it when he wrote his first letter back home? Happy still protests, but Sonora tells him to forgive Johnson. Minnie tells her "brothers" that there is not a sinner in the world to whom the path of salvation is barred. She throws down her gun. She is as she ever was, their sister. He and Bello, rough men but so good inside . . . they too will forgive. What will Ashby say? Sonora tells them Ashby can say what he likes. They owe this to Minnie. He unties Johnson's hands, who thanks them. Go, says Sonora. Farewell. The miners know she will never return again. She is gone forever. Minnie and Johnson depart, saying farewell to their hills and their beautiful California.

Comment: Minnie's entrance can be a great coup de théâtre or a total nightmare. I have never seen a Minnie riding in on a horse with a pistol in her teeth, as the stage directions would have it. Yet the orchestra is whipped up to a "Here comes the cavalry!" frenzy, so having her walk on the stage is not much of a solution either. It is not utterly critical, though, since only a bad Western would make Minnie's entrance itself the climax of the scene. What follows is what counts, and it is, I believe, one of the supreme achievements in opera. Furthermore, it is an achievement that could only happen in opera. The core idea in the scene is the transformation of a community. Wagner achieved this idea in Parsifal, *but that is a different case. Even the Holy Spirit Itself makes a cameo appearance in that (admittedly awesome) scene. Here, we have nothing more than an agent of that Spirit, a humble girl who has actually dared to take seriously the notion that sinners can be redeemed. We have seen that all are sinners (not least in the "Dooda dooda day" joy with which the miners prepared to string up Johnson, implicating them as would-be murderers and removing any sense of righteous justice from the scene) and so all are in need of redemption. She does it as any great spiritual leader would do it—one soul at a time. In performing her act of salvation, she is not above using every trick she knows to coax an agreement out of the men, just as she was not above stuffing a full house in her stocking to "save" Johnson. She positively seduces Sonora with a reiteration of the snippet of music, hardly remembered, that played when he gave her the ribbon. She knows he is in love with her, as they all are, and she is now cashing in that love. Sonora becomes her chief advocate with the other miners, as we might have suspected he would be from early on. If each of the miners has managed to communicate a vocal independence and a differentiated character from the beginning, then the intricacies of this ensemble become a convincing and masterful whole. Groups of the men protest the idea of pardoning Johnson, but she continues to pick out one at a time and "seduce" them, while Sonora adds a more aggressive note to others. Slowly, all change their music and move into the familiar and other whole-tone scale themes. A new "door" is opened inside each man individually (except for Rance, who sulks on the sidelines, and Billy Jackrabbit, who is likewise serenely outside of this whole process). Minnie and Johnson ride off (or walk off, or what have you), singing a monotone line of farewell. They are completely in unison. They had indicated earlier that they would find a new life on the plains, and it's hard to imagine what plains we're talking about here. There's no reason why they shouldn't move to San Francisco and open a bed-and-breakfast like any sensible Californians would. But they cannot: they will be alone, as they have already been separated from the rest of the world by their love. And miracle workers must always disappear after they perform their function (cf. Lohengrin). But whatever bright future they may have in front of them, there is a unique sadness to the finale of* Fanciulla, *despite the lack of a "body count" and the theoretically happy ending. The orchestra creates a picture of melancholy desolation with a chord of E major played from the lowest notes of the basses to the violins five octaves above, and almost the full orchestra, including the celesta and bass drum, playing pianissimo. Of course Minnie and Johnson are leaving their beloved California, and the miners have lost the one harbinger of beauty in their rotten lives, but there is more. It is sad to grow up, even if the illusions of youth were tainted and flawed, and even if growing up involves a salutary purgation. There really is no way to avoid a little heartbreak, even when things work out for the best. Yes, that is, as they say, sentimental. It is also very, very true.*

La rondine

The Name and How to Pronounce It

RON-dee-nay, three syllables, accent on the first. It means "the swallow" (the bird).

What is La rondine?

La rondine is a romance, neither high tragedy nor broad comedy, about a doomed love affair between a worldly woman and an innocent young man. As in *La bohème*, this affair is contrasted with a parallel relationship between another pair of lovers. Given the right cast and production, it is a work of great charm with a good deal of truth in it, avoiding, as it does, the body count of tragedies and the often-cloying silliness of many operatic attempts at comedy. It boasts a lovely and flattering lead soprano role and a gracious lead tenor role for one who can project a credible youthful naïveté.

La rondine's *Place in the Repertory*

At the fringes, and just barely. After an initial success in the intimate, elegant opera house at Monte Carlo, *Rondine* found only moderate success in Italy. A bad production at the Teatro dal Verme in Milan sent Puccini into a rage, and he began to tinker with the score. He had high hopes for the Vienna premiere in 1920, but the score revisions in general added nothing and the work was not successful. *Rondine* came to the Met in 1928, in a much-applauded, beautiful production by Joseph Urban, but the Depression quashed hopes of bringing *Rondine* into the repertory. It was too risky a proposition during a time when the house could ill-afford it. The great soprano Lucrezia Bori gave three performances of *Rondine* in the 1930s as her farewell vehicle, and the piece has not been heard there since. Anna Moffo scored a great success with it in Philadelphia in 1960, which began the laborious process of rehabilitation for this neglected opera. More recently, several important productions in Italy, at Opera North in England, and at the New York City Opera, as well as elsewhere in the United States and in Europe, have done much to revive interest. *Rondine* was finally heard at Covent Garden in 2001.

So what's the problem? How can a work by the mature Puccini possibly languish? There are several explanations. *Rondine* has many operatic parallels—too many for comfort. Puccini stated that he wanted to write something like Richard Strauss's *Der Rosenkavalier*, only lighter and with more comedy. It would have been better for Puccini had he never mentioned *Der Rosenkavalier* in this connection, since *Rondine* suffers greatly in the comparison. (It does, however, give us a clue as to how to approach the opera, with *Rosenkavalier*'s famous dictum of "one eye wet and the other dry.") The story of the worldly lady who relinquishes her young lover through her own wisdom hovers over *Rondine* and makes us question the real motivations of the protagonists, who are not as profoundly drawn out as in Strauss's masterpiece. Puccini even quotes Strauss's *Salome* in the course of *Rondine*, inviting further comparison. There is also *La traviata*, whose heroine renounces her great love for the sake of respectability. This is another comparison that does *Rondine* no service: *Traviata* is clear tragedy, and indeed Carner thought the lack of a truly tragic crisis in *Rondine* deprived Puccini of an opportunity to show his best stuff. Tito Ricordi Jr., who was, as we have seen, against this opera from the very start, called it "second-rate Lehar," a fatuous dismissal but one that has given much fodder to critics ever since. The operetta comparison does, however, carry some weight in relation to Johann Strauss Jr.'s *Die Fledermaus*, with which *Rondine* has some structural similarities. *Fledermaus*, however, does not attempt any deep human drama and succeeds by maintaining a veneer of charming frothiness over some very serious and difficult music. *Rondine* has no such solid tone. There are elegant scenes of Parisian life, which bring to mind *Manon* (in both incarnations) and about a hundred other repertory operas. When the story of *Rondine* moves into a tale of budding love against the backdrop of the racier elements of Paris, we have no choice but to think of *La bohème*, against which no opera can survive a comparison. So one of *Rondine*'s biggest problems is that it is neither *Der Rosenkavalier*, nor *La traviata*, nor *Die Fledermaus*, nor *Manon*, nor least of all *La bohème*, while making us think of all of these masterpieces.

There are other problems as well. Everyone dislikes Act III. Some fault it for sentimentality, others for lack of dramatic crisis. My feeling is that it has qualities, but it seems to belong to another opera. Still, given the right setup with a compelling lead soprano and a sympathetic lead tenor, it can be touching and satisfying.

In fact, *Rondine* as a whole can be a magnificent experience. No one doubts that there is an abundance of great music in the score: most critical complaints are more along the lines of the whole being less than the sum of the parts, rather than there being a lack of quality parts. That Puccini decided to indulge in a score with a multitude of waltzes is nothing to disdain. His handling of the waltzes, and indeed the entire score, is masterful and sophisticated. One might complain of a certain sentimentality in the libretto, but no one complains of cheap effects in the score. Indeed, *Rondine* has not historically eluded audiences because it is too schmaltzy but rather because it is not schmaltzy enough. Had Puccini compromised his art to satisfy public tastes, as some used to accuse him of doing, he would have put neon lights around all the waltzes and jammed them down the audience's throat, and probably would have written an opera with more box office life in it. The score has a charm that can please on first hearing (if one accepts right away that this will not be *Bohème* or any other opera). The real treasures become apparent after repeated exposures. It seems likely that *Rondine*'s progress toward the general repertory will continue, as well it should.

Cast of Characters

MAGDA DE CIVRY (*soprano*): A kept woman of Paris. The role is agreeable to many types of lyric and spinto voices, but it requires a certain stage presence: beauty, chic, and the ability to convey much with a glance or a sigh will go far in this role. Ashbrook went even further, comparing the libretto of *Rondine* to an early Garbo movie and suggesting that the role needs a genuine singing Garbo to convince the audience or she comes off as "a sentimental tart." Ouch! The exaggerated point (if there were ever a Garbo who could sing, the world would certainly know about it), however, does illustrate how tall an order this role can be beyond the agreeable vocal demands.

LISETTE (*soprano*): Puccini defied convention by casting the two female leads in *Bohème* as sopranos, and lyric sopranos at that. Here, the voice types are even more similar, and sing in several ensembles together. It is a truly risky proposition. The best Lisettes are ones who vary from the Magda in the color of their voice, but sometimes this goes too far. Often, one comes across rather shrill sopranos in this role, cast in an attempt to emphasize the different colors. Given her perky, to put it kindly, personality, it can become truly obnoxious. However, if she doesn't overdo the antics and trusts Puccini to show off her voice where he wanted to, the role can be very gratifying and can outshine the first soprano.

RUGGERO LASTOUC (*tenor*): On paper, Ruggero reads as the biggest nerd in all opera (no small distinction). However, portrayed by a tenor who can somehow project both erotic ardor and fresh innocence, he can come off as a very sympathetic and attractive character rather than naive to the point of idiocy.

PRUNIER (*tenor*): If Puccini was walking on thin ice with the two lyric soprano roles, he threw all caution to the wind in making the second male role a tenor. The same rules of vocal color apply here as with Lisette and Magda. The roles have sufficiently different characters to keep them clear onstage: where Ruggero is all youthful ardor (and lack of awareness), Prunier is jaded, worldly, and a little weird. Puccini actually recast the role for a baritone for the Vienna production of 1920, but this fell flat.

RAMBALDO FERNANDEZ (*baritone*): Magda's "protector," which was the elegant term for "sugar daddy" in bygone days. Rambaldo does have one distinction, however: he is clearly the nicest, most civilized "dirty old baritone" in all opera. His line to Magda when she leaves him is the model of admirable behavior. Imagine how different most operas would be if Rambaldo replaced the usual baritone. Vocally, it is best if Rambaldo can project a weary sangfroid and worldly detachment.

PÉRICHAUD (*bass baritone*): Anytime one sets an opera in Paris, it means there will be a plethora of "party guests" who must be kept busy during elegant ensemble scenes. Périchaud is one of these characters, invented, it would seem, to create employment opportunities for assistant directors.

GOBIN (*tenor*): Another Parisian party animal.

CRÉBILLON (*bass baritone*): And yet another. . . .

RABONNIER (*baritone*): A customer at Bullier's. He is often played by the same singer as Crébillon.

YVETTE (*soprano*): And what Parisian party scene would be complete without a trio of elegant strumpets?

BIANCA (*soprano*): Strumpet #2.

SUZY (*mezzo-soprano*): . . . and #3.

GEORGETTE (*soprano*): An *habituée* of Bullier's, usually doubled by the Yvette.

GABRIELLA (*soprano*): Another Bullier's customer, doubled by Bianca.

A BUTLER (*bass*): He delivers a letter. It's an important letter, but still. . . . Look for Crébillon here.

A VOICE (*soprano*): One of Puccini's marvelous "passing song" effects. This voice has her entire "song" doubled by a piccolo for an excellent sense of urgency amid the melancholy.

The Opera

Act I

Setting: Magda's elegant salon in Paris.

Magda is pouring coffee and Lisette is serving it to the various groups of guests. Prunier is chatting with Yvette, Suzy, and Bianca, who giggle and tease Prunier. He must be kidding! No, Prunier insists, he is quite serious. The latest rage in Paris is . . . falling in love! Lisette interrupts. How ridiculous! "I want you, do you want me?" There! That's all there is to it! Prunier complains to Magda of her maid's impertinence, but Magda says the unusual is the norm in her house. Yvette, Suzy, and Bianca swoon and act out parodies of sentimental love. Magda asks Prunier to continue in spite of the joking. Prunier notes Magda's interest, and continues. It is like a germ attacking all the ladies of Paris. No one is safe, not even Doretta. Who is Doretta? they all ask. She is Prunier's newest heroine in a song he has composed. He sits at the piano and strums some chords. Who can interpret Doretta's lovely dream? A king offers her gold for her favors, but she tells the king she isn't looking for gold. But Prunier lacks a conclusion. How should the song finish? Magda sits at the piano and sings. One day, Doretta meets a student, who kisses her passionately and she surrenders entirely.

Comment, scene and aria, "Chi il bel sogno di Doretta": The opera opens with a languid waltz, or actually a theme signifying a waltz more than an actual waltz. This morphs into light and vapid "chatter" music with Puccini's predictable deftness. The subject of the "outrageousness of sentimental love" is thought by many to be Puccini winking at his own career, based on this very notion. Prunier is thought by quite a few to be a parody of D'Annunzio. It is tempting to agree with this, and it allows us to apply all the eccentricities of that poet to all the obnoxious qualities of our present poet, but it doesn't quite add up. Prunier is a silly goose with an inflated sense of self, but he is hardly the toxic madman that D'Annunzio had revealed himself to be (at least to Puccini) even as early as 1916. I believe D'Annunzio is present in Prunier merely to signify "poet," since he was the most famous poet in Europe at that time. This is certainly a gentler parody than the D'Annunzio of this era might have expected to receive from any sane Italian.

The three Parisian bimbos recall Massenet's Manon, *and several other French operas as well, perhaps in an effort to create some sort of "authentic" Parisian ambience for the work. The operatic surprise comes when Prunier sits at the piano and actually plays (not really: he mimes well).*

He strums some wide-open chords, reminiscent of the whole-tone scales used in Fanciulla, *to let us know that this is dreamtime he is singing about now. The intrusion of the piano from (theoretically) the stage is quite striking: Girardi goes so far as to call it "metatheater," although Pirandellian metaphors seem a bit much for this work. And yet, we have this first act, where people talk about memories and dreams, and then the subsequent act, where those are played out in vivid detail, so perhaps Girardi is not overstating the case that much. The piano on the stage had been used by Giordano in* Fedora, *but in that opera we have an actual concert pianist (a supposed nephew of Chopin, no less) playing a set piece rather than a character in the opera playing his own song at the piano. Whatever it is, structurally, it is quite remarkable. Prunier sings the chatty first lines of the aria and then rhapsodizes in poetic speech (spoken) over the main theme, played diaphanously in the high strings. When Magda sits at the piano, she appropriates the main theme from the orchestra. It is a famous piece from concerts, made an appearance in the film* A Room with a View *(although everyone only remembers "O mio babbino caro" from that film), and is devilishly difficult. The refrain hits and hovers around high C, and the large intervals both up and down the scale require sure technique and seamless vocal production. You can tell a lot about Puccini's portent from the size of his intervals, the "distance" between consecutive notes. The score of* Bohème *is noted for its small intervals, climaxes building step-by-step up and down the scale, telling the story of real people going through the actual process of daily emotions. Magda's leaps here, conversely, tell us that she is indulging in a fantasy far-fetched from her present reality, even if we shortly find out that it is inspired from an incident in her past. As we who attend films know, and Magda will soon find out, the term "based on a true story" does not make a fact out of a flight of fancy.*

The friends praise Magda, but she tells them not to mock her. How different her life might have been! The friends insist that her dreams of romantic love are exquisite. Prunier warns that the demon of romantic love lurks in every heart, but Rambaldo insists he is immune, armed with holy water against it. He takes a box out of his pocket and blithely hands it to Magda. It is a magnificent pearl necklace. He had intended to give it to her at lunch, but forgot. Everyone except Magda is impressed. It doesn't change the way she feels about true love. "I didn't expect it to," Rambaldo blandly replies. Lisette runs in and excitedly blurts to the confused Rambaldo that a young man is here to see him. Rambaldo asks Magda how she can put up with a little windmill like Lisette, but Magda defends the maid as a ray of sunshine in her life. Yvette, Suzy, and Bianca wonder at Magda's self-pity when she has done so well for herself, but Magda remembers a night at Bullier's nightclub when she kissed a young student. No amount of money can compete with that! The student ordered two bocks and paid with a single gold coin, telling the waiter to keep the change! A voice, as though from a distance, told her to beware the dangers of total surrender. That was all that happened: two beers, a tip, and a kiss, all in two hours, but she has held on to the memory all these years. Prunier scoffs at such sordid encounters. He himself was born for higher adventures in love, and needs a Galatea, a Berenice, a Francesca, a Salome! He says he can read the goal of every woman in the palm of her hand, and offers to read Magda's. They arrange a screen by the piano, and Prunier retreats behind it with the women, leaving the vulgar commoners in the rest of the room. Prunier studies her hand. Lisette announces the gentleman visitor: Ruggero Lestouc, the son of Rambaldo's old friend, only just now arrived in Paris for the first time. He hands Rambaldo a letter of introduction. Prunier prophesizes a strange future for Magda. Perhaps, like the swallow, she will travel beyond the sea toward sunshine and love. But the fate is two-faced: is it a smile or anguish? It's a mystery. Rambaldo asks Ruggero if this is his first time in Paris, and Ruggero says yes, rhapsodizing on the city of dreams and desires. Rambaldo calls out Prunier and asks him where a young man should spend his first night in Paris. "In bed," answers the grumpy Prunier. It's true! All this nonsense about one's first night in Paris has to stop. Lisette defends her native Paris as the realm of women.

The other women suggest destinations for the young man: Bal Musard? Frascati? Cadet? Pré Catalan? It's all so glittering! No, says Lisette. Bullier's! That's where love is to be found, and light, and flowers. Anything can happen there. All agree, except Magda, who warns everyone to go easy on the newcomer. Rambaldo takes his leave and the guests follow out. Magda gives Lisette the rest of the night off.

Comment: Lisette's announcement of the visitor is a breathy but long-winded study of the limits of tonality. Surely Tito Ricordi Jr.'s dismissal of this score as "second-rate Lehar" proves what a cursory glance he must have given it, missing brief moments such as these. You won't find anything like this in The Merry Widow, *whatever its other charms may be. Magda's recollection of her big night at Bullier's is full of disjointed waltz-like themes that rather miraculously sound to our ears like reminiscences even though they are new to us. The "distant voice" takes on the recognizable form of a sad waltz. It plays again in the orchestra when Ruggero walks into the room even though nothing is said. Another "magic of opera" moment. Prunier's list of women brings him closer to D'Annunzio, whose* Francesca da Rimini *was on everyone's lips for a while (including the House of Ricordi, who had it set by Zandonai as the opera that would be everything Puccini was not). His mention of Salome is another nod at Richard Strauss, and sure enough the orchestra slyly quotes Strauss at that moment. Ruggero's soliloquy about Paris was added for the Vienna production of 1920, and it sounds like an add-on. In fact, it was a reworking of the song "Morire?" which had been composed by Puccini for a fundraising Red Cross collection of songs. Although most of the Vienna 1920 alterations have fallen by the wayside, tenors do not easily relinquish this bit since they have so little solo time in this opera. If we do not scruple to wonder why the innocent man who will soon express disdain for Parisian tarts is so effusive about Paris as the city of love, then we can appreciate this moment for the chance it gives us to understand the tenor's vocal characteristics early in the opera.*

Magda repeats Prunier's mysterious prophesy "toward sunshine and love." Suddenly she is struck by an idea. "Bullier's!" she says, and runs into her boudoir. Prunier and Lisette tiptoe back into the room. Prunier declares his love, insisting it pains him to insult her in company. They decide to go out, and Lisette puts on a hat she has "borrowed" from Magda. Prunier doesn't like it, and she leaves to find another. Alone, Prunier begs the Muses to forgive him for stooping so low. Lisette returns with a different hat and a cloak. Prunier remains unimpressed. Lisette scampers off to change again, and Prunier again asks the muses to forgive him for being such an aesthete and condescending to advise such a creature on these matters. Lisette returns in another outfit, and Prunier advises her on her makeup. They pass out of the room, kissing and declaring their love. "I kiss you because I am you!" they say. They leave.

Magda comes into the salon dressed simply as a grisette with a simple coiffure. "Who would recognize me?" she asks. She reminisces about Doretta's dream, putting a single rose in her hair, and leaves.

Comment: So, we discover, Prunier and Lisette are secretly lovers, and their banter is a smoke screen. Yet even alone they are a strange pair, with his control issues extending even to her details of makeup. Some directors find this too tempting to resist, and have Prunier play it as a flaming queen, a sort of "Queer Eye for the Grisette." This comes off as a cop-out. If Prunier isn't sexually attracted to Lisette, there's nothing left to justify their odd relationship. And the score tells us they are genuinely involved. The music here is among the most beguiling of the score: a repeating ostinato, melancholy and somewhat mechanical, that wanders around the various instruments while the singers' comments surf above it. What does it all mean? Budden thought it a good portrayal of "love on the sly." Girardi heard a self-propulsion that reminded him of Tristan. Granted, scholars hear Tristan everywhere, and the comparison seems a bit de trop, yet it is mysterious and ambiguous and Girardi comes closer to the mark when he suggests they are performing some familiar action, like playing a game. I certainly hear that, and it makes these two lovers, whatever their eccentricities, "fit" together in a way that will continue to elude Magda and Ruggero. The conclusion of the act is very quiet and understated, with Magda's glance in the mirror perhaps yet another reference to Richard Strauss and his fascinating heroines.

Act II

Setting: Bullier's nightclub.

A great crowd mixes at Bullier's: students, grisettes, prostitutes, tourists, flower-sellers, while waiters bustle between tables and lovers stroll into the adjacent garden. Georgette and Gabriella, two young ladies, search the crowd for rich men. Magda appears at the top of the grand staircase, hesitating before descending. Students try to flirt with her, but she spots Ruggero at a table and she takes refuge there. Not recognizing her from the salon, he says she is not like the other aggressive girls there, but more like the modest young ladies of his hometown, Montauban. She takes his arm and they stroll into the garden for a dance.

Prunier and Lisette mingle among the crowd, he trying in vain to instill a sense of decorum in her. She tells him she is flirting so he will clamp down on her and stop her. Magda and Ruggero return, hot and tired from dancing. He orders two bocks, and she is transported with joy. She asks him to humor her by paying with a twenty-sou coin and telling the waiter to keep the change. He complies, laughing. He toasts her health, she toasts his loves, but he protests. He will fall in love only once, and it will be forever. They flirt but they don't even know each other's names. She writes hers down on some paper: Paulette. They are drawn to each other, and kiss.

Lisette thinks she recognizes Magda across the room, and cries out. Magda shoots Prunier a look, who immediately nods. He will play the game. They sit at the table, Lisette completely confused and explaining that "Paulette" looks just like her mistress, if Paulette were elegant. Magda admires Lisette's outfit (really her own clothes) and sarcastically compliments her on her elegance. She then asks Prunier if Lisette is Salome or Berenice. Ruggero is oblivious, and the champagne arrives. He proposes a toast to love, which has brought them all together. They and the crowd toast this moment of love and friendship.

Comment, scene and quartet: The opening of this act cannot fail to bring to mind Act II of La bohème, *with its vision of all Paris in the streets. We do not have "all Paris" here, but enough of it, minus the children. It is managed with Puccini's predictable economy and sophistication. Instead of having Magda and Ruggero sing a standard love duet when they meet (again), all is understated and the growing erotic attraction is depicted by the background crowd, an excellent decision. There is a slow, quiet waltz, and then Magda and Ruggero go offstage. The waltz onstage becomes rather raucous, interjected with "whoops" from the crowd, while Magda and Ruggero interject abstract expressions from afar: "sweetness, madness!" and so forth. It's a nifty way of telegraphing all these signifiers to the audience without having to make a coherent syntactic narrative of the words of love, which usually sound kind of silly onstage anyway. The subsequent ballet is short and gets the message across. Prunier and Lisette lighten the moment with some of their comedy, although it has the effect of making Ruggero seem even more clueless than he needs to. No matter: his revenge comes shortly, when he leads the ravishing quartet, the lyric highlight of the score. Dramatically, there is no need whatsoever for the quartet, but one really must put aside such scruples when the beauty of the music is its own justification. It does have operatic precedence in* Die Fledermaus, *which hovers over this opera in some ways.* Fledermaus *contains an excellent ensemble/chorus in its analogous "party scene" in Act II, with the partygoers toasting friendship and love. The* Fledermaus *ensemble acknowledges its own fluffiness by descending into a chorus of nonsense words, "dui-du," under the pretext of everyone having drunk champagne. If* Rondine *has marks of metatheater, as Girardi thought, then perhaps we can understand the quartet as metaopera. That is, do love and beauty really require sensible explanations? Don't they pop up where least expected in real life? Pascal famously said, "The heart has its reasons the mind does not know." Had he been an opera fan, Pascal might have stated that the score has its reasons the libretto cannot know. The quartet begins with Ruggero's solo, joined by the other three and eventually by the chorus. Magda's line begins as interjected decorations to Ruggero's, but it imperceptibly becomes the core of the ensemble. The climax of the melody becomes Magda's, who takes it up to a high C, repeated and supported by Lisette and eventually by the chorus. Ruggero has "gotten to" Magda, after which she becomes the clear motivator of the relationship. Prunier and Lisette add their lines like a round, albeit a very sophisticated one. When the beauty has spread to the crowd, we have one of the most thorough indications imaginable that "love is in the air." Yet it is a certain kind of love, very different from what we experienced in* Bohème *or any other Puccini opera. The melody of the quartet is rapturous but distinctly melancholy. We can safely assume that Magda and Ruggero have no real future together, but the generalized nature of the ensemble suggests the fleeting nature of all romantic dreams. The whole world, by implication, is caught up in Magda's dilemma. No dramatic purpose indeed! The* Rondine *quartet is one of the high points of Puccini's art, and audiences never fail to respond enthusiastically.*

Rambaldo appears, and Prunier tries to distract him, unsuccessfully. Alone with Magda, he forgives her this indiscretion and orders her home. She tells him she loves Ruggero, and will not return home, adding that she is sorry and didn't mean to hurt him. Calmly, he hopes she does not regret her decision, and takes his leave. The place is empty. Magda sits at the table, lost in thought. Dawn is breaking. A passing woman on the street sings to beware of believing in love. Ruggero returns and asks if she cares to leave. They go together, promising to love each other forever.

Comment: Magda's breakup with Rambaldo is surely unique in all opera. He remains calm, even blasé throughout their little scene, while she vacil-

lates between excitement, tenderness, and calm resignation. No wonder this opera must take place in Paris rather than in Italy, and no wonder the Italians had less stomach for it than the French in its initial run. The passing woman's voice is excellent: she sings a simple pentatonic melody that intrudes on the previous lyricism, as primal as erotic attraction itself. The voice is doubled by the piccolo playing very quietly, which adds a subtly shrill quality to her warning. One can almost feel the butterflies in Magda's stomach, and here some mute acting ability is called for. The denouement is played against a soft reiteration of the quartet theme in the cellos and then the violins because, well, how could it not be? They depart the stage and sing "Amor!" from afar—an absolute dare to the audience to compare and contrast this moment with La bohème. *It's almost as if Puccini himself were trying to put some perspective on the romance of his own youth and the most emblematic product of his younger self (just as the debate about romantic love at the opera's beginning seems like a debate about romantic opera in general). Whatever its baggage, the finale of the act is poignant as only Puccini can be, and causes a lot of humming in the lobby during the subsequent intermission.*

Act III

Setting: The garden of a hillside villa outside of Nice.

Magda and Ruggero admire the view of the sea, murmuring words of love and reminiscing about the night they met in Paris. Ruggero interrupts the idyll with a confession and a secret. The confession is that he is out of money and being hounded by creditors. Even the landlord of the villa is starting to get irritated. Magda pities him. He admits his secret: he has asked his parents' permission to marry Magda. She is startled. Isn't she pleased? She hesitates. She just . . . she wasn't expecting. . . . He tells her of his home in the country, with an orchard. They could walk there, under the sacred protection of his mother, and, who knows, maybe someday a child of theirs will reach out a hand to that sunshine . . . Who knows? He strokes her hair but runs off to check the mail. She is in a quandary. Should she tell him the details of her past? No, she cannot. Yet, neither can she be silent. She goes into the summer house.

Comment: Musical reminiscences of their first meeting are abundant in this scene, suggesting that the lovers, however happy they may feel in their present situation, are outside of real time and therefore separated a bit from reality. The orchestra softly plays waltz themes throughout their dialogue as well, and we sense that Magda, for all her honeyed words, seems to have a bit of nostalgia for her former life. It is an important motivator for subsequent events, but generally too subtle to convince the audience. Ruggero's description of his simple country house is in the form of an aria, but it is very static in its forthright structure. This is, of course, meant to contrast with the Byzantine complexity of Parisian life, but it takes some real artistry in the hands of the tenor to avoid sounding banal. Verdi pulled off this trick in La traviata *when the father sings an actual lullaby ("Di Provenza") to try to convince his son to leave Paris and return to his respectable home in the country, but the situation was different enough in that opera to make the gimmick foolproof. The trick of contrasting the two lifestyle choices before Magda is problematic if the audience is not to root for her to run from Ruggero's dreary offer like a bat out of hell.*

Lisette and Prunier wander into the garden, bickering. She had made her debut as a singer the night before in Nice—and flopped! She blames Prunier for putting her up to it, and looks for Magda. Prunier defends himself: he only wanted to make her a star to improve his conquest! She tells him to stop putting on airs. She would endure anything except another night like the night before! Even now, she seems to hear voices. Are they chasing her to mock her again? Prunier gets her to relax in the calm of the garden. The voices she heard were only a butler with a letter for Ruggero. Magda appears, surprised to see the guests. Prunier apologizes for interrupting her solitude. Magda is spoken of in Paris—no one believes this solitary life is right for her. Magda protests with sadness that she is perfectly happy. Lisette asks to return to Magda's service, and Magda immediately accepts. Prunier sneers. Lisette is nothing but what she has always been. Perhaps Magda will make the same discovery about herself. Magda tells him to be quiet, but Prunier protests that it was his duty to tell her this, and now he has performed that duty. Rambaldo, who has heard about Magda's problems, asked Prunier to let her know that he was available to resume their prior relationship whenever she desired. He begs his leave, making derogatory comments to Lisette, who returns in kind. Farewell forever, he bids her, and she expresses satisfaction at his parting. Before he leaves, he asks her in a whisper what time she is off work. "At ten," she answers. "I'll be waiting for you," he replies, and exits with great dignity.

Comment: The intrusion of Lisette and Prunier in the scene is a deft touch of comedic contrast. Listen for the off-sounding piccolos in the orchestra as Lisette is tormented by the memory of the boos and whistles of the previous night. The orchestra plays some themes reminiscent of Paris while Magda is denying any present unhappiness, one of those marvelous moments that can only happen in opera. She is already moving back to Paris in her mind. Lisette and Prunier's parting lines are parlato *and always get a welcome laugh.*

Lisette asks for work to do: she wants to keep busy. Magda tells her she missed her. Lisette runs off, dons her maid's outfit, shows up again to show it off, curtsies, and leaves. Ruggero runs in, excited. His mother has written him and assented to their marriage. Won't Magda read the letter herself? She begins: "Son, you tell me that a tender creature has touched your heart. May she be blessed if the Lord has sent her." Magda hangs her head, but Ruggero urges her to continue. "It brings tears to my eyes to think that she will be the mother of your children, since children make love sacred. If you know that she is good, gentle, pure, and has all the virtues, God bless her. Your parents' simple home awaits your return with your chosen bride. Kiss her for me." Ruggero bestows his mother's kiss on Magda's forehead, but she recoils. She cannot accept it. She cannot deceive him. Her past cannot be forgotten, and she cannot enter his parents' house. She was not pure when she met him. He protests that he does not care, but she insists there is more that he doesn't know. She passed in triumph between shame and gold. He does not want to hear any more. Doesn't she realize that she is ruining his life? And doesn't he think that this is tormenting her? she counters. But she must tell him the truth now, and they must part. He begs her not to leave him, but she tells him she must, and asks him to remember her sacrifice for him. She strokes his hair and speaks to him as a mother to a dear son. Let him go on, she will bear all the pain in her sad life. Church bells toll in the background for vespers. Lisette appears from the summer house, and without a word surmises the situation. She takes Magda by the arm, wiping her tears with a handkerchief. Magda gives one last, tender glance back at Ruggero, who is sitting with his head in his hands, sobbing. She and Lisette leave together.

Comment: The letter reads like it would be a great climactic musical moment, but Puccini must have wanted to maintain the lighter touch. The result is not entirely satisfying. In opera, paradoxically, highly senti-mental dramatic moments must be matched by analogous music or they will appear more sentimental. There is also a bit of a problem with the breakup, as Carner noted. Ruggero says he does not care about Magda's past, so there is no great compelling reason for her to break up just then. Yet Puccini did not want to make her a coldhearted bitch and say flat out that she was bored (as, say, Carmen might have said if she were in this opera), so she can come across as rather insincere when she speaks of her sacrifice. (Here there is more unnecessary comparison with the heroine of Traviata, *who speaks much of "sacrifice" and who has every reason to use the word.) Budden asked the salient point, in his most piquant British way, "What did Magda suppose she was about anyway?" It's a hard ques-tion to slough off. Ruggero's response is likewise a bit mystifying. He pleads with her not to leave him, but only a little, and acquiesces rather too quickly and quietly. There are none of the threats (force, suicide, etc.) that one might expect from a tenor who is being dumped. Of course this is not Ruggero's style, which is why it is so important that he convince us of his utter sincerity and integrity in the previous acts. Otherwise he will just appear as a wimp. This sounds cold and macho, but it is true. It is all very well to complain of the standard tenor role in Italian opera being stupid and prone to testosterone-driven, impulsive action, but the fact is that if the tenor lacks an opportunity to demonstrate some resolve, his high voice might make him sound whiny and rather self-pitying. Only an excellent tenor can keep us from having contempt for Ruggero at this point, and few excellent tenors get around to singing Ruggero. (There recently have been, thank God, exceptions.) As for Magda, the answers are in the orchestra, assuming those can be embodied by the soprano and transmitted to the audience. We hear reminiscences of the "romantic love" music that accompanied the opening of the opera at the beginning of their confrontation. Magda's decision is based on the realization that she has been living an illusion. If only she had found a way to say precisely that in plain Italian, perhaps this moment would be more convincing. However, a fine soprano will find a way to communicate that idea—a change of vocal color, perhaps—and then we do not need to fault Magda for being coldhearted or hypocritical. She can, under the right circumstances, come off as having the weary wisdom of the Marschallin in* Der Rosenkavalier, *even if she gets no help from the libretto and only the subtlest help from the score. The bells tolling at the end are haunting and a good indicator of Puccini's intentions in this scene: the most poignant eulogies are not necessarily for dead people, but rather (as we saw in* Bohème) *for dead illusions.*

Il trittico

The Name and How to Pronounce It

Just as written, accent on the first syllable of "trittico." Try to use the long "e" sound for the "I" vowels in "trittico" to avoid sounding like turn-of-the-century Englishmen touring Italy. Linger over the double "t" for full proper Italian effect. The name means "The Triptych," referring to the medieval altarpieces in three separately framed panels.

What is Il trittico?

Il trittico is a collection of three one-act operas meant by Puccini to be given in a single night. As we have seen, he was quite annoyed with various attempts at dismantling the piece into component parts. Although he conceived of the first opera, *Il tabarro*, separately and took a while before hitting on the final formula, he was adamant that the three worked together and only together. Very few have credited him with enough knowledge of his own work to follow his wishes in this regard, and the three operas have had varying fortunes in the intervening years since their premiere at the Metropolitan in 1918. Nowadays, people have come to agree with Puccini's verdict that the three work best together, when it can be managed. The operas move from grim (*Il tabarro*), to enigmatic (*Suor Angelica*), to a masterpiece of ensemble comedy writing (*Gianni Schicchi*). Taken as a single opera, it is by far Puccini's longest, and in many ways his most ambitious opera. Audiences today appreciate the flow of mood in the work even though one still reads critics who complain that there is no thematic unity between the works and who see it more as a potpourri than a unit. Nothing could better illustrate the gulf between Italian and American sensibilities than this point of view. Any Italian, or anyone sensitive to the whole issue of Italian culture, would instantly recognize the model for a tripartite work that goes from redemption to hope in the single defining work of Italian art: Dante's *Divine Comedy*. Indeed, the hint, if one were needed, is made explicit since *Gianni Schicchi* derives from a brief episode in Dante subsequently elaborated by others. *Gianni Schicchi* even playfully asks the indulgence of "Father Dante" for this little romp in the epilogue that completes the evening. The connection to Dante is not original to this book: Carner pointed it out decades ago. However, it receives little consideration from critics and program notes and is worth looking at.

Il trittico corresponds perfectly to Dante's three "realms" of hell, purgatory, and paradise: *Il tabarro* is a study in changeless hopelessness, *Suor Angelica* presents pain and suffering as part of the process leading toward final redemption, and *Gianni Schicchi* is a celebration of joyous love.

So much for the similarities to Dante: the contrasts are more fascinating. The despair of *Tabarro* is caused more by economic and material realities than by moral turpitude. Angelica's redemption comes entirely from within without any outside influences. The love of *Schicchi* is not Dante's abstracted, scholastic philosophy but sensual, sexual love as experienced by two young people and mirrored both in the flowering nature of spring and the flowering culture of proto-Renaissance Florence. If we call Dante's work "divine," we might do well to call Puccini's "earthy."

The changes from Dante represent changes in the understanding of human nature. Marx and Freud are well represented by *Tabarro* and *Angelica*, respectively. Schicchi suggests that salvation is to be found by participating in life rather than attempting to transcend it, a marvelously Renaissance idea. The gentle subterfuge of these evolutions is evident in the fact that in Dante, Schicchi has been consigned to hell (and a very deep level of hell at that) for his fraud. In the opera's point of view, Schicchi has been the agent of life and more life, and therefore is an agent of salvation when looked at through modern sensibilities. *Il trittico* is the *Divine Comedy* turned upside down by modernity. It is a beautiful statement of faith in humanity and a wonderful journey, and the modernity of the piece is composed of much more than a clever use of chromatics and a tooting automobile horn (in *Il tabarro*). *Il trittico* can be astoundingly effective if given the resources it deserves: great singers who can act, more great singers who can act, a good production, and a sensitive conductor.

Il trittico's *Place in the Repertory*

Outside of the basic canon of repertory, but not quite obscure at this point in history. There is the tremendous difficulty of casting the work. In essence, one needs three separate large casts. Some doubling of casts is possible in certain roles. Occasionally a star baritone will appear in both *Tabarro* and *Gianni Schicchi*, and the tenor roles in those operas can be (although rarely successfully are) sung by the same tenor. Even more occasionally, a very ambitious diva will assume all three lead soprano roles, but this is foolhardy in the extreme and even questionably rewarding, since the final role is much smaller in scale and scope than the middle one. In any case, *Il trittico* only began to resurface as a complete opera in the 1960s, with important productions in San Francisco and elsewhere. By the 1980s it was being seen in more and more companies as an opportunity for that company to show some of its muscle. Presenting *Trittico* as a whole is still considered an "event" for most companies, but fortunately it is an increasingly common event.

Il tabarro

The Name and How to Pronounce It

Just as written, accent on the second syllable. The only question is how much you want to roll the double r's. It means "the cloak," referring to the baritone's article of clothing, with which he used to wrap up his wife in happier days but which becomes something else entirely. Don't bother translating it in conversation. If you call it "The Cloak," no one except a few people in the English National Opera's marketing department will have any idea what you're talking about.

What is Il tabarro*?*

Tabarro is a gritty tale of workers on the Seine River in Paris, their desperate lives, their search for moments of happiness, and, ultimately, a murder. It is based on a one-act play called *La Houppelande* by Didier Gold that caused some chatter in Paris and had impressed Puccini when he saw it there in 1912. Adami fashioned an excellent libretto out of the play, retaining all its grunge and ironic contrasts but with a taut craftsmanship that prevents the piece from falling over into the maudlin or exhausting us with self-pity. Puccini's score nears perfection. Technically daring and masterful, it belongs more to the advanced world of *Turandot* than to the earlier melodic outpouring of, say, *Bohème*. It may be Puccini's most "modern" piece, both musically and dramatically. This score has an economy to it that is impressive even among Puccini's corpus of work: there are "special effects," but used sparsely. There is melody in the score, but it too is used sparingly and for maximal effect to the drama rather than for its own sake. Given a charismatic baritone and attention to the smaller roles, the piece as a whole has a sweep and a dramatic inevitability that recall some of Wagner's best single acts.

Tabarro's Place in the Repertory

Tabarro was a true rarity for many years, the most unknown of the three *Trittico* operas (*Angelica* had the advantage of being occasionally sought out as a diva vehicle). Lately, besides the generally higher profile of *Trittico*, *Tabarro* has likewise been seen more and more often, often in curious double bills. It often appears with *Cavalleria rusticana* or *I pagliacci*, which seems like overkill. Even though both *Cavalleria* and *Pagliacci* are about murders, they have an organic symbiosis with each other that make them flow together, somehow, when they are performed together on a double bill. *Tabarro* is just different enough from those two operas, musically, to create a problem. It neither contrasts nor complements. Occasionally, *Tabarro* will be seen with a short opera of an entirely different nature: Opera North in England performed it with a reworking of a one-act Rossini comedy, while the fringe Montepulciano Festival in Italy recently paired it with Poulenc's *La Voix humaine*.

Cast of Characters

MICHELE (*baritone*): The owner of a barge on the Seine River, a man of about fifty. Michele is not a monster, but rather can be kind and patient with those around him. It is a plum of a role for a star baritone, the only lead Puccini wrote for the baritone range except for Gianni Schicchi. He must be able to communicate the man's transformation from a nice, average schmo to a homicidal maniac in less than an hour.

GIORGETTA (*soprano*): His younger wife, about twenty-five. Although not as vocally heavy as Suor Angelica (not to mention Minnie in *Fanciulla* or Butterfly), Giorgetta has the challenge of portraying someone who had had more than her age's portion of life's burdens, yet is still young enough to crave romantic love. She must be weary of life and want more of it at the same time. This is not something one can rightfully expect from a twenty-five-year-old soprano, so there is the additional challenge of looking the part as well.

LUIGI (*tenor*): Despite the brevity of the role, Luigi must also (like Giorgetta) be able to convince you that he is heartily sick of life and yet be convincing in his passionate outbursts. Star tenors will sometimes be found, and occasionally an up-and-coming tenor will claim his stardom with the role.

TINCA (*tenor*): A stevedore on Michele's barge, with an unfaithful wife and a propensity to drink. He is about thirty-five—that is, neither young enough to assert his desires nor old enough to be resigned to his lack of fulfillment. His name means "tench," a kind of fish, as in "he drinks like a . . ."

TALPA (*bass*): Another stevedore on Michele's barge, an older man of about fifty-five. His name means "mole," which is proverbial Italian for a dull man.

LA FRUGOLA (*mezzo-soprano*): Talpa's wife, a ragpicker and rummager through the trash cans of Paris. The name means "the frugal woman," but it also means an "imp" in Italian. Indeed, La Frugola is a character, and though she does not cause any impish trouble, she is full of little moments of philosophy and otherworldly observations. She is quite a refreshing character in opera—a mezzo who is neither a shrew nor an ancillary vocal part with no life of her own.

The Opera

Setting: A barge docked on a quay of the Seine River in Paris. There is a single act.

Giorgetta is doing her chores on the barge while the workmen are carrying sacks from the barge's hold to the quay. Michele is standing apart, silently, contemplating the sunset and the end of another hard workday. Sounds of the city interrupt the reverie—a car horn, the loud horn of a tugboat. Giorgetta suggests she offer the workers some wine. They worked so hard today, and emptied out the storeroom. Michele approves. Giorgetta is so good, always thinking of everything. Doesn't she have a thought for him? She claims not to know what he is talking about, but when he tries to kiss her, she avoids him. He goes below.

   Giorgetta calls over Luigi, Tinca, and Talpa, and pours them glasses of wine. Luigi calls over a strolling organ-grinder on the quay and asks for music. Giorgetta suggests she only cares for dance music. She looks at Luigi, but Tinca interrupts and offers to dance with her. He is clumsy and eventually steps on her foot. Luigi now takes Giorgetta in his arms and dances with her until the others warn that Michele is returning. The men return to work. Giorgetta asks Michele which of the men he will keep on for more work. Tinca? Talpa? Yes, both, answers Michele. And Luigi too. Luigi will starve if they don't keep him on. A song-peddler appears on the quay, followed by a group of girls. He sings the story of Mimì, who loves greatly but dies alone, abandoned. Meanwhile, Michele asks Giorgetta if he has ever beaten or abused her. No, she admits. It might be better if he did. Anything but his damned silence. What is it that bothers him? "Nothing," he mutters. "Nothing."

La Frugola arrives with her bags full of the day's scavenging. She gives Giorgetta the best loot of the day—a pretty comb. In another bag, she has a beef heart as a treat for her cat, Corporal. Ah, the cat is a perfect lover! Just purrs, never gets jealous, no scenes. How much better to eat an animal's heart than to sit around eating out your own for love! The men come on deck, and Michele asks Luigi to return to work the following day. He returns below.

Comment: Puccini insisted on raising the curtain in silence and then begin-ning the soft, insinuating music. It's the only time he ever opened an opera in silence, and it's a far cry from Tosca *or* Fanciulla. *The soft murmurs of the river become the underlying musical metaphor for the whole piece. The use of the automobile and tugboat horns is economical and superb. People rarely think of Puccini as a pioneer in the use of the grating sounds of mod-ern life in music, but this score predates the more famous uses of this idea by Hindemith and many others. If Puccini had been German, there'd be vol-umes of essays written on it. The tugboat is especially evocative, cutting across the background music like the Nightwatchman's horn in Wagner's* Meistersinger. *It seems to have some relation to Michele's brooding, as we will see again later. The organ-grinder's dance music is a study in bitonality, meaning two different keys playing at once. It sounds marvelously "off" and is an idea Puccini borrowed from Stravinsky's ballet* Petrouchka, *which he knew. The passing music peddler is another excellent touch, fraught with suggestion. His song is about Mimì, and Puccini drives home the point by quoting (but very cagily) a passage from her aria in* La bohème. *But here, Mimì dies abandoned and alone. A warning to the audience, perhaps, not to expect another* Bohème? *La Frugola is the "character" of the piece, an "amiable freak," in Budden's terms. She is usually played by an aging mezzo with a keen sense of camp. Her little solo about her cat "Caporale" is dis-turbingly formless, like the character herself, and includes a repetition of "ron, ron ron" (which is Italian for "purring").*

La Frugola berates Tinca for being a drunk, but Tinca defends his vice. Drinking beats thinking, he tells her, laughing cruelly. "You're right," says Luigi. Better not to think. Just bow your head and curve your back. For us, that's all there is. Every joy becomes pain. Better not let the higher-ups see you! Any love, any pleasure has to be stolen between spasms of pain and fear while the end of the workday becomes the beginning of the next. Bow your head, bend your back. . . . You're right, Tinca. Better not to think. Tinca feels vindicated, but Giorgetta tells them that's enough. Tinca goes in search of a bar.

Talpa suggests he and La Frugola leave as well. He's dead tired. But she needles him to quit this life and let them move to the country. "That's her fixation," remarks Giorgetta. "I've had this dream," La Frugola explains. A house, four walls around a small space, two pines for shade, the "old man" nearby, Corporal on her lap, all just waiting to die, and that solves everything. Giorgetta has a different dream—to live in the suburb of Belleville again, where she grew up. Luigi knows it. He was born there too, and they have the city life in their blood. To walk on sidewalks again instead of rivers, with the neighbors waiting for their loved ones to come home from work, everyone chatting, gossiping, walking arm in arm to the Bois de Boulogne! It's hard to explain this great homesickness, this melancholy. La Frugola understands. Life is different here at the river. Talpa tugs her to leave again. He is tired. They leave, musing on the little house, a couple of trees, the cat on the lap, waiting for death, which solves everything. . . .

Comment: Tinca begins to sing of the pleasures of drinking, and we think he is about to launch into a happy drinking song. No such luck: he cuts himself short with a bitter, hysterical laugh. It's not something we come across in Italian opera, and seems more like something we'd find in German expressionist drama (or even "Action's" psychotic laugh in the "Cool" number in West Side Story*). In the play, he goes off to kill his wife rather than get drunk. Adami and Puccini rightly toned down this detail, focusing the drama on the protagonists and adding to the realism and in a way*

*to the despair: in real life, people are generally incapable of any action to
escape their misery, even desperate action. La Frugola's little lines about
her ideal life are muttered mostly around a single note. In a way, she provides the key for the whole opera. A significant amount of this score is
built around "flat" vocal phrases that never "go" anywhere. The characters
are clearly "stuck" at these moments, as Giorgetta underscores when she
says this is La Frugola's "fissazione." Dreams are nothing but part of the
prison for these people. The present is even worse. Luigi's aria "*Hai ben
ragione,*" where he recounts the misery of their rotten lives, likewise is
constructed around monotonic phrases. This aria is devilishly difficult—
the monotones linger in the* passaggio—*and can be extremely effective. I
remember hearing a very good house tenor sing this role one night and
thinking, "Oh, that's nice." A few nights later, however, he was replaced by
a truly great star tenor and I was completely devastated. The star tenor did
not have more voice, he just knew that there was something more to this
passage than a young man kvetching. Smart man: if Puccini, of all people,
is avoiding gorgeous melody, there must be some reason brewing. Melody
comes along shortly, when Luigi and Giorgetta sing of their idealized
memories of their Belleville. These people are capable of feeling, but only
in certain moments of the imagination. Even this moment of melodic
imagination is cut short and broken, "stolen," as Luigi states, scored in
nervous triplets in the orchestra, framed again by a simple repetition of La
Frugola's little phrase. Reality never soars for these unhappy people.*

Two lovers pass on the quay, and a tugboat toots its horn in the distance. Alone, Luigi and Giorgetta kiss passionately, but she backs off.
Being discovered would mean death! Luigi does not care. Death
would be better than this sharing. They swear to be together, always.
Michele is coming, and Luigi backs off. He asks Michele to drop him
off at Rouen when the boat gets there. He wants out. Michele talks
him out of it. There's no work in Rouen. Fine, says Luigi. He will
continue to work for the boss. Michele returns downstairs to light the
lamps. Luigi takes Giorgetta in his arms. They promise to meet again
in an hour. She will give him the same signal—lighting a match—and

he will come aboard the boat. He wants no other man to have her. He shows her his knife. He would gladly kill any man who touched her, and with the drops of blood, make her a necklace. Luigi rushes away. Giorgetta remarks how hard it is to be happy.

Comment: The "love music" is represented by two other lovers passing by in the background. These two only sing "la la la" as they pass, effectually mocking any hope of love for Luigi and Giorgetta and perhaps parodying the idea of love itself. Even with two more chances for a love duet, Puccini denies any sense of fulfillment to Luigi and Giorgetta. There is melody here—real feeling, that is—but it wanders elsewhere rather than forming a cogent whole as in Madama Butterfly. *The climax is Luigi's grotesque outburst about his knife and the blood-necklace he'll make for Giorgetta. Again, the whole long phrase is divided between a mere two notes, E and F-sharp, the* passaggio. *The inherent emotionality is present, but we know even this depraved fantasy is nothing but a fruitless attempt to escape the present reality. It isn't "going" anywhere. As a "coda" to this, Giorgetta mutters "com'è difficile esser felice" in a sort of sigh ("sospirando"), again with an interval of only two notes (C-sharp, D-sharp), but at the bottom of the soprano register. The sense of pure "letdown" must be unique in the annals of operatic "love scenes."*

Budden can't resist a bit of moralizing over Giorgetta's sigh. Of course it's difficult to be happy, he says, if one wants it both ways, as she does. Well, true, in a perfect world, but this negates the careful scene-painting with which Puccini sets up the characters' situation, as careful a sociological portrait as any I can think of in lyric theater. It also misses one of the chief hallmarks of verismo, in all its forms: namely, that happiness is elusive. Unseen forces conspire against it—social codes, in Cavalleria rusticana; poverty, in the film Bicycle Thief. The same idea is very much central to Dante's Divine Comedy, which, I maintain, has more in common with Il trittico than most commentators imagine. Several characters in the Inferno command our sympathy. They are not damned because they are "bad." They are damned because it is very, very difficult to be saved. The most notable of these characters is, of course, Francesca da

Rimini, the subject of D'Annunzio's play, which Puccini considered set-
ting as an opera and which was used by Riccardo Zandonai. This may, in
fact, be the very essence of verismo, and the reason why Zandonai's opera
is often categorized as such despite its grand opera format. Think again of
Bicycle Thief. *The "hero" tries to be good, and fails, even though we are*
given glimpses of opportunities when he might have changed his destiny.
Yet can anybody "blame" him for snapping? Moralizing seems superflu-
ous. The purpose of these stories is not to show us what people should do,
but the poignancy of what we actually do in real life.

Michele comes on deck, lighting lamps. They discuss work. Perhaps
there are too many men. Giorgetta suggests letting Tinca go. He's
always drunk. "His wife's a whore," says Michele. "He drinks so he
doesn't kill her." Then suddenly he asks why Giorgetta doesn't love
him anymore. She protests that she does, but it's so hot down in the
boat, she can't sleep there. He reminds her of their old life, how she
loved him, how he would wrap her and the baby in his cloak, rocking
them both, in those days before the baby died. She tells him to be
quiet. She can't bear to think of those days. He begs her to come
back, back to his love, and back to her old self. "We're older now,"
she says bluntly. Things have changed. "We've changed." She bids
him good night, and goes downstairs.

"Whore," he mutters. The pair of lovers sings in the distance, and
the bugle call from the barracks sounds from afar. Michele peeks in
the cabin. She is there, still dressed, waiting. But who is she waiting
for? Talpa? Too old. Tinca? Too drunk. Luigi? But he asked to be let
go at Rouen. Anger overcomes Michele. How he longs to discover
her lover and confront him, and say to his face, "It's you! It's you!"
before he kills him. And then there would be death, and peace. He
lights his pipe. Seeing the match, Luigi jumps on board. Michele
grabs him and forces him to admit he loves Giorgetta. Luigi denies it
while Michele's hands tighten around his neck. "Admit it," says Luigi,
"and I'll let you live!" "I love her!" Luigi gasps, and Michele strangles
him to death.

Giorgetta comes up on deck. Michele throws his cloak around Luigi's corpse. Giorgetta can't sleep. She is frightened. Can she sit with Michele? "Wrapped in my cloak?" Yes, she answers. It's like he always used to say. . . . Every man's cloak hides a joy and a sorrow. "And sometimes," Michele adds, "a crime!" He reveals Luigi's corpse and forces Giorgetta down onto her dead lover.

Comment: Michele begins his reverie of the happy days within the mono- tone format, almost a lullaby. He develops into melody, though, signify- ing that he too can only come alive within selected memories. The score directs the baritone toward "crescendo" and "allargando," growing and lengthening the phrase. It ends with his plea to Giorgetta, "resta vicino a me, la nott'è bella!" It is a beautiful phrase all sung on G, the baritone's passaggio—emotional and pulsing, but monotonic nonetheless. He is back in flat present, where hopes "go" nowhere. She answers in low monotones: people grow old. Her rejoinder is the nail in the coffin of his hopes. His comment "squaldrina!" ("whore") is muttered rather than sung or yelled. It is, however, the departure point for his soliloquy, which is the high point of this remarkable score. Its rare accomplishment is in showing a character develop, think, and change points of view rather than the usual function of an aria, which explores a single emotional state. Here, the various condi- tions morph as seamlessly as anything in opera, with pizzicato strings for his "thinking" music, and contrast of interior thoughts with exterior effects (the subtle bugle call, like a call to action, and the "la la la's" of the passing lovers again, this time a thorough mockery of Michele's condition). When he expresses his longing to confront the lover, he comes truly alive at last. His soaring vocal line is scored against a rush of all the strings playing descend- ing chromatic figures in thirty-second notes. That sounds a bit like sliding the finger (rapidly!) down the strings, but in fact it's much more difficult than that since the written notes are not exactly sequential. I have no idea how musicians manage such feats of legerdemain, but the effect is astound- ing: it's as if Michele's soul is being sucked into the depths of the rushing river, or into hell, even as his spirit (voice) rises into an ecstasy of killing. The business of the murder is handled very quickly, which is appropriate.

*Depicting a man working himself up to murder is a much richer domain for
an opera composer than the actual murder itself. (If only Hollywood could
grasp this same insight!) Hiding Luigi's body in the cloak is an absolute
nightmare to stage without falling into slapstick, but it can come off if the
baritone is large enough to hide a tenor under his overcoat. In any case, the
scene is dark and the orchestra thunders out the final chords while the curtain rapidly descends. Whatever the problems might be in staging the details
of the actual murder, the overall arch of the work is superbly crafted and
supremely effective. In less than an hour, there is a thoroughly convincing
depiction of a man driven to murder, and also of a man, in a sense, driven to
being murdered. The power of the action is also heightened by the sudden
curtain. There is no denouement, as in* Carmen, *or even a view of the effect
of this murder on the community, as in* Cavalleria rusticana. *There is nothing but the intractability of human damnation. When people attempt to
sound educated by belittling the range of Puccini's art, it is always effective
to ask them when they last attended a good performance of* Tabarro.

Suor Angelica

The Name and How to Pronounce It

The first work is a lot like the English word "swore." It means "sister"
and is a common title for nuns in Italy. Angelica has a soft "g," accent
on the second syllable.

What is Suor Angelica?

Suor Angelica is a unique opera, a single act of all women (except for a
touch of men's chorus in the very end). Nowhere is Puccini's preference for the soprano voice more in evidence, not only in the casting of

all women but in the role of Angelica herself. Consequently, it has become something of a vehicle for prima donna sopranos of the old school, those who can wring an audience's collective neck with their combinations of vocal presence, acting gifts, and sheer chutzpah. Alas, there aren't a lot of those around these days, and performances of *Angelica* and the opera's reputation tend to suffer for it. The opera itself is admittedly problematic. It tells the story of a young nun who, we find out in the course of the work, was shut up in a severe convent by her noble family as a punishment for having hooked up with an unsuitable young man. A child was born of this union, and this child has been taken away from Angelica. Whether or not Angelica had married this man is not discussed and is not important for the present story. In many ways, *Suor Angelica* is a protracted mad scene, with all the challenges of that genre of expression. The climax of the work is especially difficult, since it might be a mad scene or it might be an actual miracle, which is always a difficult thing to pull off onstage. More than any other Puccini, even more than *Butterfly*, *Angelica*'s success depends entirely on the performance of the title role.

Angelica's *Place in the Repertory*

Angelica has a life, barely, outside of *Il trittico*, and is often seen in smaller companies and at the universities. One reason for this is that women who sing are easier to come by in this country than men who sing, and it is easier to round out the ensemble for this work than for, say, *Billy Budd*. Its pairings in non-*Trittico* performances are even more recherché than those of *Tabarro*. Of course, it is often paired with the inevitable *Cavalleria* and *Pagliacci*, but has been given recently with such divergent works as Ravel's *L'Enfant et les Sortilèges* and Mozart's *Bastien und Bastienne*. This reflects the difficulty in categorizing *Angelica*: it's hard to call it verismo, yet the score has a verismo feel to it that is hard to avoid (and harder to perform). It will always be called on the carpet for its sentimentality. Even the performance of the prima donna will only go so far since she does not sing in the climax. Stage directors feel obliged to interpret the "miracle" in any number of ways, from a hallucination to breakdown to an outright heroin overdose (which I've never actually seen, but would not doubt in the least that it has been done). Still, the very centrality of the lead role and its extraordinary demands, and the various and magnificent methods employed by the greatest sopranos to meet them, assure that *Angelica* will always hold a high place of honor among the most devoted Puccini fans.

Cast of Characters

SUOR ANGELICA (*soprano*): She is about twenty-five, and must convey a sense of mystery about her in both presence and voice.

LA ZIA PRINCIPESSA (*contralto*): Puccini's unique foray into the contralto voice, and perhaps the single biggest bitch in all opera (no mean accomplishment).

SUOR GENOVEFFA (*soprano*): Although not as young as many of the nuns in this cast, Genoveffa has a sweet disposition and therefore is portrayed by a soprano.

SUOR OSMINA (*soprano*): A young nun who has a weakness for beautiful flowers.

SUOR DOLCINA (*soprano*): A very innocent young nun, whose guilty pleasure is tasty morsels.

THE ABBESS (*mezzo-soprano*): A figure of authority, full of understated gravitas.

THE MISTRESS OF NOVICES (*mezzo-soprano*): No particular type of voice is required for this worthy sister beyond a sense of decorum.

THE SISTER MONITOR (*mezzo-soprano*): The "Sora Zelatrice" voices the severity that is the soul of this convent, although there is no need (as one often sees) to overdo the role and play her as a dominatrix.

THE NURSING SISTER (*mezzo-soprano*): This mezzo gets to sing one of the few phrases of excitement, an undecorous energy in the score, and her voice should stand out like an alarm.

TWO NOVICES (*sopranos*): Young and innocent, nothing more.

THE ALMS SISTERS (*sopranos*): As the sisters who go out into the world to beg, these two sopranos chatter a bit and talk about food, and have earthier music than the other sisters.

TWO LAY SISTERS (*soprano/mezzo-soprano*)

The Opera

Setting: The action takes place in a convent in northern Italy in the seventeenth century. There is a single act.

Bells announce the beginning of prayers, and the nuns are heard from inside the chapel singing an "Ave Maria." Sister Angelica is heard singing more fervently than the others. Two novices rush toward the chapel, late. They hesitate for a moment to listen to a bird singing, then enter. The sung prayers continue, after which the sisters emerge into the garden. The Sister Monitor hands out the penances: for the two novices who were late and neglected to kiss the chapel threshold as a sign of contrition, twenty prayers for the afflicted. For Sister Lucilla, who made everybody laugh in chapel, some spinning in silence. And Sister Osmina, who hid a flower in her sleeve and then impudently denies it, is confined to her cell. She is ordered not to delay—the Virgin is watching! The other sisters pray for Osmina. Penances dispensed, the Abbess grants an hour of recreation.

Comment: Four measures of a simple bell tolling, and the curtain rises, the bell theme moving to a celesta (a kind of spooky-sounding keyboard glockenspiel) and drawn out by the strings. It is a serene, if not severe, mood that lasts throughout the opening. The nuns' singing is likewise austere, with only Angelica departing from the strict division of harmony. It is another case of Puccini making us listen to the soprano before we can see her, as in Bohème, Tosca, *and* Butterfly, *although even more important here. Once the stage is filled with the nuns, there is nothing visual to set her apart, and we will need the "sound bite" to distinguish her, visually and emotionally, from the others. The Sister Monitor makes clear the severity of the community—this is no country-club convent.*

Angelica tends to the garden while the others admire the sunset. Sister Genevieve explains that this is the time of the Golden Fountain, the three days a year in May when the sun hits the water directly as they leave the chapel in the evening, turning the water gold. But since that happened last year, a sister has died. They all think about the departed sister for a moment. Sister Genoveffa suggests they take some of the golden water and bless the sister's grave with it. The others praise the suggestion, except Angelica. The dead have no desires, because the Virgin anticipates them all. "Sister," she explains to Genoveffa. "Death is life made beautiful!" The Sister Monitor expounds that even in life, desire must be mortified. "Even innocent desire?" asks Genoveffa. She was once a shepherdess, and sometimes longs to feel a soft, bleating lamb against her breast. If this is a sin, may Christ, who is the only Lamb she should desire, forgive her. This prompts Sister Dolcina to begin a confession of her own, but the others interrupt. They know she likes tasty food! And what about

Angelica? No desires? "No!" she answers. Now they pray God to forgive Angelica her lie, because they know she has a great desire for
news from home. They know she was a noblewoman when she was in
the world, but in seven years has never received a single visitor. What
is she being punished for? The Nursing Sister runs in from the infir-
mary, asking Angelica, who is so knowledgeable about herbs, to gather
some for another sister who has been stung by wasps. Angelica immediately prepares a remedy and the Nursing Sister withdraws, praising
Angelica's skill with herbs and flowers.

*Comment: Our first glimpse of Angelica in action shows that she is on
a separate spiritual plane from the others. She is even more zealous in
her mortification of desire than the Sister Monitor, not even allowing
Genoveffa her poignant moment to hold a little lamb (little bleats in
the orchestra bring home the moment). Her phrase around "Death is
life made beautiful" becomes an important theme later.*

The Alms Sisters enter with their gifts: it was a good day for collec-
tions! Lentils, bread, nuts, even some red currants, which they dis-
tribute as a treat. They casually mention that there is a magnificent
coach outside the walls. Some rich, noble visitor is with the Abbess.
Angelica nervously asks questions. What were the arms on the carriage? What colors? The Alms Sisters did not notice, only that it
looked rich. The other nuns pray that the visitor will be for Angelica.
The Abbess enters, calling Sister Angelica and dismissing the others.
Angelica presses her for information, but the Abbess orders Angelica
to master her emotions. "I am calm and obedient," replies Angelica.
"Your aunt, the Princess," the Abbess announces, withdrawing.

   The old Princess enters, offering her hand for Angelica to kiss but
never once looking at her. The Princess icily explains the reason for
her visit. When Angelica's parents died twenty years ago, they left
her, the Princess, in charge of the estate. Now she wishes to divide
the estate. She presents the document. Angelica is to read it, discuss
it, sign it. Angelica searches the Princess's face in vain for any sign of

affection. After seven years, doesn't this sacred place move her? This place of mercy, of forgiveness . . . "Of penance!" interrupts the Princess. The only reason for her visit now is because of the business matter. She wishes to divide the estate to provide a dowry for Angelica's sister. "Little Anna Viola is to be married!" Angelica cries out. But to whom? To one who found it possible to overlook the stain Angelica brought on the family honor, is the Princess's cold reply. "Oh, sister of my mother," Angelica erupts angrily, "you are unrelenting!" "How dare you invoke your mother against me!" is the Princess's answer. Calming herself, she explains that she often visits her dead sister's grave, and somehow they seem to be able to talk. And in their conversations, one word is repeated . . . "Repent! Repent!" Angelica must offer unceasing expiation to the Virgin. For seven years, Angelica answers, she has offered everything to the Virgin—everything except one thing: the memory of her son. That she cannot give up. She demands news of her son. The Princess is silent. Angelica warns her aunt that the Virgin is watching, and the aunt will be damned forever if she does not answer her question. "Two years ago," the Princess replies, "he came down with a fever. Everything possible was done for him. . . ." "Dead!" Angelica exclaims, collapsing and sobbing. The Princess moves toward her, but steadies herself with prayer. She calls for a desk, pen, and ink, which are brought in. Angelica signs the document. The Princess collects it, and, as she is leaving, turns toward Angelica, who recoils from her. At the threshold, she glances again at Angelica, but says nothing. After a moment, she leaves.

Comment: The chirpy music of the Alms Sisters grinds down to the oppressive musical palette of the confrontation scene. Puccini wrote elaborate stage instructions for the Princess's entrance, the most elaborate, in fact, that he ever specified. The upshot is that Angelica moves; the Princess does not, except to enter, staring straight ahead and never once meeting Angelica's eye. The Princess, the only true contralto role Puccini ever wrote, is introduced in the orchestra by string figures in C-sharp minor, which terminate in a muted horn chorus in C minor. This is a dissonance that can set your teeth on edge in an instant. Her vocal palette is built around chromatic increments. It creates an effect Girardi rightly calls both "snakelike" and suggesting a "motionless figure whom time has frozen in a past full of hidden rancor." Very true and perceptive. Or you can just listen and know instinctively that this woman is one mean old bitch. Several commentators have cruelly cited Puccini's wife Elvira as a model for the Princess, which seems excessive (though perhaps not). Despite the brevity of the role, it is a plum for contraltos or campy mezzos who can at least fake a good chest voice. There is no aria, much less a duet. Her lines are basically declamatory, many of them on the same single note pattern that was so prominent in Il tabarro, *though they tend to end on downward plunges in the register. Vocally, she is the millstone around the neck of Angelica, whose efforts to "rise up" are futile. The denouement is remarkably subdued.*

Angelica, alone in the almost-dark garden, thinks of her lost son. Without a mother, he died, never knowing a mother's love. But now he is an angel in heaven. When can she see him again? She begs him to speak to her, speaking of love.

Comment, aria, "Senza mamma": Angelica's aria is hardly an aria at all. It is more of a narrative, and it's one of Puccini's great accomplishments. One keeps expecting it to turn into "Vissi d'arte" or "Un bel dì," but it keeps fooling the listener, changing melodic and emotional direction in every measure. The aria, like the character who sings it, has lost its center. It is structured in two parts. The first part shows Angelica demonstrating some emotion. Then, just when we would expect fireworks from another composer (or a younger Puccini), a great sense of calm takes over. Puccini wrote the second part after the New York premiere. The vocal line soars in G major (a "bright" key), but the muted orchestra recalls the Zia Principessa's prayer in the previous scene—an awesome example of sublime fantasy departing from reality and taking leave of dreary reason.

The sisters pass through the dark garden, telling Angelica that the Virgin has heard her prayer. Angelica agrees: grace is falling down from heaven. She runs off to her cell, repeating from afar that grace has come down from heaven. All is quiet and the garden is empty. Soon, Angelica reappears, picking flowers and preparing them into a potion. The flowers were always her friends, she notes. Now they will provide the poison for her. Her son has called her. She says farewell to her sisters, who are in their cells, and, embracing the foot of the cross, drinks the poison. Anguished, she cries out, "Ah! I am damned!" She begs the Virgin to forgive her for this mortal sin for love of her innocent son. She hears the choirs of angels interceding for her, and begs for a sign of grace. Light radiates from the chapel door, and the Virgin appears, with a small child. The child takes three steps toward Angelica, who reaches for him and dies.

Comment: "Grace" *is depicted in the orchestra by great swirls on the harps and muted trumpets. It is grace but also madness, as Angelica herself says when she is praying desperately shortly afterward. In fact, grace and madness seem very subtly connected at this point. Angelica repeats her desperate pleas for salvation while the choir is singing, her voice rising higher and settling firmly over the staff, yet this scene is more effective if it avoids falling over into the shrill. Puccini calls out all the musical forces for the finale: two pianos, organ, glockenspiel, celesta, triangle, bass drum, cymbals, and the rest of the traditional orchestra, and yet the melodic framework is surprisingly restrained for the miracle. He's been roundly trashed for it ever since the premiere. He once referred to this moment as the "Royal March of the Madonna" and commentators have understood his flippancy to signify that he did not believe in the moment himself. The New York Times critic at the premiere likened the effect to "an illuminated Christmas card" and faulted it for false religiosity. Only Girardi, among the commentators, figured out that the moment is not religious at all but psychological, so there's no need to accuse it of spiritual shortcomings. Parsifal this isn't, nor is it trying to be. Puccini fulminated against this finale being "misunderstood," but unlike Wagner he did not write two dozen volumes of paranoid prose to attempt to explain it. Again, a referral to Dante might help clarify: if this episode of* Il trittico *is analogous to the* Purgatorio, *then we are in the realm of process, not resolution. And it is worth noting that the* Purgatorio *climaxes with a march in the form of a resplendent procession. It is the Church on parade, so to speak, culminating in the figure of Beatrice as a representative of the Virgin. None of this is otherwordly in Dante's understanding: the Church is a "vehicle" to get this world into the next. There is no Church in* Paradiso *since there's no need for one. Wagner was working outside of this paradigm in* Parsifal. *I, for one, admire Puccini's and Forzano's solution here precisely because it is a human process rather than a cosmic event. It brings to mind Verdi's* Requiem, *which resolutely rejects answering the question of what happens after death and focuses instead on the poignancy of the human need for salvation. Yet all this can clash, it must be admitted, with what we see on the stage. It falls to the soprano to make this convincing, in her final vocal lines and then in her acting. Expect to see anything—absolutely anything— onstage as a prima donna attempts to communicate a moment that lies somewhere between a mental breakdown and a transcendent miracle.*

Gianni Schicchi

The Name and How to Pronounce It

Gianni Schicchi is a man's name, Gianni being a very common abbreviation of Giovanni. Schicchi is pronounced "SKEE-kee." Gianni presents more problems to Americans. It's two syllables, not three: "JAH-nee." On the television series *Everybody Loves Raymond*, there is a character named Gianni, and the cast stress the three syllables, "gee-AH-nee," to signal, presumably, that his name is not "Johnny." It's a strange dynamic: trying to honor Italian culture by violating it. Gianni Versace got the same treatment, as does Jason Giambi (attention sports announcers!). Don't emulate them. Pronounce Gianni correctly and score big points for international détente and diversity sensitivity.

What is Gianni Schicchi?

Gianni Schicchi is an ensemble comedy in one act, an acknowledged masterpiece of Italian opera. The structural model is clearly Verdi's *Falstaff*, which has impressed musicians and audiences alike since its premiere. Speech patterns form the basis for the sung music. Melody is present but, for the most part, it is formless and morphs organically with the situation on the stage, without discernible breaks between recitative, solos, ensembles, and so forth. Puccini did interject two set arias in *Gianni Schicchi*, one of which is perhaps his most familiar melody, but the ensemble spirit pervades the balance of the work. In addition, he infused the score with a light insouciance that not even the august *Falstaff* can claim. It is a thoroughly satisfying work.

Schicchi's *Place in the Repertory*

When performed within *Il trittico*, *Schicchi* is almost always the audience's favorite of the three. It also has a healthy life outside of the *Trittico*. It has been paired with many different operas to form a full evening's entertainment. Some of the pairings, even in major companies, have been bizarre: Bartók's *Bluebeard's Castle* (huh?) and, my personal favorite bad idea, Richard Strauss's *Salome*. Mind-boggling. Small companies and universities love to perform *Schicchi* since, although the lead role soars in the hands of seasoned pros, it can still succeed with a rookie cast. The tenor role is small and can be accomplished by a lighter *leggiero* tenor, which is much, much easier to find than the usual Puccinian tenor requirements. Besides, it is an easy opera for audiences to swallow, and *Schicchi* gets trotted out frequently by many ensembles trying to find that elusive "new audience" out there. Sometimes the earnestness can be overwhelming. You can almost feel these companies saying, "Look, see? This opera stuff is really great fun!" However, there is a darkness in this opera, Puccini's only actual comedy, that prevents it from cloying and is in fact part of what makes it quite irresistible.

Cast of Characters

BUOSO DONATI (*corpse*): That's right, a corpse, present onstage for the whole first half of the opera. This is among the easiest roles in Puccini's operas to cast.

GIANNI SCHICCHI (*baritone*): A rich Florentine of the emerging merchant class. Any variety of baritone voice will work in the role, but it is essential that he have the gift of diction (not very common) and a serious sense of timing.

LAURETTA (*soprano*): His twenty-one-year-old daughter. Lighter soprano voices will work in this role too, and she must sound young, but a little heft will make her showstopping aria more than a bit of fluff.

ZITA, LA VECCHIA (*contralto*): "The Old Lady," Buoso's cousin, about sixty years old. A chance for a contralto to camp it up. Zita makes an interesting contrast to the Zia Principessa in *Suor Angelica*, yet the two roles are not always played by the same contralto.

RINUCCIO (*tenor*): Zita's twenty-four-year-old nephew. This role is also amenable to *leggiero* voices, yet it has been sung by Plácido Domingo and, more recently, Roberto Alagna. As with Edmondo in

Manon Lescaut, Rinuccio must be young and bumptious, which is harder to portray than most tenors assume. His attempts to be young and bumptious can be a trial on one's nerves, and the clip-clop nature of his aria does nothing to mitigate this potential problem.

GHERARDO (*tenor*): Buoso's cousin, forty years old.

NELLA (*soprano*): Gherardo's wife.

GHERARDINO (*contralto*): Their son, seven years old. Try to find a good contralto who can pass as a seven-year-old boy. No wonder opera producers tend to be such nervous wrecks.

SIMONE (*bass*): Buoso's cousin, seventy years old. The basso buffo (comic bass) role is a stock-in-trade of the bel canto tradition.

MARCO (*baritone*): Simone's son, about forty-five.

LA CIESCA (*mezzo-soprano*): Marco's wife, thirty-eight years old.

BETTO DI SEGNA (*bass*): Buoso's brother-in-law, a "poor unkempt person of uncertain age."

SER AMANTIO DE NICOLOA (*baritone*): A lawyer.

MAESTRO SPINELLOCCIO (*bass*): The doctor always has a Bolognese accent, since the University of Bologna was the chief medical school of the Middle Ages. The doctor with the Bolognese accent is one of the stock characters of the commedia dell'arte tradition.

PINELLINO (*bass*): A shoemaker.

GUCCIO (*bass*): A dyer.

The Opera

The relatives are loudly mourning the death of Buoso Donati, who lies motionless in his bed. They each try to outdo the others in demonstrations of grief. Betto whispers something in Nella's ear. "Really?" she asks, surprised. "It's what they're saying at Signa!" Betto answers. Others ask Betto what it is they're saying at Signa. He whispers in La Ciesca's ear, who is as shocked as Nella, and then in Marco's ear. Zita la vecchia demands to know the secret. Betto blurts out that the gossips at Signa say Buoso left all his fortune to a convent. The relatives can't believe this, and turn to Simone. Simone explains that if the will has already been filed with a notary, there could well be a problem. They all look high and low for the will, and in the confusion Rinuccio expresses a wish in an aside that matters will work out so that he can marry his beloved Lauretta. Betto finds some silver but no will. Soon all the drawers and closets are emptied, to no avail. Rinuccio finds the will: jumping up and down, he yells out his discovery, but before handing it to Zita he demands a promise that, if everything works out well, he can marry Lauretta, Gianni Schicchi's daughter, who has no dowry. Zita answers him evasively and snatches the will as the relatives gather around. Rinuccio quietly bribes Gherardino to find Schicchi and Lauretta and bring them back with him. Zita reads. The rumors were true! Everything is to go to the monks at the Santa Reparata monastery! All imagine the monks living well off their inheritance and laughing with scorn at the impoverished Donati family. If only the will could be changed! Not even wise old Simone has any idea what to do.

Comment: The brief orchestral introduction sets the tone of the opera: heavy on the pizzicato strings and little tweets in the winds. Light rhythm has been the marker of comedy in Italian opera for centuries. Nothing is going to be too serious here. This sets up the initial scene of the mourning relatives. We know their grief is false from the introduction, but also from the contrasting heavy-handedness of the scoring (little descending phrases consciously recalling the death chant "Miserere" from Verdi's Il trovatore*). The phrases are shorter here, however. They never soar because they're not real. Anyone who has ever doubted the sincerity of a mourner at a funeral, especially an Italian funeral, will find the parody apparent and delicious. The voices are introduced individually. Even in ensembles, the soloists tend to sing a beat or two apart from each other, and we have a perfect picture of several people working at cross-purposes. When Rinuccio demands recognition of his right to marry Lauretta, he does so in an expansive lyrical phrase that will repeat at interesting times later in the opera. The relatives sing in unison when they deplore the monks getting "their" money. These people are only on the same page when they are united in hate.*

Rinuccio suggests they get advice from the clever Gianni Schicchi. Zita sneers at the very name: these peasants who come to Florence and get rich are the bane of respectable noble families like theirs! The relatives concur: Schicchi is an upstart, a mere parvenu! How could one of the Donati marry a peasant's daughter? Rinuccio defends Schicchi: he's smart and knows all the tricks of the law. So what if he's from the countryside? Florence is like a blossoming tree, with trunk and branches spreading out from the Piazza della Signoria, with new roots growing out to keep it nourished and strong, able to reach for the skies with its slender towers! The Arno runs by, singing and kissing the Piazza Santa Croce, bringing in its course new men learned in the arts and sciences: Giotto from shady Mugello, and the Medici. Long live the new men and Gianni Schicchi!

Comment, scene and aria, "Firenze è com'un albero fiorito": Rinuccio's solo is in two distinct parts. In the first, "Avete torto" ("You're all wrong!"), he sings a little theme that will be recalled later when Schicchi's "wheels are turning," so to speak. The second part, "Firenze è com'un albero fiorito" ("Florence is like a blossoming tree") is written as a Tuscan stornello, or folk song, typically sung to a flower. It is in 6/8 time (that is, clip/clop). In America, this rhythm is instinctively associated with cowboy ballads and the country-western songs derived from them, and therefore is at a slight disadvantage. Indeed, the aria has never been as popular in America as in Italy. (Of course, the words are very flattering to the Italian identity, which may account for the difference in popularity as well.) It always works better when the tenor strives for a certain legato quality and does not let the bounciness of the 6/8 beat force him to punch out the notes. It is, in any case, an aria of small scale, and there's no use decrying the presence of an aria here in this ensemble piece since it is woven rather skillfully into the surrounding score.

Schicchi arrives, impressed at the family's genuine grief concerning Buoso's death, and soon finds the true explanation for their tears in the disinheritance. Schicchi and Zita exchange unpleasantries, and their argument heats up. Schicchi refuses to help such people, despite Rinuccio's urgent pleadings. Lauretta speaks to her father: dearest Daddy, she says, she wants to go to Porta Rossa and buy her wedding ring. Yes, yes! She wants to go there, and if she can't, she'll go to the Ponte Vecchio instead and throw herself in the Arno! She is struggling, she is tormented. Won't Daddy have pity on her?

Comment, aria, "O mio babbino caro": From the night of the premiere to the present day, the critics and audiences have been at war over this moment: the critics deploring the inclusion of a flat-out aria in an otherwise seamless ensemble opera, and the audience eating up the irresistible tune. Indeed, the tune, hammered into the world's consciousness by the film A Room with a View *(shortly after it entered the public domain) is probably at this point even more ubiquitous than "Musetta's Waltz" from* Bohème. *It constantly appears in television commercials, hawking everything from champagne to bargain tours to Italy. (Oh the humanity!) Yet to my knowledge no one has ever questioned why Puccini thought to include it here. Critics insist it was a concession to popular taste, while fans docilely accept it as a concession. It is more than a pretty tune. It is a consciously forthright one as well. The structure draws attention to its formality: First line (A), second line (A with a soaring conclusion), third line (A repeated without vocal accompaniment in the strings—a very old trick here), and fourth line (A without a soaring conclusion, ending on the same note where it began). Not even* Bohème, *the mother lode of melody, dared such a simple structure for any of its solos. One must turn to the most rudimentary hymnals to find anything analogous. It sets Lauretta apart from everyone else as a pure character, simple, to be sure, and untainted by any "art" or artifice. It is also very obviously old-fashioned, which may at first glance seem a curious choice for the ingenue. It is, in fact, nostalgic, playing on the audience's nostalgia for youth and youthful delusions of love and for everything that has been swept away (including, perhaps, opera that uses melody). It is the very center of the opera, which alone tells us something. The man who wrote* "Senza mamma" *could certainly have written something else at this point had he wanted to avoid charges of debasing his art.*

Schicchi takes the assignment, prudently sending his daughter out onto the terrace. He gives orders: remove Buoso's body. There is a knock on the door and Schicchi hides behind the bed curtains. The doctor Spinelloccio enters and asks after his patient. Schicchi imitates Buoso's voice, faintly, and insists he's doing much better. The doctor can leave now and return in the evening. Spinelloccio brags about his own medical prowess and exits. Schicchi bursts forth, praising his own skill. He divulges his plan. Rinuccio must get a notary. Schicchi will put on Buoso's gown and nightcap, get in the sickbed, and dictate a new will, leaving everything to the family. The delighted relatives are in perfect agreement about the division of the cash and minor items but begin to bicker over the three prizes of the inheritance: the house in Florence, the mills at Signa, and the best mule in Tuscany. A death knell rings from afar. Can news of Buoso's death have made it outside of the house? No, it turns out to be for the majordomo of a rich neighbor. In relief, the relatives agree to leave the disposition of the three prize items to Schicchi. As Schicchi is getting dressed as Buoso, each of the relatives passes by him and offers him a bribe for one of the prize possessions. He assents to every offer. Zita, Nella, and La Ciesca assist Schicchi in changing clothes, flattering him for his brains, his looks, his goodness. Before he hides behind the bed curtains, Schicchi reminds them all of the penalty for falsifying a will: a hand cut off and exile from Florence! Banished from the divine Tuscan sky and forced to wander like a Ghibelline! Do they all understand this well? He makes them repeat the penalty, and they mutter: Farewell, divine sky of Tuscany!

Comment: When Schicchi bursts forth after the doctor's exit, he sings fortissimo and in short phrases. This is the New Man who is going to define the Florence that will shortly rock the whole world with its creativity. If there were ever a moment for a fireworks aria for the baritone, this would be it. Yet it is only artful recitative. So much for concessions to public taste. The passing relatives offering bribes is accomplished with a delicious stealth and sense of ritual as Schicchi replies "E sia" ("so be it") to each one. The real highlight of the scene, and of the score for many people, is the marvelously lyric trio for the three women as they flatter Schicchi. In its lush harmony, the trio is a parody of every female seduction in opera, made comic by the cloying tune, the setup of these characters' music at the beginning of the opera, and their combined advanced (for operatic seductresses) age. There is much harmony in the orchestra's winds, drawing attention to the insubstantial nature of their words. The little harp glissandi even put Ashcroft in mind of Wagner's Rhinemaidens, who are also, in a sense, seductresses. Schicchi's subsequent spelling out of the penalty for falsifying a will is a sad tune built on a descending phrase, a classic trope of lovers' parting. The lover in this case is, of course, Florence, whose beguiling nature is at the center of the plot. The Ghibellines were banished from Florence by this point in history, as were half the victorious Guelfs within three years of the date of the setting. Exile was a real fate for many Florentines, and Dante, who would experience it, found it the worst imaginable punishment.

Rinuccio returns with the notary, Ser Amantio, and two witnesses, Pinellino the shoemaker and Guccio the dyer. The notary mutters in Latin: "In the name of our God Jesus Christ in the 1,299th year of his salvific incarnation, I . . ." and so on. Schicchi, as Buoso, announces also in (bad) Latin that he is nullifying, revoking, and provoking any previous wills. The relatives praise this foresight. Schicchi sets aside two florins for his funeral, and all praise his modesty. He leaves a mere five lire to the monks at Santa Reparata, and is praised for his piety. Ser Amantio asks if this sum is perhaps too little, but Schicchi insists that people gossip if you leave too much money to the Church. The relatives agree with his wisdom. He divides the money among the relatives, and gives them each a little prize: some fields in Prato, and so forth. They all thank him and mutter that now the three big plums are coming: the mule, the house, and the mills. Schicchi bequeathes the mule, the best in Tuscany, to . . . his devoted friend Gianni Schicchi! What's that? the relatives ask. The notary repeats the bequest in Latin. Simone asks why Gianni Schicchi would want the mule, and Schicchi slyly replies that he knows better than Simone what Gianni Schicchi wants. He then bequeaths the house in Florence to . . . his dear, devoted, loving friend Gianni Schicchi! All grumble loudly but Schicchi reminds them, "Farewell Florence, divine sky!" And as for the mills at Signa (farewell Florence!), to his loving friend Gianni Schicchi! *Ecce fatto!* He instructs Zita to pay the notary twenty florins from her purse and the notary and the witnesses leave, praising Buoso's goodness. The relatives turn on Schicchi: thief! traitor! knave! trickster! wicked! He casts them all out of the house, and they continue the abuse, taking whatever silver they can get their hands on as they leave. Rinuccio takes Lauretta by the hand to the window. Isn't Florence beautiful? He points out Fiesole on the distant hilltop, where they shared their first kiss and first vow of love. Florence seems to them a paradise.

Schicchi turns to the audience. Tell me, he asks, could Buoso's money have served a better end? "And for this, I have been consigned to hell. But, by leave of great Father Dante, if you have been

amused tonight, please grant me the benefit of extenuating circumstances!"

*Comment: The writing of the will is a parody of every ritual in opera,
always built on the number three, and in this case introduced in Latin to
drive home the point. The tension is marvelous as the relatives can only
grumble under Schicchi's repetition of the sad phrase of exile from Florence. After the notary leaves, the relatives sing in unison until they leave
the stage, another instance of what it takes for these people to unite in
common cause. We can only sympathize with a thief if he is stealing from
a worse thief (cf. the film* The Sting*), and the score reveals more about
the "bad guys'" corrupt natures than words alone ever can. The theme
from Rinuccio's first exclamations about his right to marry Lauretta now
appears in full lyric effusion as the lovers unite and regard Florence, their
paradise. Young love, the creative ambition of the Renaissance, praise for
the achievements of the human mind (even a somewhat devious one such
as Schicchi's), and the beauty of the city of Florence are all united in one
sentiment. If all those things together aren't paradise, what could possibly
be? Schicchi's address to the audience is spoken, not sung. This is a sure
step away from verismo practice and a nod toward the new trends of
theater, shortly to be seen in such artists as Pirandello, who acknowledge
the "staginess" of drama. If the ensemble of the opera has been effective in
creating a tense "noise," the finale can work as a charming close to the*
Trittico, *Puccini's longest night in the theater and his last completed
opera.*

Turandot

The Name and How to Pronounce It

Let's settle this right now: it is pronounced as it is written: TOO-rahn-doat. You pronounce the "t" at the end. For years, there has been a tendency among some to drop the final "t." This is affected at best and slightly racist at worst. In Italian, every written letter is pronounced (except "h"). English speakers find it an imposition to say anything in a Latin language, but the general idea out there seems to be that if we must say something in Italian, then we must give it a French twist, since French is as far as we will go away from our own language. (We do this with Spanish too: note the sports announcers who persist in saying Sha-VEZ and Pe-REZ for Chávez and Pérez, as if shifting the accent makes it more elegant or something.) We use French names for most Italian cities, but that dates from a time when the only people in England who had reason to mention Italian cities were French speakers themselves. Let's not make the problem any worse than it is. Pronounce the final "t." And that's a long "o" in the third syllable: don't let it rhyme with "polka dot." If anyone corrects you, stand firm and call them insulting names. Incidentally, do not pronounce the first syllable "Tyu" unless you're the general manager of the Royal Opera House.

What is Turandot?

Turandot is Puccini's last opera, unfinished at the time of his death in 1924. It is perhaps the grandest of grand operas, a huge spectacle with a prominent role for chorus and one of opera's most sophisticated orchestral scores. It is usually cited as the last grand opera of the great tradition. *Turandot* is Puccini's only foray into the realm of the fairy tale, as far away from verismo as one can get. And yet, all of Puccini's trademark glories are present: a beautiful lyric soprano role (not the title role, for heaven's sake, but the other one), a lusty if unreal tenor with some dreamy solos, marvelous ensemble work, and so forth. Still, there is much in *Turandot* that is unique in Puccini's output: a commedia dell'arte trio who, ironically, form the most human core of the work, a massive and ritualized face-off between tenor and soprano, and, most remarkably, a title role written for a soprano of Wagnerian proportions. *Turandot* also affords opportunities for the most gargantuan stagings imaginable. It is simply impossible to overdo this opera, although many have tried. Performances of *Turandot* are always an event.

Turandot's *Place in the Repertory*

Solid, and growing. Despite initial success at La Scala in 1926 and at the Met the following year, *Turandot* remained something of a curiosity for a long time. London audiences were thrilled by Eva Turner's interpretation of the role in 1937, but the opera was left aside for several decades. The Met, too, put *Turandot* on the shelf until a series of legendary performances with Birgit Nilsson and Franco Corelli blew off everyone's wigs in 1961. At least since the 1960s, *Turandot* has been a staple of the repertory. If it isn't in the *Bohème/Tosca/Butterfly* category of most frequently performed operas, it is not for any lack of public affection. It is simply a matter of logistics. *Turandot* is grand opera and requires grand resources—a huge chorus needing a lot of rehearsal time, big productions, and so forth. While many smaller companies like to show their creativity with cleverly reimagined interpretations of the big operas, *Turandot* is better left to the power-horses. (There have been some successful *Turandot*s in the smaller companies, but generally they tend to be depressing affairs, like a friend's first attempt at a chocolate soufflé.) Then there is the title role. She sings very little and doesn't even open her mouth until well past the halfway point of the opera—but then she had better blow everyone out of their collective somnolence or there isn't really much point to this opera. While some lyric sopranos have been able to acquit themselves decently in this role, the performances people remember best are those sung by the great leather-lungs of vocal history. There's really no way around it. Sopranos like that don't grow on trees, and the ones that exist rarely have the capacity to sing in what remains, after all is said and done, the Italian style.

Cast of Characters

THE PRINCESS TURANDOT (*soprano*): The bloodthirsty moon goddess of myth and legend, a cosmic avenger of women. The role calls for a unique voice type in Puccinian canon: a full dramatic soprano. Yet she has very little to sing in terms of actual time onstage. Still, a soprano can become a legend in her own right with a memorable performance of this curious role.

CALAF, EXILED PRINCE OF TARTARY (*tenor*): Calaf is as wooden and unreal as any tenor in Italian opera (and that's saying a lot). However, his music is sublime and nuanced and reveals depths not indicated in the libretto (although few are the tenors who are able to discover them). In theory, the role does not require a voice any heavier than the standard Puccini tenor, but clearly the more heroic the voice, the more impression he will make.

TIMUR, DEPOSED KING OF TARTARY, CALAF'S FATHER (*bass*): A sympathetic character and a bit of a moral center.

LIÙ, A SLAVE GIRL (*soprano*): The self-sacrificing soprano role and a difficult role for the audience to digest, as Puccini and his librettists conceived it. Still, she has the most beautiful music in the opera and often steals the show. The role requires a lyric soprano of great focus and clarity (to be heard in ensembles), as well as dreamy floating vocal abilities.

PING, THE GRAND CHANCELLOR (*baritone*); PANG, THE GENERAL PURVEYOR (*tenor*); AND PONG, THE CHIEF COOK (*tenor*): Three characters, always together onstage, derived from commedia dell'arte tradition. Ping, Pang, and Pong interrupt the action in Act I before weaving into it, appear on their own in Act II, Scene 2, and are fully integrated in Act III. The roles require supreme musicianship and voices that, while not necessarily large, have enough character to be heard through ensembles and then have the ability to blend with each other.

THE EMPEROR ALTOUM OF CHINA (*tenor*): A very ancient personage, whose voice must project an otherworldly quality.

A MANDARIN: The "announcer" of the opera. He makes only two appearances, but must convey all the authority of Confucian order.

The Opera

Act I

Setting: A public square in Peking, with the Imperial Palace to one side. Legendary times.

"People of Peking!" the Mandarin announces to the throng. "This is the law! Turandot the Pure will be the bride of any suitor of royal blood who solves the three riddles given him, but should he fail, he pays with his audacious head!" The crowd gasps. "The Prince of Persia," the Mandarin continues, "was not favored by fortune. He dies by the executioner's hand when the moon rises!" The bloodthirsty crowd calls for the moon to rise and the executioner to hurry to the palace. Guards strike at them. In the confusion, old, blind Timur is knocked over and Liù, a young slave girl who is his only companion, calls for help. Calaf, among the crowd, recognizes Timur as his father. Each had thought the other dead after the far-off battle that cost Timur the throne of Tartary. He tells Calaf how he wandered all the way to Peking as an exile, accompanied only by the faithful Liù. Calaf asks Liù who she is and why she alone has remained loyal to Timur. "I am nothing," Liù tells him. "A slave." Once, many years before, Calaf had deigned to smile at her at court, and she has never forgotten. The executioner's men come to sharpen a sword on the grindstone, urged on by the crowd, who call for more death. The executioner will never lack for work in Turandot's kingdom! But why does the moon delay? Let the severed, bloodless head rise in the sky! A glimmer of moonlight appears and the crowd ecstatically calls for the executioner, Pu-Tin-Pao. A group of boys walk past, singing of the spring that never came and the snows that never melted. The Prince of Persia is led on toward his execution: he is young and handsome, and the crowd's bloodlust immediately turns to pity. They call for Turan-

dot to reprieve the Prince, joined by Calaf, who curses the woman
who would kill such an innocent. Turandot appears on her imperial
balcony, and with a silent gesture orders the execution to proceed.
She disappears, and the procession moves on. Calaf is smitten by the
sight of Turandot. Do the others not smell the perfume that perme-
ated the air when she appeared? Timur and Liù urge Calaf away from
this place of death, but he insists that life is here, and can only repeat
the name "Turandot!" "Turandot!" cries the Prince of Persia from afar,
cut off by the executioner's ax and the gasp of the crowd. Is that
how Calaf wants to end up? asks Timur. Calaf is not dissuaded but
approaches the gong to declare himself a suitor.

Comment: The opening scene of Turandot *is a magnificent and thrilling
panorama that assaults the senses while never losing its command of subtleties for an instant. Loud, dissonant chords bring up the curtain (sort of*
Tosca, *sideways), followed by a series of repeated chords wrung out of
the orchestra in an excellent depiction of anarchic tension. The Mandarin's
pronouncement sets the tone, musically and dramatically, of severity and
otherworldliness. Listen for the weird bass xylophone figures: besides
sounding like rattling bones, they are a direct quote from Richard Strauss's*
Salome. *It is followed by two descending sighs of "ah" from the chorus,
who then dominates the rest of the scene. Their first chorus, beginning with
the fortissimo cries of "Muoia!" ("Let him die!) establishes their volatility.
Liù, Timur, and Calaf can interject their lines between waves of choral
sound, appropriate for individuals almost crushed by a throng. The chorus
"fades out" for Liù's simple explanation of the smile she received at court
years ago. She floats up (on a good night) to a pianissimo B-flat, which is
enough, in the world of Italian opera, to indicate to even the dullest member of the audience that she is thoroughly in love with Calaf. This brief
moment is interrupted by the chorus in full strength, singing "Gira la
cote!" ("Turn the [sharpening] stone!" for the executioner), a rolling piece
of music culminating in four jarring, offbeat laughs. All this adrenaline
suddenly transforms (celesta, harps muffled with pieces of paper between
the strings), into the hymn to the moon, an extraordinary piece of choral*

writing. The peaceful, meditative beginning belies the rather twisted words, as the people compare the moon to both a bloodless, severed head, and the distant, virginal Princess Turandot. It's interesting to compare this lunar hymn to Mascagni's "Hymn to the Sun" from his Japanese opera Iris, *which was very popular at one time in Italy (and we know every success of Mascagni's rankled Puccini a bit). The* Iris *hymn is a giant wall of sound, an impressive mass of music that of course couldn't be more un-Japanese if it tried. Puccini, conversely, here has a diaphanous, seemingly formless collection of exclamations from small divisions of the chorus, punctuated by unlikely interjections from the orchestra (a snippet of melody in the strings here, some taps on the xylophone there). The loud climax is both surprising yet inevitable—a great accomplishment for any composer. It is the executioner's name decried on three repeated notes, a "dah-dah-dahhhh" construction that is a certain sign of death in the vocabulary of Italian opera (cf. the Judgment Scene in Verdi's* Aida*). The massive sound evanesces and we hear the last thing our ears expect: a small boys' chorus singing the lovely Jasmine Flower song, "Mou-Li Hua," one of Puccini's discoveries from Baron Fassini's invaluable music box and one of the most important themes in the opera. Some commentators say the theme, as Puccini uses it, represents the innocent aspect of Turandot, but if that's true, then the converse must be true as well: perhaps the "innocent" children are indicted in the general bloodlust. In any case, their sudden vocal intrusion is marvelously eerie and an ingenious and rare use of boys' voices, quite unlike the usual annoying brats who appear in so many operas. (Granted, at least in* Bohème *and* Tosca *the boys are supposed to be annoying brats, but boys' choruses in opera are generally a trial on the nerves.) The tune takes various forms throughout the opera: in this first instance, as Girardi has rather brilliantly demonstrated, Puccini has lightly harmonized the authentic, pentatonic Chinese tune in a Western manner. Specifically, the notes he adds create a scale in the mixolydian mode—a Gregorian scale that strikes the listener (who need not know squat about Gregorian modes) as being both ritualistic and archaic. The eeriness is accentuated by two alto saxophones hidden in the wings providing part of the harmony for the children.*

This change of tone leads into the appearance of the Prince of Persia, a very curious role. He struts nobly and elegantly across the stage and off the other side. There is another chorus to mark his progress, only this time the crowd is lyrical, full of pity, and begging the Princess to spare the young man's life. This is not a subtle change of heart, as Puccini created, one by one, with the community in Fanciulla*: it is the fickleness of a bestial crowd. What is astounding about this chorus, besides its sheer beauty, is the way that Calaf's voice emerges from the wall of sound, the beginning of individual characterization in this opera from amid the vast panorama. The Princess appears on the balcony of the royal palace with the orchestra thundering out the* "Mou-Li Hua" *theme while the chorus repeats* "Principessa! la grazia!" *to the same notes they had cried out in their previous climax, summoning the executioner Pu-Tin-Pao. It is exciting music and connects the Princess to the executioner implicitly rather than saying they are the same—that is, in a way spoken drama could not. (It's also a good time for the production team to conjure up some great coup de théâter to match the swelling music and the direction in the libretto that says she appears "like a vision.") Mimì, Tosca, and Butterfly were all heard before they were seen: Turandot not only reverses the order—she only makes a silent gesture here—but delays her actual singing until the second scene in the next act. The music diminishes to a creepy quiet (the strings bang out a few bars col legno and then add mutes) as Calaf admits his change of mood: he has fallen in love with Turandot. The morbidity of his change of heart, and a sly comment on the toxicity of love, is underscored by a three-measure chant (a four-note Chinese melody from the edition of folk songs Ricordi had provided) by some priests (basses) for the soul of the Prince of Persia—a tad premature, but operatically apt. Calaf continues his pining for Turandot in a crescendo that climaxes with the triple repetition of "Turandot!" The final cry ends on a high B-flat, answered by the Prince of Persia, offstage, with almost the same cry: he ends a half-tone lower, A-natural. There is a "smush" sound (I know of one production where they used a large hammer and a watermelon offstage for this aural moment), followed by a grotesque sudden tumbling effect in the orchestra, neatly depicting the severed head rolling off the scaffold. That's right: the producers must pay a tenor the scale wages for* *standing in the wings in his T-shirt and jeans, hitting a single A-natural. If you thought the note was produced by the same guy who floated across the stage looking pale and poignant, then you're every director's ideal audience member. The visible Prince is usually a dancer, or, in the Met's case, a "professional movement specialist." By the same token, don't expect the prima donna of the evening to get all tarted up in imperial drag an hour before her real entrance just to make an "Off with his head!" gesture. A body double will usually be used instead.*

Calaf's trip to the gong is interrupted by Ping, Pang, and Pong, the Emperor's ministers. Fool! they tell him. This is the way toward the slaughterhouse, nothing more. Does Calaf wish to be cut into little pieces? And for what? For Turandot? Take away the crown and the robes, and there's nothing there. Just flesh, and you can't even eat it. They will give Calaf a hundred wives, with two hundred lovely legs. Turandot's maids order silence from the balcony. The Princess is sleeping. Ping, Pang, and Pong approach Calaf to dissuade him from the gong, but shades of dead suitors arise to urge Calaf on. Let him strike the gong that they may see her again! The ministers assure Calaf that Turandot doesn't exist. Only the executioner is real. Just then, Pu-Tin-Pao appears with the severed head of the Prince of Persia. There's love for you! Timur begs Calaf not to leave him alone. Liù begs one word: she could not bear it if Calaf died, and she and Timur would have to die alone on the road of exile.

Comment, scene and aria, "Signore, ascolta": *Ping, Pang, and Pong cut through the musical texture of the opera like a hot knife through butter. Their first entrance is derived from another of Baron Fassini's music box tunes—and it's tricky stuff. The meter alternates in every measure, and their interjections are sometimes in unison but often are fractions of a beat off of each other. You don't need the biggest voices in the world to sing these rules, but you need first-rate musicians who can count. It is effectively comical music (not a moment too soon in this heavy atmosphere) and chattily philosophical. The offbeat, curiously off-balance music for these three paradoxically make them, at least at this point, the voice of sanity in an insane world. It is the intrusion of comedy (represented, in the Italian tradition, by rhythm, as we saw in* Gianni Schicchi*) as well as pithy little bits of philosophy (whereas all that we have heard previously is pure emotion). Their appearance blurs the lines between comedy, madness, and true wisdom, an interesting trope of the commedia dell'arte tradition. The maids who call for silence (nine sopranos, sometimes in unison and sometimes divided) change the tone yet again. Ping, Pang, and Pong try again with Calaf with another rhythmically charged Chinese tune played in pizzicato tweets in the oboes. Liù's aria* "Signore, ascolta," *the first aria of the opera, is one of Puccini's "hits": a wonderfully diaphanous melody built on a pentatonic scale but making no other attempt to be Chinese. It plainly establishes Liù as the most genuine human being in the opera.*

Calaf tells Liù not to weep: if that smile meant anything to her years ago, she must be strong and stay with Timur. By tomorrow, perhaps, they will be alone in the world again. Timur, Liù, and the ministers urge Calaf to back down, but he imperiously bangs the gong three times, and is led off by the guards to face the riddles of Turandot. Ping, Pang, and Pong laugh at the madness.

Comment, scene and aria, "Non piangere, Liù": *Calaf's solo here begins as a typically Puccinian effusion of lyric tenorial beauty but shortly becomes the central thread of a wildly elaborate ensemble. During the* "Prince of Persia" *ensemble, Calaf "surfed" off the waves of choral sound: here, the chorus provides the interjections. He has become the motivator of the action. The ensemble builds, in a swaying motion (like a tug of war between Calaf and the other soloists, with the chorus entering bit by bit in a sort of tug of war with itself, both warning of death and encouraging Calaf to bang the gong so they can get another execution). The orchestra builds with the complex vocal line, adding xylophone, tuned gongs, timpani, harp arpeggios, tam-tam, and a whole lot of noise before Calaf finally strikes the (untuned, onstage) gong. The* "Mou-Li Hua" *theme bursts out again in the chorus before Calaf is led off, the curtain falling on Puccini's most ambitious act and one of the greatest sweeps of music ever unleashed in the theater.*

Act II

Scene 1

Setting: A pavilion in the Imperial Palace.

Ping, Pang, and Pong ponder the situation in their royal pavilion. They prepare lanterns for a wedding and incense for a funeral. They are ready for either outcome, although so far it has been nothing but death. Oh China! How peacefully she once reposed in her seventy centuries of serenity according to the ancient rules! Now, nothing but three bangs on a gong, three riddles, and a head falls off. What miserable work! Once, they were respected ministers. Now, nothing but ministers of death. They reminisce about their peaceful country palaces. Will they ever know such peace again? No, not with all the madmen in love who keep coming to Peking! Remember the Prince of Samarkand? Of Burma? Kirghiz? The Indian? All dead. Crowds are heard murmuring for another execution. Oh, farewell China and her divine lineage, until she who knows no love shall lie naked and intoxicated by the joys of passion! Only then will there be peace again in the sacred kingdom. They hear the drums and the crowds assembling, and depart for yet another execution.

Comment, Ping, Pang, and Pong: First-timers at Turandot *often have a certain amount of trouble with this scene, which lasts about twelve minutes. It certainly requires more focus than any of Act I. Equally predictable is the response of certified Puccini fans (like me) who will invariably tell them that this is the best part of the opera. The critics have had a rough time with it until recently. W. J. Henderson of the* New York

Sun, *reviewing the Met premiere in 1927, found them "a perverted dream of Gilbert and Sullivan," and their music an "incoherent babble." Indeed, without benefit of in-house translations or familiarity with the libretto, the talkiness will be bewildering to non-Italian-speaking audiences. It also must be admitted that many performers (or, more likely, their diabolical directors) will exacerbate the problem by a great deal of unnecessary prancing around. The best productions sit them on the stage in clear view of the conductor and let them sing. This, however, elicits the most common and tired critical complaint about this scene: that it stops the action. Who cares? Verdi and Wagner strove, spectacularly, to free opera from its bel canto forms and separate the line between recitative and aria—which is to say, between action and reflection. But that doesn't mean any subsequent opera that chooses to do otherwise is a failure. This is a complaint voiced by people who don't have an idea in their heads newer than 1860, and it's high time it died. If this were still an issue, every panoramic shot in films would have to be jettisoned. Since the days of Verdi and Wagner, we have experienced Einstein, Pirandello, and science fiction in all its forms, and it's pretty clear that some moments in time take longer than others. There's really no such thing as real time. Perhaps this is why baroque opera has made such a great and unexpected comeback in the last twenty-five years. Perhaps the "mannerisms" of that era were a form of insight that only becomes clear now. The critics don't question the issue of "stopping the action" in baroque opera, however, but you will read it frequently regarding this scene. Maybe it's because it's Puccini, a composer rooted in verismo whose every opera takes place in "real time." There is no standing back from the action and commenting on it. But* Turandot *is a departure for Puccini in every way, and this fantasy opera requires a moment to stand back and reflect on the goings-on.*

Musically, it has the form of a complicated sonata. It begins with a scurrying theme (Chinese, harmonized curiously with more tweets in the oboes) as the three comment. This gives way to a stately, gorgeous theme as they have their dreamy nostalgia for the peace of their country homes. The final section brings in more rapidly rhythmic Chinese themes, here in unison, there in an interwoven counterpoint. There is a gush of melody as the three bid farewell to the China of the ages, "Addio, amore! addio razza!" *doubled in the strings as sentimentality briefly overlaps philosophical resignation. The finale is another fast Chinese theme as they try to imagine Turandot succumbing to love. The orchestra here is muted but seemingly almost at war with the singers: listen for the insanely "offbeat" pizzicato, chromatic run up the strings as the three sing their final salute to the ecstasies of love,* "Gloria all'ebbrezza e all'amore." *The pulses of a march, in drums and muted harps, keep growing under the melodic line, and we go directly into . . .*

Scene 2

Setting: The courtyard of the palace.

The crowd gathers in the courtyard of the Imperial Palace to witness the latest suitor try the three riddles. They point out Ping, Pang, and Pong, who remain silent. Soon, the Emperor appears and the crowd greets him with the Imperial Anthem. The Emperor, very old and with a distant voice, announces that he is bound by his terrible oath to go through with the ceremony, but he asks the stranger to leave before facing the questions. Calaf hails the Son of Heaven and asks to face the test. The Emperor asks the stranger to let him live out his fading years with no more bloodshed, but Calaf asks the Son of Heaven to let him face the test. No more blood in the palace! says the Emperor, but Calaf asks the Son of Heaven to face the test. So be it, the Emperor acquiesces. The crowd repeats the anthem, and the Mandarin repeats the law: Turandot the Pure will wed any man of royal blood who answers the three riddles, but if he fails, he will pay with his head. The boys sing for the Princess to appear and make everything shine with her splendor. Turandot advances toward the throne.

In this palace, she announces, many thousands of years ago, a cry rang out that has lodged itself in her heart. Princess Lou-Ling, who reigned in peace and joy, defying the tyranny of men, now lives in

Turandot! The people mutter that this was when the king of Tartary unfurled his battle flags. The story is known to all, Turandot continues. China was conquered and Lou-Ling was dragged away by a stranger—a stranger like you! she says, pointing at Calaf. The people say that Lou-Ling has rested for centuries in her giant tomb. O princes, Turandot cries, I take revenge on all of you! "No man shall ever have me!" She tells the stranger not to tempt fate: the riddles are three, but death is one! "No," Calaf counters, "the riddles are three and life is one!" The people ask Turandot to let the stranger face the test.

Comment, scene and aria, "In questa reggia": The transition to the palace takes place within a few bars of a march. Ideally, the revelation of the imperial grandeur should make the audience squeal with delight, and Puccini has obliged with "dum-dum-dums" in the brass to let us know precisely when to squeal. Expect every visual shtick the opera house can come up with in this moment—I wouldn't be too surprised to see a high school marching band onstage someday. The crowd sings the Imperial Anthem, "Diecimila anni," another theme harmonized in the mixolydian mode and thus adding to the ritual atmosphere that is the essence of this scene. The score says the Emperor is lowered from above the stage amid clouds of incense, but don't count on that (singers hate it). The voice of the ancient Emperor should always sound strange and, if possible, old. In 1987, the Met hired the Swiss art song and specialty-role tenor Hugues Cuenod to make his somewhat belated Met debut in this role at the spry age of eighty-four. He was great. Bizarre castings in this role are to be expected. His interaction with Calaf accomplished, we are prepared for the long-awaited entrance of Turandot by a repetition of the Imperial Anthem (this time in hushed, reverential tones) and a reiteration of the "Mou-Li Hua" tune (more alto saxophones in the wings). She begins her great narration, "In questa reggia," in a deceptively simple declamation, although the orchestra quiets down and her voice should ideally be laser-focused and chilling even if she has yet to crank up the volume. The two mutters of the chorus each push her louder and higher, with a few changes of key. When she sings "Mai nessun m'avrà" ("No man shall ever have me!"), she shifts into F-sharp minor, which was the executioner's key. The dullest member of the audience will get the point. The final third of the aria demands full volume while hovering well over the staff. This is dramatic soprano range, the sort that is demanded by the most challenging Wagner and Strauss roles. Puccini seems to have obliged by writing music that is not, on the written page, among the most compelling or beautiful in the corpus of his works. What matters here is whether or not the soprano in question can muster the sound and size of her voice to portray Womanhood in its fiercest aspects: the blood-drinking virgin moon goddess who accepts the sacrifice of young men as her due, and the all-too-human woman who is exacting revenge for a crime thousands of years ago that somehow lives on in her. By this denial of the passage of time, there is the implication that she is avenging all women for all the crimes committed on them since the beginning of time. Now we must be convinced that she has met her match in Calaf, since the aria ends as a sort of duet, if you can call it that. It's more of a battle to the death. She sings (or rather declaims) her line "Gli enigmi sono tre, la mort'è una" ("The riddles are three, but death is one"), he answers a step higher, and they repeat their versions of the line together for the third time, climaxing on a fermata high C that lasts until one or the other turns blue or motions the conductor to stop the torture. Don't worry about what they're saying, since the most you'll be able to make out will be "Wha-WHAH-wha-WHAH-wha-Whah." The chorus rushes in as the phrase mercifully concludes after another fermata high A, effectively covering any applause, lack thereof, or, most likely, gasping on the part of the singers. The whole passage is, on face value, a somewhat cheesy vocal circus act, but in the hands of truly great singers appropriate for these roles, it is astounding. It can encapsulate, better than any painting, movie, or any other piece of art I can think of, all the hostility that has ever existed between Man and Woman in both their fleshly and cosmic dimensions.

Turandot announces the first riddle: "What soars above all humankind, and all call to it, is reborn every night and dies every new day?"

"Yes!" Calaf cries out, "It is born in my heart now! It is hope!" The wise men consult the scrolls: hope is the correct answer. "Yes, hope, that always disappoints," adds Turandot. She continues: "It smolders like a flame, but is not a flame. It is a fever, a passion, sometimes a delirium! Inertia makes it sag. It grows cold with faintness or death, but dreams of conquest make it flare up. You hear its voice in fear, and it glows like the setting sun!" The Emperor tells the stranger to take heart, and the crowd encourages him. "Yes, Princess!" Calaf says. "It burns in my veins when you look at me. It is blood!" The wise men concur: it is blood. Turandot orders the guards to strike the crowd, who now are wholly on Calaf's side. She continues: "Ice that gives you fire and from your fire takes more ice . . . white and dark, if it frees you it makes you a slave, and if it accepts you as a slave, it makes you a king!" She tells the stranger to hurry with his answer . . . his paleness shows he is lost! "Victory gives you to me!" Calaf says. "Turandot!" The wise men consult the scrolls. The answer is Turandot. The people hail the victor and their glorious Emperor. Turandot begs the Emperor not to throw her into the arms of the stranger like a slave. He stands firm that his oath is sacred, but she counters that she is sacred. She insists no man shall ever have her. Does the stranger want her like this, reluctant, trembling? No, Calaf answers, he wants her aflame with love. The crowd urges her to accept the stranger, who risked his life for her love. She offered him three riddles; now he will offer her but one: tell him his name. If she can discover it by morning, he is prepared to die. The Emperor hopes that by dawn he may call the stranger his son. The people hail the Emperor.

Comment: The fused-voice hostility that was the end of "In questa reggia" *becomes a ritualized standoff here. All of the questions and answers sound similar but are individualized in details: listen for the creepy clarinet figures in the second question. The questions themselves are rather goofy, but it fits the fairy-tale quality of the story. Busoni got predictably brainy in his version, and it works against the story as a whole. Still, it's rather amazing that Calaf can answer even these riddles, since there is nothing in his music or what he says to indicate that brains are included in his list of ostentatiously functioning organs. His offer to die for Turandot if she finds out his name makes us further question where he summoned the brains to answer the riddles. It does, however, offer an opportunity to return to some very lyrical singing (despite an optional high C that really never comes out right when he says he wants her burning with love) and is what we would call a "tease," since it includes strains of the celebrated Act III aria "Nessun dorma." The act concludes with a very noisy and a more complicated harmonization of the Imperial Anthem, this time including stage brass and even an organ to conclude the act with a massive sense of ritual.*

Act III

Scene 1

Setting: The gardens of the palace.

Heralds announce the law: On pain of death, no one shall sleep in Peking this night until the stranger's name is discovered. People pass to and fro, repeating the command: no one sleeps! Calaf appears. No one sleeps! Even you, Princess, he says, are awake in your cold rooms, staring at the stars this night. But his secret is shut inside him. No one will know his name. No, no, he will reveal it only on her lips, when he kisses her as the day breaks. Women are heard from afar, bemoaning that they will be killed unless the stranger's name is found. Calaf orders the night to flee and the stars to set, for at dawn he will be victorious!

Comment, aria, "Nessun dorma": This last great tenor aria of the Italian tradition is beautifully set up by the heralds (eight tenors, offstage) and the lamenting replies of the sopranos, also offstage. The first part of the aria is lyrical and very much at odds with what we have heard of the score so far while maintaining the C major of the introduction. There is a miraculous transition to the subsequent "plateau" of the aria: four notes in the violins, a plunk in the strings, and a quiet sigh in the bassoons, and we are in the "triumphant" key of G major. A lesser composer might have taken a minute or two to achieve the same transition and still not convince us well, as Puccini did, that all was right with the world, or soon would be. The climax of the aria, driven by the offstage chorus, is the last word, "vincerò." The second syllable, a B-natural, is marked in the score as a sixteenth note, but you'll never hear it sung that way and the tenor would probably be booed if he attempted it. Tradition (or decadence) dictates that this is the moment for the tenor to grab whatever organs he must and belt out a war cry of the ages. It's funny, but many tenors who have no trouble nailing the high C in the riddle scene will completely shipwreck on this note, and he's alone onstage and the orchestra is a mere murmur. It can be very painful. Not to reinforce the audience's baser instincts, but it must be admitted that on the rare occasion when the tenor actually nails this note without sounding like a scalded cat, the effect is tremendous— like the passing of a communal kidney stone. The fact that the aria itself is hackneyed by overexposure in inappropriate places speaks to its quality. It was, I recall, used as the background music in a TV commercial for a luxury hotel in Los Angeles, probably the single worst instance ever of matching music to an intended message ("No one sleeps . . ."). In the context of the opera, however, it is a superb breath of fresh air. The orchestra sweeps directly into the following scene, theoretically eliminating the opportunity of an ovation. If the audience doesn't at least try to interrupt the performance with applause, however, the rendition in question may be considered a failure.

Shadowy figures appear among the bushes: Ping, Pang, and Pong try to encourage the stranger to leave China. Does he want love? They present dozens of scantily clad girls to him. Let him take them all! Riches? They open caskets of the finest jewels in the world. Glory? They will lead him to vast empires. Calaf remains firm. The ministers, joined by the crowd, now beg the stranger to have pity on them. He doesn't know what cruel tortures Turandot will inflict on all of them, but he is not dissuaded. Guards drag in Liù and Timur. These two were seen with the stranger. They will reveal his name! "They know nothing," sneers Calaf. The crowd calls Turandot and tells her they have witnesses who know the stranger's name. She orders Timur to speak, but Liù steps forward, saying she alone knows the stranger's name, and she will never reveal it. This secret is her supreme joy. Soldiers restrain Calaf and begin to apply torture to Liù, demanding the name. She begs forgiveness but cannot obey. She cries out under torture. The Princess asks Liù what gives her strength to endure such pain. "Princess, it is love!" "Love?" Turandot asks. Yes, Liù explains. Her secret love makes these tortures sweet, because she endures them for him. They call the executioner, and Liù worries that she will break under the pressure. She demands Turandot hear her. "You who are wrapped in ice," she says, "will love him too before the night is over. But alas I will see him no more." She pulls a dagger and stabs herself. The crowd gasps, imploring Liù to reveal the name before she dies. She dies at Calaf's feet.

Comment, scene and arias, "Tanto amore segreto" and "Tu che di gel sei cinta": Although the music for the "presentation of the hoochie-koochie girls" is exotic and interesting, the visual presentation onstage is usually embarrassing rather than titillating or even offensive. No matter. The moment soon passes and the mood shifts when Timur and Liù are dragged onstage. Here we come across a major problem: nearly all commentators have complained that the onstage torture of Liù was totally unnecessary, and they're right. Armchair psychologists have a field day exploring Puccini's kinks through this scene (the torture was, in fact, his idea). Leaving aside the issue of Puccini's "Neronian instincts" for the moment and focusing on the drama at hand, we can see that the story does not in any way benefit from this protracted abuse. It all flows better when the torture is minimized and we can move directly to her two solos, but fat chance of that. Today's theater is firmly committed to "shock and awe" tactics, and you can expect a hefty dose of dungeon slave antics, or some director's con-

ception of the same, in this problematic moment. Liù then must sing two beautiful arias, a hell of a way to make a living. The first, "Tanto amore segreto," is a mostly gossamer-thin lyrical flight of fancy, doubled by solo and then unison violins. It sounds quite a bit like some of Mimì's music, and therefore as shocking in the context of this score as "Nessun dorma." It's also a good time for the soprano to lay on all the tricks in her magic vocal bag since, let's not forget, she will be using this moment to try to steal the show from the much louder lead soprano. After a bit more torture (Pu-Tin-Pao comes back), she has her second and more famous aria, "Tu che di gel sei cinta" (the lyrics were Puccini's own). The orchestra pulses quietly like a stifled sob (timpani, bass drum included). This gorgeous aria requires all the upper range, pianissimo lyricism of the previous aria, plus a dose of heft in the lower ranges. See if the soprano can pull it off without resorting to fake chest tones. If she can, nine times out of ten she actually will win the bigger ovation at the end of the night.

Timur approaches the body, telling Liù to get up . . . dawn is coming and they must wander the highways of exile yet another day. "Old man," says Ping, "she is dead." Timur berates the crowd for this crime and tells the people to pay homage to her spirit so she does not return to haunt them. Ping, Pang, and Pong are stirred by the death—they, who have seen so much death! All leave to bury Liù, begging her shade for mercy. Only Turandot and Calaf are left.

Comment, Liù's funeral: Timur is the center of this ensemble, built around the same lines as "Tu che di gel sei cinta" with the pulse in the orchestra amplified. It is the sort of musical connection that cannot be explained by logical deconstruction, yet it makes perfect sense in performance and is truly moving, never failing to make an impression on the audience. It ends with all but Calaf and Turandot leaving the stage, the celesta holding a strangely piercing chord before resolving. This is the end of the score as completed by Puccini, and the moment where Toscanini made his famous pronouncement (whatever it was, exactly) on the night of the premiere.

Calaf turns on the "Princess of Death," accusing her of Liù's death. Turandot is offended: she is the daughter of heaven! Calaf tells her her body is right here on earth, beside his. She resists, but he succeeds in kissing her passionately as the dawn begins to break. She sheds her first tears and admits how stirred she was when first she saw Calaf. His eyes shone with a hero's light, and he has conquered her. Her glory is done. He tells her her glory only now begins. Ecstatically, he tells her his name: Calaf, son of Timur. She calls him before the people with her as trumpets announce the sunrise.

Comment: Poor Alfano, stuck with the rotten assignment of the century, and it shows. His conclusion of the opera, contracted by Ricordi and accomplished with Toscanini's help, was then cut by Toscanini. It was in this edited version that the opera was given at La Scala after the dramatic opening night and at the premiere performances in New York, London, Buenos Aires, and elsewhere. After the superbly weird conclusion of Liù's funeral, loud brass introduces the tenor's "Principessa di morte!" solo, a straightforward, less-than-inspired tenor solo. The brass and the outline of the theme are both Puccini's, so Alfano was stuck with them, although God alone knows what Puccini might have done with them. Alfano composed Turandot's aria "Dal primo pianto," and it is quite good. Toscanini threw it out the window, and it has only recently been heard with regularity. The old feeling was "Let's get this over with as quickly as possible," while the new thinking says that with the complete ending as Alfano wrote it, one has a chance of at least hearing a completed thought process by a very good composer. The love duet exists in long and short versions. In either case, it is loud and difficult to sing and again hampered by being neither Puccini nor first-rate Alfano. One thing is clear: the transformation that Puccini wanted, with Turandot becoming an actual human being, never happens. It's one thing for a composer to write "Then, Tristan!" in the margins of an uncompleted manuscript, and another to write a new version of Tristan.

Another ending to Turandot, *including the subsequent scene, has recently been composed by the Italian composer Luciano Berio. When Berio announced his intention, many gasped: the great contemporary composer known for his serialism, electronic music, and collage tech-niques did not strike many people as a logical person to complete Puc-cini's final masterpiece! Berio surprised the gaspers, however, with a score that is melodic and true to Puccini's spirit, as well as infused with many touches that Puccini would not in all likelihood have imagined but of which he may well have approved. The Berio ending has won great praise but has not yet become standard. Time alone will tell if it will survive as is or as only another interesting footnote to this well-footnoted opera.*

Scene 2

Setting: The courtyard, as in Act II, Scene 2.

The people hail the Emperor. Turandot says she knows the stranger's name: it is Love! The people hail Love as the light of the world.

Comment: We return to the palace, usually with much pageantry and waving of flags and other silliness to help us forget the problems of this behemoth. The chorus sings a verse of "Nessun dorma" for the finale. Ending with "Nessun dorma" is not unprecedented—Tosca ends with an orchestral outburst of the big tenor tune, much to the horror of most critics. The problem is that Puccini would have done something with the tune here if he had chosen to use it as the finale. He never wrote straight-forward, unison choruses but always had something interesting going on at the same time, even if the average listener would have to hear it a few times to notice. What a sad irony that the whole magnificent tradition of Italian opera should end, not with a bang or a whimper, but a big, fat question mark.

Part Three

THE PUCCINI CODE

Issues in Puccini
and the Perception of His Works

The Myth of Tosca:
A Key to a Fresh Perception of Puccini
(and Everything Else)

KERMAN'S DISMISSAL of *Tosca* as the "shabby little shocker" is hardly unique. Many find the melodrama and the character of Tosca herself perfectly ridiculous. The problem, I believe, lies in the understanding of verismo, and therefore is worth looking at not only for *Tosca* but for the rest of Puccini's works and a great many other Italian works of art as well. Verismo is not "realism," but would be better defined by the inelegant term "truism." Thus the film director Rossellini, whom we will have reason to discuss in later chapters, once remarked that neorealism was "simply the artistic form of the truth."

But what, as the ancient question asks, is truth? Do we Americans define it the same way as the Italians, who constantly use the motto "Se non è vero, e ben trovato"? (Roughly, "If it isn't true, then it's well founded.") Can there be a difference between truth and fact? And what does Rossellini's inclusion of the word "artistic" allow within the definition?

Verismo in film and opera (cinema being the artistic heir of the Italian genius when it fled the opera house after Puccini's death) is not, at core, about scruffy poor people who have a tendency to shout their emotions, although that is a common component of it. Indeed, *Tosca*, for example, would not wholly qualify as verismo (the characters may shout, but they're very well dressed) if that were the only definition. Yet anyone who attempts to sing it can instantly recognize the work as verismo. I suggest that at the core of verismo there is a search for the mythic in everyday life. The best definition of myth I ever came across was Norman O. Brown's: it is an old, old story. Old, old stories are more present and vibrant in Italy—even in modern, capitalist, Americanized Italy—than they are in America. And nowhere are they more alive than in the city of Rome itself.

Looking at this dimension of *Tosca* might open up new (actually very old) ways of appreciating this admittedly "over-the-top" work and, by implication, the rest of Puccini's corpus as well. Specifically, Sardou's and Puccini's insistence on the locale of the Castel Sant'Angelo and the presence onstage of the statue of St. Michael the Archangel caused me to wonder what issues might lie beneath this "little" melodrama. It requires a look at the background as Puccini, a nineteenth-century Italian and a fourth-generation church musician, would have seen it, which entails some discussion of Catholic Church politics and mythos and their roots in the ideas of the Roman Empire. It's also interesting to note how incomprehensible this point of view is to the Anglo-Saxon mentality, which is the prevailing mode of thought in the world today. None of these ideas were discussed openly in Sardou's or Puccini's correspondence. Neither of these men were theoreticians. They were men of the theater who used only the theater to say what they had to say. They weren't Wagner. But they do remark on their immediate rapport about the story, they are in full agreement about the symbols needed to make the story come alive, and they speak much of the *Romanità* (Romanness) of *Tosca*. Sardou was also quite candid about the fact that this opera would have to be written by an Italian and that Puccini's opera was infinitely better than his play. Sardou pointed the way and Puccini found the treasure, so to speak. In order to begin to mine (and this long chapter is, trust me, only a beginning) the true *Romanità* of *Tosca*, we need to spend a little time looking at someone we don't often think about these days, Pope Saint Gregory the Great.

The Gregorian Ideal

Gregory was born into a notable family of the senatorial class in AD 540. His maternal grandfather was Pope Felix III (taking holy orders after his widowerhood) and his mother and two aunts were later canonized as saints. The Roman Empire of the West had ceased to exist sixty years before, and the city that had once ruled the known world and boasted a population of over a million was now a half-ruined backwater with perhaps 50,000 residents. Yet the city had not vanished altogether. The aqueducts still ran with fresh water and there were even occasional meetings of the Senate. Moreover, as Gregory well knew, there was still power in the idea of Rome. And it was the seat of the pope, which counted for something at the Imperial Court of Constantinople and even with many of the barbarian tribes who were reshaping Western Europe. In this atmosphere, Gregory began his remarkable career. He became a Benedictine monk, despite the wealth of his family, and used the family palace on the Caelian Hill (near the Coliseum) to serve meals to the poor. Despite his monastic calling, Gregory's destiny was not the cloister or the hermitage. His talents were too worldly, and he rose in the city's decrepit but still extant administrative ranks until he became the prefect of Rome, or, in effect, the mayor. He was noted for efficiency in this capacity, sometimes bordering on the ruthlessness that the anarchic times demanded. For example, he dealt very harshly with the slaves on his family's large estates in Sicily. The produce of these estates was used to feed the hungry of Rome, so his motives were beyond reproach. But Gregory believed in order, plain and simple. The alternatives were apparent throughout crumbling Italy, and Gregory would not tolerate them.

Gregory was sent by the pope as emissary to the Byzantine court at Constantinople, to which Rome, in theory at least, was still subject. Gregory loathed everything about the parvenu capital: its effeminacy, its luxuriousness, its endless debates about theological minutiae, and its intrigues so excessive that we still use the word "Byzantine" to describe extreme complexity. Most surprisingly, Gregory did not speak Greek while at the capital, either from ignorance (hard to imagine in a person of his class) or, more likely, from inclination. He proudly expounded the papal position in plain, untheoretical Latin, which had legal status in that city, whose official name was, after all, New Rome.

He returned to Rome after two years. When Pope Pelagius died of the plague raging through Rome in 590, the populace and the bishops alike, we are told, acclaimed Gregory pope. Three times Gregory refused but in the end accepted, with tears and lamentations. Once installed as pope, his zeal and his abilities were almost boundless. He provided for Rome itself, and the hapless Romans knew a few years of relative peace and near-prosperity, but Gregory's vision was truly international, truly "catholic." He sent a monk named Augustine to England to introduce Christianity to the Germanic and Celtic peoples there. Augustine's mission, based in Canterbury, met with phenomenal success. Then Gregory wrestled with the Arian heresy, which had important adherents, paradoxically, among the barbarian chieftains of the north and west and in the Imperial Court of Constantinople. His success spelled the end of Arianism as a viable movement, while the Visigothic (and Arian-leaning) kingdoms of Spain were stamped with a Catholicism so orthodox that it survived and flourished throughout the subsequent 750 years of conflict with the Moors. Gregory turned the attention of the Catholic Church away from the eastern, Greek world toward a newer world in the west and north of Europe. Either Gregory sensed that the future of the Catholic Church lay in these new directions, or his actions caused this to be true.

This much is history, or at least as historical as anything from that murky era can be. Even scholars of Gregory have complained of the lack of a critical biography of the man. Nor would it be possible, from existing contemporary evidence, to write one. Much of what we know of him was written 200 years later by the Venerable Bede, that English chronicler-monk who is the bane of early-literature students and hardly reliable as a biographer. Yet the historical facts and issues are a problem for others: what concern us are the legends of Gregory's life and work and their implications. Whether such things "happened" or not is quite irrelevant.

Bede himself is the source of a legend dear to Englishmen. He tells us that Gregory was moved to evangelize Britain when he encountered some young boys in the slave market of Rome. Struck by their blond beauty, he asked the race of these lovely creatures. "They are Angles," he was told. "Truly, for they have the appearance of angels. And from what country do these Angles come?" "They come from Deira," came the answer, citing a name for Britain supposedly current at that time. "Truly, then, they must be saved *de ira*" ("from the wrath [of hell]"). None of this sounds remotely like the Pope Gregory of history, who had no faith in appearances, abhorred attractions of the flesh, did not think one race was closer to God than any other, and who never used puns in his writings, let alone puns as bad as these. Yet such was the legend as the English liked to hear it, and the fact remains that he was the pope who Christianized their country. Another tradition names Gregory as the tutelary saint who will call the English nation, living and dead, to judgment on the Last Day.

Aside from whatever singular memories the English nation may have of him, Gregory is primarily remembered for his accomplishments in three areas. The first is his role in church music. Most scholars will rush to tell us that the Gregorian chant, still the official music of the Church, has very little to do with Gregory. True and false. Most of the music in the Church's official books came from France two to four centuries after the time of Gregory. Yet it was Gregory who began to codify notions of proper church music systematically. He was tireless in his attention to detail in this area, naming eight modes that were specifically approved for liturgical use (including one, the mixolydian, that is the basis of the chords in *Tosca* that represent Scarpia). He wrote at some length about the importance of music in worship, and a specific kind of music that would channel the Holy Spirit to the congregants. He propagated the chant as a tool of liturgy. We know he set up several *Scholae cantorum* (schools of singing), in churches in Rome (the term may simply have referred to what we would call choirs). One of them was in the church he had built on the site of his former monastery, now known as San Gregorio Magno, where the choir area by the altar can still be seen. Among Gregory's possessions that are preserved as relics in this church is a whip he was said to use on lazy or unmusical choirboys. His interest in music was intense and personal. The idea that there was morally good and bad music is emblematic of Gregory.

The second area where Gregory holds a symbolic role is as the founder of the Papal State, the monarchical, independent nation of the City of Rome and its environs. This, too, is hard to prove as the sort of historical fact that would satisfy the modern scholar: popes asserted their authority in Rome as the emperors' power declined. By Gregory's time, any authority in Rome would have de facto independence. Even the papal tiara, the symbol of the pope as head of state, is thought to predate Gregory. Pope Leo I, who saved Rome with a prudent payment to Attila the Hun in the middle of the fifth century, is usually depicted wearing the three-tiered tiara. (Pope St. Leo is the only pope besides Gregory to be awarded the title "the Great." He also makes an appearance in Italian opera, in Verdi's *Attila*.) Yet again we must credit legend with insights that elude hard history: Gregory's acumen and his ability to stand firm against the emperor in Constantinople made the political notion of the Papal State a fact as well as a concept. Later representations of Gregory, including famous paintings by Rubens and Goya, invariably depict him wearing the beehive-shaped tiara.

The third memory of Gregory, and the one most patently present in *Tosca*, is as an ender of plagues. The well-traveled legend tells us that on the day of his elevation to the papacy, while the plague that killed Pope Pelagius raged through the city, Gregory formed the people into seven processions through the city. While they chanted the *Kyrie eleison* ("Lord, have mercy"), eighty of the faithful died in the streets. Finally, Gregory greeted the processions at the bridge leading to St. Peter's, and he heard the antiphon *Regina caeli* ("Queen of Heaven") sounding from the skies. At that moment, the Archangel Michael was seen atop Hadrian's Tomb, sheathing his flaming sword to signify that God's wrath was withdrawn and the plague was over.

None of Gregory's writings make any reference to such an event and the earliest account of it we have dates from a few centuries later. But the legend became enormously popular throughout the plague-ridden Middle Ages. The key role of music in ending the plague made perfect sense to people who saw Gregory as the man who made music itself sacred. Several representations of the miracle are to be found from all over the continent, including a particularly beautiful one in the illuminated manuscript the *Très Riches Heures du Duc de Berry*. A statue depicting the appearance of the archangel adorned the top of Hadrian's Tomb since at least the tenth century, and it has been known as the Castel Sant'Angelo since that time. The bronze statue that is there today was installed by Pope Benedict XIV in 1748.

These three aspects of Gregory—arbiter of music, head of state, and ender of plagues—are not three discrete aspects at all to the ancient, mythic mind. They are in fact one, in that they are aspects of the Roman god Apollo. Apollo is the patron of music—not of rustic music, which belonged to Pan, nor of the theater, which was the realm of the rival god Dionysus (in Greece) or Bacchus (in Rome)—but of civilized music as represented by the seven-stringed lyre, which was sacred to him. He has the power to begin and to end plagues, as we read in the *Iliad*, the *Aeneid*, and elsewhere, by the virtues of his arrows. Music also played a role in health in the Greek mind: disease was understood as a form of disharmony. Sick people went to the shrines of Asclepius, Apollo's son, to seek cures from finely tuned lyres. Here we might pause to remember Schaunard's escapade in *Scènes de la vie de bohème*, where his repeated playing of a single chord badly on the piano is meant to drive the neighbor and her offensive parrot mad, according to the Englishman who hires him and is convinced the plan will work because he "knows something about medicine." Even today, one hears much about the "healing power of music," and there is no disaster that is not followed by a slew of concerts intended to "begin the healing process" for the survivors. Above all, Apollo was the patron of the political state, the patriarchalist par excellence. In his benign form, Apollo was the source of the world's refinement, of moderation, of order, of reason, of patient methodology. In his extreme avatars, his influence was suffocating, overbearing, repressive of primal human instincts.

Augustus Caesar, perhaps the greatest manipulator of symbology in history, well understood the importance of Apollonian imagery in creating his own cult of state, which had no legal basis and needed all the symbolic help it could get. Once he even appeared at the games as Apollo, but this was considered overstepping his bounds, and Augustus later contented himself with appropriating Apollonian symbols.

Gregory's rise to political power had much in common with Augustus's consolidation of power six centuries earlier. Like Augustus, Gregory needed the sacred attributes of a king but could not use the name of king. In effect, he had to be both more and less than a mere king: more in that he would have authority over other kings, and less in that he could maintain the fiction of humility (*princeps inter paros* for Augustus, "servant of the servants of God" for Gregory). Gregory appropriated the title "Pontifex Maximus," with all its pagan connotations, from the defunct emperors of Rome. Even the title "Vicar of Christ" was boldly expropriated from Augustus's successor, the Byzantine emperor.

Nor is the association of Apollo with Christ gratuitous: the *Ovide moralisé* saw the myth of Apollo and Daphne as a figure of Christ's obsessive love for the Church, while Dante three times calls Christ the "buon Apollo" in his *Paradiso*. Apollo and Christ have conferred authority on rulers at various times in European history, and both their attributes have been co-opted by European rulers. Then, as now, style equaled authority. Thus Gregory, like Augustus, could perform all the acts of a sacred king without having to call himself a king. One of the most important functions of a king is to prevent disease, and so the statue atop the Castel Sant'Angelo is a sign of the divinely ordained legitimacy of temporal, political papal rule. The statue is also an implied threat: the Archangel might just as well be unsheathing his sword as sheathing it, and plague would be the result of challenging papal rule of Rome.

Similarly, Shakespeare's Richard II, at the moment when he is forced to abdicate, says, "Yet know—my master, God omnipotent, / Is mustering in his clouds, on our behalf, / Armies of pestilence; and they shall strike / Your children yet unborn and unbegot, / That lift your vassal hands against my head, / And threat the glory of my precious crown" (Act III, Scene 3). It is a striking image, with plague as the punishment for upending the divinely ordained legitimate political structure. Conversely, the king can bestow health, and English monarchs practiced the "laying on of hands" for the health of a subject until the Stuarts. Apollo, although not originally the sun god, became identified with the sun in antiquity, and as such was appropriated by the French king Louis XIV, the Sun King, who dared to do what Augustus recoiled from, appearing in pageants as Apollo the Sun God to centralize and legitimize his shaky political authority. Nor was healing absent from the attributes of the French kings. Even many in the crowd who cheered Louis XVI's beheading ran to the guillotine to dip their handkerchiefs in the sacred blood for use against disease. The sun stands for power, order, and health, and the sun, like Gregory's policies, moves from east to west.

Thus St. Gregory the Great, partly by his own savvy and partly by the accretions of time, came to be identified with the Apollonian ideals of order, reason, and legitimacy. He and his institutions also came to be identified by detractors with the toxic aspects of Apollonianism in extremis: oppressiveness, abuse of power, and everything that we would now call totalitarianism. The connection of St. Gregory the Great to totalitarianism was reinforced by Pope Gregory XVI, elected in 1831. History has not been kind to this Pope Gregory: he is remembered for his use of secret police and a general obscurantism.

(In fairness, it must be pointed out that Pope Gregory XVI also abolished the use of torture, once and for all, in the Papal State.) This was the era truly represented in Sardou's play, rather than the supposed setting of 1800. There were no police, let alone secret police, in June 1800. It would have taken weeks to approve an order of torture. Mario Cavaradossi might have been shot outright in 1800, but we would not have had the play as we read it now. Men like Scarpia ruled Rome in the middle of the nineteenth century, rather than at the start, with the full support of the retrogressive Pope Gregory XVI. He famously banned gaslights and locomotive trains from the Papal State as being "prejudicial to religion." Furthermore, he fetishized St. Gregory the Great beyond the selection of his own papal name. He founded the Order of San Gregorio Magno, which still exists, and spoke at length of the Gregorian ideals of legitimacy and submission to authority, even at the expense of Christian charity. When the French reformer Lammennais finally managed to wangle an audience with this pope, and presented him with his radical ideas for the renewal of the Catholic faith, he was disappointed to be sent away with a lecture on the virtues of obedience and given a medal of St. Gregory for his troubles. The more Pope Gregory entrenched the increasing anachronism of the Papal State, the easier it became to see all Gregorian ideals critically.

All this would have been perfectly apparent to an Italian of the nineteenth century, and, to a certain extent, to the French, who were politically central to the Rome Question throughout the era. It would have been less apparent to an Englishman, who would have a different set of meanings for the symbols in question. St. Gregory the Great is not loved by the Italian people. The name Gregory does not appear on any list of the hundred most common names in Italy, but it has consistently ranked in the top fifty in English-speaking countries, landing at thirty-seven for the twentieth century. Such lists are unreliable, but the fact remains that you can live many years in Italy without ever meeting a man named Gregorio. Of course there are other factors involved in the giving of names, but affection or antipathy for the source influences, consciously or otherwise, that name's use or neglect.

If an Englishman (or, by implication, an English speaker, since language carries with it the baggage of history) thinks of St. Gregory at all, it is as a lover of music, an efficient administrator, and a drooling admirer of the Angles/English. A recent English-language *Lives of the Popes* by Richard P. McBrien has appendices ranking the ten best and ten worst popes (this in itself being typical of the northern European predilection for order). Number One on the list of the best is Pope John XXIII, followed in second place by Pope St. Gregory I (the Great). No Italian could come to the same conclusion. Gregory is regarded as the founder of the Papal State. Pope John XXIII officially ended it, formally retiring the tiara as "prejudicial" (interesting word) to the true mission of the papacy. Any Roman would perceive the two men as polar opposites. As much as the English maniacally loathe the papacy, the English imagination simply does not associate St. Gregory the Great with the historical fact of the Papal State as clearly as Italians do. This is part of the reason why English speakers have consistently missed the point of *Tosca*.

But it's only part of the reason. Mythic significance is more accessible to the Roman mind, even today, than to the more literal Anglo-Saxon mind. (Pasolini, for one, was convinced that the ancient sense of myth survived into the modern day most authentically among the uneducated urban subproletariat of Rome—more on him later.) And the point of *Tosca* is in its mythic significance. Scarpia is a *minister* of the Papal State, which is to say he is a Gregorian minister. In short, he is a priest of Apollo, and one who has run amok in his abuse of power. Consider his entrance in Act I and its effect on the choirboys who were having fun. It is not a stretch to recall the whip on display at San Gregorio Magno. His first line is rarely translated properly: "Tal baccano in chiesa!" A *baccano* is a mess, a riot, but the root of course is "bacchanalia," or an orgy in honor of Apollo's rival god Dionysus/Bacchus. Clearly, Dionysian rites have no place in Scarpia's worldview.

In Greek mythology, the Olympian Council of Twelve Gods sat in serene splendor until a newcomer god, Dionysus, demanded a seat. The humble Hestia, goddess of the hearth, resigned her seat in favor of the wild Dionysus, who taught men the art of winemaking and "conquered the world" with this knowledge. The priests of Apollo often resisted the raucous newcomer, whose rites included drunken orgies. When these priests denied the divinity of Dionysus, they met their death—usually by dismemberment—at the hands of his devotees: nymphs, satyrs, and other humans inflamed with wine, variously called maenads, Bacchae, or bacchantes. Most famously, this vision of worldviews in conflict is found in Euripides' *The Bacchae*, where inflamed maenads tear Pentheus, king of Thebes and a priest of Apollo, to pieces. Interestingly, the battles are not fought by the gods themselves but by their devotees. The Greeks never suggested that Dionysus should replace Apollo or rule over him, only that a complete system would have to acknowledge the divinity of both ends of the spectrum.

Tosca the Maenad

Tosca is the maenad who challenges the absolute rule of the Apollonian Scarpia. For starters, she is a "diva," one of remarkably few in opera. Diva means opera star (it has come to mean any notable woman), but of course it really means a pagan goddess. Tosca is called a diva in the course of the opera (though not in Sardou's play) by Scarpia (Act I), not by Mario. Scarpia recognizes Tosca's mythic identity in a way that eludes Mario. Even if she had not been so named explicitly, she would still qualify as a priestess of Dionysus just by virtue of being a woman of the theater. The theater is the realm of Dionysus: the Athenian Drama Festivals of antiquity were sacred liturgies performed in honor of Dionysus, a channeling of the spirit of the earlier drunken orgies into a (barely) more respectable form when the god attained Olympian recognition. The Athenian dramas

were sung to some extent—how much is not known—and accompanied by percussion and other instruments. It was the desire to re-
create the spirit, if not the details, of the Athenian Festivals that led
to the creation of opera itself by the Florentine Camerata in 1597. At
the same time Sardou was writing, Wagner was attempting to redefine opera with his Bayreuth Festival, the clear model of which was
the ancient Athenian Drama Festival. Nietzsche wrote at great length
(and with some twisting of history) of the ancient Athenian rites, of
the Apollonian and Dionysian urges, and of Richard Wagner as the
long-awaited synthesis of these conflicting urges. Later, of course,
Nietzsche choked back all his words and pronounced Bizet's *Carmen*
the salvation of mankind, but the damage was done and we still
speak of the Apollonian and the Dionysian much as Nietzsche imagined them. To this day, people speak of "music purists" as very distinct from mere "opera fans"—a distinction of Apollonian versus
Dionysian allegiances.

Nietzsche was not the only one who strove to see a resolution of
the ancient conflict in the theater: infusing the theater with a modicum of Apollonian reason and moderation was a goal then and still is
today. The old Tor di Nona Theater of Rome, founded in the seventeenth century by the remarkable émigré Queen Christina of Sweden
in direct violation of the pope's wishes, was in constant trouble with
the censors and frequently shut down. Finally, someone had the
bright idea to rename it the Teatro Apollo, and as such it flourished
under papal rule until it was finally demolished in the 1880s to make
room for the Tiber River embankments. But the name is an oxy-
moron. You can't have an Apollo Theater any more than you can
have a Bacchus Health Clinic. The name was meant, consciously or
not, as a sop to those who found theater itself inherently immoral
and anarchic. Perhaps this was deep in the subconscious of the people who opened the Apollo Theater in Harlem and all the other
Apollo Theaters in the world as well. Even the august Paris Opera
House, the Palais Garnier, was officially known as the Académie
Nationale de Musique, as if they hoped no one would notice it would

be an opera house. A statue of Apollo holding his lyre tops the grandiose edifice.

There is more that associates Tosca with Dionysus. Her name, Floria, is not a standard Italian name. It identifies her as a vegetation goddess, as Dionysus was a vegetation god, and allies her with all the dismemberment and bloodletting rituals once reserved for the Powers who brought forth nourishment from the earth. She even makes her entrance carrying flowers, a detail no director can ignore, no matter how iconoclastic the production. She does not shoot Scarpia, nor poison him, but cuts him open and makes him choke to death on blood. She traditionally wears a red dress in the second and third acts, as do the bacchante in paintings of Burne-Jones and others from Sardou's era. The blood color is known to designers as "opera red."

Then there is the whole issue of wine. In the libretto, we read that Tosca, in the climax of Act II, goes to the table to take the glass of wine Scarpia poured for her, with a trembling hand, and sees the knife. No further details. Maria Callas and the director Franco Zeffirelli famously worked out a compelling bit of stage business for this moment in an important production at London's Covent Garden in 1964. Tosca poured herself the glass of wine, trembling, and knocked it over. Tracing the flow of the wine on the white tablecloth with her fingertips led her eyes to land on the knife. Supposedly, Callas worked for hours on this bit to make sure the timing would be exact with the music. It was a thrilling moment, and not only because it was executed with her legendary attention to detail. She imbued the wine with a greater significance than the libretto recognized explicitly. In fact, the wine reminds Tosca, as a Dionysian, of her own true identity. It is as if it reminds her that no maenad need suffer abuse from any skanky little priest of Apollo—she can always dismember him! This would explain the otherwise puzzling lines Tosca then utters: "Killed by a woman! . . . Look at me! I am Tosca!" Why the sudden need to identify herself? Might Scarpia perhaps have mistaken her for, say, Lizzie Borden, wandering onstage from another opera? No, this moment is a bloodletting orgy of Tosca's self-actualization as a maenad whose trail was, as ever, blazed by wine.

Callas, like Pasolini (the only director with whom she made a film, *Medea*), always grasped the mythic dimension of her characters, and in fact a greatly disproportionate number of her most celebrated roles involved a pagan priestess performing a ritual: *Norma*, *La vestale*, *Medea* (in both operatic and cinematic incarnations). Even Lucia di Lamermoor and Lady Macbeth dwell, as archetypes, on this same plane. If there was an inherent "Greekness" in any character, Callas would reveal it, and she understood that Tosca's Greekness is one of the attributes that put her at odds with the Westernized Gregorian, Scarpia. Their conflict is not situational. It's not about who's doing what to whom. Tosca never mentions Mario as she hurls abuse at the dying Scarpia. Theirs is a conflict of opposing natures.

Luther vs. the Quadriga

If Tosca and Scarpia represent the conflict of Dionysus and Apollo (or Isis and Osiris, or Yin and Yang, or Gestalt and Reason, or Nature and Culture, or Id and Ego, or however one chooses to define it), then why not simply write an opera about Dionysus and Apollo? One could—some have—but this would not be the Roman way to address the issue. Everyone from Sardou to the present has stressed that *Tosca* is a Roman story. Surely they mean something more than the setting: *Tosca* is Roman in a deeper way than, say, *Bohème* is Parisian.

There is a line across western Europe that separates the northern and southern sectors. It is not a perfect line, much less a visible border like those prized by modern mapmakers, but it exists all the same. It follows, very roughly, the ancient border of the Roman Empire. This is also the line that divides—again roughly, with aberrations—the Protestant North from the Catholic South. Historians tend to focus on the political reasons that caused the religious rift of the Reformation, but the primary reasons were actually cultural, perhaps racial, in the broadest sense of the term, and it would seem determined, to some extent, by which countries were once part of the Roman Empire and which were based on Germanic inhabitants. The two camps, to oversimplify grotesquely, had and have two different ways of looking at things, which in turn engender different religious beliefs (rather than vice versa, as many people tend to believe if they think about such things at all).

Greek mythology does not separate human endeavors into discrete spheres of the sexual, the political, the spiritual, and so forth: all are mixed together in a holistic vision of the human condition. In many ways, the Roman mind held on to this. Bernini, the man who basically created the baroque Rome we still love to visit, caused a scandal with his statue of *Saint Teresa in Ecstasy* in the Cornaro Chapel of Santa Maria della Vittoria. The saint is being prodded by an angel with a spear, and is frankly and undeniably experiencing a very fleshy orgasm, amplified by the shimmering ripples in her robes. The setting of the statue is even more shocking to some than the action depicted: the chapel has trompe l'oeil boxes along the sides, containing members of the Cornaro family sitting in contemplation of the miracle. It is a theater, which, in Italy, traditionally meant an opera house. The various Cornaros are not in fact watching the saint. Their heads are turned elsewhere, yet they appear to be paying attention. In fact, they appear to be hearing the miracle, as if it were an opera. The statue and setting were castigated by many for its theatricality. The melding of sexual and spiritual was shocking enough for many visitors, but it is the addition of the theatrical that threw the most rabid critics over the edge. And most of these critics were from the hordes of transalpine art junkies who descended on Rome in the eighteenth and nineteenth centuries. The Romans themselves seemed to take it all in stride. To this day, one sees pious Roman women praying in the chapel as if it were the most natural thing in the world.

When Luther preached his message of emphasis on the Word, the Germanic peoples responded. Some went even further than Luther in their literalism. The literalist message felt right to northern Europeans, and literal interpretation of Scripture (and therefore, by implication, of everything else) became a hallmark of some strains of the Protestant movement. It fell on deaf ears south of the Alps. You can't make an Italian believe in the literal truth of anything, least of all a text. Catholic theologians maintained (and still officially maintain) the Quadriga, the fourfold layers of interpretation of Scripture (and therefore of everything else). The layers of the Quadriga are (1) literal/historical, (2) allegorical, (3) moral/theological, and (4) anagogical. This last meaning is perhaps the most interesting for critical purposes. This split survives—is emphasized, even—in English translations of Catholic and Protestant ideas. Catholics speak in English of the Holy Spirit, a living, breathing (*spira*) entity, while the traditional Protestant term is the Holy Ghost, with all its implications of something that is not alive in quite the same way it once had been.

The nature of the Eucharist was the focus of a great debate that reveals the divergent predilections of Protestant and Catholic Europe. Luther favored the literal/historical aspect of scriptural exegesis, and though he believed Christ was present in the Eucharist others went further: Calvin taught that Christ was present spiritually but not physically, and Zwingli taught that the Eucharist was symbolic only, taking literalism to its natural conclusions and rejecting any other possibilities of interpretation. The literalist strain in Protestantism has at times far exceeded that of the founders of the movement. The idea one encounters among literalists is that bread and wine on the altar, being bread and wine, cannot be anything else. The Roman theologians agreed that of course they are bread and wine (meaning #1 of the Quadriga), which means that they are something else as well (#2), which is crucial for us to do over and over again for our own salvation (#3), and, since this was so many times before—at the Last Supper, the manna in the desert—then it can continue to happen all over again every time the rite is performed (#4). This is the difference between Protestant and Catholic Europe. It's really not about the pope. It's about the best way to interpret a text—and everything is a text.

This duality continues today and is still the chief reason "Latins" and "Anglo-Saxons" often fail to understand each other. Rome remains the place where multiple layers of interpretation are most possible, and therefore where the term *verismo* will have a different implication than our word "realism." Look at the great movie *Bicycle Thief*. Is it a veristic, near-documentary made with an invisible, non-editorializing hand of the director about an ordinary person facing quotidian problems, or is it an allegory of the cyclical alienation of the human condition? Of course it is entirely and authentically both at the same time, which is why the movie must take place in Rome. In director DeSica's subsequent film, *Miracle in Milan*, he tells a fable, clearly "framed" as such. It even has a "magical" ending, with all the homeless of Milan being chased on bicycles [!] by the police and taking off into the sky, a vision that must have been very clear in the mind of Steven Spielberg for his American übermyth, *E.T.* Such an ending would make more sense in the industrial Lombard city of Milan, while *Bicycle Thief* is only possible in the equally gritty yet mythically vibrant city of Rome.

This is why Rome has always been regarded as a sacred city. It is not, even for Catholics, because the pope lives there. There are many more convenient, pleasant places for the pope to live. That was tried. It didn't work. No, the pope must live in Rome because it is a sacred city. Likewise, some of us were taught that Rome is sacred because St. Peter was martyred there and the Church was literally and figuratively [!] built upon him. Perhaps, but that puts the cart before the horse. Peter could have been—and nearly was—martyred in any number of spots throughout the empire. The legend says that Peter, already an old man, was leaving Rome to escape the persecutions of Nero when he encountered a mysterious stranger. Asking the stranger where he was going ("quo vadis?") he was told, "I am going to Rome to be crucified again." The stranger immediately vanished and Peter realized he had encountered the risen Christ. He knew he had to return to Rome to face his death. A small chapel on the Appian Way marks the spot, although I must tell you that it is usually surrounded, in classic Roman fashion, with prostitutes and drug dealers. But the point, I maintain, was not that Peter had to die. He could have identified himself as the leader of the Christians to any soldier or official anywhere and been dispatched on the spot without further ceremony. The point was that he had to do so in the city of Rome in order for his martyrdom to have anagogical resonance with Jesus' own death. In Rome, Peter can become Jesus, or some version of him. For some reason, events and ideas in the city of Rome resonate in a unique way, and have done so for a very long time.

So the *Romanità* of *Tosca* is more than a travelogue of picturesque locations. And the fact that it is about the Sleazy Police Chief and the Jealous Opera Singer does not prevent it, in the Latin mind, from being about great cosmic confrontations. Northern Europeans would—and have—treated the same issues quite differently. Germans (and Germanics) excel at fairy tales and fables: you can tell an "impossible" story and remain a literalist if you draw a frame, so to speak, around the action and say something along the lines of "Once, in the Magic Kingdom of ___," or, for that matter, "A long, long time ago, in a galaxy far, far away. . . ." Italians have been faulted for failing at the genres of fantasy, science fiction, or anything dealing with the supernatural. (Recently, in our homogeneous world, this is of course less so, as witnessed by the magical realism of Italo Calvino—which is, significantly, more highly regarded in America than in Italy.) The fact is that Italians have not traditionally needed to place their tales "out there" to tell tall tales. A very ordinary person walking down the streets of Rome, viewed through the methods of the Quadriga, contains all possible universes within himself or herself.

The conflict of Apollo and Dionysus appears in the opera *Death in Venice*, composed by the Englishman Benjamin Britten and based on the novella by the German Thomas Mann. The hero Aschenbach looks at the boys playing on the beach and has a frank hallucination of a contest between the rival gods. The dream sequence is further identified as surreal by balletic choreography. One of the very few operas in which an opera diva makes an appearance is Richard Strauss's and Hugo von Hofmannsthal's *Ariadne auf Naxos*, in which Dionysus (Bacchus) also appears. In its original form, *Ariadne* presented an opera based in the mythic world of antiquity in which the action was invaded by a "lost" troupe of Italian commedia dell'arte performers. It was not a success, although there were several reasons besides incomprehensibility for its failure. Hofmannsthal and Strauss went back to the drawing board and added a prologue dealing with the backstage politics before the "opera" itself. The Diva appears, and the Tenor (albeit briefly) in their "normal" forms in the prologue before they "reveal" their mythic identities as Ariadne and Bacchus in the opera-within-the-opera. At the end, we have a type of mystical marriage between Ariadne, formerly the Diva, and Bacchus. A frame—quite literally, in most productions—must be drawn around the real-life characters before their mythic identities can be explored. The Italian clowns, significantly, move freely between both worlds without any great change in their manner.

So the Anglo-Saxon critics say that Italians fail at the supernatural, when the failure is actually a different point of view. There are many cases of this in opera. Everyone dumps on Verdi's witches in his *Macbeth*. They're right. Verdi wasn't interested in witches. He was more interested in an actual human being, Lady Macbeth, acting like a deranged witch, and he certainly did not fail in creating her character. Budden, usually astute in issues of Italian cultural perceptions, finds Verdi's devils' choruses in *Giovanna d'Arco* pathetic compared to what Weber and Wagner were achieving with the supernatural in their operas. The *Giovanna* devils' music, he sniffs, "reeks of the Neapolitan café." Quite right. Where better to encounter the Devil than a café in Naples? The idea that the Devil must wear black and act spooky is a specifically German idea: "Gothic," as they used to say, or even "Goth," as the hipsters now say. But since the German notion is at the root of the American mentality (even more than the English, due to the huge numbers of Americans who trace their recent ancestry to Germany), it becomes to us the right notion. As the world becomes more and more American, it becomes the only notion. All Americans are Protestants—even those of us who are not Protestants. We have complete faith in The Word. The Italians who do not rush to emulate seem to have fallen behind and gotten "lost in the past." You can imagine the gulf this creates in German and Italian notions of opera productions, which will be explored further in the appropriate chapter.

Apollo's Revenge

Let's assume that people in Rome in 1900 understood *Tosca* as a conflict of archetypes rather than a mere bodice ripper. What did they make of it? Above all, what did the archpriest of Apollo make of this? Pope St. Pius X was elected in 1903. He was regarded as an intellectual and had been known for piety in his time in Treviso, Mantua, and Venice. He was also a reactionary. He regarded the presence of the Italian government in Rome as a foreign occupation, railed against Modernism in all its forms, and set about to "restore all things in Christ." In short, he was a perfect Gregorian. Only those popes who fit the oppressive Gregorian mold got canonized these last hundred years. Pius received his enrollment in the Canon of Saints in 1954 by Pope Pius XII, another Gregorian whose beatification process is being rushed through its various stages at present despite his highly questionable role during World War II. (Pope John XXIII, the most popular, charismatic, and probably most holy pope in memory, languishes in the process. Perhaps he should have held on to that blasted tiara.) Nothing was more important to Pius X than music. Among his very first acts was the issuance of a papal bull *Tra le sollecitudine*, the famous *Motu proprio* of 1903. (A *Motu proprio* is a bull issued by a pope who is *self-moved* to speak on a given topic, which shows the personal stake Pius X had in this area.)

In the first paragraph, Pius maintains the necessity of spelling out the proper rules for liturgical music due in part to the "fatal influence exercised on sacred art by profane and theatrical art," and warns of the "pleasure that music directly produces, which cannot be easily contained within the right limits." He lays out the principle that the Gregorian chant is the official music of the Church and all other music must be considered in how closely it "approaches in its movement, inspiration and savor the Gregorian form." He admits the polyphony of Palestrina, saying it agrees with the Gregorian model. Those who debated Palestrina's music in his own day (the sixteenth century, in which it was a terrific cause célèbre) would have been surprised to hear a pope say so, but Pius could hardly be so reactionary as to bar Palestrina. Besides, he would have been instantly denounced even by conservatives as ignorant and coarse, which he was not. Pius also recognizes that the Church has a role in fostering new art, but spends two paragraphs making sure that any new music "be free from reminiscences of motifs adopted in the theaters, and be not fashioned even in their external forms after the manner of profane pieces." He then states the case bluntly: "Among the different kinds of modern music, that which appears less suitable for accompanying the functions of public worship is the theatrical style, which was in the greatest vogue, especially in Italy, during the last century. This of its very nature is diametrically opposed to Gregorian Chant . . . and therefore to the most important law of all good sacred music." The theatrical meant the operatic, plain and simple. It is an issue of sound, not sight, for how else can a pope as addicted to pageantry as Pius rail against the theatrical? Then comes a list of prohibitions: women's voices, the mainstay of the opera, are barred from church. The piano is likewise barred in a sentence where it is ranked with "noisy or frivolous instruments such as drums, cymbals, bells and the like." The use of woodwinds is severely curtailed. Pius sent this encyclical to the vicar-general of Rome with an official letter wherein he continues his complaints about the influence of the music of "*our* Italian theaters" (lowercase, meaning "yours and mine," not the royal "We") and says, "We are overjoyed to be able to give these regulations at a time when We are about to celebrate the fifteenth centenary of the death of the glorious and incomparable Pontiff St. Gregory the Great, to whom an ecclesiastical tradition dating back many centuries has attributed the composition of these sacred melodies and from whom they have derived their name."

None of this makes any logical sense at all unless we attribute ancient, mythic significance to music in its various forms. All of Pius's prohibitions (women's voices, percussion instruments—including the piano, which the musicologists assure us it is, and which is why it is lumped with drums and cymbals—and woodwinds) are immediately recognizable as instruments of the ancient Dionysian rites, both in the woods and in the theater of Athens, and therefore abhorrent to Apollo. It is not based on Scripture—indeed, Hebrew Scripture (which Gregory claimed as his basis of proper liturgical music) specifically instructs worshippers to make a "glad noise unto the Lord on cymbals and tambourines." Psalm 150 even instructs the congregation to praise the Lord with pipes and harps and specifically "loud, crashing" cymbals! Pius ignores this as blithely as Gregory had. And what could the problem with woodwinds be except Apollo's disdain of the rustic rites, the age-old hatred of the refined for the raw (even though woodwinds have become as sophisticated as anything else: Pius's prejudices are based not in the modern world but in the ancient). Pius, Pentheus-like, would admit nothing of the Dionysian to his temple, and he knew the enemy when he saw it. Furthermore, the line about Italian theaters shows that Pius was not ignorant of the opera, and the opera that people were talking about in Rome at that time was *Tosca*. The issues at stake in the opera did not escape him. In short, the *Motu proprio* of 1903 is a hysterical reaction to *Tosca*. There have been several important papal pronouncements on music throughout the twentieth century, but the *Motu proprio* remains the point of departure and recently has been reiterated as a tonic against the freedoms allowed by Vatican II. The Church is still reacting against *Tosca*.

At this point the reader might fairly object, "But I'm not interested in the liturgical music of the Catholic Church!" Keep reading:

there's much more going on here than what Catholics listen to while praying. We're looking at some very intelligent people exploring the meanings of music itself. And attitudes about music are never merely about music.

In our own day, the conservative Gregorian point of view is strongly articulated by no less a personage than Cardinal Ratzinger, now Pope Benedict XVI. This notable has written many of the Vatican's pronouncements on various issues, human sexuality in particular, over the last twenty years, with a consistent steering toward the Right. He has also penned two books and several articles on music, in which his tastes are apparent. Nothing would satisfy Pope Benedict more than a steady diet of Gregorian chant with occasional flings into such cutting-edge modernity as Palestrina's polyphony. He has no stomach for the reforms of Vatican II, which in fact were only half-earted reforms (they allowed for diversity in music but still acknowledged the primacy of the *Motu proprio* of 1903, which gives a lot of wiggle room for conservatives). In fact, then-Cardinal Ratzinger stated plainly that only the spirit of obedience (a Gregorian virtue) compelled him to accept such reforms at all. But his greatest enemy is anything that smacks of the theatrical. He equally loathes opera and rock in the church. It's hard to know what a man of Ratzinger's background considers "rock music," but he is definitely on to something. Rock has something in common with opera in that it is first of all theater and second of all musical. An extremely educated man with a fine nose for historical subtext, the erstwhile Cardinal Ratzinger wrote at some length about sacred music in precisely the same terms of Apollonian/Dionysian duality that we are employing here. He stated that only the Apollonian can have a rightful place in worship, because it elevates the spirit. Dionysian music, conversely, "drags man into the intoxication of the senses, crushes rationality, and subjects the spirit to the sense." Whatever the parameters of proper worship music are or should be, the implication is clearly that "rational" music is beneficial to people while "sensual" music is malignant. Pope Benedict dismisses Hebraic precedence just as Pius and Gregory had. That same Psalm 150 urges "all that breathes" to praise God. Presumably, "all that breathes" includes sopranos and rock stars, and David himself speaks and acts more like an ecstatically tanked habitué of the Burning Man festival than the Platonic ideal of a philosopher-king, but no matter. Absolute authority (Pentheus and Scarpia in literature; Augustus, Gregory, Louis XIV, et al, in history) has no room for any Dionysiac uncertainty principle.

Of course, one doesn't generally encounter rock, operatic music (whatever that means), Palestrina, or Gregorian chant in American Catholic churches. One is usually confronted with the guitar and some well-intentioned "leader of song" plugging away through the Mass. This genre is best represented by Marty Haugen, a wildly popular composer of songs for church usage. Although Haugen is himself a Lutheran, his music holds a virtual monopoly on Catholic churches in America. If you have been in a Catholic, Episcopalian, or Lutheran (among others) church in the last twenty years, you have probably heard his music. He is perhaps the most played composer in the world today.

Haugen and Pope Benedict XVI might be considered the polar opposites of the issue, but I question that. Haugen, predictably, writes and lectures much. He, too, despises the operatic, frankly blaming it for the demise of Catholic church music. He calls all Catholic music between the council of Trent (mid-sixteenth century) and Vatican II "unspiritual." So much for Monteverdi, Vivaldi, Scarlatti, Mozart, Beethoven, Gounod, Dvořák, Janáček, Poulenc, and God knows who else, but of course those composers all wrote operas as well as writing liturgical music. Their spiritual credentials are compromised. He further dismisses anything classical as elitist—a point of view that surely would have shocked Verdi, among others. The notion is that the appearance of a guitar and an unbearably sincere, unschooled, corn-fed American singer in front of an altar is supposed to imply something about the goals of that particular congregation:

populist, nonelitist, and so on. The conflict of Apollo and Dionysus does not exactly follow the political divisions of Right and Left, tempting as it often is to see it in this way. And for all the intended populist intentions of the so-called Folk Mass, the guiding spirit is Apollonian. The true nature of the Folk Mass is revealed in its meticulous excision of everything remotely erotic. The need for church music to be innocuous is akin to the need for it to imitate the calm cadences of the Gregorian chant. Both represent Apollonian fears of the anarchy and sensuality that might ensue if congregants heard music that stirred rather than calmed (repressed?) the soul. The ubiquitous guitar in American Catholic churches today is nothing but Apollo's seven-stringed lyre in its latest incarnation.

King David played the lyre like Apollo but also employed every other kind of musician and even danced in ecstatic nudity, bacchante-like, before the Ark. David knew what eluded Pius and continues to elude many: that one must seek a balance between the two poles, not try to quash one with the other.

The Leap of Faith

The finale of the opera makes the case plain. Giacosa, typically, thought the idea of having Tosca jump off the parapets simply too vulgar to contemplate, and suggested a mad scene instead. Puccini would have none of it. For starters, mad scenes were not Puccini's "thing." He never wrote an actual one, and the one time he employed something that could arguably be filed under that heading—the finale to *Suor Angelica*—everyone found it ineffective. But there was more to it than that. There is no reason for Tosca to "go mad" at the end of the opera. Mario's death is very annoying to her, no doubt, but not enough to change her character. Tosca had to leap off the Castel Sant'Angelo in order to fulfill her character.

She was not the first soprano to fly offstage at a finale. Wagner's Senta (*The Flying Dutchman*) and Brünnhilde (*The Ring of the*

Nibelung) each take some sort of redemptive jump to their deaths at the end of their respective operas. Gounod's Sapho jumps to her death over the lost love of a young man (she isn't *that* Sappho). There are others. But two are direct antecedents of *Tosca*, one a nonsinging woman and the other a tenor. The first requires a bit of staging that makes *Tosca* seem subdued by comparison. Auber's *La muette de Portici* (1828) tells the story of a doomed love affair set against Masaniello's Neapolitan uprising against the Spaniards in 1637. Just as the plot machinations become unmanageable, Vesuvius erupts. The mute girl of the title (written as a mime/dance role) brings down the final curtain by twirling out the window to her death, presumably in the lava floes below. The difficulties in staging this opera are obvious, and it rarely gets performed in concert because of the singular muteness of the lead. It is quite good, however, and in its day it was a great scandal, to say the least. The opera's 1830 premiere in Brussels, under the title *Masaniello*, stirred the audience to such a pitch that a riot ensued, which in turn is credited for lighting the spark that resulted in Belgian independence from the United Netherlands. There must have been something implicitly political in *la muette*'s self-sacrifice.

Verdi understood the orgasmic implications of a heroic jump, nineteen years later, and applied them to his opera *La battaglia di Legnano*. This work was written for the Teatro Argentina (the theater where *Tosca* is singing, according to Sardou) in Rome at a time of great tumult. The revolutions that had upset the status quo throughout Europe in 1848 finally reached Rome itself. Pope Pius IX escaped the city, and hordes of volunteers (including Garibaldi) convened to defend the city against the inevitable backlash of the French and the Austrians. Just two weeks before the short-lived Roman Republic of 1849 was declared, Verdi's opera received its premiere. *Legnano* was an out-and-out propaganda piece, calculated to move the audience to a frenzy of patriotic fervor. There is a love triangle: two friends, Rolando and Arrigo, both in love with Lida, Rolando's wife, set against the great conflict of the Lombard League and the Holy Roman (German) Emperor Barbarossa in 1182. The parallel to current events was hardly coincidental. Rolando discovers Arrigo's intentions just as the Lombards are uniting for the decisive battle of the title. Rather than kill Arrigo, Rolando decides to disgrace him by locking him in a tower so he will have to miss the most important battle in Italian history. Arrigo's patriotism forbids this, however, and the tenor wraps himself in the red, white, and green Italian flag (an obvious anachronism), cries "Viva Italia!" (on a high C), and jumps out the window. He survives the fall (Verdi had discreetly written a rippling little woodwind prelude to the act to suggest that there might be a moat) but is mortally wounded at the (offstage) battle. In the short final act, he is reconciled to Rolando before he dies, and the crowd, amid celebrating their victory, pronounces that any man who would do such a thing must be a hero. The audience at the January 1849 premiere went literally bonkers. One young patriot during that run was so moved that he emulated the Big Moment, wrapping himself in an Italian flag, crying "Viva Italia!" and leaping out of a fourth-tier proscenium box to land, unharmed, in the orchestra pit below. (I cannot verify this story, but *se non è vero . . .*)

This story is often treated by English-speaking writers with a certain condescending indulgence typical of our culture's attitude as a whole toward these cute but hotheaded and rather childish Latins. But there were other reasons why Verdi's spectacular stage effect would have resonated with a Roman audience in 1849, meanings that continue to elude the Anglo-Saxon nations today. The battle of Chapultepec had occurred a mere two years previously between American forces and the cadets of the Mexican military academy outside Mexico City. What we call the Mexican War was, in a sense, another clash of Latin and Anglo-Saxon points of view (as was the actual battle of Legnano) transferred to a New World. It is not much remembered in the United States, but the war and especially the battle of Chapultepec continue to figure in the Mexican national consciousness today. After defeating the regular Mexican troops, General Winfield Scott attacked the hilltop Chapultepec Palace, which was defended bravely by young cadets. When defeat became inevitable, the remaining eleven cadets wrapped themselves in the red, white, and green Mexican flags and leaped off the ramparts to their deaths below rather than surrender to the *yanquís*. The Americans won the war, but the moral victory, by virtue of this suicidal jump, remains Mexico's. Mexicans visit the spot as a place of patriotic pilgrimage, and every year the top eleven cadets in the military academy are wrapped in national flags and symbolically entombed as national martyrs, the highest honor that can be attained at the academy. Rome, with its active diplomatic community that included, at that time, a Mexican ambassador, must have been abuzz with this story and recognized a symbolic analogue in *La battaglia di Legnano*. Even the flags were (and are) the same colors. Within a few months of the wild premiere of the opera, the Roman Republic was gone and there was no chance to produce the opera again except under heavy disguise, which was not successful. *Legnano* had to be fully itself in all its over-the-top (literally) glory or it was nothing at all. It was put aside and Verdi, characteristically, spoke of it little or not at all. But few Romans who lived through those heady days could have forgotten about the exciting events at the Teatro Argentina, and Verdi's opera became part of the vast mythos that is the city of Rome.

With all this in mind, it seems rather impotent to criticize the score of *Tosca* as vulgar, crass, or turgid. That is exactly the point of the score. The notion of decorum (rather than sensual abandon—St. Gregory's and Pope Benedict's writings are clear on this) in music is at the very core of the Gregorian ideal, which extends into the political fact of the city of Rome and the monarchical conception of the papacy. To have written a "tasteful" score would have been to ratify the tainted ideals under attack in this work. Tosca as a Dionysian revels in an earthy vulgarity as a statement of purpose and rejects the implications of seemly music.

The much-misunderstood finale of the work illustrates this perfectly. As we have seen, Tosca climbs the parapet by the statue of St. Michael the Archangel, cries out to Scarpia to meet her before God, and jumps, presumably (in Sardou's imagination) into the Tiber. The orchestra blasts out (fortissississimo) the "big theme" from "E lucevan le stelle." No English-speaking writer has been able to make heads or tails out of this. Kerman, whose brain apparently fevered at the mere mention of this opera, calls this the final insult in an evening full of personal violations. "The orchestra plays the first thing that pops into its head," he says of this (as if Puccini, of all people, couldn't have come up with another bang-'em-up melody for this moment had he been so inclined). I wonder if Kerman had the same gripe with Wagner's *Ring of the Nibelung*, where the whole weeklong affair ends with a reiteration of the Big Theme (admittedly, one of many great themes). Other commentators have twisted common sense into absurd apologies that make Tosca a more likable gal-next-door but still miss the point in a big way, saying that the Big Theme from the tenor's aria demonstrates that Tosca's thoughts are with her dear departed Mario at the supreme moment. Really? She doesn't say so. It would have been perfectly logical and within operatic convention to have Tosca exclaim, before her grande jeté, "Oh Mario! I'll see you again in heaven!" or some such line. But of course her thoughts are not with Mario at that moment, but rather with the true representative of her eternal struggle, Scarpia. In fact her thoughts are never entirely with Mario, even when she is making love to him ("Falle gli occhi neri"). In a way, Kerman is closer to the truth. The Big Theme has meaning simply by being what it is, a sensual gush of shameless melody. The operatic word for this is *slancio*, always translated as a rush or even a fit. There is a better translation that is generally avoided: an ejaculation (from the Latin *jacula*, a spear, which in Italian is *lancia*). When she jumps off the parapet—away from the statue of the archangel— she is saying (1) I do not believe that Gregory and his ilk have the power of life and death over us, (2) therefore he and they are not the legitimate rulers of Rome, and therefore, (3) their authority to dictate appropriate music is nulled. A lovely, redemptive plunk on the harp would hardly have illustrated that point as well as a blasting reiteration of the Big Hit Theme. *Tosca* is not shocking because it is a "searing indictment" of the Roman Catholic Church—plenty of other operas do that and no one seems too upset by it anymore (*Boris Godunov*, *Palestrina*, and *Don Carlos* spring to mind). Directors who caricature the Church and its clergy reduce rather than augment the scope of the opera. *Tosca* is scandalous because it is a battle for, not against, the soul of the Church. In demanding a hearing before God, Tosca claims legal parity with Scarpia. Apollo is Christ but so is Dionysus: the man/god born of a human mother and divine father, who experienced death, harrowed hell, and rose to the heavens, seated at the "right hand of the Father," rejected by conservative religious opinion before assuming his divine stature, and whose sacrament is wine. Tosca's case before God is an echo of Bernini's *St. Teresa in Ecstasy*, an orgasm of cosmic dimensions in a setting that acknowledges the common Dionysian provenance of church and theater. Let us recall here that Puccini said he was told *by God* that his vocation (his term) was in the theater and only in the theater. The curtain falls on Tosca's orgasm of victory, a victory that is political, spiritual, and, *pace* Kerman, musical.

Puccini is always credited with "theatrical instinct," but there really is no such thing. There is, instead, the ability to manipulate myth skillfully, whether conscious or not of the degree that this is happening in one's art. Myth resonates more vibrantly in Rome than in most places, so artists use Rome to explore them, but the issues are not confined to the actual fact of the city of Rome. It's not (only) about whether the pope or the Italian government is the legitimate ruler of Rome and the surrounding area. That was basically (although not entirely) solved by the time *Tosca* hit the operatic stage. It's about differing views of human nature and human validity. Tosca's leap is a consummate act of faith in the human condition; that the whole being, in its messy, unrefined carnality, has a right to stand before God in judgment with confidence. It's a message of hope.

Productions:
What You Might Expect to See

THE ART OF OPERATIC PRODUCTION—that is, bringing a piece to life on the stage—has been to a certain extent a victim of its own success. It has become the primary issue of any new presentation of an opera, with the singers and the total musical execution generally relegated to the final paragraph of critiques. Beverly Sills spoke of the success she had with creative new productions of the classics while at the New York City Opera: fans told her it "was like seeing an old painting in a new frame." Lovely, of course, but it is a sad day for art when critics spend 90 percent of their columns discussing the frame and only 10 percent on the canvas. Nor is the emphasis on production ideas the only problem. The debate about styles of production has fossilized. It seems that either one must stick to the letter of the libretto, which is what is called "conservative" or "literal," or apply some overarching concept on the whole work and twist everything to fit the concept, which is called "creative." Whether the production is good or not doesn't seem to enter the debate. I hereby propose a new standard: Does the production in question open up the possibilities of the opera or does it diminish them? A production of any genre can do either, and we who believe in the validity of Puccini's art will be best served by productions of the first quality, whether they are "traditional" (another catchphrase) or "radical interpretations."

It can be very exciting when a daring production succeeds. The clash of egos between the director and the composer can make for thrilling theater in and of itself. But more often it falls short. Not many directors have the genius to take on a composer as established as Puccini in anything resembling a fair fight. But this doesn't stop them from trying. Wrestling with the operatic favorites is the only way to make your résumé as an opera director. That is as it should be. But we in the audience must always question the motives behind what is set before us. Half of contemporary opera production is comprised of directors trying to prove their moral superiority to the work in question. (Yes, moral.) And by implication, they are demonstrating their superiority to the people (us) who would buy tickets to such things. With Puccini, that fraction is even higher. Everyone seems to feel the need to rework Puccini. The notion is that his major operas are so familiar that they need to be presented in a new way or they will die. This is partially laudable, although it would be more accurate to say they need to be presented with respect to the issues at stake in each opera, or they will die. I also have to question what it is about Puccini that makes him above all other composers so in need of "interpretation." One never sees "radical reinterpretations" of Berg's *Wozzeck*, for example, even though at this point Berg's opera is as familiar to audiences as *Fanciulla* and *Trittico*, if not *Bohème* and *Tosca* and *Butterfly*. Deep down, I think Puccini's frank emotionality embarrasses a lot of people, who like to tone it down with a lot of extraneous commentary. I love an interesting production of a Puccini opera, but I resent directors trying to save me from Puccini.

With Puccini, we also have the whole problem of realism (except, perhaps, in *Turandot*). Bits of stage business are not incidental; they are the core around which the score is constructed. When Wieland Wagner removed the props from his grandfather's operas, there was no loss to the drama. Indeed, Tristan and Isolde were discovered not to need a cup to be understood as drinking from the cup. The cup was a metaphor to begin with. In Puccini, the prop onstage can be a metaphor—the sword of Cio-Cio-San's father, for example—but it is also very much what it purports to be in real terms. Thus the candle and the key in Act I of *Bohème*, the deck of cards and the drops of blood in Act II of *Fanciulla*, and the eponymous overcoat in *Il tabarro*, for example, must be visibly present onstage unless total confusion is to ensue. Therefore, whatever updating is involved, or whatever concepts are grafted onto the original stories, there is a sameness to most productions of Puccini's operas. And when anyone attempts to do something different, which is laudable in and of itself, it often fails to address the core of the work in question. Puccini is difficult that way.

Manon Lescaut gets less interpretation from directors and designers than most of the Puccini repertory. It is a story that is firmly rooted in a time and place, not merely as a detail of its libretto but at its very core. The issue of luxury is inherent to Manon's nature and therefore to the story. If there has ever been a moment in history better equipped to explore the conflicts of love and luxury than rococo Paris, it has yet to be discovered. The only issue at stake is how much one wishes to comment on the luxury itself. This subject arises specifically in European productions, primarily in France, Germany, and the United Kingdom. The impetus came from German productions, particularly those of Götz Friedrich in Berlin from the '70s through the '90s. In his Wagner productions, most notably *Tannhäuser* and *Meistersinger*, the aristocracy and the bourgeoisie (respectively) were represented as corrupt. Well, duh, one might say, but again this is the German predilection for making explicit that which is implicit. Crippled, eye-patched well-to-do's crossed the stage making their nefarious plans. It seems apparent to me that this is in fact an endorsement of the ancient prejudices rather than a rejection of them, since it supports the idea that corruption is evident to the naked eye. Conversely, if it looks good, then it is good. Oh well, it was a phase, and one must applaud Friedrich and his imitators for attempting to wrestle, however clumsily, with their culture's difficult history. But the "ratty wallpaper aristocracy" idea has since been done to death, in Mozart's *Marriage of Figaro*, in Verdi's *Don Carlos*, and probably everywhere else. In *Manon Lescaut*, it makes no sense whatsoever. Geronte's palace must seduce us as it has seduced Manon or she is nothing but a flighty slut, which is another story altogether and one that does not work with the music provided. If you come across this idea in a staged version, either shrug it off as passé and tedious or boo the production team, according to your own preferences.

The ur-production of *Bohème*, and a good point of departure for any discussion of this opera in stage, is the Met's. It was conceived in 1977 by Franco Zeffirelli and is still going strong. Zeffirelli is excoriated in many circles for being visually overcooked, hopelessly traditional, and generally retrograde (his right-wing political affiliations in Italy have not helped this perception). There is no doubt that he can be—usually is—all of those things, but taking the Met *Bohème* on its own merits helps us to understand its enduring popularity. It is big, overblown, and punctiliously traditional, but it is well done on all those counts. Zeffirelli solved the problem of the small garret on a huge stage well in Acts I and IV, with a module room against a backdrop of the rooftops of Paris. The protagonists can be seen well within this module from every corner of the Met, which is nothing short of miraculous. Act III looks like any other Act III, basically, except perhaps for more snow than has probably ever fallen on Paris at one time. The controversy comes from Act II, which has always been the problem in staging *Bohème*. Zeffirelli noted that Puccini and Illica defied logic by placing this scene outdoors, and took them at face value. So he gave us the Latin Quarter—*all* of it—on the stage. There are throngs and throngs of Christmas Eve revelers, all appropriately attired in hoopskirts and whatnot, with many children running about and no end of "business." In fact, it calls for more people onstage than any other Met production, which is saying something—210, compared to a mere 204 for *Aida*. Parpignol arrives on a pony cart, and Musetta arrives in a horse-drawn buggy, which always brings forth applause from some people and makes the hipsters twitch. Fun and games for both camps, so far. One may like such extravagance or not according to one's preferences, but it must be admitted that Zeffirelli was in command of his resources on this occasion. The protagonists can always be seen and heard within all this by a series of clever redeployments, lighting, even a moving wall or two, all having the effect of "close-up" shots. This is all that is needed to make the scene a success. Paradoxically, I have seen much smaller, more sober productions where the leads got lost, visually and aurally, in this scene.

The Met production is the ne plus ultra of one way of producing opera. (We saw in the previous chapter how labeling this method "traditional," "conservative," or "realistic" does not entirely explain the situation, but such terminologies are inevitable for the moment.) Not only is it "traditional," but it is monumental. Only the Met could have done it on that scale. One benefit this has on other American opera companies is that it forces them to come up with new ideas, in theory, at least. There's no way another opera company in America (or anywhere, for that matter) could out-Zeffirelli the Met's Zeffirelli. They shouldn't even try.

If one wants an alternative to the Zeffirelli approach, what are the options? The most common idea is to update the action to any time between 1840 and the present. Updating can be good or bad. Usually it is neutral, in and of itself, although critics still discuss the issue as if it were the trendiest point of the cutting edge. Directors eager to be discussed (a redundancy) therefore know they can get some attention by this not-so-new ploy. But a production must be judged on whether or not it brings out the drama, not by how terribly shocking it is to see Mimì in a leather harness (or whatever). Lately there has been a trend to suggest (or say flat out) that Mimì's deadly illness is AIDS rather than tuberculosis. Of course, *Rent* went all the way with this idea, but *Rent* is another story for another chapter. The AIDS card is played in order to create that most dreaded of all words in the theater, relevance. But *Bohème* is not, at heart, a plea to the audience to fund a cure for tuberculosis, and therefore there is no gain by changing her disease. (*La traviata* suffers this fate as well.) Incidentally, tuberculosis is the leading killer of people with AIDS throughout the world, so in fact one could be even more relevant by leaving it as it was.

The most elaborate updating conceit I have seen was in a New York City Opera production by James Robinson in 2000. We were moved to 1915, and the action was set in contrast to the background of the Great War. Children played with gas masks in Act II, and newspapers hawked the names of the dead from the ongoing battle of Verdun, which ran up to thousands a day and whose casualties eventually exceeded the incomprehensible number of 700,000. Act III was set in a train station, where coffins—dozens of them—were piled on high as the lovers broke up. Translations in the supertitles were changed although the original libretto remained in the singing, which is another strange phenomenon of modern *regietheater*, and one fraught with problems. From the staging, we learn that Schaunard has been drafted and will shortly be packed off to Verdun, presumably as cannon fodder. Throughout Mimì's death scene, Schaunard sat slightly apart, smoking, and pondering his own sure death. The cue for this departure does exist in *Bohème*. Schaunard's hovering just outside the door while Mimì is expiring is curious and makes us wonder what Puccini had in mind for this character that never made it to the stage. I suspect it was this moment in Act IV that cued Robinson for the whole concept. But the result was not wholly satisfactory.

If the point of all this was to underscore the power of *Bohème* to make us consider our own mortality, the actual effect was, at best, of going all around the block to get to the house next door. The death of Mimì was made to seem insignificant. Perhaps they were trying to disprove Stalin's adage that one death is a tragedy but a million deaths are a statistic, using the sadness of Puccini's score to do so. Or perhaps *les bourgeois* were being *épatés* yet again, as in "How dare you sit there and weep for Mimì while you consign tens of thousands of young men to die at places like Verdun, and don't think twice about it?" Schaunard's death in war is posited as preventable while Mimì's is an act of God, inevitable and therefore less tragic—a point that could be argued on many levels.

And leaving aside, for the moment, the traditionalist argument that the work in question is *La* (as opposed to the masculine *Le*) *bohème*—that is, it's about her, not Schaunard—there may be a well-intentioned point in there somewhere beyond proving the director's moral superiority to the always-despised opera audience. However, the hundreds of thousands of corpses at Verdun really ARE just a statistic unless we can see each of those bodies as a human being, as an individual whose life mattered. And Mimì's life must matter as much as Schaunard's or none of it matters at all. In other words, either Mimì's death breaks your heart, or you haven't got one to break.

Baz Luhrmann has been interested in *Bohème* for some time. His movie *Moulin Rouge* is, of course, a gloss on *Bohème*, but that, too, is a story for a later chapter. In 1993, Luhrmann staged a successful production of *Bohème* itself at the Sydney Opera House. The action was set in the 1950s which created no major problems (all right, the candle shtick was a bit of a stretch, but no big deal). The unbearably attractive leads (Cheryl Baker and David Hobson) were good and looked ripping in a pillbox hat and leather jacket, respectively. The sets were practical and appropriate, the major gimmick being the red neon sign proclaiming "Amour" in Acts I, II, and IV and letting us know this was about love in, well, neon lights. But the Sydney production was, in essence, quite conventional. All the everyday objects of the libretto were there onstage (hat, muff, herring, etc., etc.) and the "business," like the hunt for the key, was handled creatively and with an attention to detail surpassing the obsessive Zeffirelli. You could tell Luhrmann liked this work, and it is well worth watching.

Luhrmann one-upped himself with his much-discussed production of *La bohème* on Broadway, which was very like the Sydney production, only more so. The basis of the production was Luhrmann's desire to have young and attractive leads playing the protagonists. This is laudable, but it would appear that that alone was not enough to make it a smash. Opera is funny that way. Luciano Pavarotti looks truly ridiculous as Rodolfo, and cannot—indeed, has never even attempted to—act his way out of the world's largest paper bag. Yet people will be talking about his Rodolfo as long as people will be talking. He remains a paragon who—somehow—can bring the story to life. Name the babes on Broadway who took the lead roles. I dare you. And of course they were amplified, which doesn't help, no matter how "tastefully" it is done. Amplification creates a disconnect between singers and an audience that can only be bridged by an art form (rock, perhaps) that inherently relies on amplification as part of its mode of expression. In opera, fat and ugly with a voice beats young and pretty with a mike every time. Furthermore, it is rather rude, to say the least, to suggest that attractive leads have never graced the roles of *Bohème*. For my money, José Carreras and Teresa Stratas were as good-looking as people can be in their *Live from the Met* in 1979, and their acting was top-notch. Really. By any standards. Now, if we could have some sort of operatic time machine and connect those two in their primes with a Baz Luhrmann, then we would really have quite an exciting performance.

At least Luhrmann tried something, and since his love for this work is patent, I, for one, applaud him. The news headlines at the time, though, were enough to annoy any opera fan and apparently were not enough to lure in that elusive, entirely imaginary public-who-would-go-to-the-opera-if-only-the-singers-were-younger-and-prettier. The sense was that something truly revolutionary was going on, that *Bohème* was being freed from the clutches of the lorgnette-wielding Robber Barons of the Jurassic Operapark and being revealed, at long last, to the masses on Broadway. Actually, *Bohème* has been on Broadway (Lincoln Center) for years, so the whole issue really involved moving it south twenty blocks. Nor was it an issue of pricing. Top ticket prices may be higher, but low-priced tickets are cheaper at City Opera by far and even at the Met than on Broadway. So the Great Social Issues at stake existed only in the minds of the *New York Times*.

The issues of Protestant literalism vs. the Quadriga explored in the previous chapter become most evident, predictably, in current productions of *Tosca*. It is axiomatic that "interpretive" production values come from Germany while Italians have remained mired in "literal" productions. Those terms are not merely useless. In fact they are exactly wrong if looked at this way. In an Italian (or Italian-derived) production, you might see a *Tosca* where Scarpia wears a peruke and shoe buckles and Tosca a red gown and a tiara, so that you will know they are something other than a guy in a peruke and a woman in a tiara. A German (or a German-inspired) production does not allow for multiple layers of interpretation and therefore any meanings the director wishes to make clear must be patently visible onstage. If Scarpia is into kinky S&M sex, which he clearly is, then the peruke must go and the leather harness must come out. All of which is fine, as long as the Germans and Italians who create in these different ways have a grasp on their own cultural vocabularies. The real problems come with us Americans, who generally speaking have no grasp whatsoever on cultural nuance (and we are heartily hated by the world because of this). Mark Lamos in his slightly scandalous New York City Opera production of *Tosca* had to show Scarpia masturbating in church to let us know that Scarpia is a hypocritical pig. Of course this has the advantage of shocking the bourgeoisie, yet again, but the real problem is that it is too literal for a story such as *Tosca*. If we must see this to know what Scarpia is, then it is we, and not our Victorian predecessors, and least of all the Italians, who have repressed our sexuality into nonexistence. Across Lincoln Center, the Met continues to trot out Zeffirelli's production, which re-creates the familiar Roman landmarks in question almost identically. Indeed, the apartment in the Palazzo Farnese is an exact replica of an actual room in the Farnese, in precisely the same scale. Lamos's production, whether praised or panned, will be called "creative" and "progressive" while Zeffirelli's will be called "literal." Neither is either. Each reflects a whole stack of historical-cultural baggage on the subject of textual interpretation. To constantly praise one method while always decrying the other is nothing short of racism, pure and simple. I wish directors who write (at great length) about their work, and the critics who review it, would finally grasp this idea.

The fault may not lie entirely with the directors, who often are trying to get to the core of the opera in question, even if their ideas take them in other directions. *Tosca* was shocking in 1900, and it should be shocking now. It is shocking, if one is listening carefully. The violent clashes of the score, not to mention the libretto's details of Scarpia's ideas of fun ("spasms of hate, spasms of love . . .") ought to be enough information for any audience. But is it, nowadays?

Lamos's production moved the action to Fascist Italy, an idea that has become almost "Option B" for any production of *Tosca*. The film *Roma, città aperta* (*Open City*, 1945) used much glossing of *Tosca* for its story of the last days of the Nazi occupation of Rome, as we will see in the "Permutations" chapter. And there was a film version of *Tosca* made in Italy shortly after the war called *E avanti a lui tremava tutta Roma* that did this, and many other productions have followed suit. It is not a bad idea in and of itself, and it generally works, although one does weary of always seeing Nazi and Fascist uniforms used to telegraph "bad guys" to the audience. How much more subversive and insightful when the bad guys look rather elegant and potentially charming! Besides, if one is searching for (shudder) contemporary relevance, it must be admitted that Fascist Rome is basically as remote as Napoleonic Rome to these elusive audiences who must be developed. Ultimately, it will matter much more how the characters interact than what outfits they wear. I'm sure fine directors like Lamos know this, and they too must fret over the lack of attention these aspects of their directorial prowess receive in the press compared to the sets and costumes. In general, the Big Concept will always be a problem with productions of Puccini operas because the concepts tend to quash the details. And nowhere is the adage that "God is in the details" truer than in Puccini's work. We've already seen this in the case of *Bohème*, which is all about details, but it remains true for the rest of the corpus as well, even the "big" works like *Tosca* and *Turandot*. How Tosca communicates to Mario that he should color the painting's eyes black, "Falle gli occhi neri," is infinitely more important than how the Roman Catholic Church is represented, or parodied, in the Te Deum.

The great problem in *Madama Butterfly* is to frame the story in such a way that it is not a thoroughly offensive reduction of Japanese culture. This is difficult, since there is something inherently oppressive about projecting one culture onto another. Making the characters express themselves in Italian and in an Italian art form creates a problem right away. Directors and designers sometimes create new problems by bending too far backward trying to prove that they are not cultural imperialists. If this recent craze for "crossover" and "fusion" is anything but the latest incarnation of cultural imperialism, then I'm too dense to understand. The search for Japanese authenticity can only solve so much in what is, like it or not, an Italian opera based on an American play. Companies assume that hiring Japanese directors will act as a de facto defense against any accusations of missing the point, and this has been in fashion for some time. Even Geraldine Farrar hired a Japanese actress to coach her on movement and gesture.

In the 1950s, the Met hired a Japanese team to produce a new *Butterfly*. The first thing jettisoned was the gimmick at the end of Act II, where Butterfly pokes three holes in the rice-paper walls to keep vigil. This was thought to be "wholly un-Japanese." Of course, so is singing "Tu! tu! piccolo iddio" in Italian before committing ritual suicide, so where does one draw the line? In extreme forms, we have "Kabuki" or "Kabuki-inspired" (whatever that's meant to mean) productions of *Butterfly*. These tend to create a clash of aesthetics that, while interesting in itself, overwhelms the opera. Yet there are exceptions.

Robert Wilson directed a production of *Butterfly* for Los Angeles and Paris using his hallmark stylized gestures and stage movements (or nonmovements), which are derived from Japanese theater. At this point in time, it is fair to say Wilson has made a mark by sticking to what appears to be one idea, involving near-motionless characters striking poses and moving, if at all, like chess pieces pushed by an unseen hand. Of course a man of Wilson's talents has more ideas than that, but there is a sameness to the experience of a Wilson production whether it is *Butterfly* or Wagner's *Lohengrin* or Tom Waits's opera *Alice* or. . . . That is now. In 1993, it was a revelation for *Butterfly*, and many people who have only seen Butterfly trying to negotiate authentic geisha movements would still be blown away by Wilson's production. Generally speaking, no Puccini opera blooms if it is stifled, and Wilson's stage ideas can be stifling, but the production was entirely successful. Paradoxically, by restricting the movement and the stage "business," it focused concentration on Butterfly herself and her inner journey. Any production that accomplishes that is working within the spirit, rather than the letter, of this opera. I doubt that even Wilson would suggest that his method should become the one and only new way of putting *Butterfly* on the stage, but it was a new way of appreciating this work and is therefore to be applauded enthusiastically. I only wish it had toured more cities.

Wilson's production was also a good format for deriving from Japanese tradition. Again, he used ideas of the Japanese theater, but did not attempt to replicate the exactitudes of Japanese theater. As stated above, authenticity is elusive in a work like this. Besides, it spills over into the reductive and even the unintentionally comic. W. S. Gilbert understood this when he directed the first run of his and Sullivan's *Mikado*. Gilbert insisted on spending a fortune on authentic Japanese costumes and hired any Japanese person he could find in London to teach gestures. He even raided the staff of the Japanese tea shop in Knightsbridge for tutors. Then, when the character of Pooh-Bah struck an authentic pose dressed in magnificent robes and introduced himself as the "Archbishop of Titipu," the effect was hilarious. Directors and designers need to remember this—"authenticity" can backfire.

Then, of course, there is the whole problem of *Fanciulla*. How does one address the California Gold Rush without eliciting howls of laughter? The best productions, in my experience, rush this problem head-on. Embrace the clichés, since Belasco and Puccini certainly did. That is, stage a "horse opera," as Stravinksy called it, and let everyone howl away. A certain giddiness is appropriate to this piece—think of Minnie's outburst at the end of Act II—and there are some wry and comic touches in it, particularly in Act I. The problem of Minnie riding in on a horse to save the day is even more acute now than it was at the premiere. Few are the sopranos who can add horsemanship to the other requirements needed for this role. Yet having her walk on with pistols waved in the air falls short of the big buildup in the orchestra. The best solution I ever saw was Hal Prince's for San Francisco in 1980, his first opera production after being enshrined as the King of Broadway Directors. It was also his best opera production. He brought Minnie on for her big Act III "Here comes the cavalry!" moment on one of those pump carts used on rails in mining, the kind Wile E. Coyote likes to use for chasing the Road Runner. It brought down the house. I wouldn't have been surprised to see some hats tossed in the air and pistol shots fired from the audience as tokens of approval. In Act II, Prince used the long, moody orchestral introduction for a shtick where a bear rummaged through the garbage cans outside of Minnie's cabin. Everyone who had ever spent a weekend at Lake Tahoe or Yosemite, which is to say most of the audience, guffawed, and in the right way. As Shakespeare well knew, a little laughter does nothing to diminish real drama. In fact it heightens it, not merely by ironic contrast but, I believe, by loosening up some of the audience's well-guarded emotions. The important thing was that the old pro Prince never lost sight of the principals. The details in *Fanciulla* are every bit as important as they are in *Bohème*, and even more devilish to manage if stage directors are to be believed. The half-smoked cigar in the ashtray, the deck of cards (with three aces and a pair readily available), and, above all, the drops of blood landing on Rance's hand in cue with the music must all be readily perceived by the audience if this is not to devolve into farce. Prince accomplished this, and *Fanciulla* was the hit of the season.

Il trittico is such an expensive and risky proposition to begin with that companies generally opt for reasonably safe productions. There are exceptions, however, especially since the three operas are often given separately. *Tabarro* generally doesn't get a lot of reinterpretation. The scruffy denizens of Paris's seamy underbelly don't seem to need a lot of disguise to be made digestible to modern audiences. The only visual suspense, when the curtain rises, is how scruffy they are, and how hard the point is driven home that manual laborers are underpaid in this world. *Angelica*, though, has its own problems. Moving it out of the convent is sometimes tried. New York City Opera's production moved it into a children's hospital, which seemed like a compromise and didn't really come off well. The hospital idea should work in theory—it's a close relative of a convent. But shouldn't it have been a mental hospital? This would have at least underscored the opera as Angelica's private hallucination, which seems much more palatable than the straight sentimentality of the convent-based story. The religiosity was lost, of course, and *Angelica* is not much without the religiosity. Most productions of *Angelica* retain the convent setting, even if only to make rather banal digs at Catholic ritual. This serves the double purpose of making the production "edgy" yet leaving all that theatrically delicious Catholic ritual intact. We can be involved and above it all at the same time. Beware of this tendency in productions. Either you take *Angelica* on its own sentimental terms, or you had best put something else on the stage. However, it is best to avoid the outright kitsch of the original productions: Geraldine Farrar's false eyelashes really must have made them howl even in 1918. They were a greater offense to religion than any Andrés Serrano art installation. And the statue coming to life amid a shower of glitter never comes off well anymore. In fact, it didn't come off too well in 1918 either, judging from contemporary accounts. A little magic from the lighting crew will work the true miracle at this problematic moment. The best *Angelica* productions go for an austerity that is appropriate to the setting: this convent is a severe place, not an early version of St. Trinian's. Besides, austerity in design highlights the soprano, who must bear almost the entire burden of this work if it is to succeed at all.

Gianni Schicchi gets produced very frequently, and is a favorite of universities and other smaller companies. But it's not an easy opera to produce. Comedy is always tricky, and *Schicchi* can be very funny when directed right. Unfortunately, too much slapstick usually detracts from the comedy in this case. Since *Schicchi* has the reputation of being a good introduction to opera, you will often feel the director almost begging the audience to like this art form. Furthermore, no great shtick is worth compromising the ensemble's musical timing, without which there's no point to this opera. If you have a great Schicchi with real presence, the comedy will take care of itself without making it necessary for the aged aunts to do backflips. As for messing with the setting, the medieval Florentine ambience of the libretto is hard to ignore, and the much-tufted outfits of the epoch make good opportunities for comedy. Besides, the relatives are money-grubbing climbers. So if the rented costumes are a bit ratty, all the better. Yet *Schicchi*'s setting is not sacrosanct. Film director William Friedkin had a success at the Los Angeles Opera with his *Schicchi* done in a high-Victorian Florence, with much white linen and straw hats in evidence. It was a smart idea, because the Florence of E. M. Forster is every bit as mythical a time and place as the Florence of Dante—perhaps even more so. The essentials of the Florentine setting are still there—that is, a place where young love with all its hormones are ready to burst forth and sweep away all the old hypocrisies. Pay attention to the issues in a given opera and one cannot go wrong. And yes, folks, even Puccini has "issues."

La rondine is so rarely given that productions tend to be rather straightforward. The main issue at stake is how glitzy to make it. The New York City Opera has been trotting out a rather simple production of *Rondine* for years: it's neither this way nor that way, and as such it works fine. Conversely, critics complained that the notable Covent Garden production of 2000 was de trop: Magda's salon was a palace; the sordid Parisian nightclub where she meets Ruggero was too grand, and so forth. Of course, audiences like seeing lavish sets, and *Rondine* is a bit of a hard sell in the best of times. The problem is that this places it firmly within the camp of operetta, since such sets are perfect for, say, *The Merry Widow*. *Rondine* has always suffered from comparisons to Viennese operettas, and it is better if the issue is avoided. *Rondine* is a small, intimate opera and thrives when it is presented as such. The very modest and intimate premiere in Monte Carlo in 1917 was a success. They didn't overdo it. The score, as always, is the best indicator of an appropriate production format.

Then there is the other end of the spectrum: *Turandot*. We learn from contemporary accounts that the Met premiere of the opera in 1927 called for "120 opera chorus, 120 chorus school, 60 boy choir singers, 60 ballet girls, 30 male dancers and procession leaders, 30 stage musicians, 230 extra supers—650 persons in all, beside the eleven-star cast and a hundred orchestra players in the pit" (Tuggle, quoted in Phillips-Matz, p. 310). So basically it's impossible to overdo a production of *Turandot*.

Not that people don't try. I worked on a production in San Francisco many (ahem) moons ago that featured a giant Buddha onstage who shed tears of blood. Never mind the muddled history of the conceit—statues of the Buddha in China belong to historical rather than legendary times, and the libretto is careful to avoid specific religious allusions. It was unbelievably ugly, not to mention a bit offensive. You would think there would have been some comments from the large local Chinese community, but perhaps everyone was distracted by the casting of Eddie Albert as the emperor. That's right, the guy from *Green Acres*. He wasn't half bad, actually.

Zeffirelli took on two important productions of *Turandot* in the 1980s in his own inimitable way. The first was at La Scala in 1982. The centerpiece of the production was the huge, and, from the sketches, beautiful rendition of the Throne Room in Act II. I didn't see it live, but the buzz was that he built the set as a series of bridges over a real pool of water, and stocked said pool with large, expensive *live* goldfish. I can't verify the live goldfish part of the story, but friends who were there swear to it. Maybe Zeffirelli's real genius lay in making people think there were live goldfish in the pool. He dispensed with the pool and the goldfish, or rumors of goldfish, in his 1986 Met production, although the rest of the Throne Room set remained the same (if slightly enlarged, taking advantage of the Met's Brobdingnagian proportions). The critics hurled abuse at Zeffirelli's excesses, and we were getting rather a lot of him just then. But lost in the howling was a good critical analysis of what worked and what did not. Act I was singled out as being excessively vulgar, with raggedy throngs mulling about and heads on pikes mounted throughout. Hey, read the libretto, people. That's the least of the problems! The bamboo walkways on which half the population of China scurries about are a bigger problem, acoustically, than mute disembodied heads. On the plus side, Zeffirelli took advantage of the Met's elevating stages to make the Royal Palace rise up in the background in Act I (again, the libretto . . .). It never fails to elicit gasps, even twenty years later. Act II is big and monumental and basically quite effective. Some of the more outrageous touches have been toned down over the years. Originally, Turandot made her entrance with three banner-bearing poles inserted into the back of her costume. As each of the riddles was answered, a single banner was unfurled and taken off, as Turandot is symbolically raped of her secrets. Sounds good, but it was a total mess. Manuela Hoelterhoff said the flags "looked like those things they stick in bulls." The flags are long gone. Another "touch" in the premiere season was the casting of gay porn star Frank Vickers (no relation to the famous tenor—at least I don't think there's any relation) in the nonsinging role of Pu-Tin-Pao the Executioner, complete with a leather hood and an ample bare chest. None of the reviews caught this detail, or admitted that they caught it. Act III was utterly inexplicable—two little pagodas with a bridge between them. Whatever.

Turandot can shine in big, outdoor productions like those at Verona and Caracalla in Rome. Okay, so the backdrops aren't authentic Old China, but they are monumental and very old, which is half the fun. Some performances have been timed so that the moon will rise at the appropriate moment. I can only imagine what the logistics for this would be in a large production in Italy. For monumentalism combined with some level of authenticity, it would be hard to beat the performances mounted at Beijing's Forbidden City itself in 2000, the *Turandot 2K*, available on DVD. Many of us rolled our eyes when we first read of plans for this production, but it must be admitted that it all came off rather well and was, in fact, a bit of a hoot. The audience seemed genuinely entertained by the spectacle, even as they contemplated how weird European notions of China are. Zhang Yimou, China's leading film director, had been invited to create a production for the Florence Maggio Musicale the year before. There were some wonderful touches in that production. In Act I, the choristers huddled under little roofs, in groupings of two or three. It was an excellent solution derived from Chinese tradition, suggesting *all* of the city onstage more effectively than a huge throng of choristers tripping over each other (and bamboo walkways). Or at least it looked like a wonderful solution. The little roofs mounted on poles turned out to be heavy for the choristers to carry, and there was no end of complaining about directorial impracticality. Oh well, at least they got to sit still. An even better solution, also in Act I, was Yimou's idea for the Executioner. No hulking porn star in leather for him! Yimou gave the role to a woman, a tiny firebrand acrobat/gymnast/dancer who performed an amazing sword dance. The director explained her as the spirit of execution, with much scholarly metaphor. His explanation went entirely over my head, but I could appreciate the energy of the moment. Furthermore, her dance made sense with the music, bringing out the ferocity and violence of the score much better than a sweaty muscleman walking about, snarling and flexing and otherwise trying to strut the time away until he can walk offstage. I admit it—it was an instance of "crossover" that worked. But it worked because it was a way of opening up the possibilities of the score, not a way of forcing them to conform to imposed ideas.

The idea came to move the production to the Forbidden City itself, and score a great coup in international relations and artistic cross-pollination. The Chinese government jumped at the chance and threw open the resources of the world's most populous country to the international production team. Eight hundred extras were engaged. Actually, "engaged" might be too loose a word, since the Red Army itself was pressed into stage duty. Thousands—literally thousands—of people worked on the costumes. Whole villages were pressed into sewing service. The entire affair was done with a totalitarian spirit that must have made every other opera director in the world gag with envy. There were clashes of temperament and aesthetic values. The lighting designer, a certain Guido Levi, strongly disagreed with Yimou about lighting the background of the scene (and what a background!) at certain moments. Yimou could not resist. He had done it before for some pageant at the Forbidden City, and it had been a great success with the audience. Besides, who could argue with wanting to see the Forbidden City, for heaven's sake? Levi continued to argue. Puccini, he explained, is about characters, even in *Turandot*. To sacrifice the human for the monumental was, for him, a "monstrosity" he would not tolerate. (Who *is* this guy? Why isn't *he* directing opera somewhere?) Emergency diplomatic summits were called. Yimou refused to back down, feeling that he knew what to do with the Forbidden City better than any Italian. In the end, Levi acquiesced, but only partially. For the moments he felt most strongly about, he actually sabotaged the lights, so that they couldn't function, and played apologetically dumb. Damn, opera is fun.

Sometimes a more minimal approach is tried, with varying success. David Hockney came to the rescue of San Francisco's "Bleeding Buddha" production with a new production of *Turandot*, a vision in dark blue and red. Flats replaced statuary, and the protagonists seemed outlined in color, and the opera was beautifully filmed for television. Less successful was the introduction of Chinese acrobats in the brief interlude between Act II's Scenes 1 and 2. One sees this sort of thing every now and then, and it always proves that "overdoing it" in *Turandot* isn't really a question of too large a chorus or set, but too many ideas. Authenticity is an even more spurious goal in *Turandot* than in *Madama Butterfly*, which is a modern story of real people rather than a fairy tale. I can't imagine what was meant to be accomplished by the acrobats, unless it was a sort of apology to the Chinese community for the bleeding Buddha. The Royal Opera mounted a splendidly minimalist production in the 1980s that was sent to Los Angeles for the cultural festival around the 1984 Olympics. This attempted to explore the opposite end of the Chinese aesthetic from the florid bright colors we associate with the tackiest souvenirs in Chinatown, and must have made quite an impression on people who assume that all Chinese art is busy and loud and only Japanese art achieves the minimal. The problem is that *Turandot* is busy and loud, so there was a disconnect between what one saw and what one heard. Critic Martin Bernheimer quipped, "Sometimes this is Noh *Turandot* and sometimes this is no *Turandot*." Tsk tsk.

Levi's comment about characters underscores that even *Turandot* is about people, albeit in exaggerated form. Most of the conceits in *Turandot* are applied to the sets rather than the characters, except when Liù's inherent masochism is made manifest in the most garish ways (use your imagination on this one). One recent production in Berlin, however, decided the story was too offensive as it was and added a touch at the very end to mollify the audience: after Turandot "submits" to love, she throws a wink at the audience to show that she is not going to be a docile housewife after all. Even the Berlin critics found this puerile. It's heartening to see that people are sensitive to misogyny in opera, and that's a huge issue to be addressed by each generation in its own way. I just wonder if there wasn't a better way to do this rather than with a wink. If we did not live in a tone-deaf era, then it would be clear that Turandot expresses her equality with Calaf through her voice. She sings her validity, and in fact usually comes out on top, so to speak. The Berlin shtick brings to mind every bad high school production of *The Taming of the Shrew* one must endure. Also, it does seem that directors pull out all these rather desperate ideas more for Puccini than for other composers. There is something "immediate" about what emanates from the stage in a Puccini opera that seems to demand this sort of thing. I have never seen any such shenanigans in *Wozzeck*, to repeat the example. *Wozzeck* is as misogynistic as any other opera, but perhaps the expressionist texture of its magnificent score forms a divide between the issues onstage and the audience, allowing us to digest them with more ease.

This speaks to the power, rather than the weakness, of Puccini's work. If it makes people uncomfortable, well, isn't that one of the points of theater? Isn't *Wozzeck*'s purpose to challenge its audience? And if it can challenge people with sentiment rather than revulsion, shouldn't that be celebrated rather than masked? Many directors can support their ideas with the claim that those who don't like them are traditionalists, a hateful name in the world of the arts. (In Europe, it's a code word for "fascist." In America, if you think about it, it means absolutely nothing. What tradition?) As Alex Ross has so aptly pointed out, this pose is a brilliant and foolproof defense—it protects the director from any criticism whatsoever. Anyone who would criticize is automatically disqualified from the discourse.

I believe, therefore, that we should retire the words "traditionalist," "literalist," and "avant-garde" from our perceptions of what we on stages at the opera house and everywhere else. (Is there even such a thing as "avant-garde" anymore? Is there a word with less meaning?) We should judge a production by how it makes us feel about the work in question. Does it make us want to know it better? To see it again in other incarnations? Do we leave the theater amazed at the many layers of an artist of Puccini's caliber, or do we leave feeling superior to him and to everyone who went before us? Some of the onus for forming a new dialogue on this subject falls to us in the audience. Can we experience something unfamiliar without automatically booing, or, conversely, cheering? Can we experience something very familiar and question why it must remain so, perhaps representing some significance we had not previously considered? In other words, can we sit back with open minds and ask ourselves whether or not we are engaged in the piece we are attending? Perhaps if we in the audience trusted our own instincts more, and did not walk into an opera house as if we were attending some arcane ritual to be endured for the sake of self-edification, then perhaps the critics and the directors would have to respond in kind. Then we would see a lot more truly creative productions, whether set in legendary times or in outer space.

Film Music: Puccini as Shorthand in Today's Mass Market

TO AMERICANS, NOTHING SAYS "Old Europe" like opera. Europeans, compared to Americans, are effete, frivolous, and immoral. Married Europeans have affairs, and admit them. Europeans take off for six weeks in the summer while we work, work, work. And that's not all they take off. On a recent episode of *Survivor*, a guy named Sarge (no less) reacted to one woman's removal of her bathing suit on the deserted beach by explaining, "Oh, I've seen that before. I've been to *Europe*!"

For several years, I have been making a study (if you can call it that) of the use of opera as background music for mainstream movies. I've found that opera only appears in certain contexts, and always seems to have some significance beyond being "pretty." That significance is usually pretty sinister, and this has sent me thinking about what opera means to my compatriots. Simultaneously, I have been working in arts marketing in one form or another for many years, and the question always arises why it is that the American public has a certain resistance to opera. To me, the movie issue and the marketing question seem quite obviously related, and the issue is underexplored. Therefore, I have included this informal survey of the use of Puccini's music in some mainstream movies. The goal is not to use this as a guide for "easy ways to approach Puccini" (an excuse always cited by marketing people to justify chopping up the

classics for general consumption in pop culture, as if there were anything "hard" about Puccini's work to begin with). The goal is to continue to examine what this music signifies within our culture, and
what cultural barriers already exist among us against this art. One
disclaimer: Whenever I give talks on this subject, people are always
objecting to the idea of a "conspiracy" and wondering if I believe that
directors and other creators of films are actually thinking the
thoughts I impute to them. Of course not. There is no conspiracy.
Most directors will choose a piece of music because it "feels right."
(There are exceptions of course.) My concern is to question why a
certain piece of music would feel right in a given situation. And I am
convinced that there is much to be learned in this line of questioning.

Opera is first and foremost an indicator of the snob factor in
American movies. If movie characters go to the opera, you can expect
them to be sitting in Box One, sipping wine (a practice that vanished
from world theaters centuries ago) and surrounded by dowagers
wielding lorgnettes. None of this has anything to do with the recent
experience of attending an opera, but the image remains. Verdi gets
this treatment in the Marx Brothers' *A Night at the Opera* and the
more recent *Pretty Woman*. As offensive as it is to endure Verdi, of all
people, as emblematic of a privileged elite, those two movies are
shrewd in their vision of the effect of a bit of Italian culture on Americans. In the first, *Il trovatore* unleashes a stream of healthy anarchy in
the theater, while the eponymous Pretty Woman (Julia Roberts, as if
anyone needed reminding) has a transformative moment of self-
assertion brought on by *La traviata*. The hysterically historical film
The Age of Innocence uses Gounod's *Faust* to showcase the decadence
of our upper classes in the nineteenth century, with some historical
justification. But even now, a box at the opera remains the most powerful visual representation of the rapacious elite in television, film,
and the popular consciousness. The problem is that boxes at the
opera don't actually exist as such anymore, and I've never seen anyone using a lorgnette in real life. And the real emblems of the current
rapacious elite—luxury boxes at sports facilities, for example—go

unnoticed. Or unmentioned. Or forgiven. The problem, deep down, is not the existence of a carnivorous plutocracy. We simply resent our rich masters when they try to act like Europeans. If they wear cowboy hats, we forgive them anything. Never mind that tennis is no more native to this country than opera. For some reason, tennis has been subsumed into our mainstream in a way that opera has not.

Puccini and the other veristi, with their emphases on the scruffier aspects of life, generally escape usage as signs of the elite, but not entirely. In *Hannah and Her Sisters*, Woody Allen's deft use of Puccini themes creates a background for a gallery of neurotic New Yorkers while delineating differences between them. The film opens to the strains of *Madama Butterfly*'s opening "running around" music. Sam Waterston plays a superficially attractive architect who flirts indiscriminately with two women at once and seems more interested in being admired than in connecting in any substantial way. His taste in architecture is suspect: he takes the women on a tour of his favorite Manhattan landmarks, which are all quite pro forma. Fodor's guide could do a more interesting job. He compares the beauty of one flamboyant Beaux Arts townhouse favorably with its austere neighbor, a very good example of modernism. And yes, he "keeps" a box at the opera. (No one has "kept" a box at the Metropolitan since the time of J. P. Morgan and the Robber Barons.) Carrie Fisher is the lucky (?) woman who gets invited to the Met with him, where she sips wine (!) and pays half-attention to a performance of *Manon Lescaut* (the aria "Sola, perduta, abbandonata!" is performed onstage). Now, Woody Allen knows New York. While other directors might have a character sipping wine in "his" box at the opera because they simply don't know any better, we can be assured that Allen intended to tell us something in this moment. Allen is parodying the wannabe-elite, an even more contemptible class than the actual elite and a group that received a fair share of film humiliation in the self-conscious and flamboyantly rich 1980s. (Oliver Stone, a director who sends his messages with cinematic sledgehammers, played snippets of Verdi's *Rigoletto* in the background in 1987's *Wall Street* while hot-shot arriviste Charlie Sheen cavorted with trophy girl Darryl Hannah in their new penthouse over imported food items whose names they could barely pronounce.) It's just too bad that Allen had to put down opera and Puccini to justify and elevate his own character (self-justification being a main concern of most of his films). Later in the movie, Allen's character successfully flirts with Barbara Hershey in the classical section at Tower Records, where he is buying Bach recordings. The inference is that Bach is intellectual and substantial while Puccini is superficial, appropriate for men who may be hand-somer than he but less challenging and ultimately less of a catch. Oy.

Ultimately, it is this very idea—that Italian-style emotionality is false and superficial—that encapsulates the verismo school in Anglo-American film. Proper Anglo-Saxon men don't cry. It's a Latin aber-ration that can lead to the breakdown of everything we hold sacred. The forthright emotions of verismo must be ridiculed and held up as a caution.

In *The Untouchables*, we see Al Capone (Robert De Niro) crying at the opera (the first box from the stage, of course) while the tenor wails the famous "Vesti la giubba" from Leoncavallo's *I pagliacci*. The irony is intended—how can this man cry over the fate of the sad clown while blithely murdering dozens of people? First of all, he's crying in public, an inherently un-American thing to do. Butch and Sundance killed people but they didn't cry. There's a right way and a wrong way to be a criminal in this country. Furthermore, these must be crocodile tears, since Americans seem incapable of fathoming the idea that bad guys sometimes have tender feelings. (And vice versa: we remain genuinely shocked and appalled every time our political or sports heroes are found in possession of cocaine or caught in sexual indiscretions.) But there is more. The immorality of opera and specif-ically of verismo—that is, of women and even men expressing their full range of emotions without any regard to decorum—has some relation to the immorality of organized crime. Is this an exaggera-tion? Why, then, name the hit series *The Sopranos* when Soprano is not an Italian last name? (Look it up, you won't find it, anywhere.)

Prizzi's Honor has a steady stream of Puccini in the background. Perhaps many mobsters do attend the opera. I suppose Capone did as well, but that's not why the scene was there. Many different people attend the opera. Colonel Shaw of the Massachussetts Fifty-fourth attended the opera on the night of his wedding, his one night of leave from the front in 1863, but you wouldn't have seen that in the movie *Glory*. It's not a matter of who is at the opera, it is a matter of what opera—Italian opera, and verismo specifically—signifies. It remains the sign of un-American, unmanly, scofflaw mores.

The Godfather III is built around a performance of—big stretch here—*Cavalleria rusticana*, the definitive Sicilian opera (written, of course, by the Tuscan Mascagni). The whole world basically comes apart during the performance at Palermo's Teatro Massimo. In the house, several operatives are knifed or shot, while mafia capo Eli Wallach gags on a poisoned cannoli, no less. At the same time, in the Vatican, an archbishop is shot to death and the pope himself drinks poisoned tea and dies. Another capo somewhere gets a knife in the throat à la Scarpia (cutaway to shot of the Ponte Sant'Angelo in Rome in case we didn't get the reference). Oblivious to all this, Al Pacino leaves the theater and is shot in the shoulder on the steps of the Massimo, while the hapless Sofia Coppola takes one in the chest and dies. Talia Shire puts her shawl over her head and Sicilian life goes on. Pacino then dies of old age in his garden while reminiscing to the strains of the famous intermezzo.

The problem isn't crime, it's disorder. And once the lid comes off of order, anything is possible. Which brings us to sex, which brings us back to Puccini. His music can barely be dissociated from the erotic, and therefore tends to represent the disorder that comes with the unrestrained erotic. That's not always a bad thing, as many movies have pointed out. In *The Mirror Has Two Faces*, literature professor Barbra Streisand lectures toward the beginning of the movie on romantic love as a social construct with no anthropological basis. She defends it, though, for the sole reason that "it feels so fucking good," and specifically champions the idea of hearing *Bohème* or *Turandot* in our heads when in contact with our love object. (I must here give Ms. Streisand a gentle slap on her elegant wrist for leaving off the final "t" in her pronunciation of the latter opera.) She then enters into a non-sexual marriage with math professor Jeff Bridges, who finds sex to be too disruptive to his vision of an ordered universe. The whole story, then, is a case of delayed-aria-gratification, until she finally gets Bridges to express love the old-fashioned way. A gray dawn spreads over Park Avenue while the two cavort in the middle of the street and "Nessun dorma" blasts as if from the air. Mutual orgasm achieved. Not subtle, but not without charm.

The most genteel use of Puccini in this trope is, of course, *A Room with a View*. This is, of course, a British film based on an English novel, but the issues remain similar to American points of view. (Hey, we got our notions from somewhere, and most of them came to us along with our language and laws.) The film is very much about "proper" Anglo-Saxons confronted with unruly, unkempt, but undeniably appealing Latins and their culture. "O mio babbino caro" from *Gianni Schicchi* and, less famously but no less relentlessly, "Che il bel sogno di Doretta" from *La rondine* drip from the air throughout the first half of the movie while the English tourists attempt to repress their libidos in turn-of-the-century Florence. The second half of the movie returns to England and Puccini is set aside for the while—only moody Beethoven banged out on the piano for the rainy island. Our heroine, Helena Bonham Carter, is to marry the correct young gentleman, who is of course all wrong, while secretly pining for the raffish wrong young man, who is of course all right. Propriety is, in this case as so often in E. M. Forster's work, a toxic illusion, a falsehood that stifles the erotic life force. After much plot-twisting and some help from the potty group of Italophile friends, she does of course marry the wrong (that is, right) young man and returns to Florence for her honeymoon, opening her balcony doors wide (get it?) and positively swimming in the sunshine and a reprise of "O mio babbino caro." Her spiritual malaise was a case of *aria interrupta*.

The Mirror Has Two Faces uses Puccini as a motif and *A Room with a View* employs it in the background, like the subconscious feeling Streisand describes in her movie. But Puccini, and *La bohème* in particular, are the very core of the plot and the point of *Moonstruck*. Cher copped an Oscar for her portrayal of a young widow in a rather mythical yet not unrealistic Italian American household and community in Brooklyn. She listlessly accepts the proposal of the listless aging mama's boy (Danny Aiello) but succumbs to the unruly passions of his younger brother, the googly-eyed, dopey-faced yet dripping-with-hormones Nicolas Cage (a scion of the opera-conscious Coppola family who even had a small role in *Godfather III*). Cage plays a baker who has lost a hand in an oven accident, and there are many clever uses of "Che gelida manina" while his prosthetic hand grasps for Cher. *Bohème*, in the form of the superb Tebaldi/Bergonzi recording, plays through much of the movie. Cage rants about love as a destructive yet life-giving force. He states bluntly that he loves only two things: Cher and opera, and gets her to attend a performance of *Bohème* at the Met. She undergoes a much-anticipated transformation from reasonably attractive frump to, well, Cher. If ever a coiffure could be described as an aria, it would be Cher's in this scene. They have a box, naturally, and we are not to question how an apprentice baker can spring for two parterre box seats at the Met, since this is near-myth. Her transformation moves from the externals of hair and clothes to her very core during the performance, which visibly moves her. As she says of the opera, "I knew she was sick but I didn't think she was gonna DIE!" This tough cookie's crust has been delightfully cracked by *Bohème*, her true, beautiful, sexy, risk-taking nature revealed, and her ultimate choice for the "wrong" guy Cage is decided at the Met. The night would be perfect if she had not also run into her father in the lobby, attending with his mistress and reminding us of the dangerous side of all this emotional messiness.

All is resolved in this comedy: Cher and Cage announce their union to a startled but quite pleased family, and Dad (a brilliant Vincent Gardenia) even agrees to drop his mistress when challenged by his all-knowing wife (Oscar-winner Olympia Dukakis) to accept the onset of age and death with grace. Another operatic in-joke for cognoscenti: the slightly potty grandfather, who walks the dogs, speaks little English, and occasionally howls at the diva-esque moon, is played by Feodor Chaliapin Jr., whose more famous father was celebrated for his great bass roles but who also recorded "Vecchia zimarra" from Act IV of *Bohème* before World War I.

The salutary effects of opera and "the operatic life" are patent in this movie, but only within a clear framework. *Moonstruck* is set within a discrete community whose colorful separateness from the American norm is clearly delineated—to the point of caricature, some felt at the time. Opera makes sense for *these* people, the movie implies. The visuals corroborate the sound track. Cher and her family live in a remarkable brownstone full of deep, faded red tones in the carpets, draperies, and upholstery. When Cher walks into the Metropolitan Opera House, with its emphasis on brilliant red trappings and glitzy crystal chandeliers, it's as if someone had turned on the lights in her own house. But the issues at stake wouldn't work in mainstream America, which Brooklyn and Lincoln Center clearly are not. First of all, no WASP hero (think Brad Pitt, for instance) could wax poetic about the life-affirming passion of *Bohème* and be taken seriously as a heterosexual. Remember *Breaking Away?* The collegiate hero develops an Italomania, which his corn-fed dad eyes suspiciously as analogous to homosexuality. Rossini provides the sound track for that movie, but only because the velocity of that music matched the freneticism of the bicycle racing that was the central plot. If the boy had been a gymnast or participated in a less peripatetic pastime, the music would have been Puccini. For all its charm and wisdom, *Moonstruck* reinforces the same idea as *Breaking Away*—all this "carrying on" is fine for those kooky Italians, and even for Italian Americans, but these are a separate breed from mainstream (real?) Americans.

The "Real" America, with its white church steeples and white people, has a different relationship altogether with this music. *The Witches of Eastwick* are three ladies (including our favorite chameleon, Cher) in various stages of feminine crisis who fall prey to an unscrupulous man (Jack Nicholson, of course). Puccini plays in a single scene here, when the women move into his mansion and abandon themselves to a rather decorative metaphor of depravity. They cavort around a room full of balloons in slow motion while "Nessun dorma" provides the aural component. Pretty tame stuff, but, oh, did I mention that the man is actually the Devil himself?

The Witches of Eastwick is sarcastic, self-knowing, and in on its own joke. The butt of parody is precisely American notions of erotic propriety, and Puccini makes his appearance as part of that gibe. For an over-the-top look at our fears of "foreign" sexual mores and their malignant effects on our wholesomeness, we must turn to Puccini's ultimate film incarnation, *Fatal Attraction*.

Michael Douglas is the upstanding married man who is seduced by Glenn Close, a successful and attractive woman who is, however, a carnivorous, predatory maniac with an absolute obsession for *Madama Butterfly*. She listens to it constantly, even while slashing her wrists, and manages to drag Douglas to a performance of it at the Met. (Hey, at least they don't sit in Box One.) Her secret desk drawer of blackmail materials even contains a libretto (of all things) of the opera. She turns murderous and must finally be killed by Douglas and his wife.

Close is not foreign, nor is she a complete sociopath right from the beginning. She is a successful businesswoman who gives in to her self-destructive impulses and is destroyed by them. In the process, she comes close to destroying a good man whose only crime was giving in to his lower impulses once. And the culprit is, or is embodied by, *Butterfly*, which simultaneously signifies victimhood and hysteria. Close is literally out of control, like a diva in a *grand scena*. And here we must pause to take a second look at the word diva as examined above in "The Myth of Tosca" chapter: a goddess, a life-and-death force who demands blood offerings. She is the sexual aggressor—already a perversion of the patriarchal order. She bites a lot during torrid sex scenes and draws blood à la Tosca, albeit, in this case, her own. (No matter: suicides and suicide attempts are generally under-stood as acts of aggression and revenge at another person that turn toward the self when all else fails, as in *Butterfly*, *Tosca*, *Turandot*, and hundreds of other operas.) The startling murder scene drives home the point. Audiences gasped when Close, apparently finally drowned in the bathtub, heaves up again one last time and practically requires a stake through her heart to put her out once and for all. Woe to any American male who allows himself to be charmed, even for a moment, by such a woman, such a diva, such a "Soprano."

The toxicity of Puccini plays a crucial role in the film *Heavenly Creatures* (which also is not American, though certainly New Zealand can be considered within the same category in terms of cultural anthropology). In this extraordinary account of a historical incident, two teenage girls form an intense and neurotic friendship that culmi-nates in their murder of one of their mothers who posed a threat to their relationship. Director Peter Jackson relies much on dream sequences and exploration of the subconscious in this film. That opera would play a role here is a foregone conclusion, but that Puc-cini should be so central to his depiction of matricidal crypto-lesbian teenagers is remarkable. The girls have an active fantasy life, invent-ing stories of knights and dragons for each other and so forth, that becomes more all-encompassing throughout their descent toward crime. They also share a passion for Mario Lanza recordings. Beyond Lanza, "E lucevan le stelle" (*Tosca*, Act III) makes an appearance, and, when they are separated, there is a dream sequence of one of the girls singing "Sono andati?" (*Bohème*, Act IV) to the other. (It is sung by Kate Winslet herself, all white gauze and gel lenses, and a truly, ahem, unique vocal delivery.) The murder itself is a cinematic "aria"—the girls are hiking with the mother, the camera follows them around the leafy paths and shady trails, there is a brick, and . . . the "Humming Chorus" from *Butterfly* is the only sound. It is beyond creepy. But what does it all mean? Jackson himself has been quite cagey in interviews, insisting he had never heard the "Humming Chorus" until it was suggested to him for this scene. Where, then,

did he come up with "Sono andati?" This much is clear: the "unreality" of opera has some association with the process that moves these
girls from healthy fantasy into homicidal delusion.

The themes of sexual and social upheaval represented in these
movies overlap and move into overdrive in *The Sum of All Fears*, Tom
Clancy's tale of international terrorism set against a Cold War background. Although American relations with the Soviets are tense in
this film, we know from the beginning that there are worse bad guys
behind this plot to detonate a nuclear bomb at the Super Bowl. The
mastermind of evil turns out to be Alan Bates, whose very presence
in a film is enough to telegraph nasty things to audiences. His chief
operative, however, is a suave and slimy foreigner with an indefinable
accent (Afrikaans, in fact) who lives in a very well-decorated apartment in Damascus and deals with very bad Arabs. The story functions almost as a self-help guide for Americans who need guidance in
morphing their traditional hatred of Russians into a more up-to-date
irrational hatred of Arabs. When we think of the Super Bowl being
attacked, we know this is war—even closer to our collective heart
than the Pentagon and the World Trade Center combined. That the
chief slimeball terrorist instigator is a South African is incidental—he
just reads as a suspiciously overrefined foreigner with a vague accent.
And an undetermined sexuality. While each of the other characters—
our CIA hero Ben Affleck, the American president, the Russian president, and even Ron Rivkin as the American secretary of state—are
all seen with wives or girlfriends or make reference to them, the
South African alone is unpaired with a spouse. This is subtle yet
effective. (The same technique was used in *The Sting* to distinguish
between the good crooks, Redford and Newman, each given pro
forma scenes in bed with a woman, and the bad crook, the accented,
unattached Robert Shaw.) Instead of seeing the South African with a
woman or being assured that he has one somewhere, we see him
alone in his apartment listening to the arietta "Io la vidi" from Verdi's
Don Carlo, of all completely random selections. You can barely hear
it, but it is there, and somebody chose to pop in opera rather than,

say, Reba McEntire or Tim McGraw. And there sure is no opera play-ing in Ben Affleck's apartment! Later, when the CIA finally gets the upper hand, there is a montage of carnage while the South African and each of his evildoer cohorts is blown to bits, one by one. The music played during this bizarre episode is "Nessun dorma," which covers a lot of issues. First off, "Nessun dorma" is great "triumph" music, as Streisand knew in her film. But it also, in this context, rep-resents the man who is getting killed and everything he stands for. The film, in its muddled mythography, both uses Puccini as a sign of anti-Americanism that must be stamped out and yet co-opts the power of his music for its own brand of American triumphalism. It's rather galling.

It may also be an indicator of current directions in American thought. The notion that those who are not with us are against us will not be contained to political manifestos but seeps into the rest of our whole neurotic relationship to the "Old World," and to every shred of inherited or imported culture we have. The classics, and at this point in time we may rank Puccini in that group, will endure, but we who find enjoyment in them may well continue to encounter strange atti-tudes of resistance from others.

Puccinian Permutations

IF WE LOOK AT IDEAS and images in Puccini's operas reflected in subsequent works by other creators, we get an idea of the depth of his art in the communal unconscious. Looking at these other works, in turn, gives us insights into the multilayered and unsuspected depths to be mined out of Puccini's operas.

Let's begin this look at Puccinian permutations by flailing Tosca and her leap a bit more. Certainly the setting of the Castel Sant'Angelo, repeated at virtually every performance of this frequently performed opera, has managed to register as a significant spot. It's now one of those places whose very presence in, for example, a film, seems to be full of portent. Pasolini understood the overlap of myth and reality and felt that the mythic consciousness was most authentically present not in the rural poor but within the urban subproletariate of Rome. His references to *Tosca* become patent in his early masterpiece *Accattone* (1961), a film that remains spectacularly misunderstood by American critics when they have bothered to notice it at all. Perhaps they all need a good dose of *Tosca* to clarify the whole thing for them. At the beginning of the film, Accattone (the name means "beggar") dives off the Ponte Sant'Angelo into the dirty, dribbling Tiber River for the coins this earns from onlookers. The camera makes a clear juxtaposition between Accattone and the statue of the saint on the bridge before he jumps off. Of course, this is only the

Ponte (bridge) Sant'Angelo, not the neighboring Castel of the same name, and these are statues of mere human saints rather than an archangel. But then, Accattone is only a pimp and a thief, not a celebrated prima donna. He is lower than she, even though they end up in the same place. Accattone lives, and even gets some money out of it. Virtually every English-speaking critic names this striking initial scene as Accattone's "fall from grace," but this is the wrong interpretation. He is still reasonably successful as a pimp and a thief at this point. In the course of the film, he talks of his diving for money and laughs, "I'm going to end up like Tosca!" ("Vado finire come la Tosca"). Later, he attempts to jump off the bridge for money again, but can't do it. He falls apart, and is run over by life. He doesn't die, he just becomes the walking dead one sees in any city. His tragedy is that he doesn't end up like Tosca. There is no grace for him. He cannot make the leap of faith. In opera, as in so many ancient myths, suicides are a form of moral victory. Even this act of dignity is denied a modern Roman street bum.

A much more glamorous and glib, if no less mythic, use of the Castel Sant'Angelo is to be found in the charming Billy Wilder film *Roman Holiday* (1951). Here we have the stunning Audrey Hepburn in her first lead role as a royal princess of some unnamed country on a goodwill tour of European capitals. A princess, of course, serves no practical function in the modern world but serves as a touchstone for a great many pent-up aspirations and dreams. In fact, a princess is a sort of priestess, a near deity whose very existence and interaction with the rest of us mortals is some type of divine grace that truly touches people, as we witnessed in the world's unprecedented and traumatized grief over the demise of the late Princess of Wales. *Roman Holiday* is very much an American film (albeit directed by an educated Euro) and puts forth modern American claims on the ancient myths. The American claim is embodied in Gregory Peck, no less, a hard-bitten reporter whose ridiculously unlikely romantic encounter with la Hepburn results in a bout of self-actualization for both of them. They manage to sneak away from the palace (the Palazzo Barberini, in fact) for a night on the town, like any other romantic couple in Rome. They dance on one of the barges that occasionally still appear in the Tiber in the spring with a small band and Japanese lanterns, in this case moored directly across from the Castel Sant'Angelo, with our favorite archangel prominently lit against the Roman night sky. When they are spotted by palace guards, they escape into the Tiber, jumping in and swimming away. It is her defining moment, an action of self-definition that makes her fully a woman. We know this because they subsequently escape to Peck's little apartment and there is much midcentury coy action involving getting undressed out of wet clothes, donning the man's bathrobe, and so forth. It is her first time ever alone with a man, and they discuss the possibility of being a married couple. She promises she could learn to be a housewife and is in fact eager to be, swearing that she will learn to sew and do whatever is necessary to be a "real woman." Funny. We tend to think of women's rights advancing in a direct continuum to the present day, but this expression of postwar ideals must give us pause. In 1900, what *Tosca* suggested as an alternative escape from constricting social roles for women was the dismemberment of patriarchal authority figures. A half century later, the best Hollywood could offer was vacuuming. Fortunately, the princess does not morph into June Cleaver. She returns to her world, wiser and more self-assertive for the experience of her leap into the Tiber. The film ends at her farewell press conference. She has rehearsed a tactful speech about her favorite cities in the tour, saying that each in its own way blah blah blah, but abandons the speech and interjects, "Rome, definitely Rome," to the amazement of the press and her advisers. She has discovered the ancient magic, where princesses can be common women and common women can be anything, and could only have made such a discovery in Rome.

La Hepburn's dip in the Tiber is an overt reference to *Tosca*. Other films use the idea of a "leap of faith" without any conscious reference to *Tosca*, but the impact of the image is nevertheless amplified by the communal experience of *Tosca*, conscious or otherwise.

Crouching Tiger, Hidden Dragon (2000) was directed by Zhang Yimou, whom we met as the director of a notable production of *Turandot*. The music for the film was written by Tan Dun, who is, not incidentally, also a composer of operas. In fact, *Crouching Tiger* is an opera, replete with arias, duets, trios, and choruses (albeit not sung), and full of outlandish situations that somehow become plausible within their context. The film ends with the "bad girl" taking a leap off of a waterfall, and, by the magic of film, gliding and somehow soaring away. There is no "splat" in this leap. Many were baffled by it, but the sense (corroborated by the musical score) was that it was a redemptive act of atonement. Anyone who had some sense of opera, however remote, would have been convinced of this interpretation.

This, of course, brings to mind a few other notable leaps in film: *Thelma and Louise* do not even need to drive the car off the banks of the Grand Canyon (an American icon) since the police are chasing them to tell them they're actually out of trouble. Their death is more than a suicide dictated by necessity. It is a choice, a preference to this rotten world and all the humiliations they can expect as women if they stay in it. In this way, it is a moral victory, an analog of Tosca's death with an additional nod to Butterfly's. Perhaps the most notable, character-defining leap in American film is in *Butch Cassidy and the Sundance Kid*, where the characters are also evading the police. They assume the jump will kill them and it doesn't, although they must leave the country afterward. It is therefore a rejection of their society no less than Tosca's. When they jump, Sundance (Robert Redford) lets out a prolonged cry of "whoa, shit!" that made quite an impression on audiences of that time. This seems to be an American cinematic equivalent of a *slancio*, an ejaculation filled with raw, unedited emotion. It's a convincing analog of the big theme from "E lucevan le stelle" that we hear at the end of *Tosca* and that caused Kerman so much aggravation. Elegant it's not, but it strikes one as very appropriate and true in the circumstances.

Tosca has more in it than one jump, of course, and there are other aspects of *Tosca* that are important in subsequent pieces of art. We already saw how *Bicycle Thief* used Rome as both a background and a key to its own interpretation, and gave us a deeper understanding of the term verismo. The film that launched the brief, midcentury vogue for neoverismo, *Open City* (*Roma, città aperta*, 1945), is also a Roman story in every sense. It looks at small, inconsequential people caught up in epic struggles to survive and unwittingly playing major roles in history, or at least in modern mythology. There is a boy named Romoletto (little Romulus), a priest named Pellegrini (Pilgrims), and so forth. This is not exactly symbolism as we tend to understand it: there must be many actual boys in Rome named Romoletto, and a great many priests named Pellegrini, for instance. It is in its method of looking at the multiple dimensions of everyday people and places in Rome that it recalls *Tosca*, and being a definitively veristic work of art, it teaches us how to look at anything that can be classified as verismo. This is the formula that I explored previously: a search for the resonance of myth in common contemporary settings.

Yet there is more than tone in *Open City* that draws our attention back to *Tosca*. There is a comic sacristan with a penchant for stealing pastries. The hero is a partisan priest fighting the Nazis, and therefore a sort of composite of the revolutionary Cavaradossi and the priestess (in my reading) Tosca. There is a torture scene very like *Tosca*'s, with the lead forced to watch the torture of his companion. The bad guy Nazi is very much like Scarpia—punctilious, courteous, and sadistic. He's also homosexual for good measure, but this is almost just icing on the cake within the codes of this pageant (although it adds the threat of sexual abuse to the torture scene). There is even elegant music floating into the room between the officers' salon and the torture chamber where the priest sits enduring his friend's torture while the villain watches with gratification, exactly as in the Palazzo Farnese scene in *Tosca*. The priest is eventually executed by a firing squad atop the Gianicolo, the hill that overlooks Rome from the Vatican side of the river. The camera pans to the group of boys, led by Romoletto, who march away and down the hill.

We see the panorama of Rome and the dome of St. Peter's in the background. It is a moment of hope for the future, vested in the children. It is a curious juxtaposition of imagery—here it is the priest who is martyred to liberty, and the dome of St. Peter's is bathed in light while the music swells before the final credits. It does not convey the same message as *Tosca*, but it counts on the audience's familiarity with the symbols in *Tosca*. The primary symbol being explored is Rome itself, the place of extreme opposites: republican/imperial, Catholic/Communist, partisan/Fascist, and so forth. The issues at stake are extreme—in fact they are the extremes of the human experience.

Open City no less than *Tosca* has been criticized for compromising on "realism" and dipping into melodrama, yet who could separate melodrama from realism when the issues at stake are so large? *Open City* represents a different moment in Italian history than *Tosca*, although the conflicts to be resolved remain much the same as they always have been. *Open City*, made at the moment of liberation of Italy from the Nazis and the Fascists, offers a vision of hope that the remnants of Italian society might find common ground in the children to rebuild this beautiful, *sacred* country. The Church and the Communists might have found that they were not enemies after all, having fought together to rid the country of this foreign-based evil (at least in the world of *Open City*). All the opposite urges that pull apart the city and the world are exposed and apparent in the panorama of Rome. Perhaps these impulses are not so opposite after all, the film dares to suggest. Of course, this moment of hope passed almost immediately after the end of the war, and the old hatreds erupted anew and continue to the present. The finale to *Open City* is more dated than that of *Tosca*, in this sense, but is perhaps even more poignant because of the vanity of this moment of hope. But it would have made no sense—indeed, it surely wouldn't have been filmed in the same way—without the precedent of *Tosca*.

Tosca embodies certain ideas that will get bandied about as long as people are talking, and in particular the persistent concept of Rome.

It is not, however, the only work of Puccini to lodge itself in the public's mind. *Madama Butterfly*, beyond the woman-as-victim idea in *Fatal Attraction*, has become a flash point for the whole fraught issue of East-West relations. The film *My Geisha* (1961) used snippets of the score because, well, how could it not? On Broadway, there was David Henry Hwang's *M. Butterfly*, which was very much about the myth of the submissive Asian woman in the Western mind. The play was a fascinating gloss on a complicated subject, made even more complicated by the twist of the heroine in question being an anatomical man, unbeknownst to her Frenchman lover of twenty years. The story of the play was said to be based on a true story, although *Madama Butterfly* is also said to be based on a true story, and really everything is based on a true story in some sense. Audiences were quite fascinated by the technicalities: how could a man make love to someone for twenty years and not know his lover's sex? Hwang correctly glossed over that with a few comments ("Asian women are bashful," s/he says) and allowed everyone to use their imaginations. The point of the play was not the nature of genitalia but the functions of power, and of course the hero/ine becomes the character with all the power by the end. The Frenchman goes from sexual imperialist to a broken and bereft remnant of a man, which is what I, for one, imagine will happen also to Pinkerton when he returns to the States. Hwang gives the *Butterfly* myth its full due and looks beyond the victim idea, as I believe the opera does too, as anyone can say if they actually attend a performance of it. Elsewhere, Hwang has said that it is common among the Asian community to say that one of them who has fallen in love with a white guy has "pulled a Butterfly." These myths run deep, and it is fascinating that a community that has been saddled with another culture's perceptions of them can take the stereotype and run with it. The sarcasm is implicit and cutting. It makes me think about how Spaniards deal with the whole idea of *Carmen*.

M. Butterfly embraced the ambiguities of the story. *Miss Saigon*, which owes a great deal to *Madama Butterfly*, chose to ditch them.

This hit musical opted for a true love story, which is to say a rather unrealistic story. The protagonists are good, honest people (he's American, she's Vietnamese) who are genuinely in love. The conflict is entirely around them (the Vietnam War) and not at all within them. This happens, of course, and is worthy of stage presentation, but one learns less about the darker recesses of human nature when confronted with a story of this type. It also must make us wonder if there is any progress at all in our national capability for critical thinking about our role in the world. A century ago, even in the era of Teddy Roosevelt and the Great White Fleet, a popular Broadway playwright such as Belasco was able to present an American naval officer as a cad and sexual opportunist with a culpable sense of entitlement. Eighty-five years later, audiences on that same Broadway needed, and got, a likable, good-looking American chap with a high moral standard. All characters onstage are representations, and we seem to have even less stomach for seeing mirrors held up to our own failings than our supposedly more bigoted Victorian antecedents.

Bohème, of course, is the emblematic Puccini work, and it has not gone unnoticed in popular culture. Snippets of *Bohème* are everywhere, even beyond such thorough explorations of the opera as a whole as *Moonstruck*. Della Reese's best-selling hit of her career was 1959's "Don't You Know," which was "Musetta's Waltz" sung as a fully honest love song. There's no complaining about what la Reese did with the world's most abused melody. She sings it well in her own style and seems to believe every word. The only problem one might have with it, if one is aware of the original, is the utter lack of irony involved. This was, of course, a tune written for the launching of a battleship. How curious that it became emblematic of a love song by some transitive property ("Musetta's Waltz" = Puccini = Romantic Love, perhaps). But the waltz appears everywhere. Currently, the piano solo version is the background (and virtually only sound track) of a New York State Lotto television commercial about a neglected dog who buys a lottery ticket, wins, and drives past his previous owners in a limousine attended by three dolled-up poodles. Somehow, it's charming and funny. (Of course the dolled-up poodles are especially funny to anyone familiar with the character of Musetta.) Like the opera from which it comes, "Musetta's Waltz" always works, often to its own detriment.

Bohème, however, is so well known as a cultural icon that it can be telegraphed to an audience without any (or with hardly any) reference to the music. In this way, it is almost unique among opera—*Carmen* is the only other opera I can think of that comes near this level of recognition. The film *Moulin Rouge* virtually is *Bohème*. Everyone called the movie an update of the *Camille* story, which it is in many ways: the heroine Satine is a prostitute rather than a grisette like Mimì, and the hero Christian is tormented with bourgeois guilt over his liaison. (Interestingly, the hero becomes an Englishman for no apparent reason except that the mores of the bourgeoisie have become synonymous with the English-speaking peoples in the world's view. Having a Frenchman feel pangs of conscience for loving a whore would simply make no sense to anyone nowadays.) It may take the template from *Camille* (and *Camille*'s operatic offspring, Verdi's *La traviata*), but the whole ambience is *La bohème*: the fetishization of poverty as moral/political identity, the celebration of the Artist as a spiritually superior shaman, the camaraderie of the band of bohemians are all in our subconscious because of Puccini. Director Baz Luhrmann even brought the red neon "L'Amour" sign that he had used in *Bohème* productions since at least 1993 into the film. The film makes Satine a showgirl so we can have spectacular production numbers, all very anachronistically jumbled up with a sense of dizzying glee. *Moulin Rouge* uses the imagery of *Bohème*, but makes no attempt to be *Bohème*. Thus we are able to enjoy its own strange postmodern whirligig without having to compare it to *Bohème*.

This is not the case with *Rent*, the late Jonathan Larson's rock opera set in the 1990s' East Village of New York City and based deliberately and relentlessly on *Bohème*. At least Larson wrote his own music for his updating—well, mostly his own music. *Rent* has its passionate partisans and violent detractors (Sarah Schulman wrote a whole, fascinating book against it), and there's no need to take sides here. What matters for our purposes is what *Rent* teaches about its role model *Bohème*—a comparison the audience is dared to make at every conceivable opportunity. While the self-consciousness of *Moulin Rouge* is urbane, *Rent*'s is deadly "relevant" and digestibly hip. There is a whiff of preachiness about the whole thing, suggesting that if you really cared about people today, you would respond to *Rent* and leave *Bohème* behind. This is where I reach for my guns.

Puccini wrote a shamelessly sentimental little mood piece about a solitary tragedy, knowing full well that he would be castigated by the cognoscenti for his choice. But he believed in it to the end and created a musical vocabulary that allows others to take the journey with him. *Moulin Rouge*, on the other hand, is an assault of impressions that, by its very detachment, still manages to tell a vaguely human story. *Rent* seems to want it both ways. Self-consciously hip and sassy (Mimi—accent on the first syllable—seduces Roger with the line, "Don't I have the hottest ass on Fourteenth Street?" Not much of an accolade, frankly, since she'd be competing mostly with fast-food guzzling bargain-hunters on that august thoroughfare), it counts on delivering an emotional coup de grâce but has no means to do so when the time comes. The moment of Mimi's death is "represented" by a loud wail on the electric guitar of the big theme from "Musetta's Waltz." The World's Favorite Little Tune happens to sound great as an electric guitar riff, but so what? It always sounds great. Ashbrook assures us that it even manages to work in an edition rewritten for sussuraphone. That's not the problem. Quoting the opera at this moment literally and figuratively puts quotation marks around the emotional climax. Moreover, Mimi rejoins the cast for the final number, further distancing the audience from any emotion. Such a gimmick is an intended statement in *The Beggar's Opera*, not to mention the "framing" techniques of a master like Bertolt Brecht, but here it is a big fat cop-out. And why, why, why the "Waltz Song," of all things? Simply to telegraph *Bohème!* to the audience? (What if the guitar played "Sono andati?" Would the audience have mistaken that for, perhaps, *A Chorus Line*?)

This flaw, however, probably tells us more about the times we live in than any failures on Larson's part. There is no way to convey sheer tragedy with music that could be called "contemporary" by the critics. Our loss. And to think we tend to imagine audiences of the 1890s as uptight and repressed. . . . Still, there remains something about the characters in *Rent* that do not seem as real somehow as those of *Bohème*, even if they are wearing Levi's rather then hoopskirts. Both the bohemians and the Rentkids do their share of preening about their superiority to bourgeois conformity, but it's more natural in the first instance. The bohemians don't sing about not paying rent—they simply don't pay the rent. By the end of the evening, the bohemians are forced to get real. Larson's kids are never required to pay the rent, emotionally speaking. They are largely the same people at the end of the evening as they were at the beginning, and still preening. If this is what the partisans mean by insisting that *Rent* is more relevant to today's world than *Bohème*, one can only sigh for today's world. *Rent* has much to commend it, and some lessons from *Bohème* were well applied. There is a deft seamlessness in many of the songs, with characters coming in and out and returning to the dominant melody that recalls Puccini's accomplishments in the same area. This is rare on Broadway, and even rarer in a rock musical, whose very musical structure tends to restrict it to 4/4 time and glaring breaks between songs. No doubt Larson would have gone on to great heights had he lived longer, and it would have been wonderful to experience his work, especially when it was not saddled with comparisons to *Bohème*.

Puccini lives on Broadway beyond *Rent*. He can be heard every night in (slightly) altered form in *The Phantom of the Opera*. The climactic phrase of the love duet "Music of the Night" was so similar to the climax of the love theme in *Fanciulla* that the Puccini estate sued Webber. The case was settled out of court, and the details are murky. But obviously the Puccini estate had a good case, and in fact it is instantly recognizable as a "lift" to anyone who has heard *Fanciulla*. Even though I am sensitive to plagiarism in composers I confess I'm not sure what all the fuss was about. I doubt Webber was hoping no one would notice: *Fanciulla* isn't *that* obscure. And this is a story about an opera house, so why wouldn't there be a quote here and there? (I'm not sure why Webber would have quoted *Fanciulla* to make that point when Gounod's *Faust* is there for the taking, but that's not for us to say.) Besides, as Sir Arthur Sullivan said, there are only eight notes between all the composers (well, the composers of the European tradition at least). Puccini himself plagiarized at will. There is the enigmatic quote of Richard Strauss's *Salome* at the beginning of *Turandot*, and I distinctly hear Debussy's *Prélude à l'après-midi d'un Faune* in the "Principessa, grazia!" ensemble in the same act. (No one else seems to hear that, so perhaps I'm imagining it, and yet . . .) I'm sure there are other instances. Every other composer does the same. I wonder why the Puccini estate got so riled up about this one instance. If our courts were more sensitive to artistic property issues, then the Puccini estate could have sued Webber for his entire career. Webber increasingly tried over the years to become Puccini, and it does a disservice to both composers. Webber is a great songwriter, but opera is a different animal. Let's recall the π formula: it's not the numbers themselves, it's the spaces in between them and their relationship to each—that's where God is. There is nothing shameful or inferior about being a great songwriter and not an opera composer. Schubert, Brahms, Mahler, and Schumann, to name just a few from the German classical tradition, and not to mention every other great songwriter of history, all managed to make marks "merely" as songwriters. We can learn lessons from Puccini without having to try to become him.

These forays out of the opera house are merely a small attempt to give context for Puccini's work and see where it has resonated beyond the admittedly marginal world of opera. Or perhaps it is also an attempt to see that the world of opera might not be quite so marginal as it sometimes appears (or is said to be). But the best resource for diving into Puccini's work remains Puccini's work, and the following chapter looks at the wide availability of this work on recordings and videotape/DVD.

Part Four

EXPLORING PUCCINI

Singers, Recordings, and Performances

ULTIMATELY, OPERA IS about the singers. Shakespeare's words have power on the printed page, no matter what delirious heights can be reached by interpreters. Opera is different. Opera is uniquely capable of expressing the most abstract ideas, but those ideas are black dots on paper until they are brought to life by artists. This is the Great Fact for all opera composers, whether they are the type who appeal to academicians (Ferruccio Busoni springs to mind) or the guy on the street (Puccini springs to mind). It's what people who love the form will discuss (and argue, and discuss some more). And, it will be admitted, this is especially true for Puccini's style of opera. He lived in the theater, knew the singers for whom he wrote (in most cases), and belonged to a tradition where he expected them to include their own personalities in their interpretations in the roles. It is all very well for commentators (like me) to ramble on about the inherent issues at stake in, say, Butterfly's cry of "he loves me!" But then a great diva will come along, hit the note in a certain way with a certain tone and a certain manner of diction and a certain gesture of her hand, and all philosophical inquiry must remain silent. In short, it is the singer who keeps Puccini's art alive.

Before discussing recordings or videos of recommended performances, it is necessary to list a few dozen of the singers who have made a mark specifically in the operas of Puccini. This list is not complete by any means. The connoisseur will find cherished names missing from the list, and I have some personal favorites who are absent. The point is to give the reader a familiarity with the names most often encountered in recordings, in discussions of Puccini's art, and, in a few cases, of legendary names we come across in articles and books. My list is intended to give an idea of what particular singers were and are cherished (or vilified) for rather than to tell you (yawn) how moved I myself was when I heard so-and-so sing such and such. Please go to the Internet for that—there is no shortage of opinion and personal testimony there. Granted, it is impossible not to let personal preference seep through. The reader must get accustomed to that if he or she is intending to enter this most opinionated of worlds. Before jumping into the hobby (or addiction) of collecting recordings, the fan will perhaps find some key words that pique interest. Some people prefer dramatic intensity. Others melt over the tone of a particular voice. There is no right or wrong in preferring one artist to another. It's what keeps opera interesting.

Alagna, Roberto (1963–): One of the most notable international tenors of recent times, Alagna combines a robust stage presence with a beautiful, passionate voice and a refreshing style. Alagna did not follow the usual path for a singer, and has met with some opposition from those who prefer the standard conservatory training. He was born outside Paris of Sicilian parents and sang cabaret (specializing in the songs of Jacques Brel) before turning to opera. (He wasn't, as some journalists would have it, a singing waiter.) Alagna declared he would never use rubato in his singing, and a minimum of portamento, and his recordings are evidence of his aversion to these techniques. Ironically, he has chosen many of the roles where a heavy dose of such singing gimmicks are expected, such as Rodolfo in *Bohème* and Cavaradossi in *Tosca*. The passion in his tone has made the addition of vocal effects unnecessary. Alagna's interpretation of the role of Ruggero in *Rondine* has been especially revelatory.

Albanese, Licia (1913–): A cherished fixture of the New York opera scene since anyone can remember, Albanese was born in Bari in 1913 where she debuted as Butterfly in 1934. She settled in New York after the war and was chosen by Toscanini for an important *Bohème* recording shortly after. Essentially a lyric voice, she managed to be a success in the weightier role of *Manon Lescaut* as well. For decades, opening-night Met audiences have cocked their ears during the group-sing of the National Anthem to hear Albanese's high C at the end, a sign that all is right with the world.

Amato, Pasquale (1878–1942): This famous baritone was part of the Met's unparalleled roster of the pre–World War I years. He created the role of Rance in *Fanciulla* in 1910. Interestingly, he had previously been noted for his interpretation of the role of Pelléas in Debussy's *Pelléas et Mélisande*, which he had sung at that diaphanous opera's Scala premiere in 1908.

Bergonzi, Carlo (1924–): Bergonzi is synonymous with Verdi—he hails from Verdi country and, in his retirement, opened a hotel in Verdi's hometown of Busseto named I due Foscari, for heaven's sake. However, he must be included in this list for his marvelous Pinkerton in *Butterfly* as well as several fascinating assays at Cavaradossi in *Tosca*. Bergonzi had a pleasant, basically lyric voice and a ton of style. One can't always be sure what he is doing, but one is always convinced by the end.

Bjoerling, Jussi (1911–60): A beloved Swedish tenor with a ravishing voice and an abbreviated career, Bjoerling brought a fine focus to his vocal projection without sacrificing any richness of tone. He was celebrated in his day for his Rodolfo in *Bohème*, although I feel his interpretation of Des Grieux in *Manon Lescaut* holds up even better.

Caballé, Montserrat (1933–): A statuesque lady with the loveliest voice imaginable in a human being. Her long legato line is a revelation, and her rendition of the role of Liù in *Turandot* is almost unbearably beautiful. Conversely, some find her cold, although this is incomprehensible to me, and many have criticized her interpretation of the title roles in *Turandot* and *Tosca* for this reason. Admittedly, Caballé did not engage in diva histrionics on the stage—she hardly moved, preferring to "act" entirely with her voice (and a little bit with her hands). She raised eyebrows in New York in the '80s when she merely walked off the stage at the end of *Tosca*. Her voice records particularly well.

Callas, Maria (1923–77): A judicious discussion of Callas's voice and place in vocal history is quite impossible: she is a legend, the ur-diva, and nearly three decades after her premature (and mysterious) death she still commands fanatical loyalty among fans. On the other hand, she is often abused for a stridency of voice (especially in later years), and her presence in the opera world has been conflated with her persona as an international glamour figure and real-life tragic heroine. This much can be said: Callas's musical intelligence and dramatic genius remain unique, and she rethought everything she did from the ground up. Fans adore her intense interpretations of Manon Lescaut, Butterfly, and Turandot, although in general she was not a Puccini specialist and avoided most of the roles onstage. The one Puccini role that was central to her career was Tosca, and at this point all other Toscas must be compared to hers.

Carreras, José (1946–): One of the most truly beautiful voices of all time and a striking stage presence made the Barcelona native one of the star singers of his generation. His career was interrupted by a near-fatal bout with leukemia beginning in 1987. He cited Rodolfo in *Bohème* as his favorite role, and was also a magnificent Cavaradossi in *Tosca*.

Caruso, Enrico (1873–1921): Legendary tenor whose impact on the opera world (and on music in general) can hardly be overestimated.

Caruso arrived just as the art of recording voices was coalescing, and his clarion tenor tones made him the first superstar of the recording industry. Despite the technical limitations, Caruso still sounds good on recordings (transferred to newer technology with varying levels of success. Do a little homework to find out what the critics have to say about specific recordings before laying out the cash). Art and technology merged well for Caruso: the short, intense arias of the verismo genre were perfect for the wax cylinders and then for the 78s he made. Puccini's arias were well represented in Caruso's catalog from the start. Beyond the recording arts, Caruso reigned at the Met and London's Covent Garden (he avoided Italy after his youth, and positively refused to sing in his native Naples) before his premature death in 1921. Caruso had a rather dumpy figure, and never attempted any level of "acting," yet such was the power of his voice that audiences went wild over him all the same. He even managed to outshine the Butterfly when he sang Pinkerton at the London and Met premieres of the opera, which is no easy task. He created the role of Dick Johnson in *Fanciulla* in 1910, and was also celebrated as Des Grieux in *Manon Lescaut* (hard to picture, but he was a sensation), Rodolfo in *Bohème*, and Cavaradossi in *Tosca*. He was an affable man who loved practical jokes and was often less serious about his art than colleagues would have liked. For his first assay in the role of Des Grieux, he had not completely learned the music for the final act, and demanded the soprano lie on her side for the entire act while he sight-read the music he propped up against her behind. Caruso acted as Puccini's tour guide around New York during his visits, and the two shared addictions to flirting with women and smoking tobacco (both died of complications from throat cancer).

Cavalieri, Lina (1874–1944): Called "the most beautiful woman in the world," Cavalieri's face graced souvenir postcards (many of which can still be found in antique shops and online) during her reign at the Met and elsewhere in the early years of the twentieth century. Legends and notoriety attached themselves to Cavalieri from the start:

she was reputed to have bestowed her favors on any number of the crowned heads of Europe before sailing to the New World. Puccini was reputed to have shared this trophy on his trip to New York in 1907, but then again, she was also said to be Mussolini's mistress in much later years, so perhaps all the tales need to be taken with a grain of salt. When could the woman have found time to sing? Her lighter, lyric voice had its critics, yet she was a sensation in the heavier role of Manon Lescaut at the Met premiere in 1907. Cavalieri was killed in an air raid outside Florence in 1944.

Corelli, Franco (1921–2003): The Ancona, Italy, native's confidence and vocal swagger added a unique dimension to his roles and thrilled audiences. His Cavaradossi in *Tosca* was a force of nature—without having to intellectualize the issue (which he never did), Corelli conveyed all the inherent archetypal issues in the opera. This is even more apparent, and more important, in *Turandot*, where Corelli reigned supreme. They simply don't make them like this anymore.

dalla Rizza, Gilda (1892–1975): Puccini heard this soprano in *Fanciulla* and was impressed. He gave her the *Rondine* premiere (after Raisa turned it down), and the important Rome premiere of *Il trittico* in 1919. Dalla Rizza starred in the legendary Scala production of *Manon Lescaut* in 1923. In 1924, she was singing in Santiago, Chile, when news arrived of Puccini's premature death. The schedule was altered, and dalla Rizza sang Suor Angelica as a tribute. The performance had to be interrupted twice because of emotion on both sides of the footlights. Dalla Rizza quit the lyric stage while still in command of her voice, and taught at the Venice Conservatory. Anna Moffo became one of her students.

de los Angeles, Victoria (1923–2005): A Catalan soprano with a gorgeous voice and a complete command of her own abilities and limitations. De los Angeles surprised audiences with her choices of roles, switching from Mozart to Verdi to new works and back to the baroque with great ease, and always, in retrospect, with wisdom. Her Mimì in *Bohème* still sounds great on recording, as does her recording of *Suor Angelica*, which did much to rehabilitate that opera with the public.

del Monaco, Mario (1915–82): A heroic tenor primarily known for the dramatic roles of Verdi, the clarion del Monaco delved into the heavier Puccini repertory in *Turandot* (appearing with Callas at the Colón in 1949), as Des Grieux in *Manon Lescaut* at the Met in 1950, and especially as Dick Johnson in *Fanciulla* with Eleanor Steber at the Florence Maggio Musicale in 1954 that is still discussed today among fans.

Destinn, Emmy (1878–1930): A great Czech soprano who introduced *Butterfly* to London, and who was the creator of Minnie in *Fanciulla* in New York in 1910. Puccini thought her voice a bit light for Minnie, but, excuse me, whose voice isn't? Destinn returned to Prague after the creation of Czechoslovakia in 1919 and dedicated herself to the development of music in her country. She is still revered in Prague.

Di Stefano, Giuseppe (1921–): A Sicilian tenor who, in his brief prime, had arguably the single most beautiful tenor voice of the century. It was damaged early on, some say by overexposure, others fault some riotous living habits, and one will want to do a little research before buying his recordings. The good ones are without equal, the bad ones are painful. He is most noted for his rendition of Cavaradossi in *Tosca*, particularly in a number of legendary performances with Callas. His singing of "E lucevan le stelle" from Act III might change your life. It's been known to happen.

Domingo, Plácido (1941–): The Madrid-born, Mexican-raised tenor superstar's contributions to the world of opera are so numerous and outstanding that they cannot be listed here. Conductor James Levine put it best when he called Domingo a "one-man Golden Age of opera." He has sung everything, recorded everything (several times over), runs not one but two opera companies (Washington, D.C. and Los Angeles, both of which were considered provincial backwaters in the opera world before he stepped in), and has expanded the opera world with his innumerable "crossover" appearances. Still, on nights when he isn't singing, conducting, or running the opera world, Domingo is often seen in the audience, throwing his support to younger singers. As difficult to appraise with a level head as Callas and Caruso (the only singers of the century with whom he can be reasonably compared), it can be said that Domingo's assays into the Puccini repertory have been uniformly successful and often awesome. He has sung all the lead tenor roles, including, believe it or not, the bouncy *leggiero* Rinuccio in *Gianni Schicchi*. Domingo is a great actor by any standards, and perhaps the only great tenor one could name who could have had a career in film had he so chosen. This has helped him in numerous television productions of operas (*Manon Lescaut* in the 1980 *Live from the Met*, for example) and filmed versions of operas (Jean-Pierre Ponelle's *Madama Butterfly* of 1974, where he actually *walks* like an American sailor). Somehow, the role of Dick Johnson in *Fanciulla* must have been written for him. His assays into conducting have taken a beating from critics, and yet, whatever his shortcomings as a conductor, it is curious how the singers on the stage always seem to give better-than-usual performances when Domingo is in the pit (particularly with *Tosca*). Hmmmm. . . . It is impossible to conceive opera in the world today without him.

Farrar, Geraldine (1882–1967): A huge star in her day, Farrar was also a great actress and a marvelous stage presence with her own legions of fans, especially among the young ladies known as "Gerryflappers." Born in Melrose, Massachusetts, she transferred to Berlin and made a sensational debut there in 1901. She was also said to have had a flagrant liaison with the Crown Prince of Prussia, but of course such tales are always indispensable to the development of a soprano's career. She moved to Monte Carlo in 1904 and debuted there in *La bohème* with Caruso. A member of the Met roster from 1907 to 1922, she introduced the role of Butterfly there with Puccini present, although he was quite unimpressed with her and remained so throughout his life. It became her signature role, despite his complaints that her voice was too small for it. Farrar's relationship with Toscanini was well documented and a bit tempestuous, as one might imagine. At one dinner party later in their relationship, she served caviar. Toscanini grumbled to his table companions, "I slept with that woman for seven years. You'd think she'd remember that I hate fish." Charming. After a hiatus (aided by World War I), the two ex-lovers did manage to maintain a warm friendship throughout their old age. Farrar had a second career in silent films, including a filmed version of *Carmen* (1915). She did not make the silent movie version of *La bohème*: that was left to the younger Lillian Gish in 1926, and was a great success. (The viperish film columnist Louella O. Parsons memorably commented that *Bohème* was "woefully bereft of sunshine and smiles." And we wonder why arts marketing is such a challenging field in America. . . .) Farrar retired to Connecticut and supported local charities until her death.

Favero, Mafalda (1903–81): The lovely Favero was known as a light lyric soprano in her youth, yet was chosen by Toscanini to debut at La Scala as Eva in Wagner's *Die Meistersinger von Nürnberg* in 1929. She had a success, but then wisely retreated to roles more congenial to her voice. She rarely left Italy but did venture forth successfully in 1937. She made her Met debut that year as Mimì in *Bohème* opposite Bjoerling, who was making his Met debut in the same opera. She took Mimì to Covent Garden that same year, and also sang Liù in the legendary Turner/Martinelli performances of *Turandot* there. Favero then took on the role of Butterfly, against advice, and her voice was severely compromised by the demands of the role. Attention sopranos and coaches: she survived Wagner but not *Butterfly*. You have been warned. Favero was given the honor of appearing in the famous concert that reopened La Scala after the war with Toscanini returning home in triumph. Favero was assigned Act III of *Manon Lescaut* (in which, indeed, the soprano has relatively little to sing).

Fleta, Miguel (1897–1938): This Spanish tenor made a sensational debut when he was chosen by Zandonai to take the grueling role of Paolo in *Francesca da Rimini* in 1920. Fleta continued with the role and also met Puccini during the busy 1920 Vienna season. Fleta was noted for his interpretations of Rodolfo in *Bohème* and Cavaradossi in *Tosca*. Fans determined him to be the greatest tenor in the world, surpassing even the late Caruso. We must take their word on this, since Fleta recorded very little and the few snippets that do exist are said to be compromised and giving no hint of his real sound. Fleta traveled much, was popular throughout Europe and North America, but absolutely idolized in Spain and Latin America. (He easily sold out a concert at a 10,000-seat bullring in Mexico City.) He had the temerity to fight with Toscanini over the correct interpretation of passages in Verdi's *Rigoletto*, and yet he was chosen by Toscanini for the all-important posthumous premiere of *Turandot* in 1926 (over Beniamino Gigli, who was reputed to have been Puccini's preferred tenor for the role). No recording of that night or that era exists. Fleta's voice showed signs of wearing out shortly afterward, and his only recordings date from this troubled period. He returned to Spain hoping to play a role in his country's musical establishment after the declaration of the republic in 1930. Disillusioned with the republicans' failures in the arts, Fleta got very cozy with the Fascists and enthusiastically supported their cause during the civil war. He died of renal failure in 1938.

Freni, Mirella (1935–): Is there anything not to love about La Freni? Rich tones, idiomatic phrasing, sense of style, and basically one of the most honest and complete singers in opera. Critics still manage to complain of her detachment, and indeed she never indulges in "effects." She exacerbated the perception by her self-deprecating good nature, calling herself *pigrone* ("lazy") as the key to her long-lasting success. (She claimed she disliked learning new roles, and this helped her voice, yet the facts belie this.) A native of Modena, Italy, she even shared a wet nurse as an infant with her fellow Modenese Luciano Pavarotti. ("You can see who got all the milk," she never tires of joking.) Triumphant in *Manon Lescaut*, *Bohème*, and *Butterfly*, audiences have been less impressed by her subdued interpretation of *Tosca* (which is a mistake—there is much more to *Tosca* than chewing up the furniture). A great artist whose recordings should be welcome in any collection.

Gheorghiu, Angela (1965–): A Romanian soprano with beautiful looks and a supple, intense voice that seems to convey emotion even when relaxed, Gheorghiu has made many important appearances and recordings with Alagna, whom she married in 1996. Mimì in *Bohème* and *Tosca* are among her favorite roles, but her rethinking of Magda in *La rondine* for a production and recording in London in 1997 is perhaps her greatest contribution to the Puccini world.

Gigli, Beniamino (1890–1957): One of the foremost tenors of the post-Caruso generation, Gigli's young voice was said to be a revelation, combining strength and lyricism in perfect proportions. Some insisted Puccini had written the role of Calaf in *Turandot* with Gigli in mind, although the honor of the premiere went to Fleta. Celebrated in New York for *Manon Lescaut*, *Bohème*, *Tosca*, and even *Rondine* (which he introduced there in 1928), Gigli spent a good deal of time in Italy as well. He became the official darling of the country in the 1930s—too much so for many people, since his involvement with the government struck many as exceeding patriotism and bordering on enthusiastic Fascism. Gigli even continued to appear in official functions during the troubled time of the German occupation and the Republic of Salò. At the war's end, he was banned from appearing in the city of Rome, but he pleaded his case well and was allowed to appear there in *Tosca* (significantly) in 1945. London also forgave him early on, and he appeared in *Bohème* opposite his daughter Rina as

Mimì, sure evidence that Gigli's lapses in tact were not confined to the political realm. America, perhaps feeling instructed by Toscanini, wanted none of him, and he did not sing here again until a series of concerts in 1953. Gigli wrote several pamphlets arguing his case before the public, and his autobiography is said by critics to be the last word in deep denial, if not outright lying. In any case, he left us with several recordings: the earlier ones clearly demonstrating the power of the voice. The later recordings are naturally more compromised vocally, and quite full of the sobs and other effects so prized by verismo traditionalists and abhorred by others. Gigli's existing recordings are always instructive, often quite pleasing, and occasionally demented.

Gobbi, Tito (1913–84): This great baritone sang over 100 different roles, but would be remembered by history if only for his interpretation of Scarpia in *Tosca*, which he sang onstage almost 1,000 times. His incisive delivery of text through the music remains astounding: people who do not understand any Italian can feel as if they are following every word. He was a natural foil for Callas, and his performances of *Tosca* with her are legendary. In his autobiography, he even concocted a background bio for Scarpia, since he felt he "knew this guy pretty well." In later years, critics can rightly complain that he became somewhat breathy and perhaps a bit mannered in his delivery, but this cannot change the fact that one must always start with Gobbi when discussing the great Italian baritone tradition.

Homer, Louise (1871–1947): A true contralto voice who held her own, and then some, among the mighty Met roster in the early twentieth century. Born in Pittsburgh, Homer studied abroad, sang at Covent Garden and elsewhere, and returned to New York. She took lead roles and even managed to get the Met to resurrect some long-forgotten baroque masterpieces to show her off to best advantage. Melba called her voice the most beautiful she had ever heard. She is included here solely because she created the role of Suzuki at the

Met premiere of *Butterfly* in 1907, which demonstrates either how much the Met was willing to spend on the production or how important people used to think this role was. The very opposite of the temperamental "diva," Homer had six children and would think nothing of leaving a rehearsal early to return to the suburbs and observe her housewifely duties. This sometimes annoyed other singers, notably Farrar, who did not have the same priorities. Quite incidentally, Homer was the aunt of the great American composer Samuel Barber.

Jeritza, Maria (1887–1982): Glamorous, elegant, and undeniably beautiful, the Austrian soprano was Puccini's favorite *Tosca*. (It was Jeritza, as we have seen, who "invented" the "fall-to-the-floor-and-sing" shtick with the aria "Vissi d'arte." Was it an accident, or great artistry? God alone knows.) Jeritza also created a sensation with her Met premiere of the role of Turandot in 1926. Less well known was her role in horse breeding: Jeritza brought the first Lipizzaner horses to the United States, setting them to breed at her California ranch in 1937.

Kirsten, Dorothy (1910–92): This all-American soprano from Montclair, New Jersey, had a lyric voice that was so focused and clear that she could succeed where more dramatically equipped sopranos failed. Her Met debut in 1945 was in *La bohème*, but she soon added a still-discussed Manon Lescaut, Butterfly, and Tosca to her repertory. More surprisingly, she succeeded in the role of Minnie in *Fanciulla*, to the delight of audiences. Sadly, she did not record the role, although snippets exist of one performance in New Orleans in 1960. Kirsten remained a particular favorite in San Francisco.

Malfitano, Catherine (1948–): This native New Yorker studied dance in her youth and brings complete dramatic portrayals to all her work. (She even nabbed an Emmy Award for her *Tosca* broadcast of 1992.) Besides the inevitable Toscas, Malfitano has been thrilling as Butterfly and has recently been singing Minnie in *Fanciulla* around the world. Always exciting and committed, Malfitano is one of the rare breed of opera singers who will take any risk rather than give a "boring" performance. She has been key in the propagation of new operas by American composers, and indeed approaches even standard repertory roles as if they were world premieres.

Martinelli, Giovanni (1885–1969): This heroic tenor made a great name for himself in the heaviest dramatic roles of the romantic (that is, pre-Puccini) repertory. He is included in this list for the impression he made as Calaf in *Turandot*, especially in London in 1937 with Eva Turner. Recordings of segments of these performances exist. Martinelli's voice is quite unusual by today's standards—there is a beat in the voice that earlier audiences took in stride but grate on our contemporary ears. Yet the power of the voice is undeniable, and any tenor who could stand up to Turner in the Act II "face-off" is to be admired if not worshipped.

Melba, Dame Nellie (1861–1931): The great Australian soprano, born Helen Porter Mitchell, devised her operatic last name as an Italianate tribute to her hometown of Melbourne. She sang internationally, and managed to sing at both the Met (1893–1910) and the rival Manhattan Opera Company (1907). Her true artistic home, however, was London, and she sang at Covent Garden from 1888 to 1926. She absolutely owned the role of Mimì in *Bohème* in London, refusing to allow any other soprano near it and causing Puccini much distress and a little embarrassment. When the sixty-year-old Melba finally stepped down for a few performances of *Bohème*, Puccini wrote privately that Mimì would be thrilled to be "un-sung" by Melba. The famous peaches to which her name has been eternally attached, incidentally, were an invention of the famous chef Escoffier, who was in charge of the kitchens of the Savoy Hotel (Melba's preferred residence in London). The dessert was the result of an argument over the menu for a dinner party the diva was hosting. She wanted flamed peaches to finish off the night: he, quaintly, wanted to serve ice cream. La pêche Melba was the compromise, and peace was gloriously maintained.

Merrill, Robert (1917–2004): This agreeable American baritone retains such a degree of popular affection that we are still treated to his (recorded) rendition of "Take Me Out to the Ballgame" during the seventh-inning stretch at Yankee Stadium. Besides this bit of vocal glory, Merrill is still remembered for his many exciting performances in the '50s and '60s, especially those with his good friend Richard Tucker. Merrill's rendition of Marcello in *Bohème* is masterful in its sly humor and vocal blending.

Milanov, Zinka (1906–84): As if Callas and Tebaldi duking it out for the public's affection weren't enough in the 1950s, let us not forget that the semiofficial prima donna of the Met was this Croatian soprano, born Zinka Kunc. Milanov specialized in Verdi roles, and her major contribution to the Puccini repertory was a series of *Tosca*s, where she made a great impression with her powerful and instantly recognizable voice.

Milnes, Sherill (1935–): This great American baritone from Downer's Grove, Illinois, was a fine, snarling Scarpia in *Tosca* and a superb, snarling Rance in *Fanciulla*. Milnes appeared and recorded with Domingo frequently, and their ability to blend their voices created some marvelous effects. (The shared upward line toward the end of the duet in Act IV of *Bohème* was positively demented with these two, and they never failed to include that "bit of fluff" in their many recitals together.)

Moffo, Anna (1932–): A beautiful lyric voice and fine acting abilities made this Wayne, Pennsylvania, native popular in the 1960s. The new medium of television was a boon to Moffo's particular gifts, although audiences tended to take her for granted after a while. This is a shame, because her recordings hold up well, and she was a superb Liù in *Turandot* and Mimì in *Bohème* and even mastered Butterfly at one point. Most significantly, she resurrected *Rondine* for some successful performances in Philadelphia in 1960. We could use an Anna Moffo today.

Muzio, Claudia (1889–1936): This great soprano had a most unusual voice: a wide range but afflicted throughout with a curious beat in it. Many complained of it, yet her live performances were always thrilling. She had a natural flair for the stage, perhaps aided by her father, who was for a time the stage manager at Covent Garden. In her still photographs, she looks very much like Sarah Bernhardt, and it will come as no surprise that her signature role was Tosca. She also, however, sang Turandot, of all things, and created the role of Giorgetta in the Met world premiere of *Il tabarro*. One of her great admirers was the poet Eugenio Montale, who dubbed her "La divina." This is a title that later generations would bestow on Callas, and indeed Muzio might be understood as a sort of proto-Callas in many ways. She has left us with some recordings that are sometimes bizarre but always compelling.

Neblett, Carol (1946–): This thoroughly agreeable personality from Modesto, California, has graced us with over 400 performances of Tosca, no two of which have been quite the same. (That's a good thing in live theater.) Neblett's choices in roles have been curious, switching, as she does, from Mozart to verismo to everything in between, but you can actually tell that she always feels a connection to her role on some level or she does not sing it. Neblett has made Musetta in *Bohème* one of her signature roles, and woe to the Mimì who goes up against her! Most notable for Puccini fans were Neblett's wonderful portrayals of Minnie in *Fanciulla* in the early 1980s in San Francisco, London, and elsewhere. San Franciscans know their Gold Country gals, and Neblett convinced everyone in the prickly audience. Her natural personality made her one of the few divas who could do the talk show circuit without appearing like a total freak. (Favorite moment: Johnny Carson asks, "So what's new, Carol?" She answers, "Oh, I'm getting another divorce!" bursting into tears as if on cue. What audience could fail to fall in love?)

Nilsson, Birgit (1918–): The great Swedish soprano wowed the world with her interpretations of the heaviest Wagner and Strauss roles from the '50s through the '80s, convincing everyone that she could blow off the roof of the opera house without exerting too much effort. This one-of-a-kind voice then turned her attention to the then-neglected role of Turandot. A series of legendary performances with tenor Franco Corelli ensued in New York, London, Buenos Aires, and elsewhere. They simply have to be heard to be believed. Nilsson recorded Minnie in *Fanciulla*, but avoided the role onstage. She also sang Tosca, because, well, who can resist? Her most notable performance of *Tosca* was in Los Angeles in 1974, back when the New York City Opera used to do a fall season there every year. Reigning City Opera diva Beverly Sills had arranged a gala performance of one of her specialty roles for the opening night, and then suddenly came down with the flu. Sills was irreplaceable in many of these roles, but the next night's repertory selection was *Tosca*. Hmmm, what to do . . . ? Sills, from her bed, called Nilsson, who happened to be in Los Angeles (doing what, God only knows). "How would you like to make your City Opera debut . . . tonight?" she asked. And the gala audience was treated to a nice surprise. The emergency, on-call Cavaradossi that night, incidentally, was José Carreras. Sigh.

Olivero, Magda (1910–): Often called "the last verismo soprano," Olivero is known for being the opposite of the general trend in modern opera singing. She threw everything but the kitchen sink into her portrayals, using rubato and portamento by the ton and not disdaining gasps, *parlato*, and the occasional shriek for effect. Yet—and this is an important yet—she was always convincing and her involvement in her roles was beyond question. Olivero has maniacal fans (you know who you are), and not without reason. She must be heard in order to understand what it is that so many people complain about in today's "boring" singers. Her roles included Manon Lescaut, Mimì in *Bohème*, Tosca, Minnie in *Fanciulla*, and a remarkable Suor Angelica. Olivero made her belated Met debut in *Tosca* in 1975 (do the math). There can be no discussion of the optimum interpretation of Puccini without reference to Olivero.

Pavarotti, Luciano (1935–): Pavarotti has captured the imagination of the general public better than any tenor since Caruso, and opera fans likewise thrilled for years to his uniquely gorgeous, instantly recognizable voice and instinctive phrasing. Although the large man never "acted" in any sense of the word and hardly looked like any of the heroic parts, his singing was enough to convince anyone. He may have also had the salutary effect of forcing modern audiences (which are addicted to visual imagery but not accustomed to listening with the same intensity as our predecessors) to hear opera in a new way. His Rodolfo in *Bohème* remains unequaled. His early renditions of Cavaradossi in *Tosca*, also, were magnificent, although it must be admitted that his insistence on singing this role too long did not help his reputation. Pavarotti also made recordings of Des Grieux in *Manon Lescaut* later in his career, which hard-core fans appreciate but which do not display him to his best (and Pavarotti's best is as good as it gets).

Pertile, Aureliano (1885–1952): A tenor with a huge if not precisely beautiful voice but who nevertheless thrilled audiences and was a particular favorite of Toscanini. Pertile sang several Puccini roles, including Pinkerton in *Butterfly* (Naples, 1914), an important *Fanciulla* (Bologna, 1915), Cavaradossi in *Tosca* (Madrid, 1917), and—difficult to imagine—Ruggero in *Rondine* (Bologna, 1917). He was popular in South America, where he scored a great success with Des Grieux in *Manon Lescaut* (Santiago, 1923). His North American ventures were less successful: his Met debut in *Tosca* coincided with Jeritza's in the title role. Ignored in the press, Pertile sang a couple of performances in Philadelphia and Brooklyn and then left the United States for good. He returned to La Scala and was rewarded with the title role in the famous premiere of *Nerone* in 1924.

Price, Leontyne (1927–): One of the greatest American singers of all time (which is to say one of the greatest singers, period), Price combined a rich tone with a dramatic delivery to make every performance memorable. You couldn't always understand every word she said, but you could always believe it. Her Tosca is imbued with passion and conviction, and she also sang Minnie in 1961 (and famously walked away from the role several years later), Manon Lescaut in the 1970s, and Butterfly.

Raisa, Rosa (1893–1963): Born Rose Burchstein in Bialystock, she fled to Italy in 1908 after a violent pogrom. After several different variations, she settled on Rosa Raisa as her stage name. Her powerful voice and intense delivery attracted attention almost immediately. Puccini offered her the premiere of *Rondine* in 1917, which Raisa had the temerity (or foresight) to refuse. Raisa's career after the war centered mostly in Chicago, where she was the reigning prima donna during the 1920s. Raisa did return to La Scala for three notable seasons in the 1920s, participating in the famous premiere of Boito's *Nerone* in 1924 and, most impressively, creating the role of Turandot in 1926. Raisa was underrecorded in her prime, believing that her focus on Chicago prejudiced the New York companies against her.

Sayao, Bidu (1902–99): Born in Rio de Janeiro, the great, beautiful soprano with the supple lyric voice made a specialty of French and Mozart roles. She wisely kept her forays into the Puccini repertory to Mimì in *Bohème*, but she positively owned the role at the Met from the 1930s to the 1950s.

Scotti, Antonio (1866–1936): Officially known as the "best Scarpia ever," Scotti was known for his smooth yet incisive delivery and his great dramatic skills. The brief recordings we have of him reveal his vocal and dramatic power.

Scotto, Renata (1933–): A controversial Italian soprano whose musical and dramatic intelligence remain undisputed. Scotto's beautiful, if hard-edged and sometimes wild, voice was often pushed to the limits. Audiences became jaded on her unpredictable sound in later years, and she became the butt of much carping. This much must be said about Scotto: she gave some great performances, and she gave some bad ones, but she never gave a single boring performance in her life. Many other sopranos should only be able to say the same thing. For Puccini, Scotto had a knack for finding the significance in the tiniest phrases and delivering her discoveries to the audience with a vehemence appropriate to the verismo genre. Her Tosca set your nerves on edge, but isn't that the point of *Tosca*? Her early portrayals of Butterfly remain monumental, her Mimì in *Bohème* should be studied by everyone, and her Manon Lescaut is one of the high points of (operatically speaking) recent memory. Her love for opera continues in master classes where she shares her considerable genius with young singers and audiences alike. (Favorite line to a young singer in a master class: "I prefer the legato here rather than there, because [pointing to the score], well, here it is *written* . . .") Why do I not see everyone from the opera world at these events? This includes audiences. I guarantee no one would be able to use the words "boring" and "*Bohème*" in the same sentence again after ten minutes under Scotto's tutelage.

Spani, Hina (1896–1969): A favorite in her native Argentina and elsewhere, Spani had a most curious career. As a teenager, she went to Italy to study and made notable debuts with the greatest stars, including Caruso and Pertile. She then stepped back from performing for several years, rejecting tons of cash to restudy her technique. When she reemerged, she felt capable of singing a wide variety of roles, from Wagner, to national operas, to (then) new and experimental works. Her favorite role of all, she confessed in later interviews, was Butterfly, however. Her second favorite was the title role in Catalani's *La Wally*. Perhaps this ability to juggle Puccini and so many others, and her fond affection for Catalani's music, endeared her to Toscanini, who chose her as one of two soloists at Puccini's state funeral. She is still remembered as something of a national hero in Argentina.

Steber, Eleanor (1914–90): This Wheeling, West Virginia, native sang noted Butterflies and other roles at the Met in the 1950s but felt she was being passed up in favor of Callas and Tebaldi. Beyond New York, Steber sang a notable Minnie in a legendary *Fanciulla* with del Monaco at the Florence Maggio Musicale in 1954. She also famously stepped into the role in 1966 when Leontyne Price backed out, although this was considered well past her prime and the appearances did not help her career. A great talent who should not be forgotten despite her abbreviated and uneven career.

Stratas, Teresa (1938–): One of the most intense sopranos ever to fill the stage, the Canadian Stratas always brings something unexpected (and usually quite disturbing) to her roles. Her Liù in *Turandot* was something of a crazed stalker, while her Suor Angelica was compelling, slightly revolting, and thoroughly unforgettable.

Sutherland, Joan (1926–): The Australian powerhouse with the astounding dramatic voice puzzled and thrilled audiences for years concentrating primarily on the bel canto repertory. One of her notable forays outside that genre was her legendary recording of the title role of *Turandot*.

Tagliavini, Ferruccio (1913–95): There once was a breed of singer, now quite extinct, called the *tenore di grazia*, or a "grace tenor." A small voice with an elegant sound, and a vocal production so refined it hardly classified as human, let alone as tenorial. (The closest surviving tradition may well be that of the so-called "Irish tenors" who are making themselves heard these days.) Tagliavini was the *tenore di grazia* par excellence. He made his debut in Florence in *Bohème*, whose poetry suited his particular voice-type superbly. More surprisingly, Tagliavini was also successful in *Tosca*, *Butterfly*, and even (gasp) *Manon Lescaut*. While a tenor of Tagliavini's type would come as a shock to audiences today, there is no doubt that many young singers could benefit from familiarity with his style.

Tassinari, Pia (1909–95): A graceful lyric soprano who transferred to the mezzo-soprano repertory in later years. In 1941, she married the tenor Ferruccio Tagliavini, appearing with him internationally. Her most cherished Puccini role was Mimì in *Bohème*, in which she appeared with Tagliavini in memorable performances in London, Paris, and New York as well as throughout Italy after the Second World War.

Tebaldi, Renata (1922–2004): One of the great sopranos of the century, a perennial favorite in New York, La Scala, and elsewhere. A voice of gorgeous tone (particularly in the middle of the register, where so much of verismo "happens") combined with a feel for the legato line to make Tebaldi unforgettable. There was a great rivalry between Tebaldi and Callas, partly imaginary on the part of journalists and fans, and partly inevitable because of their conflicting personalities and artistic approaches, yet it is not accurate to say that Callas was "all art" while Tebaldi was "all voice and only voice." Obviously Callas had a voice to be reckoned with and Tebaldi was not lacking in artistry in any way. Her Tosca is as intense as anybody's, although it is not always as extroverted as some. The same is true of her other Puccini roles: Manon Lescaut, Mimì in *Bohème*, and Butterfly, which may have been her best role. A beloved figure who, thank God, left us many memorable recordings.

Tucker, Richard (1913–75): The popular tenor who remained mostly in his native New York because "he liked to eat lunch at home," Tucker was the favorite tenor at the Met in the '50s and early '60s. Onstage, Tucker had a rather stiff presence (and a tendency to look as if he were smirking, which of course he couldn't help), but his clear voice recorded well. No one thought of him as an especially poetic soul, yet his Rodolfo in *Bohème* holds up marvelously on several good recordings. His Des Grieux in *Manon Lescaut* sounds especially suited to his clear tone and vocal style.

Turner, Eva (1892–1992): This dramatic soprano, born in Lancashire, sang Musetta in *Bohème* at Covent Garden before taking on *Butterfly* there in 1920. Her large voice made an impression, although some critics found her "cold and strong" for the role. She fell in love with Italy and moved there in 1927. "Cold and strong" may have been a problem for Butterfly, but they were a perfect recipe for *Turandot*. She sang the role to enthusiastic receptions in Italy and a couple of "tease" performances in London. The critics disliked her at La Scala in 1929, however, accusing her Turandot of having too much force and lacking in the lyricism that was central to all of Puccini's characters, including this one. Taken aback, Turner looked beyond the Alps, and had a big season in Caracas in 1930. Her biggest triumph was in London in 1937, in a series of legendary *Turandot*s with Giovanni Martinelli and Mafalda Favero. Cold and strong, perhaps, but unforgettably so. She devoted herself to charities and war work during the war, and sang some more *Turandot*s in English after the war.

Recordings and Video/DVDs

Rating favorite recordings is not a pleasant pastime among opera fans—it's a blood sport. One can never recommend. One must arbitrate and simultaneously assassinate the characters of any who disagree. If you think this is overstating the case, post an innocent question on any Internet group relating to this subject. Something along the lines of "Which *Butterfly* recording should I buy?" Check in a week later and be amazed at the hostility generated by your apparently innocent question.

Appreciation of voices is as subjective as appreciation of faces, and arguing with someone who finds a given voice attractive is as futile as arguing that person's taste in looks. The extremely brief (trust me) outline of recommended recordings here is meant as the roughest guide to what you might find in a particular choice, and why people rave about particular ones. One last disclaimer: Be prepared to collect multiple recordings of Puccini operas. You will be amazed at how different each one is. I have not included "highlights" recordings—don't even think of buying a highlights recording of a Puccini opera. It's a waste of time. The list is skewed toward the newer recordings, since they are more readily available and represent current trends (for better and for worse) in interpreting Puccini's art. It is all very good for people like me to insist that Eva Turner is really the ONLY Turandot, but this would not be of much help for the reader who is wondering which is the best first recording to buy.

Manon Lescaut

There's no definitive recording of this opera: each one has high points and missed opportunities. Mirella Freni toured this role around for a few years, and she succeeds with musical intelligence and focus rather than the wild passion of traditional verismo singers. Her recording with the late conductor Giuseppe Sinopoli is a good choice. His reading of the score is solid and remarkably free of the quirks of tempo that often made him so frustrating. Domingo is one of the all-time greats as Des Grieux, and baritone Renato Bruson turns the enigmatic role of Lescaut into an intellectual exercise. Pavarotti is the Des Grieux on Freni's other major recording with

James Levine and the Met forces. This is one of those roles that mysteriously eluded The Great One—more on a temperamental level than anything else, I would imagine (he avoided it onstage). Even though the Met recording has an almost ostentatious casting of the minor parts (Giuseppe Taddei, Ramón Vargas, and even Cecilia Bartoli as the Madrigal Singer, for God's sake), go with the Sinopoli recording if you choose Freni. Dame Kiri TeKanawa also sang this role onstage whenever she could, and her gorgeous face and creamy vocals were well suited for the elegant, lacy parts of the score. The womanly passion, however, does not come through on the recording with Carreras, who is not at his best either in their recording with conductor Riccardo Chailly. For those who want to know what people are talking about when they discuss the histrionics of the grand Italian style, you might want to check out Magda Olivero's recording. She was at the end of her great career and is paired with Domingo, who was just at the beginning of his, so this is more of an operatic *Harold and Maude* than *Manon Lescaut*, but her sobs, shrieks, and bellows are quite instructive. Many fans of Maria Callas treasure her recording of this opera and go into raptures over her cri de coeur in the line "Non voglio morir!" in Act IV. Amazing as this moment is, this is not a good choice of a recording for the casual fan and is best reserved for the hard-core Callas people (who already own it anyway). For historic, midcentury recordings, Albanese/Bjoerling is excellent. She is warm and committed, while his clarion voice cuts through the thick orchestration marvelously.

There may not be a definitive recording of *Manon Lescaut*, but there is a video that every fan has to have: the *Live from the Met* 1981 performance with Renata Scotto, Domingo, and Pablo Elvira, Levine conducting. If you haven't seen this yet, put down this book and run to get it. Scotto was loved and hated, but even with a few high notes that get away like runaway trains, this is full-blooded Italian opera. The Act II duet borders on the pornographic (if one can hear eroticism instead of just seeing it). Domingo's rendition of "No! pazzo

son! guardate!" in Act III elevated him from merely one of the greatest tenors in the world to a living legend. Pablo Elvira alternates
between being cuddly and slimy as Lescaut, which is perfect. The
extraordinary mezzo-soprano Isola Jones (who once stole the show in
Porgy and Bess as the Strawberry Woman, merely walking across the
stage while hurling forth a chesty vocal line) is the Madrigal Singer.
Watch it—now!

La bohème

Bohème suffers from the same malaise on recordings that it does live:
it always works. This means everybody and their mother (literally, it
seems, in some cases) has recorded it, and it's hard to imagine an
out-and-out bad recording of it. Still, some are more notable than
others. An excellent standard choice for a first *Bohème* recording
remains the Renata Tebaldi/Carlo Bergonzi from 1965. The tempi are
generally slow, which would not be welcome in a live performance,
but it makes for a good audio experience and one gets the sense that
everyone was taking this opera seriously. Tebaldi was not famous for
her "acting" skills (in the operatic, vocal sense), but this rendition
shows how unfair that assessment of her was. She means every line
she sings, and the sheer, legendary beauty of her voice brings much
of the score to life by its own virtue. Bergonzi is a tad more adven-
turous and quite successfully so. The overall texture of sound is lush
and rich. No fan would be ashamed to have this recording on their
shelf. The Freni/Pavarotti recording from 1976 is likewise gorgeous
and shows off the two protagonists at their best. Nobody ever
accused Pavarotti of intellectual insight into his roles, but his command of the idiom of the role of Rodolfo is authoritative enough to
win any listener. Karajan's conducting is a revelation. It is probably
the "standard" *Bohème* at this point, and it has not "aged" one iota in
the last three decades. If beauty of the human voice is a primary con-

cern, one cannot fail with the Montserrat Caballé/Domingo recording from 1979. Caballé's ability to carry the listener's soul into a better world is obvious from her entrance, while her rendition of
"Donde lieta uscì" is transcendental. One of the great paradoxes of
the opera world is the fact that Domingo, who can sing anything, was
always famously stumped by "Che gelida manina," which is considered appropriate repertory even for amateur tenors. His rendition of
the aria here is no more convincing than it was in his many, many live
performances of the role, so buyers who think the entire role of
Rodolfo depends on that aria will want to opt for another choice.
However, it would be a huge mistake to dismiss Domingo in this role
and pass up this recording: his singing in Act III is phenomenal. He is
not only ravishing in tone, but he is also thoroughly compelling in
character. One of Domingo's unique virtues is the ability to convey
guilt in his voice, which has also put him ahead of the pack in many
other roles as well (cf. *Fanciulla*, Mascagni's *Cavalleria rusticana*,
Wagner's *Lohengrin*, etc.). He alone has found, or has been able to
communicate, the dramatic issues at stake in Act III. There is an
interesting recording from Rome in 1961, with Anna Moffo and
Richard Tucker. Moffo became such a familiar face around the New
York opera scene in the 1960s that audiences and critics became blasé
about her talents, but in retrospect those talents are clearer and we'd
be lucky to have a diva of her caliber on the scene today. Tucker
recorded the role many times and most of them are very good, some
excellent. Tucker was not in any way the romantic young tenor on the
stage, and yet there was poetry in his voice and he acquits himself
well in the role. Robert Merrill is the excellent Marcello. This recording was made according to the latest recording notions of 1961. Sir
Georg Solti was in the process of making his famous first complete
recording of Wagner's *The Ring of the Nibelung* with tremendous
attention to the audio details of the drama. That is to say, effects such
as sword fights and even setting cups down on tables were given their
full due. It was what we used to call "Vinyl Theater" in an earlier age.

The Rome *Bohème* applies the same ideas to Puccini's masterpiece of commonplace details, and no doubt the recording was at least as difficult in its own way as Solti's *Ring*. (Well, that's exaggerating a bit, but still . . .) Uncorking of wine bottles, dropping of keys on a wooden floor, and so forth, can all be clearly discerned here. Conductor Erich Leinsdorf had even paraded a marching band through the studio at several different angles before getting the exact "marching by" effect that was wanted in Act II. A fascinating recording. More recently, conductor Antonio Pappano joined forces with Leontina Vaduva, Roberto Alagna, and an excellent supporting cast for an excellent addition to the existing *Bohème*s. Alagna famously declared that he would never use rubato or extra portamento in his singing, and he earned a lot of scorn for daring to go against the "great tradition." This recording proves how good Rodolfo can sound without the extra dollops of "effects" that have become traditional for the role. "Che gelida manina" alone should convince all but the grumpiest that Alagna knows what he is doing. Vaduva is melting and convincing but likewise rejects many of the maudlin effects that have accrued around the role of Mimì over the years. Ruth Ann Swenson is a bit wholesome and cheery for Musetta, but this is a minor quibble. Baritone Thomas Hampson sometimes strikes people as mannered and affected in his delivery, but this is perfect for the self-conscious painter Marcello, and star baritone Simon Keenleyside is a nuanced (and funny) Schaunard. To complete the luxury casting, we get power-bass Samuel Ramey as Colline. The man who has won ovations in Boris Godunov's death scene can be expected to make the most out of the single minute of the aria "Vecchia zimarra." This is a fail-safe choice among the newer recordings.

For *Bohème* on video/DVD, the Stratas/Carreras *Live from the Met* in 1979 is a classic. Both protagonists look and feel the parts in a unique way—Stratas perhaps too much so, since critics complained that she seemed on the verge of death from the moment of her entrance. Stratas may have been the first Mimì in history to make her coughs sound like last gasps. Never one to underplay a role, Stratas is in total command of the role, and even those who thought they were jaded on *Bohème* sat up for this one. Carreras may have been the perfect all-around Rodolfo. He himself claimed it was his best role and the one he related to best on a personal level. (A potentially mind-boggling comment, but who are we to argue?) Like Tebaldi, the ravishing timbre of his voice itself is enough to expose new depths in the score at every turn. This is not to say he couldn't act—far from it. No stage actor could have delivered the role more convincingly in a spoken drama than Carreras does here. (He was slated, in fact, to make an actual film of the opera with director Luigi Comencini but was prevented from doing so by his near-fatal bout with leukemia in the very prime of his career. The film was made with Luca Canonici filling in on very short notice. Canonici was handsome and ardent and lyrical but was not Carreras. The film is worth a rental, however. Barbara Daniels is the stunning Mimì, even though she was as hale and healthy as Stratas was moribund.) The *Live from the Met Bohème* also shows the power of the Zeffirelli production when it was new and attention was paid to the all-important details. And of course there was Renata Scotto as Musetta, who clearly had no intention of being upstaged by Stratas. She comes on like gangbusters and only pumps it up from there. This woman knows how to smash a plate! Her delivery of the single word "Rospo!" ("Toad!") in the Act III quartet sounds like the most obscene word in the Italian language. (It isn't.) Scotto has all the life-affirming energy of Anna Magnani in *The Rose Tattoo* in this role, and yet her brief prayer in Act IV is perfectly understated and nuanced. If there were ever one performance of *Bohème* that came close to showing everything this opera has to offer, this surely was it.

Tosca

The numbers are unreliable, but it seems that *Tosca* has been recorded at least as much as *Bohème*, if not more. Every diva wants a recording of it, and they all want new ones every time they discover new aspects to the role (which seems to be about every third year). Maria Callas remains legendary in this role, even thirty years after her death and a half century since she last performed it. Listeners must familiarize themselves with her interpretation of the role even if they will want other, newer (and technologically better) recordings as well. There are many "pirated" editions of Callas in the role, and still other editions with questionable sound. It is also quite possible to find Callas performances that did not show her in prime form and are best left to Callas archivists. One excellent choice remains the 1953 recording produced by London Records boss Walter Legge, who was pioneering the art of opera on record at the time. Although in mono, the sound is rich and smooth. Callas was in excellent vocal shape at this stage of her career, and she is superbly joined by Giuseppe Di Stefano and Tito Gobbi. (This is important, since many other of her *Tosca*s seem to go out of their way to utilize mediocre tenors.) Everyone is excellent here. You can actually see their facial expressions just by listening. Note the incidental details as well: the loud shots of the firing squad, and so forth. Di Stefano got wilder and less reliable later in his career, but he still has glorious moments in his 1962 recording with Leontyne Price and the venerable Giuseppe Taddei. Karajan conducts superbly: he was often accused of being too slow ("Wagnerian" was the meaningless term often applied), and indeed the Te Deum in Act I, for example, is excruciatingly slow. But what tension! Price is awesome in this early recording, with passion and artistry in equal proportions. The production sound is great. Price recorded the opera later with Domingo and Milnes: she is wilder but no less exciting in that recording, and the young Domingo sounds like the vocal embodiment of the French Revolution. Milnes's Te Deum is not to be believed. Where did the guy breathe in those four minutes? Of the newer recordings, the Gheorghiu/Alagna is perhaps the most satisfying. Again, Alagna proves that passion can be attained without schmaltz. His "Recondita armonia" is one of the best there is. It's just *right there*! This tenor actually trusts Puccini as a composer. It's about time somebody did. Gheorghiu got complaints about pitch problems on this but her involvement in the role is exciting and occasionally harrowing, contrasting lyric singing with intensity.

Tosca has been filmed several times, which makes sense. It practically is a movie anyway, so you can count on the various versions to be exciting. The Tosca/Scarpia confrontation in Act II is available with Callas and Gobbi from Covent Garden in 1964. This was late in Callas's short career, but everything came together that night, and it is crucial viewing for anyone who wants to know what Callas-mania (not to mention Gobbi-mania) is all about. The full opera was filmed using the actual locations with Domingo and Raina Kabaivanska, who was an imposing Tosca. The idea sounded a tad better than the reality, but I, for one, appreciate that somebody out there realized the importance of the locations in the opera. There was a 1956 Italian film of *Tosca* directed by Carmine Gallone conducted by Oliviero de Fabritiis. The celebrated Maria Caniglia dubbed the title role, Gian Giacomo Guelfi dubbed Scarpia, and Franco Corelli was himself in the film (what actor could look better than Corelli?). An interesting effort, mostly for Corelli in action. You can't exactly say he was a great actor, but he is mesmerizing, and he seems to transcend acting. Caniglia's voice can be better appreciated in historic recordings. A recent (2002) film of *Tosca* was directed by Jacques Benoit featuring Gheorghiu, Alagna, and the always stupendous Ruggero Raimondi as Scarpia. The film opts for a sort of impressionistic style somewhere between "traditional" and "avant-garde." The feeling (I don't know if this is the case or not) is that some wonderful effects were achieved to meet a limited budget. Example: the Te Deum cuts between close-ups of Raimondi's face and a chorus, wearing T-shirts and jeans and filmed in grainy black and white. Reading comments on Internet message boards, one would think this heralded the End of Civilization or, conversely, was the cutting edge of Radical Chic. It was neither. It was an interesting effect that paid homage to the staginess of

Tosca (something that can be explored on many levels) and, not incidentally, saved a fortune on the rentals of half the ecclesiastical drag of Rome. The camera loves the Alagnas, and Raimondi always films well. You may love it or hate it, but most likely you will enjoy it on some level. It is definitely worth a rental.

Madama Butterfly

My favorite *Butterfly* recording, and one that I can recommend without any hesitation, remains the 1965 Scotto/Bergonzi conducted by Sir John Barbirolli. Scotto's voice was fresh enough to convey the youth and vulnerability without any stretch of the imagination, yet her intelligence and understanding of the dramatic issues at hand were in full flower. The sound is excellent, and Bergonzi and all the other roles are nearly flawless. Barbirolli conducted in the "old-school" style, and he is not afraid to lay on the schmaltz. Fortunately, Scotto and Bergonzi were too great to be swamped by the orchestra, and the result is an emotionally and musically satisfying *Butterfly*. If all this sounds a bit too extroverted for your tastes, you may want the newer Karajan recording with Freni, Pavarotti, Christa Ludwig, and the Vienna Philharmonic. Freni knew everything about the role that Scotto knew, and she projected every nuance, but in a subtler style. Pavarotti is particularly ravishing in the Act I duet. Karajan is amazing: the emotions are there in the orchestra, but they seem organic rather than stuck on as an afterthought. Either of these two recordings should be welcome in any collection. Renata Tebaldi was justly celebrated for her Butterfly: she made two recordings of it. The first was in 1951, the second in 1960. Opt for the later recording if you are a budding Tebaldi aficionado, and leave the first one for later in your addiction spiral. The 1960 recording also features Bergonzi as Pinkerton (charming, persuasive, eager), and Tebaldi's full maturity is evident. I can't imagine why the cliché persists about Tebaldi's "coldness" compared to Callas. It simply isn't true, as one hearing of this recording will prove. Perhaps what people are misunderstanding is the awesome economy of expression in Tebaldi's art. When you have a voice like that, the tone can express much in itself. Of course, the listener must be able (and willing) to hear meaning in tone and phrasing. Here's the test: are you not moved at the end? If you are not, then Tebaldi's art will never be for you. All the recordings listed here are decades old at this point: sad but true. For this opera, it is necessary to go back a generation or two to get the best performances. The historically minded can go back yet further: the first full-length *Butterfly* recording, from 1939, is available on CD. It features Toti dal Monte and Beniamino Gigli. Both of these singers knew Puccini and performed before him, so we can learn much from their interpretations. Dal Monte will sound particularly unusual to the modern listener. Her voice is not the fully rounded, almost dramatic sound we tend to hear in the role. Instead, it is lighter and smaller yet laser-focused. This allows her to sound fifteen years old and yet to cut right through the molten-lava orchestration of much of the opera. Fascinating and quite worth hearing. But get Scotto, Freni, or Tebaldi for your first choice.

The Ponelle film of *Butterfly*, from 1974, features much the same cast with the exception of Domingo for Pavarotti. Snap it up. Freni's acting and face are in perfect sync with her vocal delivery: she can say with a lifted eyebrow or tilt of the head what other sopranos would need a smashed vase to convey. I have already raved about Domingo in this role. Some of the directorial touches in the film are extraordinary without addressing the audience as if we were stupid, a common fault with so many directors with a "message" to convey. The small portrait of Jesus over that of Pinkerton on Butterfly's cabinet is seen, just barely, over Butterfly's head as she sings "Un bel dì." There are directors who say less with piles of corpses. The entrance of Butterfly and her relatives, emerging from a hillside fog, is stunning, and something that could not be achieved on a stage in quite the same way. It justifies the making of a film from an opera, without resorting to bombastic special effects. Ponelle's film is thoroughly satisfying on all levels.

La fanciulla del West

For years, the favorite studio recording of this much-neglected opera was with Franco Capuana conducting the Academia Santa Cecilia in 1958, with Birgit Nilsson, Mario del Monaco, and Cornell MacNeil. Finally, voices as big as all outdoors! It remains excellent, and there is no arguing with the voices of Nilsson and del Monaco. Still, the newer "standard" recording is Zubin Mehta's 1978 recording with the Royal Opera House, featuring Carol Neblett, Domingo, and Milnes. Some quibble with Neblett, and I can't imagine why. She channels Minnie brilliantly, in my opinion. No, she was not Tebaldi or this one or that one, but she is Minnie. She flies convincingly over the staff for Minnie's "freak-out moment" at the end of Act II (sounding utterly insane, which I'm sure is the correct approach), yet every smaller phrase gets its full due as well. Her snarl of the single word "Rance!" in Act I is priceless Americana. Milnes gets to snarl in return: his Act II line "Non sono Jack Rance, son lo sceriffo" ("I'm not Jack Rance, I'm the sheriff!") embodies the Bad Guy Dressed in Black in every Western movie ever made. But, moments later, his reaction to the drops of blood on his hand, "Guarda! c'è ancora sangue!" sounds like it's coming from another world. Marvelous. Domingo, I insist, was put on earth by God to be Dick Johnson. The various miners are delightfully diversified in vocal color, which is one of the most important aspects of this difficult score. Mehta conducts the score with broad strokes. You can't go wrong with this recording. The legendary Eleanor Steber/Mario del Monaco performance at the Florence Maggio Musicale in 1954 is available on a live recording, but the sound is severely compromised (especially when the singers turn around, as they seem to do a lot in this opera, what with cheating at poker and so forth). We only get a vague notion of the excitement that must have accompanied these performances.

Since everyone seems to agree that *Fanciulla* has a protocinematic quality to it, it works well on videos of live performances. The main videos of *Fanciulla* all feature Domingo as Johnson. He can be seen with Neblett in a tape of performances at Covent Garden from 1982. The production is dreary and the leads get lost frequently in the darkness, but Neblett and Domingo remain terrific. They are well supported by the underrated and gorgeously lyrical baritone Silvano Carroli. Nello Santi conducted. This affable man got a lot of flak for his "dull" conducting, but he was one of those conductors for whom singers always magically seemed to give their best performances. You won't hear every amazing aspect of the orchestral score, but on the other hand, you can hear the singers, which is not always the case with this opera. Jonathan Miller directed a notable production of *Fanciulla* at La Scala in 1992, which is available on video, featuring Domingo, Mara Zampieri as Minnie, and Juan Pons as Rance. The production is better than Covent Garden's and at least you can see everyone, but Zampieri is not entirely convincing, vocally or otherwise, in the lead role. Lorin Maazel conducts, and seems quite pleased with himself at the curtain calls. One is not entirely sure why. Pons is wonderful. There is also a fascinating *Live from the Met Fanciulla*, also from 1992. Domingo and a rather tired Milnes team again with Barbara Daniels as Minnie. Daniels's Minnie is a very interesting case in point. A pure lyric soprano, Daniels dominated the role of Mimì in *Bohème* at the Met throughout the 1980s. When she was announced as Minnie, tongues wagged. "She must be nuts!" was among the kinder comments. And yet, she did it! No, not the Minnie of the ages, but honest and valid performances all the same. Previously, Dorothy Kirsten, also a lyric soprano, had succeeded splendidly as Minnie, using focus and phrasing where she lacked the traditional volume. Daniels did the same, and her gorgeous stage presence and fine acting aided her. Paradoxes like these keep opera interesting. Birgit Nilsson, who could belt out Wagner's Brünnhilde without breaking a sweat, walked away from Minnie because she was intimidated by the vocal demands, yet a certain kind of lyric voice, with the right approach, can succeed in the role. Rent this video, and also enjoy the excellent supporting cast and the insightful conducting of Leonard Slatkin.

La rondine

For years, one had basically a single choice when buying a recording of *La rondine*: Anna Moffo's excellent portrayal of the role from 1966. It remains a good choice—the best, for many tastes. Daniele Barioni is excellent as Ruggero, hitting that youthful, eager sound that is crucial to the role. The conductor is Francesco Molinari-Pradelli, who made a specialty of recording the lesser-known operas of the Italian repertory. Critics still praise his touch on this *Rondine*, and I am always grateful for Molinari-Pradelli's work, yet I can't help the feeling that he is working just a bit too hard to "sell" us on the neglected opera. Still, a recording well worth owning. Moffo is quite beguiling.

The recent recording with Antonio Pappano conducting the London Symphony Orchestra features Gheorghiu, Alagna, Inva Mula-Tchako, and William Matteuzzi. Pappano strikes just the right note with his interpretation, merging equal doses of schmaltz and subtlety for this sentimental yet elegant score. The overall sound of the recording, and in particular the "crowd scenes" in Act II, is wonderfully engineered. Gheorghiu is ravishing, with just enough "edge" on her voice to make Magda seem substantial (and this is no small accomplishment). Some found her interpretation "petulant," yet this is a Parisian courtesan we are looking at here. A subjective issue, I would imagine. Alagna nails this difficult-to-love role, projecting the unflinching youthful ardor and idealism that turn it into something. Mula-Tchako is much less grating than the usual Lisette, while Matteuzzi is sly and intriguing as Prunier. This recording will do more to convince you of *Rondine*'s value than most stagings. It includes the "extra" aria in Act I for Ruggero, which balances the opera much better than leaving it out. An added bonus is some selections from *Le villi* to fill out the second CD. How often do you get that?

Il trittico

There is a monaural recording from 1958 of *Il trittico* treasured by aficionados. *Tabarro* is conducted by Vincenzo Bellezza featuring Tito Gobbi, Margaret Mas, and Giacinto Prandelli. Gobbi, predictably, dominates the entire recording. In fact he is the entire point of it. His rendition of Michele's monologue is astounding. That, however, is about all one can say about it. The *Suor Angelica* is more successful. Victoria de los Angeles is demented (remember, that's the highest accolade) in her portrayal of the role. Fedora Barbieri is the evil Zia Principessa. Barbieri made a specialty of bitches in opera, and her interpretation here is positively ghoulish. Tullio Serafin conducts, bringing out the essence of the score. It's the best part of this *Trittico* recording and not to be missed. *Gianni Schicchi* brings Gobbi back to the spotlight, with de los Angeles as a delicate Lauretta. Gobbi's phrasing is marvelous and his interpretation beyond reproach. It is a relief to hear this man who portrayed Scarpia almost 1,000 times onstage revel in a bit of comedy. Gabriele Santini is the conductor.

With all the merits of the 1958 *Trittico*, the 1997 recording under Antonio Pappano remains a better first choice. Pappano conducts all three operas, and finds both the unity and diversity of the works. The overall sound production is superb and subtle: offstage effects like the car horn in *Tabarro* are organic parts of the score rather than "special effects." For *Tabarro*, Carlo Guelfi acquits himself well as Michele. He's not Gobbi, but then he doesn't have Gobbi's mannerisms and problems (yes, they existed) either. Russian sensation Maria Guleghina is the soul of desperation as Giorgetta, while nobody has ever conveyed angst quite like tenor Neil Shicoff. And, speaking of luxury casting run amok, Pappano's pals the Alagnas sing the pair of lovers who walk by on the quay. *Suor Angelica* fares well in the hands of Cristina Gallardo-Domas, who has been singing the role all over the world in recent years. Gallardo-Domas trusts every note of the score and her portrayal is touching. The luxury casting continues in this opera as well. Dorothea Röschmann, who has been making a name for herself around Europe, especially in Mozart and early-opera roles, is Suor Genoveffa. She sounds young, but substantially so, not like the naive victim we often hear in this role. In *Gianni Schicchi*, there is no arguing with the monumental artistry of José van Dam. He is funny, yet not cloying, as so many Schicchis get when they attempt comedy. This man actually sounds smart, which is the core of the opera. Gheorghiu has some lovely moments as his daughter, although some hard-edged ones as well. When she says she will throw herself in the Arno in "O mio babbino caro," we get the feeling that she means it at face value. Alagna sings Rinuccio without being a bumptious minitenor trying to get a contract for bigger roles. This is, I tell you, a relief. More depth of casting appears in veteran Felicity Palmer as Zita and Patrizia Ciofi as Nella. The women's trio has never sounded better. This is a formidable recording, rendering *Trittico* the respect this wide-scoped opera deserves.

Turandot

The "desert island selection" for *Turandot* is without a doubt the 1972 Zubin Mehta/London Philharmonic recording with Joan Sutherland, Pavarotti, Caballé, and remarkable casting depth for the balance of the roles: Nicolai Ghiaurov's Timur almost steals the show in its regal presence. And one mustn't forget the otherworldly Sir Peter Pears sounding positively whacked as the aged emperor. Sutherland summons all the volume and power necessary to make this role come alive, but there is nuance as well. This is the Eternal Feminine as Goethe must have imagined it—powerful, dangerous, and impossible to ignore. Conversely, Caballé is the lyric Liù, a performance of such stunning command that Liù finally becomes something more than a victim and perhaps the real person that Puccini had in mind. If you wonder why some people carry on so much at the mention of the name of Caballé (people like me), listen to her rendition of "Tanto amore segreto" in Act III. Is she breathing through her ears? This is legato singing at its best, without any false "effects" or pushed sentimentality. Pavarotti is at his best in this recording as well, and Pavarotti at his best was something to hear. While he doesn't have the sheer ferocity to compete with Sutherland in the famous confrontation at the end of "In questa reggia," he acquits himself well enough. His legato singing in the Act I ensembles, however, is priceless. Snap up this recording. How have you managed without it this long?

Walter Legge produced a *Turandot* in 1957 with Callas in the title role, Eugenio Fernandi, and the great German soprano Elisabeth Schwarzkopf (who was, not incidentally, Mrs. Legge) as Liù. It is an interesting recording, of course. Callas had sung some reputedly sensational Turandots early in her career (e.g., Buenos Aires, 1949), and one can hear her power and dramatic sincerity in this recording. I think that for general tastes, however, it reveals more about Callas the Artist than Turandot the Pure. Just my opinion. Schwarzkopf is quite unusual as Liù. It is as if the two sopranos did a role reversal, with Turandot as the Slave of Love and Liù as the One Who is Girt in Ice.

For the Nilsson/Corelli experience, there is the 1965 studio recording, featuring a young Renata Scotto as an affecting Liù. The conductor is Molinari-Pradelli. The sound has been well remastered digitally, and you will hear all the fire and thunder of the two lead powerhouses. Here's my quibble: there are several live recordings of Nilsson and Corelli in *Turandot*, and I think their real energy was more clearly evident in those recordings, even considering the technological limitations. In the studio recording, Nilsson remains awesome of course, but there is a roughness on the top notes that is hard to ignore. Corelli's mannerisms (swoops, etc.) seem perfectly natural in live performance but a bit, well, mannered here. Of course, whether you buy this recording or the Sutherland/Pavarotti, there will always be some know-it-all who will tell you that you made the wrong choice. Perhaps it's better just to accept at the outset that you will need to buy both. (Of course, then you will be told you need the Callas recording. This game has virtually no end.)

Puccini in Print:
Books for Further Reading

NO SINGLE VOLUME CAN ADDRESS all the issues in Puccini's life and art, least of all my present effort. I hope the reader will use this volume as a departure point for further inquiry into the subject. This body of literature has grown by leaps and bounds in the last few years, and it is my intention in these pages to help the reader find books that will best suit his or her needs.

Biography

Puccini: A Biography, by Mary Jane Phillips-Matz, with a foreword by William Weaver. Boston: Northeastern University Press, 2002. 343 pp.

Phillips-Matz set a new standard in biography with her definitive work on Verdi. She brings the same acumen to her biography of Puccini: in-depth, primary source research, familiarity with Italian culture, and a heavy dose of common sense rare among music lovers. Her original detective work into the *affaire* Manfredi is a revelation. Phillips-Matz has written a biography rather than a commentary on the music itself, although she sensibly allows herself some wiggle room in this area. Her musical observations are insightful and reasonable, and she thinks *Fanciulla* is Puccini's masterpiece, so we must love her for that if for nothing else. The best biography available, and probably the best biography conceivable, for Puccini.

Monsieur Butterfly: The Story of Giacomo Puccini, by Stanley Jackson. New York: Stein and Day, 1974. 272 pp.

This author of a popular biography of Caruso turned his sights to Puccini for his next project. This was just before the biography genre blossomed and even popular biographies intended for the mass market exploded into gigantic and excruciatingly detailed microinquiries. The taste then was for chatty and charming, but this volume has its problems even within that scope. First of all, that title! What was he thinking? (It refers to a nickname that French journalists had for Puccini. Excuse me, but who cares what French journalists called him?) There are also numerous inaccuracies, all tossed off with a veneer of worldliness that gets tired fast. Some readers may find this a more enjoyably casual read than the subsequent excellent biographies, but double-check everything you read in this book before you quote it.

Biography/Critical Analysis

Puccini: A Critical Biography, by Mosco Carner. London: Duckworth, 1958/1974. 520 pp.

This is the work that started a great surge of Puccini scholarship. In fact, it was the book that made the very concept of "Puccini scholarship" a viable term at all. This Austrian author is meticulous in his methods, and his musical scholarship is beyond question: his other great book is on Arnold Schoenberg. The book is neatly divided into three parts: biography, "issues," and critical analysis of the operas. The first part, the biography, is excellent and excruciatingly researched, even if that research has since been surpassed by Phillips-Matz. The analyses of the operas are also quite impressive. The second part is a bit more fraught at this juncture in time. Carner, like a good Austrian, had a great knowledge of psychoanalysis and applies his midcentury Freudian methods to Puccini. A thorough dissection of the composer's psyche and conjectures about how this affects his art is included. Speaking strictly as a layman, I think the whole section seems quite dated now. One gets the feeling of a comic parody of the bad Viennese Freudian analyst fiddling with his watch fob and demanding of the couched patient, "Und vye do you keep dreaming about trains?" Carner's basic thesis is that Puccini was a mama's boy and therefore had a need to torture women for the rest of his life and in (almost) all his operas. First of all, the whole idea of an overbearing mother being the source of all the kinks in the world has not held up well to critical analysis. But furthermore, there is no evidence that Albina was overbearing, let alone a castrating virago, nor does Carner bother to provide examples of this archetype in her. She was, of course, a tough lady, and Puccini grieved at her death. This is why Liù must be tortured to death onstage in *Turandot*? Had Carner never seen the dynamics of an Italian family in action? If his theories rang true, the entire nation of Italy would be a sexual torture chamber. Still, we must remain grateful that Carner deemed Puccini worthy of his brand of analysis. It seemed to have had a positive effect on Puccini's standing among certain segments of the public. The operatic analyses themselves remain fascinating, and there can be no critical discussion of Puccini's work without reference to Carner. Readers are encouraged to pick up this tome with one hand while grasping a large grain of salt with the other.

Puccini: His Life and Works, by Julian Budden. New York: Oxford University Press, 2002. 527 pp.

Budden, like Phillips-Matz, made his greatest mark with his monumental work on Verdi: the indispensable *Operas of Verdi*, in three volumes. His volume on Puccini is, of course, superb and unassailable in its own right, but one gets the feeling that Puccini simply didn't fire his imagination to the same level that Verdi did. Indeed, Verdi was a three-volume artist simply in the amount of his work, whereas Puccini was not. Furthermore, Budden took upon himself the task of restoring Verdi to his rightful place among scholarly circles: *The Operas of Verdi* was the first in-depth, serious musical analysis of the complete corpus of Verdi's work, replete with printed musical examples from the full orchestral scores and lengthy paragraphs barely comprehensible to the laity. It was a historic task magnificently accomplished. It was simply not possible for anyone to disdain Verdi and maintain credibility after Budden's magnum opus. His task with Puccini was considerably less daunting. Puccini's music was already as "restored" to academic circles as it ever would be by Carner and a few others by the time Budden got around to writing about him. This allowed Budden to interject a bit more of his own personality into this book, of course, always in a sophisticated manner. So even though its scope is smaller than *The Operas of Verdi*, *Puccini* is in many ways a "better read." Budden opted for a structure that uses biography to connect the operas and then moves into musical analysis. The biography sections are only enough to transition from one opera to another, even though there are some excellent nuggets that Budden had access to with his daunting credentials. The reader will want to refer to Phillips-Matz for deeper biography. The musical analyses add some excellent insights into the existing knowledge of Puccini's works.

Puccini: His International Art, by Michele Girardi. Chicago: University of Chicago Press, 2000. 530 pp.

This prize-winning volume is an indispensable addition to the growing body of Puccini literature. The title would lead one to believe that Girardi had an ax to grind, is if trying to prove that Puccini is "equal" to northern European composers. Have no fear: Girardi's analyses of Puccini's music do place it in context of contemporary trends, but it is for insight rather than justification. In other words, Girardi can see Debussy's influence on Puccini's score of *Fanciulla* without taking the point of view that *Fanciulla* is good because it is Debussy-esque. This may sound like a pedantic distinction, but believe me, it's something to be celebrated. Girardi is a musicologist at the University of Pavia, and the book is full of musical examples and intricate erudite analyses that will be welcome by some and daunting for others, but this should dissuade no one. Girardi's examples are always in the service of making a point about the dramatic effectiveness of the opera in question. Again, this sounds minor, but it is a rare musicologist who can put his or her knowledge to the service of a greater goal than proving his or her own erudition. Girardi also includes biographical information as connections between the musical analyses, but his focus is clearly the works in question rather than interesting tidbits from Puccini's life.

The Operas of Puccini, by William Ashbrook. Ithaca: Cornell University Press, 1985. 269 pp.

Ashbrook has long been a fixture on the opera scene, and writes with an assurance and authority that are hard to resist. He also strings together analyses of the operas with biographical information pertinent to the work in question. His analyses, though, are different from the others'. Instead of going through each score page by page, Ashbrook begins with a few ideas in the given work he wants to develop, and then finds examples to elaborate his ideas. It can be pretty dizzying, skipping freely from one part of the opera to another, but Ashbrook is so concise and coherent that he always makes sense. His slim volume packs more salient information in it than many considerably longer books. Handy and interesting, if dense.

Puccini and His Operas: The New Grove Composers Series, edited by Stanley Sadie. New York: St. Martin's Press. 193 pp.

The *New Grove* series, which is the absolute Direct-from-God arbiter of Everything in Music, has never had a whole lot to say about Puccini relative to other composers. This slim volume, edited by the editor in chief of the series, is as concise and authoritative as one would expect, although it does not delve very deeply into any of Puccini's operas. One will find all the information necessary to pass a pop quiz in a history of opera class, but that's about it. One of the excellent features of this book, however, is the auxiliary section, with information about Puccini's contemporaries (Catalani, Franchetti, et al) and even literary people who figure in this narrative (Illica, Gozzi, et al). These small chapters are quite handy and sensible, and it is a pity the cover does not reveal these contents.

The Complete Operas of Puccini: A Critical Guide, by Charles Osborne. New York: Da Capo Press, 1983. 288 pp.

Osborne has been on the opera scene for years, and his contributions have been helpful to many people exploring works for the first time. His work sometimes seems a bit dated at this point: it's not really Osborne's fault. The times have changed and the issues at stake are not the same as those of a generation ago. Furthermore, Osborne is convinced of the direct connection between biography and art, which is highly dubious, and this colors his interpretations. (*Suor Angelica*, for example, is not Puccini's sin expiation for *l'affaire* Manfredi, although people like to think of it as such.) Also, much biographical information has come to light since this book was written. In general, we must remain grateful to Dr. Osborne for his lifelong dedication to opera, but may want to look elsewhere for information on Puccini and his art.

Letters of Puccini, edited by Giuseppe Adami, translated by Ena Makin, revised with a new introduction by Mosco Carner. London: George Harrap & Co., 1974. 341 pp.

This slim volume is dedicated to letters concerning productions of works and searches for libretti, and is quite sufficient for most readers' interests. Puccini in general was not a great letter writer, and his haste in writing is apparent. Scholars and those with a serious interest in Puccini correspondence will want to refer to the ever-evolving *Carteggi Pucciniani* still available only in Italian, but most earthlings will be satisfied with this concise book. The selected letters focus on the composer's work processes, and the torturous path from idea to premiere.

Memoirs and Reminiscences

Puccini Among Friends, by Vincent Seligman. New York: Benjamin Blom and Co., 1938; reissued 1971. 373 pp.

Vincent Seligman grew up with a privileged perspective on the Puccini household: he not only had an intimate, familial relationship with the Maestro, but Puccini tended to be in his best humor when the Seligmans were around. The portrait Seligman draws is therefore rather flattering to the point of naïveté, but of serious interest nonetheless for anyone needing insight into this often enigmatic man. Seligman constructed his highly personal biography around the correspondence between Puccini and his mother, Sybil, or at least as much of the correspondence as was available to him and considered prudent to publish in the 1930s. One can sense important gaps in the correspondence, and the effect can be frustrating, but we are grateful for as much as we get. (Budden gained access to more of the correspondence than Vincent had or was willing to reveal.) Interspersed among the letters are commentary on both Puccini's life and his work. Seligman did not make any pretense to musical scholarship, and indeed some of his observations into the operas reveal a touch of "group-think," but his style is as refined and delightful as one would expect from a man of his sophisticated background. It remains an excellent and important read.

Immortal Bohemian: An Intimate Memoir of Giacomo Puccini, by Dante del Fiorentino. London: Victor Gollancz, 1952. 232 pp.

Del Fiorentino's memoir of Puccini is delightful and a crucial read for any Puccini fan, even allowing for its many problems. Del Fiorentino, Puccini's "Gonnellone" ("Big Skirt," that is, priest), was quite candid in being Puccini's foremost fan, and he clearly idolized Puccini. He forgives Puccini much and his memoir has been accused of a willful naïveté toward its subject. Indeed, there was much private information that Puccini did not share with del Fiorentino, and

Puccini even made his friends tone down their racier conversations when Gonnellone was around. But del Fiorentino was not a stupid man and he was not unaware of the ways of the world, and his calling as a priest perhaps gave him access to aspects of Puccini's most secret thoughts that others did not have. It is even curious that Puccini would have had such a warm and intimate relationship with a priest, given his habit of avoidance of religious issues. In any case, *Immortal Bohemian* remains a remarkable portrait of Puccini, even if the reader must turn elsewhere for many missing details and a more judicious perspective on the man.

Special Issues in Puccini

Tosca's Rome: The Play and the Opera in Historical Perspective, by Susan Vandiver Nicassio. Chicago: University of Chicago Press, 2001. 343 pp.

I have raved about this volume in the chapter about *Tosca*; now let me rave some more. A good half of this book is devoted to examining the historical conditions of life in Rome at the crucial turning point portrayed in the opera. We learn about the governments in flux, the wars, the police force before and during the year 1800, the musical and operatic communities, and even find insights into the lives of freelance painters and designers of church pageants. If this were merely a social historian's account of conditions in Rome in June 1800, it would still be fascinating reading for the historically inclined. Dr. Vandiver has, however, correctly observed that the historical inaccuracies in Sardou's play and Puccini's opera are significant in revealing the core of the story. She gives equal analysis to the play itself, and follows the tortuous path from spoken (and screamed) drama to opera with excellent detail. Her love for the opera is apparent, but she is no blind adulator, and is not afraid to point out faults where they exist. Much the same could be said for her relationship with what I believe to be the most important character in the story, the city of Rome itself. Dr. Vandiver is neither a Catholic apologist nor are her writings filled with that repugnance at the historical fact of the papacy that color so many analyses of this subject. (This is especially a problem with the English—they simply can't help themselves.) Whatever one's personal feelings are toward history, opera, or religion, I cannot imagine anybody finding this book other than totally engrossing.

The Puccini Companion, edited by William Weaver and Simonetta Puccini. New York: Norton, 2000. 352 pp.

William Weaver has been the official arbiter of Italian culture for American audiences for quite some time now, and his credentials are flawless. Weaver has managed to maintain an extremely sensible point of view in his writings and in all his work, avoiding many fraught pitfalls in cross-cultural and musical criticism. Simonetta Puccini is the composer's granddaughter. She has made excellent contributions to Puccini scholarship, has edited two volumes of letters herself, and has been a tireless archivist of information. Their collaboration on this interesting collection was particularly fortuitous. The essays are scholarly but also make enjoyable reading—no mean accomplishment in the music world. Included among the essays are Harvey Sachs on Puccini's relationship with Toscanini, Philips-Matz exploring her laudable love of *Fanciulla*, and Arthur Groos on the genesis of the *Butterfly* story. All the essays are interesting at least and fascinating at best.

Madame Butterfly: Japonisme, Puccini, and the Search for the Real Cho-Cho-San, by Jan van Rij. Berkeley, California: Stone Bridge Press, 2001. 192 pp.

I am always a bit suspicious of titles in this format ("blank, colon, blank, comma, blank, comma, and the blank of blank"), and this book is indeed both interesting and problematic. Van Rij was a career diplomat with an interest in finding the "truth" behind the Madame Butterfly story. This is a small discipline of its own, and there are several articles, scholarly and otherwise, on the same subject. Van Rij surveys previous investigations into the story and does a good job of sifting through those that are plausible and those that are not, but he fails to make a case for why any historical precedent for Butterfly is important. How come nobody is searching for the "real" Manon Lescaut or Mimì? But for some reason the issue will not go away, and van Rij's book is a good departure point. Just don't expect any great insights into Japanese culture. The author admits to no command of the language, although his several years living in the country must count for something.

Puccini's Turandot, by William Ashbrook. Princeton: Princeton University Press, 1991. 208 pp.

Ashbrook expands his analysis of *Turandot* from his *Operas of Puccini* book and gives full rein to his speculations and musical fancies. These fancies are, as in his other book, quite lucid and interesting. This volume does presume a certain familiarity with the score of *Turandot*, (or, failing that, an incredible ability to sight-read) and is therefore not for the casual operagoer. There is also the slightest feeling that Ashbrook is attempting to justify this opera by pointing out how sophisticated it is and how much Puccini learned from Stravinsky and other progressives. Such a stance must be a necessity in musicological circles, but those of us who find the opera thrilling as it stands might wonder what all the fuss is about. Still, Ashbrook can always give the opera-lover the occasional moment of "ah-hah!" and his *Turandot* book is a good addition to the existing literature.

Tangents and Related Reading

The difficult figure of Arturo Toscanini looms large in Puccini reading, both in Puccini's biography and musical development and in the perception of his art in this country. Author Harvey Sachs has devoted himself especially to this subject, and his biography *Toscanini*

(J. B. Lippincott, 1978, 380 pp.) is a fascinating read. Indeed, how can Toscanini's life story read as anything except a good novel? Sadly, Sachs gained full access to Toscanini's voluminous letters only after this biography was written. Sachs's subsequent edition of *The Letters of Toscanini* (Knopf, 2002, 468 pp.) is a great read all on its own. All the political and business intrigue is there, as well as a ton of lurid sex letters written to mistresses. Who knew? The whole issue of interpreting the phenomenon of Toscanini and examining its effect on American musical values, for better and for worse, is compellingly explored by Joseph Horowitz in *Understanding Toscanini* (Knopf, 1987, 492 pp.). The subtitle of the book is "How he became an American culture-god and helped create a new audience for old music." The respect and the antipathy is apparent right in that sentence. Horowitz is quite comfortable going off on rants about American issues, and they are always interesting to follow even if one does not always agree with him. He is, however, quite convincing on the whole, and the whole tangled issue of America and the arts is better analyzed in this book than anywhere else I can think of. Every person working in arts marketing should have a copy of this book on their desk. The casual opera and "classical music" fan will find much of interest as well, but the book is unflinching in its challenge of cultural pretensions.

Harvey Sachs has also written an interesting and concise book called *Music in Fascist Italy* (Norton, 1988, 271 pp.). It examines the art and politics of the era through the major protagonists: Mascagni, Pizzetti, and others, with, of course, a major share devoted to Toscanini. Puccini dies off early in the story and is present in the book mostly as an icon, but it gives about as much information on the fates of Puccini's contemporaries and followers as the casual reader will want to know. It is a fine introduction to an extremely complex and perplexing issue.

A gaping hole in opera literature has recently been filled by Allan Mallach with his book *Pietro Mascagni and His Operas* (Northeastern University Press, 2002, 378 pp.). Mascagni has long needed this sort of serious consideration. Even those who are not running off to the latest production of *Il piccolo Marat* (although you should if you get the chance) will appreciate this judicious consideration of Mascagni's role in Italy's cultural life. The chapters on his involvement with the Fascist government are especially welcome, since Mascagni has for too long been dismissed as a collaborator. The facts, as always, are much more nuanced, and this book goes far in opening the subject to critical debate rather than conditioned reaction. Zandonai, too, has recently hit the bookshelves, and readers will want to take a look at *Riccardo Zandonai: A Biography* (by Konrad Clyde Dryden; Peter Lang Publishing, 1999, 530 pp.). This book is of a narrower focus than the Mascagni book and will interest fewer readers, but it is likewise valuable for its insights into twentieth-century musical life (and lack of it) in Italy.

General opera books, of course, always have to address the issue of Puccini. Books that focus on the art of the opera singer, in particular, will have much to say about Puccini. There are far too many of these to list here, but one must mention a few. Lanfranco Rasponi's *The Last Prima Donnas* (Limelight Editions, 1985, 635 pp.) is considered a classic among opera fans. A series of interviews with great female singers includes many who specialized in Puccini roles and their various insights. These include Eva Turner, Gina Ciglia, and many others. Actually, it is amazing how these ladies seem to repeat themselves. The basic idea, inherent in the title of the book, is "we knew how to sing, nobody knows how anymore, and you missed it!" This may well be true, but it can grate on one's nerves all the same. Still, it is fascinating and is occasionally a hoot. One must always listen to singers and their insights into music, even if one must roll one's eyes at the same time.

Peter G. Davis has a ton of great tidbits in *The American Opera Singer* (Doubleday, 1997, 626 pp.). Davis's definition of American is a broad one (he includes Caruso, Adelina Patti, and many others who were more American in their careers than in their beings), and along the way he gives us an informal survey of music in America. Never one to quibble about expressing an opinion, Davis must have annoyed a lot of people with this book, but hey, this is opera we're talking about.

Rupert Christiansen looks at the phenomenon of the prima donna in his aptly entitled *Prima Donna* (Pimlico, 1995, 335 pp.). Christiansen covers the whole range of the phenomenon from earliest times to (near) the present, but his passages on Geraldine Farrar and her vicissitudes with Puccini are especially good. A more casual and fun approach is taken by Ethan Mordden in his highly readable *Demented* (Fireside, 1990, 330 pp.). Mordden's personal insights (and bitchy asides) only highlight the book's readability and well-disguised intellectual viability.

For those with an interest in opera extending beyond the cult of the diva, one might get *Opera in Context: Essays on Historical Staging from the Late Renaissance to the Time of Puccini* (edited by Mark A. Radice; Amadeus Press, 1998, 410 pp.). The essays can be rather dry, but they give a good idea of the issues at stake in putting opera on the stage. There is an excellent essay in the collection by Helen M. Greenwald entitled "Realism on the Opera Stage: Belasco, Puccini, and the California Sunset." Greenwald asks some interesting questions, and one wishes she had written at greater length.

Finally, one honorable mention for interesting information from a truly tangential angle: if, after reading this book, and all the others listed here, and everything about twentieth-century Italian music, you are still confused over the term verismo, I highly recommend approaching it from the cinematic point of view. Peter Bondanella's *Italian Cinema: From Neo-Realism to the Present* (Continuum Publishing Company, 1990, 500 pp.) has more sensible insights into what the genre is and what it is not than a hundred analogous musicological essays.

Glossary

Opera has a vocabulary all its own, as does any art form (or sport, or computer games, or . . .). The language of opera has tended to reinforce the institution as foreign, obscure, and vaguely unhealthy for Americans. We have not yet, as a nation, transcended our linguistic xenophobia, but there are positive signs in that direction. One now hears words such as "latte" and "cappuccino" even at some truck stops in the heartland, and perhaps food and coffee are leading us to a greater level of comfort with foreign words. Not all the words in the opera lexicon are Italian. Some are German, others French, and quite a few are in good old English, although often no less arcane for that. It is notoriously difficult to describe music in words. Approximations are as close as we can hope for. It is even harder to describe aspects of the human voice. The basis of "opera-ese," then, is inaccuracy, mixed with generous helpings of tradition, spiced with four centuries of journalistic and literary flourish, and served with a dollop of self-referential whimsy. In short, it's really all part of the fun. No one should be, or feel, excluded from the pleasures of opera because of the words engaged by its partisans, anymore than one should avoid baseball because "knuckleball" sounds bizarre. To that end, I have included this glossary as a tool but also as a commentary on the language of opera itself. I have also included a bit of information on some of the theaters that played important roles in Puccini's career, since it would be presumptuous to assume familiarity with or interest in these places. There's also a bit of opera lore to be found in this key to the "secret language" of opera and Puccini.

arco (It., "bow"): An instruction to string players to bow the note, rather than pluck it, which is called pizzicato (q.v.).

aria (It., "air"): An aria is an operatic solo. In traditional Italian opera, there was a clear delineation between a recitative (q.v.) and an aria. All the "action" and development would take place in the recitative. The aria was a conscious suspension of time wherein a soloist would reflect on the conclusion of the recitative. Nobody thought this was strange in the eighteenth century. Indeed, no one at that time thought it strange to force gardens to grow in geometrical shapes, either. But soon the race was on to find a more natural flow between recitative and aria. The debate over which should have primacy is literally as old as opera itself. Puccini came as close as anyone to solving the problem. He did not hide from writing arias (hardly!), but their relation to the recitatives is natural and organic. If Puccini's arias were all excised from their operatic bedrocks and existed in a discrete universe, he would still be among the most celebrated tunesmiths in history. Yet his true genius was in his arias' relations to their dramatic and musical surroundings.

arpeggio: Playing the notes of a chord, or some of them, in succession in either direction. Repeats of these are often used by composers (even overused) to create atmospheric effects.

baritone: The middle, "normal" voice range for a man. The word actually means "the sound of a man" in Italian. Baritones in Italian opera vary between loving fathers, best friends, brothers, and horny villains. Puccini's two greatest baritone roles, Scarpia in *Tosca* and Rance in *Fanciulla*, are of the latter variety. (In all fairness, Scarpia is true hypocritical evil while Rance is more of an embittered and misunderstood sort of loner.) Michele in *Il tabarro* is also a remarkable, if relatively brief, baritone role. Otherwise, Puccini gave them short shrift compared to Verdi, who gloried in baritone roles. Gianni Schicchi, Marcello and Schaunard in *Bohème*, and Lescaut in *Manon Lescaut* all have a good deal to sing but seem to have gaping holes in their parts where an aria should have been (by normal Italian opera standards).

bass: The lowest male vocal register. Basses in Italian opera are generally fathers, old men, and scary clerics. Puccini seemed less interested in the bass voice than almost any other of the great opera composers. There is Geronte, the "dirty old man" of *Manon Lescaut*, who is actually a bass-baritone. The small role of Colline in *La bohème* gets a one-minute aria, "Vecchia zimarra," which is a standard of the bass repertory. And there is the Bonze in *Butterfly*. Otherwise, Puccini seemed to have avoided them. Any other opera composer would have made the role of the emperor in *Turandot* a bass (Busoni actually did in his opera on the, roughly, same subject). Puccini made the emperor a squeaky high tenor.

bel canto: The genre of Italian opera prevalent in the early nineteenth century and typified primarily by the works of Rossini, Gaetano Donizetti, and Vincenzo Bellini. More recently, scholars have come to understand much of the earlier work of Verdi as an evolution of, rather than a break from, this genre, and even Wagner's revolutionary creations have come to be seen as a progression out of the bel canto tradition. The phrase simply means "beautiful singing," and indeed the bel canto operas rely squarely on the dazzling technique of the soloists and the wealth of melodic line. Bel canto resurfaced in the mid-twentieth century when a host of great artists (Maria Callas, Montserrat Caballé, Joan Sutherland, Beverly Sills, Marilyn Horne, and others) demonstrated the dramatic depth and power previously unsuspected in these operas.

bitonality: A method of harmonizing using two strains each in different keys. The first use of this technique that impressed European musicians was in Igor Stravinsky's creepy and marvelous ballet *Petrouchka*. Puccini was a bit puzzled by bitonality, as was most everyone who heard it in 1913. Initial puzzlement for Puccini, however, often led to deeper examination of the work in question, and he used some phrases of bitonality to great effect in the score of *Turandot*. Neither Puccini nor Stravinsky was yet probably aware of the wild and wonderful contemporary experiments in bitonality by the American Charles Ives, whose interests included the effect of several marching bands playing clashing tunes in parades.

canaries: A not-very-complimentary categorization of the lightest soprano voices. Mimì in *Bohème* is a role that, for some reason, canaries think is within their realm (it isn't). Puccini always has unexpected moments of heft in his singers' parts. Canaries would do best to avoid this composer altogether, although they might be able to land a gig as one of the novices in *Suor Angelica*.

celesta: A keyboard instrument first appearing in Paris in the 1880s, producing tone by hammering steel plates. Early notable uses included Tchaikovsky's *Nutcracker* and Mahler's Sixth Symphony. Puccini used it frequently and with great effect, particularly in *Tabarro*, *Suor Angelica*, and, most notably, *Turandot*.

chest tones: As opposed to head tones. It must be understood right away that these are terms of convenience, not anatomical fact. Both men and women have a lower voice, which seems to resonate more in the chest, and an upper voice, which seems to resonate more in the head. Now here's the strange part: for some reason, in the operatic tradition, men generally sing with the chest voice, even in the higher ranges, while women tend to favor the head voice even in the lower ranges. In contemporary popular music, women almost always sing in the chest voice while men often favor the head voice. This is, of course, a sweeping generalization and there are notable exceptions in popular music, especially among the males (Barry White, for example, made a career out of wallowing in chest tones). Yet any woman who ventures into the head voice will be labeled "operatic," no matter how often you explain to people that opera is a form of drama rather than a genre of music. The best singers, operatic and pop, know when to delve into the "other" range. Many sopranos drop into lusty chest tones at the end of Act II of *Tosca* for the line "Ed avanti a lui tremava tutta Roma." Indeed, some overdo it. Conversely, Linda Ronstadt sang all of her hit "Blue Bayou" in plaintive chest tones until the very last note, when she floated into a single note in a dreamy head tone (a device she learned from the great Mexican female vocal tradition, which revels in jumping between the two "realms").

children's choruses: Generally speaking, an invention of Satan to afflict the serenity of the world, although never failing to elicit a chorus of "awwws" from sentimental sectors of the audience. Puccini's indulgence in the vice is limited and brilliant, generally as a contrast to some subsequent or simultaneous other action. Children make an appearance in the crowd scene in Act II of *La bohème*, along with the rest of teeming humanity. The choirboys of Act I of *Tosca* create a noisy background contrast for the ominous entrance of the evil Scarpia. But his ultimate use of the form is in *Turandot*, where an unexpected boys' chorus intersects the bloodthirsty crowd's call for an execution. Nobody in the crowd mutters, "Aren't they cute!" at that point.

chromatics: A fancy way of saying a scale that uses only semitones. That is, go to the piano and play all the notes, black and white, in succession. You will have a chromatic scale. It seems simple enough, but composers of the late nineteenth century caused a *scandale* every time they indulged in this curious habit. Liszt and Wagner, naturally, shocked and appalled everyone with their chromatics, but even a composer as popular as Camille Saint-Saëns used chromatics effectively and to great public approval. (The mezzo's great aria in *Samson et Dalilah* is a study in chromatics.) In Puccini's day, the use of chromatics was still considered cutting-edge. The fact that he used them effectively forced some critics to consider his music seriously despite its popularity. It can be found throughout his mature works, but most strikingly in *Tabarro* and *Turandot*.

cognoscente (It., "knowing"): A know-it-all. Generally speaking, musical cognoscenti (pl.) do not plague Puccini's world, but there is a subset of Puccinian cognoscenti. Fortunately, these will generally confine themselves to reminiscences (real or imagined) of legendary singers.

col legno (It., "with the wood"): An instruction to the string players to turn their bows around and play with the wooden part rather than the horsehair part. In Puccini and in most composers, it is synonymous with "col legno battuto," meaning "struck" with the wood, although contemporary composers sometimes differentiate between the two and ask the musicians to run the wooden part of their bows up and down the strings. Whatever the details, musicians deeply loathe this instruction and always complain of the damage to their instruments. Rossini once took this idea a step further: in the overture to his opera *Il signor Bruschino* (1813), he asked the violinists to strike their *music stands* with the back of their bows to signify the ticking of a clock.

coloratura: The elaborate and rather athletic ornamentation of vocal melody, characterized by rapid runs up and down the scale, trills, and a great ability to produce a huge number of clear and distinct notes within a brief amount of time. Coloratura was popular in baroque and, especially, bel canto opera. The higher the voice, the more agility is present for excursions into this device, although there are cases of coloratura passages for all vocal ranges including bass. When a singer is laying on the coloratura, the words (if indeed there are any beyond "ahhhhh!") are virtually incomprehensible. It fell out of fashion, therefore, in the late nineteenth century, when composers were seeking greater dramatic truth as they understood it. (Leoncavallo, however, managed to sneak some into *I pagliacci* by the clever ruse of having the soprano sing about her envy of the birds in flight.) Puccini managed to avoid it altogether, although Musetta comes precariously close to using some in her waltz "song." The word, incidentally, is not Italian but rather "opera-ese." The Italian word for this technique is *fioritura*. Please don't use *fioritura* in an English conversation unless you want to be thought of as someone working too hard at all this.

commedia dell'arte: The term really just means "professional actor" in Italian, but it has come to stand for a great tradition of Italian theater. Stock characters (such as Harlequin, Columbine, Pantalone, Pulcinella, etc.) appeared in various situations and created different sorts of havoc while always retaining recognizable traits. Improvisational comedy with topical allusions was mixed with songs and acrobatic feats. The tradition flourished in Italy and beyond from the sixteenth to the eighteenth century, although it survived as a primary source of public entertainment in rural southern Italy into the twentieth century. The influence of these troupes was astounding: the English *Punch and Judy* shows derive from them, as do our modern clowns (although let's not hold that against them). The Marx Brothers can be traced directly back to the tradition. In late eighteenth-century Venice, Carlo Gozzi wrote plays incorporating the commedia dell'arte figures, usually on fantastic fairy-tale themes in direct response to the success of his rival, the realist Goldoni. From at least that point on, the commedia dell'arte became a stylized alternative to realism. Leoncavallo managed to meld the two genres brilliantly in *I pagliacci*, which features actors performing commedia dell'arte and the fatal intersection of reality and make-believe. Shortly thereafter and perhaps spurred on by the success of *Pagliacci*, there was a surge of interest in the quaint old form in painting and the other arts, but especially in opera. Richard Strauss used a troupe of commedia dell'arte players in *Ariadne auf Naxos*, a work Puccini knew well. References to them appear in Erich Korngold's hit *Die tote Stadt* (*1922*) and Alban Berg's *Lulu* (1935). Prokofiev's *Love for Three Oranges* (*1922*) was based on a Gozzi play, as was Busoni's *Turandot*. Busoni stayed closer to Gozzi's play: the actual Italian figures show up in the imperial Chinese court and become ministers, à la Marco Polo, contrasting their plain Venetian speech with the etiquette of the Celestial Kingdom. Puccini opted to forego this plan, and instead created Ping, Pang, and Pong for his *Turandot*.

comprimario (It., "with the primary [roles]"): The secondary or "character" roles in an opera. Virtually all operas have comprimario parts, but in Puccini they can make or break the opera. Think of *La bohème*, with its emphasis on life's "little things": there is Schaunard, Benoit, Alcindoro, the kid who wants a trumpet and a toy horse, and others. Each one is important. Puccini also relies heavily on the "passing effect" of people who walk by in a seemingly random appearance, which does so much to place his stories within a given atmosphere: the lamplighter in *Manon Lescaut*, the shepherd boy in *Tosca*, Jake Wallace in *Fanciulla*, the lovers in *Tabarro*. *Suor Angelica* lists eighteen characters—all but two are *comprimarii* (pl.). So while small opera companies must base their seasons on Puccini favorites, the larger companies actually have the advantage in this area as well. Remember, since the time of *Edgar*, Puccini had the advantage of the Ricordi "machine" behind him, and later the forces of the Metropolitan as well. He did not have to write operas that were necessarily cheap to produce—a concern of many previous and subsequent composers. Some of the most interesting singing and interpretation is done by *comprimarii*, who generally do not have the most "stellar" voices but often compensate with superb musicianship and almost invariably a better sense of acting than the stars. One case in point that jumps to mind is Anthony Laciura of the Metropolitan. He has played Spoletta (*Tosca*), the Goro (*Butterfly*), Nick the Bartender (*Fanciulla*), and Pong (*Turandot*)—and that's just what I can remember offhand. I wouldn't be surprised if he stepped in as one of the novices in *Suor Angelica* one night. He almost stole the show as Nick, which is no mean feat. When you see someone of

Laciura's caliber in a Puccini performance, it reveals the amazingly detailed construction of Puccini's operas.

concertato, also **pezzo concertato:** One of the standard gimmicks of traditional opera, the *concertato* is an elaborate ensemble with several vocal solo parts and perhaps choral accompaniment. They are usually to be found at a climactic moment—the finale to Act III in a four-act opera, for example. Critics long carped about the artificiality of the form, which effectively froze the action while indulging in the artifice of writing mere [!] involved polyphony. Even Rossini, who was a master of the form, complained that he had to do it because the audiences expected it. He called it "the row of artichokes," referring to the motionless singers standing in a line at the footlights staring desperately at the conductor. The trouble is that the *concertato*, for all its structural problems, is, in its best manifestations, one of the glories of Italian opera. More than indulging in complicated polyphony for its own sake, it can reveal various points of view simultaneously, and can draw the audience along by its melodic force and allow them to follow each contrasting development. We in the audience, silly creatures that we are, were right to have "forced" Rossini and the others to provide us with our needs. Verdi struggled with the idea throughout his career. Having acquiesced to the convention in the earlier part of his career (the Act III finales of *Ernani* and of *La traviata* being superb examples), he began to explore ways to alter the form to suit his perceived dramatic needs. But he was never able to abandon the convention altogether. His mature masterpiece *Otello* incorporates a *concertato* right where one is expected, at the end of Act III. Verdi had two of the characters running among the otherwise motionless populace whispering dastardly plans to each other in an attempt to make the set piece more modern. The result is not entirely satisfactory in terms of Verdi's goal of a complete integration of drama and music. The characters "talking" in real time only accentuates the stiff formalism on the rest of the stage. (This is, of course, theoretical nitpicking, since the moment remains, like the rest of the opera, overwhelmingly magnificent.) Puccini, born later and therefore at greater liberty to fiddle with forms, was able to accomplish a more seamless union of the *concertato*'s power with an organic dramatic flow on the stage. The very arresting Act III ensemble in *Manon Lescaut* is a sort of combination of *con-*

certato and dramatic movement, although it is smaller in scope than Verdi's later attempts (four solo and up to six choral parts, compared to, for example, seven solo and twenty choral parts in Verdi's Act II *concertato* in *Aida*). "Musetta's Waltz" is a complicated *concertato* in its reprise, although few would think of it as such. The finale to *La fanciulla del West* is an awesome example of Puccini's skill in adapting old forms for new purposes and one of the most successful moments in opera. The end of Act I of *Turandot* is a monster *concertato* whose scale would have made Verdi gulp, and is thoroughly successful by any dramatic standards.

contralto: The lowest female voice, much favored by British composers, among others. Though Italian composers have used contraltos, especially for witches and other scary women, Puccini avoided them. His one notable contralto is reserved for his most extreme shrew of a character, the Zia Principessa in *Suor Angelica*.

crescendo (It., "growing," as in the "crescent" moon, and hence related to the humble French "croissant," which is actually Austrian): Getting louder. The term used for everything from individual notes to entire acts of operas. James Levine has explained to singers that every note longer than a quarter note must either be a crescendo or a decrescendo, or else one is not singing but rather stringing along notes. Conversely, Ravel's famous *Boléro* is a single crescendo. Puccini preferred to contrast loud and soft moments, most extremely in *Turandot*. One also sees *crescente*, a slightly different verb form of the same idea. The Act I finale of *Turandot* is marked *con calore crescente*, which was about as lurid as you could be in print in 1925.

crooning: To sing softly and in a sentimental style. In the opera world, it means to float sound in an unsupported manner, and is considered a very bad thing. Tenors are often accused of crooning. Of course, Bing Crosby and half the island of Ireland have shown that crooning can be an art form of its own, but to croon in Italian opera is synonymous with cheating. If a tenor croons convincingly, however, it is forgiven and then is called mezza voce (q.v.).

diatonic scale: The educated way to say "Do, re, mi" and so on.

fermata: Officially, a fermata means a pause. But ask any tenor the meaning of fermata—it means hold on to the note until you become blue in the face. The fermata is not only used by tenors, but they're notorious for making the most out of them. Puccini was careful to mark his scores with a fermata where he wanted them, so we can safely assume he did not want them in other places. Try telling that to a tenor with a good high note in his arsenal! "Nessun dorma" in *Turandot* has a particularly famous fermata.

forte, piano: Loud and soft, respectively. Early composers never wrote down the expected dynamics of passages: either they expected to be there to explain the music, or they didn't care what happened when they weren't around. The baroque singers wouldn't have paid any attention anyway. Who was a mere composer to tell them how a passage would be most effective? Improvements in music publishing technology combined with an increased stature for the composer to make dynamic marking both possible and worth noting throughout the nineteenth century. Also, instruments were capable of a much wider dynamic range (cf. the "pianoforte," the keyboard instrument [our "piano"], which could play loud or soft while the previous harpsichord could not). The superlatives of the words are fortissimo and pianissimo, and fortississimo and so forth. By Puccini's time, every detail of how music should be played and sung could be found in the printed score, supervised by the composer himself. Puccini employed Verdi's advice on these markings: if he wanted piano, he had to write pianississimo. (Did Verdi understand singers, or what?) Puccini was quite uninhibited about marking passages fortississimo and emphasizing the point by writing "con tutta forza" above that marking (cf. *Tosca* finale, the soprano's line at the end of Act II of *Fanciulla*, and almost every other page of *Turandot*).

furore (It., "furor"): A combination of an ovation and a communal panic attack that hits opera theaters once in a great while when all the elements come together. It is well beyond a success or even a triumph. This demonstrates the fine line between great art and madness, especially in the world of opera. Puccini experienced several nights in his career that could be classified under this term, but only two opening nights that were indisputably *furori* (pl.): *Manon Lescaut* in 1893 at Turin and *Fanciulla* in 1910 at the Met. The rest varied: *Rondine* was a success, *Bohème* a lukewarm success, *Tosca* and *Il trittico* barely successes, and *Butterfly* an out-and-out fiasco (which is the polar opposite of a *furore*). This shows how little effect an opening night reception has on an opera's destiny. Puccini did not live to see *Turandot*'s premiere. No doubt it would have been even more of a *furore* had he been there.

glissando (It., "gliding"): A musical direction to glide the run of notes as much as possible without differentiating between individual notes. With some instruments, like the trombone, this can actually be done. With others, such as the harp, it is an instruction to make it sound as if this were actually happening. The score of *Turandot* is replete with glissandi (pl.).

glockenspiel: The ubiquitous handheld xylophone-type instrument in marching bands is actually played vertically in orchestras. Puccini heard otherwordly rather than quotidian vibes in this instrument, and used them (often in addition to the similar celesta and the regular old xylophone) in all of his mature operas except *Manon Lescaut* and *Gianni Schicchi*.

Grand Opéra (Fr.): In the specific sense, a genre of opera prevalent—in fact, mandated by law—at the Opéra in Paris. The format was thus: an opera in five acts on a historical subject, with an elaborate ballet usually in the third act. The Paris Opéra had a huge budget and an unheard-of amount of rehearsal time (too much, Verdi thought). The chorus and orchestra were unsurpassed and the budget allowed for the best singers. The chorus, therefore, was featured prominently throughout productions at the Opéra. The great soloists each had at least one big opportunity to display their talents. The fourth act tended to be a "hit parade" of arias. Rossini was one of the founders of the style with his famous *Guillaume Tell*, and Donizetti also had some success there. Verdi wrote two actual Grand Opéras for Paris (*Les Vêpres siciliennes* and *Don Carlos*) and one very clearly influenced by the style, *Aida*. The format had obvious problems but clear strengths as well, and operas written in this genre for Paris remained popular in Italy long after they had faded elsewhere. So it would not have been outrageous for Puccini to have attempted writing one. Tito Ricordi Jr. was forever trying to get Puccini to write a Grand Opéra, and turned to Zandonai for *Francesca da Rimini* when it became obvious that the mule of Torre del Lago was not about to budge from his "little" heroines. Many scholars, however, see distinct traces of the tradition in *Turandot*.

grand scena: In traditional Italian opera, the grand scena is a specific form used at climactic moments. It entailed a soloist, sometimes (although by no means usually) accompanied by a chorus in a distinctly background role. The soloist would begin with a recitative, and then sing a cavatina, which is a melodic aria, in a slow and stately tempo. Suddenly, there would be a plot development—a messenger with bad news, perhaps—and the soloist would launch into a cabaletta, which is a fast and florid aria. Castrati and soprano divas were much addicted to the form, often putting clauses in their contracts demanding a specific number of grandi scene (pl.) per opera. It allowed them to show the full range of their talents, musical and histrionic. Thus an archtypical grand scena might run thus: Our heroine wanders on the stage, alone and dressed to the teeth, declaiming her joy on this, her wedding day. She sings placidly and in lengthy melodic lines of the fulfillment of her pious prayers. Polite applause. The court herald rushes in to inform her that her true love has been killed in battle. She resolves to avenge his death and then to kill herself (all this in recitative, which encompasses action) and then sings a fireworks aria with runs, trills, octave leaps, and a generous dollop of the words "vendetta" and "morte." She sweeps her ample skirts with a flourish and exits amidst torrents of applause and shouts of acclamation from the balcony. She returns before the drawn curtain and prostrates herself before the ovation, right hand folded before her breast like St. Teresa in agony and left hand greedily collecting the floral tributes. The audience bounces to the bar in a state of rare satisfaction. As thrilling as a successful grand scena can be, the utter artificiality of the form (exaggerated a bit in my account to stress the point) was thoroughly unacceptable to the composers of Puccini's generation, the disciples of verismo. Verdi, earlier, had also chafed at the form, even though he had written some great ones. His later works sought to incorporate the power of the grand scena into a more organic whole. Puccini continued in this manner, achieving an admirable seamlessness in his climactic solo (or quasi-solo) scenes. He did not dispense with the form altogether—he was too sensitive to effective theatrics to do that. Instead, he noted the effectiveness of the plot/reflection/plot change/climax formula and incorporated it into his own, less segmented style. It was similar to his approach to that other great standby of traditional opera, the *concertato* (q.v.). Thus, while no one in their right minds would say there is an actual grand scena in Puccini's operas, we can easily detect descendants of the form in such moments as Butterfly's triumphal outburst at the return of Pinkerton's ship in Act II and Liù's suicide in *Turandot*. In many ways, even "Musetta's Waltz" in *Bohème* can be understood as a sort of grand scena. Of course, in very general terms grand scena can refer to any scene-chewing moment on the operatic stage, of which there are many. As the bearer of both a technical and a campy definition, Grand Scena has been the name for many years of a famous opera company in New York, comprised entirely of men and women in various gender-bent guises, and headed by the redoubtable Ira Siff (aka Mme. Vera Galuppi-Borshkh). Their comedic gifts can only be imagined, matched only by their obvious dedication to and love for the source material. Among the Grand Scena's greatest "hits" are a brilliant rendition of the poker scene in *Fanciulla*, and an equally brilliant, if more irreverent, account of the finale to Act II of *Tosca*. Best moment: Tosca sips the wine offered her by Scarpia. "Quanto?" she asks, examining the label on the wine bottle. "Il prezzo?" Somebody here knows their *Tosca*, and many "serious" directors could learn much from la Galuppi-Borshkh.

grisette: The legendary working girls of nineteenth-century Paris—shop-keepers, artisans, and so on. They were not prostitutes, which were another class altogether, although they generally needed to augment their meager incomes as best they could. Their name derives from their gray dresses, gray being the color of undyed and therefore cheaper cloth. Grisettes appear at Bullier's in *La rondine*, and Magda "disguises" herself as one. Mimì is a grisette in *La bohème*. In Mürger's novel, so is Musette, as she is called, although it is hard to imagine her operatic incarnation in a gray dress. Mürger's novel has a cynical summation of these grisettes he helped immortalize: "those pretty girls, half bees, half grasshoppers, who sang at their work all week, only asked God for a little sunshine on Sunday, loved with all their heart, and sometimes threw themselves out of a window."

leggiero (It., "light"): A category of the tenor voice (primarily), reserved for a light voice of sweetness and grace rather than power. Puccini did not explore this category much, although the role of the young Rinuccio in *Gianni Schic-*

chi has sometimes been sung by *leggiero* tenors. The famous tenor Ferruccio Tagliavini managed to be called a *leggiero* tenor and still make a mark as Rodolfo in *Bohème* and even, more surprisingly, as Cavaradossi in *Tosca*.

longueurs (Fr.): The "boring parts." Leave it to the French to come up with the definitive word for this. It is a handy phrase, particularly in some second-rate French operas, which can become vague to the point of torture. Despite being crucial around the opera house, I cannot imagine this term's use regarding Puccini, whatever other shortcomings he may have had. Anyone who finds "boring parts" in a Puccini opera is either attending really bad performances or requires immediate, generous infusions of Ritalin.

libretto (It., "little book"): The "play" that is set to music to form an opera. Libretti (pl.) have long been the source of derision, getting blamed for the supposed absurdity of operas. Indeed, some opera composers have been remarkably blithe about the quality of the libretti they have set. Rossini once famously remarked that he could set a laundry list to music. Puccini, conversely, experienced the tortures of hell to get the libretti the way he wanted them. It might even be supposed that the problems of the libretto to his final opera, *Turandot*, actually killed him. A successful libretto can be an original story (e.g., *Gianni Schicchi*), an adaptation of a stage play (e.g., *Tosca, Butterfly, Fanciulla*), an adaptation of a stage play so different it might be regarded as an original composition (*Bohème, Turandot*), or an adaptation of another medium, such as a novel (*Manon Lescaut*). It must be a successful drama of one form or another on its own terms. Also—and this is the point that tends to elude our contemporary librettists—it must be composed of the sort of language that has an inherent acoustical value. That is, the words must create some sort of impression by being sung rather than by what they actually mean. Hence the much-maligned libretto to Verdi's *Il trovatore* by Salvatore Cammarano gets dissed for its tale of crazed gypsies throwing the wrong baby (oops) on the fire. Agreed, not exactly our contemporary notions of dramatic truth, but the words contain explosive power that Verdi's music catapults into the stratosphere. Admittedly, this is inherently easier to accomplish in Italian than in English. (See also versification).

lyric: As a vocal type, it refers to the lighter type of voice one might find in the opera house. It is not the lightest, which is *leggiero*. Please remember that all these categories are quite subjectively defined and seem to exist for the primary purpose of providing opera fans with conversation material on long road trips. But since the category does exist, we can say that Rodolfo and Mimì in *Bohème*, Lauretta in *Gianni Schicchi*, and Liù in *Turandot* are the primary Puccinian representatives of this category.

melody: Like love, it is impossible to define but everyone knows it when they are confronted with it. *The Oxford Dictionary of Music* gamely offers: "A series of notes, varying in pitch, which have an organized and recognizable pattern." Well, yes, that's a start. The fact is that some successions of notes (simultaneous notes are called "harmony" and are another subject) seem to resonate with people more than others. Even though people around the world use different "scales" (series of notes), melodies cross cultural and racial divisions. People either like a melody or they don't, and there is a surprising amount of unanimity in this judgment that should be, by all theories, subjective. People will complain about the production or the arrangement or the development of a melody, but it is rare that people complain about an actual tune—a unit of melody—itself. Melody fell afoul of the intellectual thought-leaders throughout much of the twentieth century. And out it went, with all who considered themselves instructed by such worthy thinkers. The vast majority of humanity ignored this decree, and the only tangible result was that the institutions that teach musicians have been forever separated and isolated from the general (and paying) public, to the detriment of both sides. The gift of creating melody cannot be taught, and those who have it often shun musical education for fear (justified) that it will be beaten out of them. Puccini was among the last humans who had both the gift of melody and a traditional musical education. For this, he has been much despised by many. Go figure.

Metropolitan Opera of New York: One of the world's "Big Four" opera houses, the Mighty Met has defined opera in America roughly since its founding in 1883. It is the world's largest opera house, and is still perhaps the most technically elaborate despite its present home being forty years old. It is distinctly "major league." The Met's reputation almost since its opening has rested on star singers, as much to the delight of audiences as to the opprobrium of stern critics within and beyond the opera world. At certain times in its history, the Met Orchestra has also soared to great heights. This can be said of our day, but during Puccini's time it was perhaps even truer, if contemporary accounts are to be believed. The musical direction was shared for a time between Gustav Mahler and Arturo Toscanini, the rivalry shortened by Mahler's untimely final illness. *La fanciulla del West* was premiered there, which was the Met's first world premiere. *Il trittico* also received its premiere there. Puccini remains by far the most performed composer at the Met—perhaps a bit too performed, by many accounts. While it is true that too many pro forma performances of the warhorses have created a sense of ho-hum around the name of Puccini, the Met must also be credited with some historic performances that have justified the composer's ubiquity. The *Turandot* performances of 1961, with Birgit Nilsson and Franco Corelli, did much to rehabilitate that opera with the public. The *Live from the Met* series, while it was on, brought many legendary performances of Puccini's works to a few million television sets: the initial Pavarotti/Scotto *Bohème*, the Scotto/Domingo *Manon Lescaut*, the Stratas/Carreras *Bohème*, the Stratas *Suor Angelica*, and many others.

mezza voce: Crooning, when done well, is honored with the appellation mezza voce, which means "half voice." A score is very rarely marked with this direction—one depends on feeling and tradition to judge when to use it. Cavaradossi's first statement of the "big theme" in "E lucevan le stelle" (*Tosca*, Act III) is almost always sung in mezza voce, although the score only says "beautifully, with much feeling." Besides sounding inherently dreamy, it also forms a good contrast for the next statement of the theme, coming only a few seconds later. A good tenor will use the mezza voce the first time around to make you think he's blowing the lid off the Castel Sant'Angelo in the repeat. By the way, make sure you pronounce this word right: METS-a-voh-chay (the double "z" is a "ts" sound, like in "pizza"). Otherwise, people will think you are mumbling *messa di voce*, which is "placement of the voice," describing a diminuendo after a crescendo, popular in the bel canto style and devilishly difficult to accomplish.

mezzo-soprano: Literally, a "half soprano," although few mezzos of my acquaintance would appreciate that reading of the word. The lower-voiced female range, though not so low as a contralto, which is relatively rare. Italian opera has a great tradition of writing for the mezzo: even many of Rossini's greatest coloratura roles were written for mezzo. Verdi also had a knack for wringing exciting drama out of mezzos, although his mezzos tended to be darker, more ominous roles than their soprano rivals (cf. *Trovatore*, *Don Carlos*, *Aida*). The French composers have greatly excelled in writing for the mezzo: predictably, "bad girls" like Dalilah and Carmen are written for mezzo, but so are "nicer" (though no less toxic) girls like Charlotte in Massenet's *Werther* and the enigmatic title woman in Debussy's *Pelléas et Mélisande*. Puccini was a sort of descendant of both Verdi and the French composers, which makes his avoidance of the mezzo voice more remarkable. Anybody else would have made Musetta in *Bohème* a mezzo-soprano—in fact, Leoncavallo did in his version of the opera. Having two leading sopranos of such similar voice types sharing the stage is virtually unique in Italian opera. He does it again in *Turandot*, although the two sopranos are of such different vocal character that it almost doesn't count. Still, Busoni wrote his version of the Liù role for a mezzo. Puccini's only lead role (as opposed to comprimario role) for a mezzo is Suzuki in *Madama Butterfly*, and she doesn't get an aria.

modes: The scales of European music from about the time of the end of the Roman Empire until the Renaissance. There are many arcane explanations of the various modes, but the simplest way to get an idea is simply to go to the piano and play eight notes in succession using only the white keys, starting with C, then D, and so forth. Each of these variations received an intimidating name based on a supposed Greek origin (Lydian, Ionian, etc.), adding to their mystique. The issue is where the scale moves a whole-tone and where it moves a half-tone. Our standard modern major scale is whole/whole/half/whole/whole/whole/half, while minor scales vary the placement of the half-tones. The major scale is the ancient Ionian mode, while the most common minor is the old Aeolian. Most European music since about 1600 has been in these two scales. Where variations were used, it was deemed easier to write them with accidentals (extra sharp or flat notes) than to change the whole piece into another mode. Only the Roman Catholic Church continued to use the mode system until quite recently, and many hymnals still use it. Partly because of this, several twentieth-century composers took an interest in the mode system for its ancient and religious sound, even though originally modes were used in popular music as well as religious. If my analyses are correct, Puccini played with modes in the score of *Tosca* to create a musical depiction of Church power run amok. Girardi noted the use of the same "churchy" modes in the riddle scene in *Turandot* (Act II, Scene 2), conferring a sense of ritual.

morbidezza (It.): Delicacy, both in the refined and the sickly sense of the word. Therefore, Renata Scotto could boast in an interview that she was an excellent soprano because she had *morbidezza*, a comment that raised a few eyebrows even among those whose Italian was fluent. But Manon Lescaut can also sing of her chambers being *morbide*, meaning both soft and sapped of energy. Be careful when complimenting someone's voice on its *morbidezza*.

ostinato: A musical phrase that repeats. The Italian word literally translates as "obstinate," which is an excellent description of the orchestra seemingly tapping you on the shoulder and saying, "Hello! We're saying something here!" Puccini used the technique frequently and usually in muted phrases, notably in the "dripping blood" moment of *Fanciulla*'s Act II and the odd little "change your hat and makeup" moment in Act I of *La rondine*.

Opéra-Comique: Traditionally, the second most important opera house in Paris, a position it retained for many years without rival after the demise of the Théâtre des Italiens in the latter nineteenth century. "Comique" originally referred to dialogue, not comedy, as "comédien" means "actor" in French. In systematic French thinking, one found different forms of opera at different theaters. Therefore, one found grand opera at the Opéra (eventually the Palais Garnier, that extravaganza in the middle of Paris), Italian opera at the Théâtre des Italiens, and opera with dialogue—a sort of forerunner of the musical—at the Opéra-Comique. So it was all very Gallic and ordered, except when it wasn't (like the French language, which is 100 percent logical and phonetic, except when it isn't). In effect, the Opéra-Comique became an alternative to the impossible bureaucracy of the Opéra, and many of its most important premieres (Massenet's *Cendrillon*, 1899 and

Debussy's *Pelléas et Mélisande*, 1902) were operas without dialogue. *Madama Butterfly* was introduced to Paris at the Comique, much to Puccini's dissatisfaction. It is open today and hosts operetta and even some Broadway musicals. The theater is well worth a visit.

passaggio (It., "passage"): Every voice has a place where it tightens as it runs up the scale. This is particularly notable in tenors, whose *passaggio* tends to be around the notes E, F, and F-sharp. This is a perilous area. It is remarkably easy to "lay an egg" when trying to attack these notes without proper preparation. On the other hand, if it is handled properly, notes in this zone have an inherently emotional appeal. The great composers knew how to make the most of it, at least for tenors who knew how to deliver on it. Puccini was a master of the art. The aria "Recondita armonia" from *Tosca*, for example, lives almost entirely in the *passaggio*.

parlato (It., "spoken"): A direction in musical scores to speak rather than sing a given word or passage. It was a device much used, even overused, by the verismo composers. The final lines of both *Cavalleria rusticana* and *I pagliacci* are spoken rather than sung. The verismo performance tradition has determined many lines to be *parlato* even if this is not indicated in the score: Tosca's Act II exit line, "Ed avanti a lui tremava tutta Roma," is not marked *parlato* in the score, though most fans would be surprised to know that. On the other hand, Puccini was not afraid to use the direction elsewhere. Marcello's poignant final "Coraggio!" to Rodolfo in *Bohème* is *parlato*. Minnie's great presentation of her winning poker hand, "tre assi e un paio!" is *parlato*. And so on. Even in such a nonverismo work as *Turandot*, the chorus indulges in *parlato* phrases frequently, most predictably during Liù's torture scene where they urge her "Parla! il suo nome!"

pentatonic: A scale that divides the "octave" (or what we Westerners call the "octave") into five notes, rather than our usual eight. Play only the black notes on a piano and you will experience a common pentatonic scale. The pentatonic scale is favored in China and Japan, and Puccini made use of pentatonic melodies in *Butterfly* and *Turandot*. The pentatonic scale is also the basic division of music in many other places, including Scotland (cf. "On the Bonny, Bonny Banks of Loch Lomond"), and much indigenous music of the Americas. The "Minstrel's Song" in *Fanciulla* is pentatonic, and is now said to have a Zuñi provenance. Now, before any modern-day Thor Heyerdahls get on a raft to prove that prehistoric musicians sailed between China, Peru, and Scotland, carrying their scale with them, be warned that the pentatonic scales of those various places are all quite different from each other.

pizzicato (It., "plucked"): Plucking a string on the violin or any string instrument, as opposed to using the bow ("arco"). Puccini uses the effect powerfully, either in a single note (i.e., when Rodolfo's hand touches Mimì's in Act I of *La bohème*), or in rather Byzantine configurations (the chromatic pizzicato scale toward the end of the Ping, Pang, and Pong scene in *Turandot*). In other spots in the *Turandot* score, musicians are required to alternate pizzicato and arco notes, a difficult effect to achieve without sounding like a train wreck.

phrasing: The difference between notes on a page and the thrill of performance lies mostly in the art of phrasing—that is, interpretation of the written notes. The individuality of voices and conductors depends largely on their ability to bring a phrase of music alive. Tastes change with the times, though. What was considered "artistic" fifty years ago is often considered excessive today. It is a subjective science, yet it remains a science. There are techniques one can use to add spice, so to speak, to the written page of music. There is rubato, portamento, *parlato*, head tones, chest tones, the *coup de glotte* (a little sob Caruso perfected), and those are just the ones singers have revealed.

plosives: The consonantal sound that separates the Germanic from the Latin languages. In English, for example, the K, P, and T sounds are accompanied by a little burst of air emitted from the mouth: hence the name. In Italian, there should be no discernible emission of air. Singers can practice this with a candle held up toward the mouth. The flame should not waver when speaking Italian. British singers, who are taught proper English locution as children, can almost never master euphonious Italian. We Americans, who are generally taught nothing at all about the English language, have an advantage here and should do better than we do. Unfortunately, diction coaches will spend days on proper German, French, and Russian pronunciation (as well they should) and ignore Italian altogether. All opera singers think their Italian is perfect anyway, and it rarely is. Why is this important? Because it will have an effect on the musical sounds being produced. Puccini was well aware of phonemes (spoken sound units) when he composed, often sending "dummy verses" to his librettists to work with for various passages. The consonants shape the subsequent vowels, which in turn affect the tone. Compare the Met or Covent Garden chorus to La Scala's in, say, Act I of *Turandot*. Anyone sitting in the first ten rows of the Met when the chorus calls "Pu-Tin-Pao!" will be covered with spit. Both choruses will have fine musicality but La Scala's will sound better at that moment. It's because of the plosives. Attention, vocal coaches!

portamento: "Carrying" a note from one to the next. Puccini marked his portamenti (pl.) more carefully and thoroughly than any other standard operatic composer, yet often singers feel moved to add additional portamenti of their own.

prima (It., "first"): Obnoxious term used by cognoscenti (q.v.) to refer to the first performance of a repertory work during a given season (as in, "You mean you weren't at the prima?"). A premiere is the first performance of the work itself or of a new production.

recitative: Opera began as an attempt to re-create ancient Greek drama in a (then) modern Italian idiom. The gentlemen involved in the project knew, as we know now, that Greek drama was sung to an extent. What they didn't know, as we still do not know, was to what extent the words of the drama were sung. Judging from the structure of the dramas, it seemed that the singing in the Greek dramas amounted to a sort of exaggerated speech pattern rather than a string of actual songs. The wailing of the muezzin from the minaret and the cadences of the synagogue cantor provide hints to how melodic such "sing-speech" can be. The gist of this idea is to emphasize the words, which are sacred to the cantor and the muezzin, and were sacred also in a sense to the Florentine scholars poring over their Greek texts. Some wanted more moments of melody in the new creation, thinking rightly that the absence of melody would be absurd in an Italian work. An argument started that has been raging for over 400 years. How much of opera should be emphasized speech and how much should be, when you get right down to it, song? The "talky" part in between the arias, duets, ensembles, and choruses is called recitative. The "opera seria" genre of baroque opera became quite formalized, with recitative done by one or perhaps two characters, followed by a solo aria, and exit, and repeat the whole formula until an evening was filled out. The recitative was where all the action happened; the aria was a moment to "stop time" and reflect on the action. Accompaniment to the recitative was, of necessity, very sparse since the words had to be understood clearly. One of Puccini's greatest accomplishments was a superb integration of recitative within the melodic structure of his scores.

regietheater (German, "director theater"): The current term for director-driven theater, which would seem to apply to all theater these days. In opera, it unfortunately tends to mean the music is given very little attention, at least in the press.

Royal Opera, Covent Garden: The main opera house of London, and one of the world's "Big Four." The Royal has had its share of offstage drama over the years, no less than the Paris Opéra, and has been teetering on the edge of closing entirely for much of its history, yet it has been, and continues to be, the site of some of opera's most exciting nights. The current building dates from 1858, with much remodeling. Puccini had a great deal of trouble with the management of the house, finding it too dedicated to its star performers and not enough to the quality of the productions, but he could never break with the house because of its stature and its fat paychecks.

rubato (It., "stolen"): A technique of phrasing, involving taking liberties with the lengths of individual notes. Literally, one steals a bit of time off of one note and gives it to another note. Without any rubato, a piece of music on a page can sound clinical and soulless. Think of the famous hymn "Amazing Grace." If one doesn't linger over some of the notes and rush others, the tune loses its power and becomes trite. Yet applying too much rubato makes singers sound like Bill Murray's hilariously cheesy lounge singer jazzing up "Silent Night." As with portamento, Puccini wrote his scores in so much detail that it is possible to sing them with feeling and not add any more rubato. Indeed, the famous tenor Roberto Alagna raised many eyebrows when he announced to the world that he never did and never would use any. Puccini sometimes marked phrases rubato, notably Suor Angelica's desperate final prayer.

schmaltz (German/Yiddish, "chicken fat"): Too little, and the soup has no flavor. Too much, and queasiness occurs. Schmaltzy (adj.) is a criticism often used against Puccini, at least in New York.

slancio: The big, gushing theme, gushed forth without inhibition. The dictionary translates *slancio* as "rush, impetus." For more on the term and one of its most notable uses, see the chapter "The Myth of Tosca."

song: In opera, where everything is sung, a song refers to a set vocal piece that is meant to be understood as a separate performed piece. That is, even if everyone onstage were talking instead of singing, the song would still be sung. If that sounds confusing, it is meant to be, since one of the purposes of songs within operas is to blur the boundaries between music and "reality." Puccini included many songs in his operas: the madrigal in *Manon Lescaut* and the "Minstrel's Song" in *Fanciulla*, for example. Sometimes the line between aria and song becomes even hazier. Are we to understand "Tra voi belle" in *Manon Lescaut* as Des Grieux singing to his friends, or just talking in such a poetic and performative tone that his "speech" becomes an aria? "Musetta's Waltz" in *Bohème* clearly begins as a song: she stands among a crowd and sings in order to draw attention to herself. But what happens when other soloists and then the chorus pick up her vocal line without any discernible break? Puccini was especially adept at incorporating fragments of songs passing in the background, as we see in *Manon Lescaut*, *Tosca*, and *Tabarro*. However hazy the boundaries may be, though, not all arias are songs.

soprano: The highest female vocal range, and one of the pillars of the Italian operatic tradition. There are specific characteristics to this vocal range that define the characteristics and roles written for them. The high soprano "head voice" can be heard clearly even when sung softly. All those pious prayers and demure arias of Italian opera are more than nineteenth-century notions of idealized submissive womanhood: no other voice can express the same idea and still be heard. Conversely, a single soprano voice in full force can be heard over anything—literally anything—including a jumbo jet taking off. It's more a matter of the quality of the sound than mere decibels. The sound slices through other sounds. The best way to look at vocal types is as aspects within each one of us. Though I may not be a soprano, I have certain thoughts and, moreover, feelings that could only be truly expressed by a soprano voice. And so do you. And the same for every other type of voice. But the soprano voice, in its ability to pierce all other noise, is uniquely qualified to represent the individual who demands to be heard against the opposition of the whole world. Verdi knew this in the Triumphal Scene in *Aida* and especially in the finale to his amazing *Requiem*. Puccini knew it too: think of Butterfly's outburst when Pinkerton's ship returns in Act II. The words may say simply, "I won!" but the sheer vocal declamation says, "I was right and all of you so-and-so's in the whole world were wrong, damn it!" A tenor voice singing the same notes would imply a very different emotional state. Whatever the actual details, there is no denying that Puccini was absolutely addicted to the soprano voice at the expense of all others. Although he wrote exquisitely and extensively for the tenor, the sopranos rule his world. All of his mature operas except *Il tabarro* and *Gianni Schicchi* are named after the lead soprano roles.

spinto (It., "pushed"): A categorization of voice, officially called lirico spinto. This refers to heavier voices than "lyric," but not full-on artillery-voice, which is categorized as "dramatic." Most of Puccini's fall within this character, although many have also been successfully portrayed by the lighter lyric voices. Discussing which lyrics were successful in which spinto roles keeps opera fans amused for hours. Case in point: Minnie in *Fanciulla* is distinctly a spinto role. Even some heavier dramatic sopranos (we're talking about voices here, not physical size) have found it unmanageable. The greatest dramatic soprano of recent times, Birgit Nilsson, recorded the role but avoided it onstage. However, Dorothy Kirsten, a lyric soprano, had a great success in the role. It's this sort of illogic that makes opera a great refuge in an otherwise clinical world.

Teatro alla Scala, Milan: Italy's most important opera house, and still one of the world's "Big Four." Puccini's career at Milan's La Scala was generally stressful. *Edgar* failed there in its much-vaunted premiere, *Manon Lescaut* was only moderately successful in its initial run, while *Madama Butterfly*, premiered there, was one of the great disasters of opera. A thirtieth anniversary production of *Manon Lescaut*, led by Toscanini in 1922–23, did much to break the ice between Puccini and the Scala public. *Turandot* received its emotional, posthumous premiere there in 1926. Any visitor to La Scala will be overwhelmed with the history, the beauty, the acoustics, and the downright fun to be experienced there. The audiences are not always friendly in the traditional ways, but they are rarely boring. Some nights are a genuine riot. There is "attitude" aplenty there, as there is in much of Milan, but at least this spot has the goods to back it up. The Scala Museum is also well worth a visit. It is not, as one would expect, in the theater but a little distance away. In fact, it's across the street from *The Last Supper*. It is well worth a trip. *Turandot* is, predictably, well represented there: Nicola Benois's gold and coral costume for Turandot would not disgrace the most over-the-top drag queen.

Teatro Argentina, Rome: The oldest extant opera house in Rome, and one of the most striking theaters in Italy. It was the site of *Bohème*'s half-successful Roman premiere, where only Acts III and IV met with general approval. In Sardou's *La Tosca*, we are told that the diva is engaged at this theater, singing an opera by Paisiello (who was not only away from Rome in 1800, but who sided with Napoleon and remained out of favor with the Bourbons). It is a quick walk from the Argentina to the Church of Sant'Andrea della Valle. Wagner's *Ring of the Nibelung* received its Italian premiere in this baroque jewel box, which must have been cozy in the extreme. It was also the site of the premiere of Rossini's *Barber of Seville*, which was, before *Madama Butterfly*'s premiere at La Scala, the most notorious fiasco in Italian operatic history. Conversely, it witnessed one of Verdi's giddiest triumphs with the premiere of *La battaglia di Legnano* around the time of the brief Roman Republic of 1849, when one audience member was so transported that he leaped from a fourth-tier box into the orchestra pit and escaped unhurt. Most tourists miss the Argentina, which is a mistake. It is now the home of an excellent state-run theater, presenting spoken dramas. For non-Italian speakers, there are also chamber music concerts there on Sunday mornings, making it one of the few open venues, other than churches, in the city at that time.

Teatro Colón, Buenos Aires: Arguably (but only somewhat) the world's most beautiful large opera house, built in 1908. Puccini never saw it, but was at the previous theater of Buenos Aires also called simply the Teatro de la Opera. A season he and Elvira attended there in 1905 amounted to a veritable Puccini Festival, with even the difficult *Edgar* succeeding relatively well there, and *Madama Butterfly* with Rosina Storchio was a great success there while its future was still in doubt elsewhere. The great tradition of traveling to Buenos Aires (with optional stops in Rio de Janeiro, Sao Paolo, and Montevideo) in the (northern) summer faded with the First World War and the rise of summer festivals in Europe and the United States, although the Colón still benefits from the relative availability of singers during the months of June, July, and August.

Teatro Costanzi (Rome Opera): As the capital of Italy and the fabled Eternal City, Rome should, in theory, have the greatest opera house in the world. It doesn't, and in fact opera has had a long but tortured history in Rome. The Teatro Costanzi, now the Teatro dell'Opera, was originally built in 1879, with a capacity of 2,212. In Rome's first flush as the capital of the Kingdom of Italy, many looked to the Costanzi as a venue for the renewal of Italian opera, free, as it was, from associations of "old Italy" like La Scala and the San Carlo. Mascagni's triumph there with *Cavalleria rusticana* (1890) seemed to confirm this new status. Puccini always held the Costanzi in high regard: *Tosca* received its famous and nerve-racking premiere there in 1900, and both *Fanciulla* (1910) and *Trittico* (1918) were given their Italian premieres there. Toscanini, however, avoided the place, and in the end La Scala, under his direction, firmly retained its traditional primacy. The Costanzi was bought by the city council of Rome and reopened, after much redesign, as the Royal Opera House in 1928. In the 1950s it was renamed the Teatro dell'Opera and thoroughly redesigned again, this time in a sort of midcentury modern, and not a very successful example of that genre. In fact, most Americans assume it is the post office. The square in front of the opera house was converted into a parking lot at some point, and an infestation of drug dealers and gap-toothed prostitutes completed the lovely picture. The parking lot was recently reincarnated as a public garden—a very rare commodity in downtown Rome. It is a welcome improvement and with luck a harbinger of better times for opera in Rome.

Teatro Massimo, Palermo: This beautiful theater had the honor of being the first place where *La bohème* was an unqualified success, after the opera's hesitant successes in Turin and Rome. This was in the theater's inaugural season, 1897, after a thirty-two-year process to design, build, and complete it. Puccini basically ignored the theater after that. The Massimo continued to have troubles after its opening, sustaining damage in the war and then remaining closed "for repairs" for twenty-five years more recently. It is finally back to its former glory and is in fact one of the centerpieces of the "new Palermo." The Massimo can be seen to full advantage in the movie *The Godfather III*, where it is the site of one of the most elaborate multiple killings in film.

Teatro Regio, Turin: This theater was important in Puccini's early career, and in fact was briefly one of the most important theaters in Italy. *Le villi*, in one of its incarnations, received a successful premiere there, as did *Manon Lescaut* (a *furore*) and *La bohème* (a bit of a disappointment). Toscanini was associated with the theater at this juncture, and gave an important Italian premiere of Wagner's *Götterdämmerung* there despite the poor acoustics. In 1906, Toscanini had a bit of an argy-bargy with Richard Strauss over the Italian premiere of *Salome*, slated for the Regio, and never really bothered with the place again. He hardly needed it after he took over the Met and La Scala, in any case. The Regio languished and burned down in 1936, replaced by a bit of Fascist realism that pleased nobody. In 1973, a new theater, designed by Carlo Mollino, was unveiled, and the new, new Regio is working hard, with some success, to put Turin back on the list of operatic capitals.

Teatro San Carlo, Naples: Italy's second most important opera house, after La Scala, and a beautiful theater. Puccini never had much luck there—*Edgar* was a disaster early in his career, which forever rankled him, and he avoided the place. Verdi also found the place uncongenial, as did even Caruso, a native Neapolitan.

Te Deum: A service of the Roman Catholic Church, giving praise to God. For some reason it became traditional to employ the Te Deum after military victories, which is how it is used in *Tosca*. Since we in the audience are expected to know that Marengo was not, in fact, a victory for the Allies against Napoleon, there is an inherent dig on Puccini's behalf against the pomp of the Church. The libretto directs Scarpia to kneel and cross himself after the first two lines of the hymn are intoned; the congregation usually does the same. The Roman Breviary, however, insists that the congregants stand during the Te Deum and are only permitted to kneel during the recitation of the later line "Te ergo quaesumus," not included in *Tosca*. You read it here first.

tenor: The highest natural range of the male voice in chest tones. There are also countertenors, who are a sort of specialized falsettist, and there were the castrati, neither of which enters into the Puccini discourse. If the soprano voice is uniquely qualified by nature to depict the Voice That Must Be Heard, the tenor voice also has unique traits. There is a very old cliché about tenors being stupid. Of course, there are stupid tenors and smart ones, but there is some insight in the old cliché. First of all, the tenor voice is not natural for a man, like the baritone's is. Tenors must first be born, and then trained. They are a rare breed, and (inexplicably, although there are many theories) become more rare year by year. If one is found who can sing with some beauty, it doesn't matter if he can dissect the inherent contradictions of Nietzsche, or even walk and chew gum at the same time. It's awesome when a tenor can act, look good, and be a thinking musician (Plácido Domingo being the obvious example of this), but the voice is precious and must be cherished where it is found. The voice itself does not sound as if it represents the intellect. It sounds inherently urgent, like it is operating on urges other than the brainy ones. Great opera composers know how and when to use this voice type. Besides always pushing for sex, tenors therefore have the voice composers turn to when there is a call to arms, a political authority figure to be insulted, or a fire to be extinguished. The temperament of some of history's leading tenors is as legendary as that of the sopranos or even the castrati, usually to the delight of the audience. In the movie *All About Eve*, Thelma Ritter names tenors as the only people in show business more temperamental than the wardrobe mistresses. Puccini wrote magnificent music for tenors even if the core of his heart was with the sopranos.

versification: The process of setting plain speech into poetic meters, with or without rhyme. The practice was all-pervasive in Italian opera until quite

recently. Zandonai's curious opera *I cavallieri d'Ekebù* (1922) was the first
Italian opera whose libretto was written in prose. It will also be noted that
the date of Zandonai's opera corresponds almost directly with the demise of
Italian opera as an international force. The Italian language, with its flexible
syntax and typical consonant/vowel alternations, lends itself extremely well
to poetic meter. It is possible to write flawlessly metered Italian and still
sound very near conversational (Dante achieves this frequently even in so
exalted a piece as the *Divine Comedy*). Rhyme, too, which always sounds a
bit comical in English, is much more natural in Italian. Thus even the ne plus
ultra of verismo, *Cavalleria rusticana*, is written with a metered libretto and a
hefty dollop of rhyme. Versification fell into disrepute among academics and
other arbiters of taste in the twentieth century, being considered as archaic
and artificial as the furrowed hedgerows of formal gardens. Ironically, we
masses, in our infinite ignorance, appear to have disregarded the academics'
attempts to liberate us from our lower instincts and have held on to meter
and rhyme in popular music. In fact, the current surge of rap music is built
on a strict adherence to formal meters and rhymed couplets that would have
made baroque librettists gag with envy.

Vienna State Opera: One of the "Big Four" of opera, in Puccini's day as well
as our own. Although marginalized for a time by the relative indifference of
the Vienna Opera's director, Gustav Mahler, Puccini achieved a true triumph there after the war. It was, in fact, the only house in which *Il trittico*
was an unqualified success, due largely to the talents of Lotte Lehmann as a
superb Suor Angelica. The present opera house is a re-creation of the previous, which was destroyed in the war.

whole-tone scale: The whole-tone scale is comprised exclusively of, well,
whole-tones between the notes (as opposed to the diatonic scale, which is
made of combinations of whole- and half-tones). On the standard piano, a
whole-tone scale can only be played in two keys: C and C-sharp. This means
the notes used are C, D, E, F-sharp, G-sharp, A-sharp, and C, or C-sharp,
D-sharp, F, G, A, B and C-sharp, respectively. Very few techniques in music
were "invented" by any one person, but the whole-tone scale is very closely
associated with Claude Debussy, who explored the technique more thor-

oughly than any other composer. Music composed on the whole-tone scale has an innately otherworldly feel to it, and as such has been used (and overused) in film sound tracks. Horror flicks, science fiction, and ghost stories tend to be addicted to the whole-tone scale. Puccini used it at various points in *Butterfly* and *Turandot*, but his primary use of the whole-tone scale is in *Fanciulla*, whose central motif is a whole-tone chord.

Acknowledgments

It is astounding how thoroughly a work like this book can be a group effort. First off, I need to acknowledge my extravagant debt to Frances Berger and Rich Lynn. Their generosity with books, recordings, videos, and DVDs is only equaled by their generosity in sharing their love for this subject. How they have tolerated the daily phone calls, requests, rants, and endless questions for these last few years, I have no idea. My gratitude to them is boundless. I must also thank Stephen Miller for, beyond the daily support, sharing his insights. His knowledge of theater and his fundamental truthfulness have allowed me to experience many of these familiar works as if for the first time. Special thanks go to Bianca Orlandi for her general support, extensive knowledge, and especially her help with my endless Italian language questions. David Groff has been a mentor and a colleague for me, and I never could have written anything without his patient support. I want to thank Alex Ross, Dr. Jason Royal, and Colin Tipton for sharing their formidable musical knowledge with me (although let me say here that any musical errors herein are my fault and not theirs) and Sean O'Toole for research and editorial help. I am grateful to Father Michael Halloran, S.J., and his seemingly inexhaustible knowledge about—well, everything, really. Almost all of the aforementioned people are the best kind of opera fans and have shared their ideas and opinions with me. In this category, I must add my debt to Harriett Leitman, Greg Lugliani, John Yohalem, and especially to Lou Ruffalo. Many people and institutions have allowed me to test half-formed ideas on them, and among these I thank Alessandra Mazzucato of Dorothea's House, Princeton, Antonio Cosenza and the Italian Cultural Institute of New York, and my very indulgent friends at our informal Italian "movie club" at St. Francis Xavier Church in New York, especially Leslie Woo, Paul Sarro, Sr. Maria Thérèse Mulieri, and again the priceless Mr. Lugliani.

I have received only the best support from everyone at Vintage Books, and now thank Diana Secker Larson (in whom the wisdom of Solomon meets the patience of Job) and a continuing thanks to Marty Asher and Russell Perreault. Additional thanks to the equally patient and excellent Cathy Slovensky for editorial help. And a continuing thanks to Al Zuckerman and the staff of Writers House for years of support and encouragement.

And my many friends and family who have supported me in countless ways—sometimes without even their knowledge—all deserve thanks, and I must mention by name Frank Angelakis, Ramón Berger, Joe Birdsong, Gustavo Bonevardi, Reuben Butchart, Ed de Bonis, John Goodman, Scott Hess, Phil Jimenez, Vinnie Maniscalco, Brandon Miller (I used your idea!), Rick Robertson, Michael Shernoff, and Kelly Webb.

Index